Attribution and Social Interaction

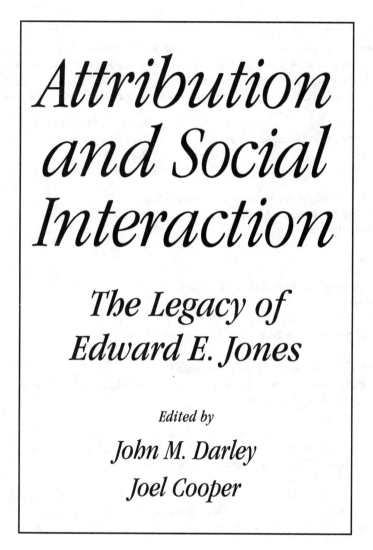

Attribution and Social Interaction

The Legacy of Edward E. Jones

Edited by

John M. Darley
Joel Cooper

American Psychological Association

Washington, DC

Published by
American Psychological Association
750 First Street, NE
Washington, DC 20002

Copies may be ordered from
APA Order Department
P.O. Box 92984
Washington, DC 20090-2984

In the UK and Europe, copies may be ordered from
American Psychological Association
3 Henrietta Street
Covent Garden, London
WC2E 8LU England

Typeset in Minion by EPS Group Inc., Easton, MD
Printer: United Book Press, Baltimore, MD
Cover Designer: Minker Design, Bethesda, MD
Technical/Production Editor: Tanya Y. Alexander

Library of Congress Cataloging-in-Publication Data
Attribution and social interaction : the legacy of Edward E. Jones / edited by
    John M. Darley, Joel Cooper.
        p.   cm.
      "The conference in honor of Edward Ellsworth Jones was held at the Psychology
    Department of Princeton University on March 23 through March 25, 1995"—Pref.
    Includes bibliographical references and indexes.
    ISBN 1-55798-475-1
      1. Interpersonal relations—Congresses.   2. Attribution (Social psychology)—
    Congresses.   3. Social interaction—Congresses.   4. Social psychology—
    Congresses.   I. Jones, Edward Ellsworth, 1926–   .   II. Darley, John M.
    III. Cooper, Joel.
    HM132.A865   1998
    158.2—dc21   97-44346
                                                                                             CIP

British Library Cataloguing-in-Publication Data
A CIP record is available from the British Library

Printed in the United States of America
First Edition

In Remembrance

Edward Ellsworth Jones died too young.

When we lose someone we love, we almost always feel his or her passing was premature. We want to be with them longer; we want to talk and to laugh, to cry and to feel sorrow. We are just not ready for the vacuum left by death. All of these sentiments and more were true when Ned Jones died in the summer of 1993. Like all who knew him, we felt shock at his death. We felt anger at his having been taken from us and deep sadness at the prospect of not being able to be with him again. Gone were the lively conversations about the latest writings in the *JPSP*, the arguments about the best of college basketball; the analysis of the best of jazz, the taunting in the latest games of squash, tennis, or ping pong. Gone were long lunches at Lahiere's and discussions of data while peering at Ned over his size 14 shoes.

We were not finished learning from Ned. He was the consummate observer of human behavior in social interaction. He had the wisdom and insight to turn those observations into theories and those theories into empirical investigations. He was the unparalleled champion for conducting the experiment that reveals the nonobvious, subtle nuance of the human experience. For more than 40 years, Jones taught all of us about how people perceive others, how they present themselves to manage impressions, and how the self is formed and changed in the process. But his mission was not complete. There was so much more he wanted to learn about human social behavior. Because he was robbed of the time to learn, so were we. We no longer have the chance to talk with him, to read his words, to see his mind turn nuance into experiment, to see the next iteration of his imaginative conceptualization.

Those of us who were touched by Ned know that Ned died too young. We were not ready to have him leave us as mentor, friend, or fellow scholar. We can never replace the insight that he brought to psychology. We can only take solace in knowing that he made our lives richer for our having known him and for our having learned from him. The work in this volume shows the enormous extent of his influence. It also shows his success at encouraging his friends, students, and fellow scholars to stretch and extend the work he began. We would love to have had more time for Ned to stretch us still farther, to challenge and inspire us in person. Ned died too young for that. We carry on with his memory and his ideas to guide us.

JOEL COOPER AND JOHN M. DARLEY

APA Science Volumes

Organ Donation and Transplantation: Psychological and Behavioral Factors

The Perception of Structure

Perspectives on Socially Shared Cognition

Psychological Testing of Hispanics

Psychology of Women's Health: Progress and Challenges in Research and Application

Researching Community Psychology: Issues of Theory and Methods

Sleep and Cognition

Sleep Onset: Normal and Abnormal Processes

Stereotype Accuracy: Toward Appreciating Group Differences

Stereotyped Movements: Brain and Behavior Relationships

Studying Lives Through Time: Personality and Development

The Suggestibility of Children's Recollections: Implications for Eyewitness Testimony

Taste, Experience, and Feeding: Development and Learning

Temperament: Individual Differences at the Interface of Biology and Behavior

Through the Looking Glass: Issues of Psychological Well-Being in Captive Nonhuman Primates

Uniting Psychology and Biology: Integrative Perspectives on Human Development

Viewing Psychology as a Whole: The Integrative Science of William N. Dember

APA expects to publish volumes on the following conference topics:

Computational Modeling of Behavior Processes in Organizations

Dissonance Theory 40 Years Later: A Revival With Revisions and Controversies

Experimental Psychopathology and Pathogenesis of Schizophrenia

Global Prospects for Education: Development, Culture, and Schooling

Intelligence on the Rise: Secular Changes in IQ and Related Measures

Marital and Family Therapy Outcome and Process Research

Models of Gender and Gender Differences: Then and Now

Occasion Setting: Theory and Data

Psychosocial Interventions for Cancer

As part of its continuing and expanding commitment to enhance the dissemination of scientific psychological knowledge, the Science Directorate of the APA established a Scientific Conferences Program. A series of volumes resulting from these conferences is produced jointly by the Science Directorate and the Office of Communications. A call for proposals is issued twice annually by the Scientific Directorate, which, collaboratively with the APA Board of Scientific Affairs, evaluates the proposals and selects several conferences for funding. This important effort has resulted in an exceptional series of meetings and scholarly volumes, each of which has contributed to the dissemination of research and dialogue in these topical areas.

The APA Science Directorate's conferences funding program has supported 47 conferences since its inception in 1988. To date, 36 volumes resulting from conferences have been published.

WILLIAM C. HOWELL, PhD
Executive Director

VIRGINIA E. HOLT
Assistant Executive Director

Contents

Part Three: Social Interaction

Contributors

Robert P. Abelson, Professor Emeritus, Yale University
Robert M. Arkin, Ohio State University
Roy F. Baumeister, Case Western Reserve University
Marilynn B. Brewer, Ohio State University
Russell H. Fazio, Indiana University
Susan T. Fiske, University of Massachusetts
Kenneth J. Gergen, Swarthmore College
Daniel T. Gilbert, Harvard University
George R. Goethals, Williams College
David L. Hamilton, University of California at Santa Barbara
E. Tory Higgins, Columbia University
James L. Hilton, University of Michigan
Ziva Kunda, University of Waterloo, Ontario, Canada
Patricia W. Linville, Fuqua School of Business, Duke University
Diane M. Mackie, University of California at Santa Barbara
Arthur G. Miller, Miami University, Oxford, Ohio
Richard E. Nisbett, University of Michigan
Kathryn C. Oleson, Reed College
Thane S. Pittman, Gettysburg College
Frederick Rhodewalt, University of Utah
Meg J. Rohan, University of New South Wales, Sydney, Australia
Lee Ross, Stanford University
David J. Schneider, Rice University
Kelly G. Shaver, College of William and Mary
Mark Snyder, University of Minnesota
William B. Swann, Jr., University of Texas at Austin
Dianne M. Tice, Case Western Reserve University
Yaacov Trope, New York University
Mark P. Zanna, University of Waterloo, Ontario, Canada

Preface

Edward Ellsworth Jones was a preeminent scholar, teacher, and colleague, who in his professional career helped lay the foundation of social psychology. His research, in which he combined elegant experimental designs, sophisticated theoretical reasoning, and the dramatic voice of a storyteller, has inspired a half century of social psychologists. We feel privileged to have known Ned as a mentor, colleague, and close personal friend. We feel lucky to have benefited from his unique vision of social psychology, from his insights into previously hidden aspects of social interaction and mental life. The enduring force and elegance of his ideas and experiments remain with us, inspiring, challenging, and provoking new insights in contemporary social psychology.

Ned was a person of boundless personal warmth and compassion, ill-concealed beneath a personal style of competitive banter. He loved his colleagues and his students as he loved his family and friends. He passed onto them his knowledge, his insights, and his wisdom. In a different way, but with no less passion, Ned Jones loved social psychology. Although Ned was modest, and often overwhelmed by the importance attached to his work, he was fiercely proud of his contributions to social psychology. He was most moved by the reference to him as "Mr. Social Psychology," declaring in a speech accepting the Distinguished Scientist Award for the Society of Experimental Social Psychology in 1987, "I'd *love* to be Mr. Social Psychology. It would be a close second to my fantasy of being able to play the piano like Bill Evans."

He remained dedicated and devoted to social psychology throughout his long and illustrious career. He proclaimed once, "those who know me at all, know how deeply I care about the future of social psychology and what an exciting field I think it is. It has never occurred to me to go into archeology like Leon Festinger, or the stock market like Stanley Schachter, or facial blood flow like Bob Zajonc. One reason is that I'm rigid and lazy and not smart enough, but another is that there just seems to be so many fascinating unsolved problems in the playing out of interpersonal relations." He embraced the creativity of social psychology, as well as its adherence to the experimental method and empirical analyses; he always sought to subject his insights to rigorous experimental tests. He imparted that love of social psychology to us.

During the years that were spanned by Jones's academic career, great strides were made in the understanding of both person perception and social interaction, and Ned was consistently one of the major contributors to these efforts. More than once, Ned used the discoveries of the attributional approach to focus on new issues, and an examination of the vocabulary of social psychology reminds us of these emerging research topics: "ingratiation," "self-presentation," "the correspondence bias," "actor−observer differences," "self-handicapping," "out-group homogeneity." Along with his new ideas, he brought new students and colleagues trained in experimental social psychology, ready to add new insights into person perception and social interaction. Ned's students, trained at Duke and Princeton Universities, are now doing creative work in departments of psychology at many colleges and universities around the world.

Ned would have been pleased, but not surprised, to see his work, his ideas, and his approach to science carried on by those whose lives he touched. Many, but by no means all, of the people he touched are represented in this volume. He would not have liked to think that he sent soldiers into the field of battle to fight for his views or to defend his every idea. To the contrary, Ned would have hoped that he challenged people with his ideas, challenged them to think for themselves, challenged them to find the flaws and weaknesses in his work and to use the empirical method to stretch, extend, and criticize his ideas.

It was in this spirit that we chose to undertake the task of organizing a conference in memory of Ned. The conference in honor of

Edward Ellsworth Jones was held at the Psychology Department of Princeton University on March 23 through March 25, 1995. The title of the conference was Attribution Processes, Person Perception, and Social Interaction: The Legacy of Ned Jones. The Psychology Department had been planning a festschrift for Ned for some years, particularly as he approached retirement. Historians of science could argue about the exact dates and occasions of the origins of experimental social psychology, but certainly Ned was one of the early contributors and one of its most articulate advocates. So the festschrift would have been an occasion to examine a good many of the exciting developments of social psychology, historically tied together by the career of a person who had been central in originating many of these ideas. Shockingly, Ned suddenly died before the festschrift could be held, a fact that we will never cease to regret. But we decided to hold a conference that would accomplish the central purpose of the festschrift, which was to review social psychology from the unifying perspective provided by Ned's career.

We found, in organizing the conference, that as we touched on the areas in which Ned had done research, we would touch on many of the important research fields of social psychology. We also found, as we sorted through the lists of Ned's students, collaborators, friends, and colleagues, that we would be receiving contributions from a remarkable number of eminent, thoughtful researchers. Thus, it seemed to us that a book derived from the conference contributions would be a valuable publication. Conference contributors were aware of this in advance and organized their contributions under the dual charge of being first an oral presentation and, after subsequent editing, a book chapter. We asked them to organize a review that took, as its starting point, a particular aspect of Ned's work. But, as Ned would have wanted—insisted—we asked that it not be a testimonial to the past, but rather, a review and commentary of the current state of the art in the area he was instrumental in inspiring.

We hope the book serves many purposes. On one level, this volume is a tribute to Ned, a chance to honor and commemorate the ideas and theoretical advances of a brilliant and enthusiastic practitioner of social psychology. On another level, the book represents the history of a very important part of social psychology over the past 50 years; the authors, each beginning with Ned's seminal contribution, have traced the achievements and unresolved issues of the subfield of person perception and attribution theory. As such, we hope this volume will serve as a useful complement to any undergraduate and graduate course on person perception and attribution theory. Finally, we hope that it will inspire contemporary and future social psychologists, leading to new insights into how ordinary people self-present, understand their own and others' behaviors, and engage and interact with others.

Both editors had the opportunity to work professionally with Ned as well as the fortune of calling him a close friend. John Darley and Ned, as colleagues at Princeton University for 15 years, never formally wrote a professional paper together, but Darley benefited from Ned's theoretical insights and verbal sparring. Darley's interest in attribution and expectancy effects in many ways mirrored Ned's and they challenged each other to more finely describe and explore how individuals make sense of their own and others' behavior, while also overcoming erroneous expectancies held by observers.

Joel Cooper not only called Ned a friend and colleague, but also a mentor. Cooper received his doctoral degree from Duke University in 1969 under Ned's supervision. They published articles together in dissonance theory and in person perception. But mostly, Ned's influence was to teach Cooper how to think about social psychology, how to look for the non-obvious in social life, and how to craft the critical experiment. It is a lesson that Ned gladly offered to all his students and colleagues.

The Department of Psychology of Princeton University gratefully acknowledges the support of the Langfeld Endowment, the National Science Foundation, and the American Psychological Association, all of whom provided support for the conference. The editors wish to thank Adam Galinsky for his assistance throughout the editing process and Mary Ann Opperman for her assistance in coordinating the edited volume. The Psychology Department of Duke University, Ned's long-time academic home, graciously agreed that Princeton University was an appropriate site for the conference. Joel Cooper and John Darley, long-time friends and colleagues of Ned Jones, structured the conference sessions, and Mary Ann Opperman ably organized and coordinated the many aspects of the conference itself. Princeton President Harold Shapiro welcomed the participants and the conference audience.

No book can give a complete account of a conference dedicated to a man loved by so many, and attended by scores of social psychologists he influenced personally and professionally. Indeed, friends and colleagues, including Kurt Back, Jack Brehm, Darwyn Linder, Robert Carson, Gregory Kimble, Terry Wilson, and Art Aron spoke to the group about some of their personal reminiscences. The conference was drawn to a close by Eliott Aronson who offered comments on the weekend's proceedings. He also spoke perceptively about what might have been Ned's major self-definition through his decades at the forefront of social psychology—Ned as mentor. Surely, the chapters in this book offer a partial but convincing testimony to Aronson's judgment. Ned's ability to teach, inspire, and lead by example, manifest in the outstanding contributions from his students and colleagues that fill the pages of this volume. We trust that reading these contributions will not only provide the reader with a highly current account of theory and research in attribution, person perception, and social interaction but will also provide a glimpse of the quality of the social psychologist who inspired this work, Edward Ellsworth Jones (1926–1993).

Editor's note. The order of editors was decided by a coin toss. Both editors contributed equally in organizing and coordinating the Festschrift, and in reviewing the submitted comments.

About Ned

Edward E. Jones, Stuart Professor (1977–1993)

When Edward Ellsworth Jones died on July 30, 1993, he was the Stuart Professor of Psychology at Princeton University. He was the recipient of numerous awards, including the American Psychological Association's Distinguished Scientific Contribution Award (1977) and the Distinguished Scientist Award from the Society for Experimental Social Psychology (1987). Ned had also been made a Fellow of the American Academy of Arts and Sciences (1982).

Ned Jones was born in Buffalo, NY, on August 11, 1926. His mother was a passionate, articulate humanist who battled social injustice. His father was a professor of psychology at the University of Buffalo. Ned's early interests were in journalism and history before he became fascinated by the mysteries of interpersonal perception and social interaction.

After briefly attending Swarthmore College and being stationed in Japan during World War II, Ned Jones received his bachelor's degree from Harvard University. He continued at Harvard, receiving his doctoral degree, under the supervision of Jerome Bruner, in 1953. Ned took his first academic position at Duke University in 1953 and remained there for 24 years. In 1977, Ned returned north to become the Stuart Professor of Psychology at Princeton University, a position he retained until his untimely death.

Ned Jones was author and co-author of over 80 articles and chapters and four books, including *Ingratiation*, which won the Century Psychology Series Award in 1963, and his most recent book, *Interpersonal Perception*, an overview of his life's work on attribution and person perception. His ground-breaking work on self-presentation, person perception, correspondent inference, and self-handicapping has inspired researchers throughout the world.

Ned was known as a dedicated teacher and mentor. The psychology departments at both Duke and Princeton prospered while he taught at those universities. He was, throughout his life, a supporter of and friend to numerous colleagues and former students around the country. In addition to his standing as a preeminent and respected social psychologist, Ned Jones was devoted to his family and took great pride in their achievements. He is survived by his wife, Virginia, six children (Sally, Carrie, Todd, Amy, Jason, and Janet), and an ever-growing population of grandchildren.

Introduction

This book originated from a conference in honor of Edward Ellsworth Jones, held at the Psychology Department of Princeton University on March 23–25, 1995. The title of the conference was Attribution Processes, Person Perception, and Social Interaction: The Legacy of Ned Jones.

Ned Jones, an American Psychological Association Distinguished Career Medalist, received his doctoral degree from Harvard University in 1953, taught for many years at Duke University, and then went to Princeton University in 1977. Jones did not burst onto center stage of social psychology with a dramatic experiment or provocative new theory. Rather, he worked carefully to understand how people present themselves in social interaction and how they make attributional sense of the behaviors of others with whom they interact. He asked, how do we know when a person's behavior helps us understand what that person is like rather than being a reflection of the power of the social situation? When can we know that the way people present themselves is a true indication of their own dispositions as opposed to a presentation thrust on them by the social demands of the interpersonal environment? By the mid-1960s, Ned and his student, Keith Davis, made systematic the insights gained from a decade of careful and interesting experiments on these questions. The publication of "From Acts to Dispositions: The Attribution Process in Person Perception" in 1965, along with similar work contributed by Ned's friend, Harold Kelley, inspired an outpouring of research and transformed social psychology in the process. Attribution theory, with its emphasis on mechanisms for determining the underlying dispositions of the actor, provided theory that was critical for the forward movement of social psychology.

NED'S THEORETICAL AND
METHODOLOGICAL CONTRIBUTIONS

Throughout his career, Ned advanced our understanding of both person perception and social interaction. Early in his career he called for future research in which "the study of person perception intersects with the study of self-presentation" (Jones, 1964, p. 199). The myriad of emergent research topics that Ned brought to social psychology was grounded in attributional logic and theory. His seminal work on ingratiation (Jones, 1964) explored how individuals accomplish the difficult task of gaining and maintaining the liking of powerful others, even when the powerful other is aware of the ingratiator's external motives for gaining that liking. Ned's discovery of the *correspondence bias*, the tendency of perceivers to view actions that had been mandated by the situation as revealing something fundamental about the actor's disposition, transformed social psychology from an emphasis on rational baseline theories of person perception to a focus on the descriptive elements and inferential errors of how lay perceivers understand their social world. In attempting to understand this pervasive tendency to attribute the causes of behavior to dispositions, Ned along with Richard Nisbett suggested that this bias occurs only when explaining the behavior of others but not when explaining one's own behavior. They documented a number of different processes (the actor's more detailed knowledge of his or her circumstances and motives, and the differential salience of information available to the actor and the observer) that conspire to produce this actor–observer difference. Ned extended his work on person perception to the perception of groups. His early demonstrations of the *out-group homogeneity effect*—the tendency to attribute greater diversity to one's own group compared with a similar out group—had important implications for research on stereotyping, intergroup relations, and social identity.

During his later years, Ned returned to his earlier interest in self-presentation, which began with his work on ingratiation. He established, with Thane Pittman, a taxonomy of self-presentational strategies and the correspondent goals each strategy was meant to satisfy. He also discovered that self-presentational strategies exert an influence on self-perception. This spill-over effect demonstrated that the "masks" people wear affect the phenomenological experience of the self. Finally, Ned also brought to the field the concept of *self-handicapping*—the motivated construction of impediments to performance designed to prevent ability attributions to the self following failure.

Ned's theoretical insights were all based on or supported by empirical work. In the laboratory, Ned sought to create a social reality that would be experienced as phenomenologically real by the research participant. He used tape-recorded scenarios, role playing, and contrived social settings to create impactful social and interpersonal situations. He followed the Lewin–Festinger tradition of experimental realism as the surest road to investigating meaningful psychological processes. He applauded the cognitive revolution in social psychology, as social cognition research extended attribution theory by focusing on heretofore hidden aspects of mental processes. But Ned regarded with skepticism the more precise research methodologies (e.g., reaction time measures) that social cognition researchers used because they removed the individual from the social context and the richness of the phenomenon from the researchers' view. For Ned, psychological processes could not be divorced from the social context or from interpersonal interactions.

The Interrelatedness of Person Perception and Social Interaction

The central theme of this book is the essential interrelatedness of person perception and social interaction. Over the years, Ned's message to the field was a consistent one: Neither field should be considered in isolation. The purpose of person perception was to allow the social actor to function in social interactional settings. Social interactions are guided by perceptions of the other actors and the interactional setting. The influence is reciprocal: Person perception guides social interaction, and social interactions revise the perceptions of persons within interactional settings.

Ned's consistent desire for a dialectic between perception and action arose from the image of the person that he held. As others have commented, social psychologists have had their theories guided by many implicit images of the person. One of the most powerful ones is of the person as scientist (Kelley, 1967), examining the doings of other people in order to understand the goals and dispositions of those persons. Another image is that of the person as a stage actor (Goffman, 1959), presenting selves to others as the circumstances of social interaction call them forth. Ned's image of the person was that of a strategist, moving through life with a number of goals to fulfill, doing what is required and learning what is necessary about others in order to fulfill those goals (i.e., the goal-driven interactant; interestingly, a view that is currently receiving a revival of attention in both social and cognitive psychology).

And so, a conference was held to honor Ned's memory and his contribution to the past and future of social psychology. In the procedure established for the conference, a paper was presented in which the author reviewed a research area with which Ned had been associated, discussed the current state of research, and sketched the challenges that remained for the future. Two other presenters commented on that paper and were asked to develop the themes they thought would supplement, extend, or modify the first contribution. We have grouped those contributions together, so that there will usually be three chapters in a set. For Ned, research and its presentation were about telling stories, and so we hope that the three chapters together further the particular story that Ned began. Other contributors were asked to extract a theme from Ned's work and, using their creative imaginations, make a case for social psychology's need to pay attention to that development. Those contributions are included in the present volume where they best fit, with the other contributions nearest to them in content. It should be noted that the chapters and commentary vary in their presentational style. The chapters tend to be strict scholarly pieces, mapping past and current theory onto Ned's contribution. The commentaries tend to be more reflective, meditating on not only Ned's theoretical contribution but also on his relationship to the research process, the growth and expansion of social psychology, and the historical waxing and waning of particular themes, theories, and methodologies.

Themes and Organization of the Book

Part 1: Attribution and Person Perception

As we previously pointed out, Jones was the first to take a systematic look at how observers decode the meaning of another person's act and how they encode that meaning in the form of an attribution, thus the book begins with attribution theory. Jones and Davis (1965) and Harold Kelley (1967) independently presented rule-based systems that allow researchers to assess the circumstances under which people can make dispositional attributions following an actor's behavior.

Sometimes, research produces fortuitous findings that cry out for explanation. The first chapter of the attribution section begins with a finding that was initially so surprising as to be seen as an artifact of experimental procedure. While conducting research with his student, Victor Harris, Ned found that people observing a debater who took a position in a speech that he or she was ordered to take by a debate coach was nonetheless perceived to believe the position espoused. Attribution theory had been designed to capture the rational decisions people make about others' dispositions. There seemed nothing intrinsically rational about using a behavior to infer a personality disposition under conditions in which it was clear that the behavior was forced by environmental conditions. Surely, this was an artifact. Or, was it? Startlingly, this finding was stubbornly robust: Perceivers continually make person attributions, assuming that the behavior accurately reflects the debater's belief. Demonstrating this "fundamental attribution error" or, as Jones later called it, "correspondence bias," and finding its psychological cause gave scientific employment to a quite remarkable number of researchers.

Dan Gilbert, in chapter 1, takes on the challenge of finding the elusive psychological cause of the correspondence bias. He offers a fanciful conversation with Ned in which they discuss the outcome of efforts to fulfill Ned's wish to find the single integrating mechanism for the correspondence bias. Gilbert concludes that there are, in truth, multiple causes for the correspondence bias and that the search for the single cause of the bias is misdirected. In his comment on Gilbert's chapter, Arthur Miller unfolds this story further and suggests how one might think about the causes of the bias. Lee Ross, who originally coined the term *fundamental attribution error* to describe the phenomenon, shows us why the effect is so central to many social processes in his comment on Gilbert's chapter.

Richard Nisbett, whose contribution comes at the end of this section, places the correspondence bias in its philosophical context and suggests that it is a characteristic bias demonstrated in Western culture, less evident in other cultures. The reason for this is that Western culture locates the causes of human action as being within the individual, the volitional agent perspective. Thus, when behaviors are witnessed, the causes for those behaviors are located in the dispositions of the acting individual.

In the second set of contributions to the attributional section, a second generational attributional model is presented. Yaacov Trope is the author of an influential two-stage model of person perception that separates the relatively rapid, perceptual inferences we first make from the later, more controlled cognitive calculations made later in the attributional process. Trope, in chapter 2 of this volume, uses his model to examine the hypothesis-testing strategies that might lead to correspondence effects. David Hamilton (see Hamilton's comment on chapter 2) begins by contrasting Jones's original correspondent-inference theory with two "post-cognitive revolution" theories, those of Trope and Gilbert. He then goes on to suggest the utility of making a distinction between two kinds of inference, suggesting that one can be thought of as preattributional in nature, whereas the other involves attributional analysis. By making this distinction, Hamilton is able to give different meanings to the correspondence bias and the fundamental attribution error. Ziva Kunda, in a remarkably original contribution, directs us toward the possibilities of drawing on a theoretical perspective that is current in cognitive psychology but just beginning to impact social psychology (see Kunda's comment on chapter 2). She presents parallel processing, connectionist thinking involving multiple constraint satisfaction, and sketches its relevance for person perception.

In the last portion of this section, James L. Hilton, Susan T. Fiske, and Mark Snyder develop a realization that we mentioned earlier, the essential interconnectedness of person perception and social interaction. This realization has interestingly complicated some of social psychology's standard stories. The self-fulfilling prophecy proves less all-encompassing than it seemed initially, for instance. Hilton begins the section with his review of how interaction goals should be categorized and how this categorization predicts the occasions in which expectancy confirming or disconfirming outcomes will prevail. He makes the case for distinguishing among goals by the degree to which they are accessible to consciousness. Fiske and Snyder report on their long-term research programs and touch on the ways in which we should taxonomize goals. Fiske provides an organization of different taxonomies, suggesting criteria for choosing among them. Snyder picks up Hilton's theme of the motivational component that is introduced into the analysis when goals are considered and points out the utility of the functionalist perspective in social and personality psychology. This section presents the best case for the claim laid out in Ned's research with John Thibaut on the interdependence of interaction and perception. The section ends with the thoughtful contribution by Richard Nisbett mentioned earlier, on "essentialism" and its possible connection to Western culture.

Part 2: The Self

Part 2 takes on a challenge that was always implicit in Ned's writings, perhaps a challenge that social psychologists do not consistently address. What are the motives that determine the actions of human beings? Relatedly, what is the core nature of the self? These are questions that all of the human sciences return to with regularity. Roy Baumeister takes issue with what one might call the "1990s answer" to that question, which is that self-esteem—an intrapsychic motive—is the fundamental source of human motivation (see chapter 4). However, Baumeister suggests that social affiliation—an interpersonal motive—is the basic motive, and self-esteem simply a marker of how well one is doing in gaining affiliation. George R. Goethals evaluates Baumeister's suggestion from the perspective of Jones's work and makes the case that the core concept for Jones was interpersonal effectiveness rather than belongingness. Thane Pittman, who co-authored with Ned the influential chapter on interactional motives (Jones & Pittman, 1982), also challenges Baumeister's contention and presents the case for the motive to have effective understanding and control of the physical and social environment as primary. Self-esteem then is a marker of how well the individual feels he or she is doing in the struggle to operate effectively in the world.

E. Tory Higgins (see chapter 5) focuses his attention on one of Jones's remarkable contributions to the literature that should not be overlooked when examining his thinking. Ned's textbook with Harold Gerard (Jones & Gerard, 1967), *Foundations of Social Psychology,* was a text like few others. It offered novel integrations to a field of study and provided theoretical clarity and new research hypotheses. Higgins examines the impact and importance of Jones and Gerard's view of what they called the *minimal social person.* Socialization, Higgins argues, produces two different self-regulatory orientations: one, an "ought based" orientation that creates security-focused strategies; the other, an "ideal self guide," producing positive outcome-oriented strategies. Mark P. Zanna and Meg J. Rohan in their comment on Higgins's chapter consider the transmission of values between parent and child and report that, when one examines the college-aged "child," the child holds the values of parents who were responsive rather than instrumental in their orientation to their child. Fazio, drawing on his own research project on attitudes, sketches how memory processes may work to transfer past learning of the sort that Higgins discusses into current perceptual and associative processes.

Kenneth Gergen closes Part 2 with a contribution on "the relational self" that looks ahead to the next section. Gergen's concern is with the conceptualizations of the self that are prevalent in psychology, and the research consequences of these conceptualizations. How are social psychologists to think about the often taken-for-granted concept of the self? Gergen suggests that researchers need to move away from psychology's customary treatment of the self as an individual containing judgment and decision-making apparatuses, to a view of self as essentially relational, engaging in culturally conventionalized patterns of human interchange.

Part 3: Social Interaction

The final section of the book places the self in a social interactional context. We feel that this orientation always seemed at the heart of Ned's concerns. (Darley often suggested to Jones that he developed correspondent-inference theory to specify the rules that the smart self-presenter knew were governing the observer's attributions. Jones admitted to the charm of the unity that this suggestion gave to his work but denied being that "planful." What self do I need to construct to accomplish my goals in this upcoming social interaction? Do I need to ingratiate myself? How can I become a sincere ingratiator? Is intimidation called for? Then, as discussed by Jones and Pittman (1982), an intimidating personality is mobilized.

Although Ned made several contributions to the theory of self-presentation, characteristically he was most intrigued by deploying that theory to account for some subtle, second-order phenomena. Since Heider, we have been aware that ordinary people realize that a person's performance on some ability-linked task is a function of that person's ability, but also a number of other considerations, such as long-term motivations to do well, short-term disturbances, the difficulty of the specific task, and a number of ill-defined determinants that we group under the heading of "luck." Ned looked at how a performer who feared giving a poor performance attempts to defeat the obvious attribution of poor ability.

Ned, as usual, was off doing something more subtle with the general notion. Ned's contribution to this field was his demonstration of the phenomenon of self-handicapping, which he, along with his student Steve Berglas, asserted was an example of a broader category of complex self-deceptive practices. A person who had done well on an ability-significant task, but who had no idea of how he or she had done so well, when faced with the requirement to again perform on that task would engineer barriers that would tend to degrade performance on the task. And, Ned continued, this was done so the performer could maintain his or her *own* perceptions of high ability.

Robert Arkin, for years Ned's friendly research antagonist, suggested that at least often, handicapping behavior was really motivated to preserve the attribution of high ability in the eyes of the observers, and thus could be the result of a conscious calculational strategy of the actor. Arkin and Oleson (see chapter 6) present a thoughtful review of how the evidence suggests that we should formulate the process, arguing for the possible existence of both of the abovementioned purposes of self-handicapping. They go on to sketch further theoretical developments in the area and some interesting future directions for research. David Schneider uses self-handicapping to illluminate the continuing themes in Ned's research (see Schneider's comment, this volume). He remarks that the self-handicapping idea was a return to Ned's early work on ingratiation, but it was a return with a thick veneer of his subsequent concerns with attributional issues. Kelly Shaver connects the notion of self-handicapping to an extension of expectancy theory that he has been developing, and to Tesser's self-esteem maintenance model (see Shaver's comment, this volume).

Certainly for Ned, and for many social psychologists, personality was constructed and reconstructed for the purpose of the next social interaction. Without denying the personality theorist's conceptualization of a relatively fixed personality structure, Ned and others were struck by the degree to which people display personalities that will assist us in achieving our interactional goals. Are we the low-power person in the interaction seeking to bring our interactant to like us? Then we exhibit the ingratiator's personality. Are our goals otherwise? Then a different personality is presented. The first-order question that arises from this is whether we convince the other of the truth of our displayed personality. This was the question that Ned attended to in his book on ingratiation (Jones, 1964). Many others have researched this general question in self-presentation, but Ned was, characteristically, heading elsewhere. Regardless of whether we are able to convince the other of the truth of our displayed personality, we may convince ourselves. Therefore, for at least some time following the interaction, we may think of ourselves as having the personality displayed in the interaction. How does this odd and interesting outcome come about? Frederick Rhodewalt began work on this problem when he was a graduate student and postdoctoral fellow at Princeton. In his chapter in this volume,

Rhodewalt examines the research on the carryover effect and what these studies indicate about the interplay between public presentations and private self-concepts (see chapter 7). William B. Swann, recalling a remark by Ned that "the self is not a bowling ball, you know" unpacks that response to show how our image of self is grounded in the interactional messages we get from others (see Swann's comment on Rhodewalt, this volume). Dianne M. Tice points out that there are a variety of audiences to which individuals give their self-presentations. Ingratiation and self-promotion, the most studied of self-presentational tactics, are the tactics most likely to occur between strangers; other tactics, likely to be used between friends and acquaintances, have been less studied.

Our review of Ned Jones's research would not have been complete without the additional perspective that concludes the final section of the current volume. As Ned showed in his pioneering work with Patricia Linville and George Quattrone (see Jones & Linville, 1980; Jones & Quattrone, 1980), our perceptions of others are very much affected by the way in which we are anchored in social groups. Linville, in her contribution to this volume, offers a systematic review of progress in what has become known as the out-group homogeneity effect—the phenomenon that people perceive members of their own groups to be considerably more diverse than people in comparable out groups. The willingness that people have to view out groups as simple and homogeneous leads to several consequences that are important theoretically and pragmatically. People are willing to make generalizations of out groups from a single instance of behavior. Thus, a behavior by a Black person as judged by a White perceiver can be used as the basis for making generalizations about the entire race—an attribution the White perceiver would resist making about his or her own racial group. Furthermore, people make more extreme judgments of out groups because, as Jones's and Linville's research shows, people's judgments are more extreme when they are judging groups that they believe are not complex. The importance of this work for issues such as stereotyping is clear and has prompted sustained interest in uncovering its causes.

Linville's chapter (see chapter 8) systematically analyzes the progress that has been made in identifying the cognitive processes and motivational issues behind the out-group homogeneity effect. She analyzes the progress in terms of successive waves of interest that have characterized the field for the last 15 years and demonstrates the impressive array of analyses that have been brought to bear on this problem, including her own work on the covariation–extremity effect. Linville concludes her chapter with a playful rumination about how Ned would have responded to the progress in this field. He would have been a bit surprised by expansion and proliferation of work in this area, he would have been quick to point out the still-missing elements of the variability story, but, Linville predicts, he would have been quite pleased.

Marilynn Brewer's commentary asks us to view the out-group homogeneity effect as part of two theoretical orientations in social psychology. The first is motivated cognition, and Brewer points out the advantages of viewing the out-group homogeneity effect as part of the motive to establish a distinctive or differentiated representation of the self. The second perspective is from her own dual-process model of impression formation. Here, Brewer offers the provocative notion that the representation of people in memory on a "person node" and a "category node" can explain the causes of homogeneous and heterogeneous attributions and place the out-group homogeneity effect in a broader context of group categorization research.

Diane M. Mackie recalls Ned Jones's belief that progress in social psychology would come from finding those few basic processes that can help to explain the diversity of people's motivational and cognitive activity in the social context. Accordingly, Mackie seeks an integrated explanation of the out-group homogeneity effect on the basis of the principles of correspondent inferences and attributional processing originally discussed by Quattrone and Jones. She makes a forceful case for the explanatory power of attribution theory and suggests that the application of another of Jones's classic attribution findings, actor–observer differences—can solve an important piece of the theoretical puzzle of explaining the out-group homogeneity effect.

The 1995 conference in honor of Ned Jones included a contribution that provides a fitting close to the book. Robert Abelson, Ned's friend for many years, presented an account of "caricature theory," which he invented for the occasion (see chapter 9, this volume). Abelson's theory is an examination of some of the "systematic occurrences of psychosocial absurdities." He delineates several social interactional processes that work to transform normal situations, events, and activities into ones that then become more extreme or overblown. For instance, sometimes it is competition that drives a phenomenon toward absurdity (e.g., as individuals compete for the role of most outrageous rap singer, or most pierced body parts). Animus between two individuals or two groups can lead each to decrease points of similarity between themselves and "the other," in order that an observer not see them as in any way similar to the despised other.

There are, of course, several interesting extensions of attribution theory that are made in Abelson's chapter, and we could hang the presence of the chapter on that connection. But we prefer to take it for what it is: A salute by Abelson, friend and contemporary of Jones, to Ned. In making this contribution, Abelson reminds us of something that was a central characteristic of Ned Jones. Ned was interested in the nonobvious subtleties of human life: The predicaments and dilemmas that we get ourselves into where our typically rational rules leave us little guidance. He was often motivated by looking at a phenomenon that he found fascinating and wondering how it could ever have arisen. Abelson, with his characteristic wisdom and playfulness, conducts his own version of this enterprise.

"My chapter is totally unlike anything Ned might ever have done . . . Nevertheless, I think my theme is one he would have enjoyed," Abelson remarked. Indeed Ned would have.

REFERENCES

Goffman, E. (1959). *The presentation of self in everyday life.* New York: Doubleday/Anchor.

Jones, E. (1964). *Ingratiation.* New York: Appleton-Century-Crofts.

Jones, E., & Davis, K. E. (1965). From acts to dispositions: The attribution process in person perception. In L. Berkowitz (Ed.), *Advances in experi-*

mental social psychology (Vol. 2, pp. 219–266). San Diego, CA: Academic Press.

Jones, E., & Gerard, H. B. (1967). *Foundations of social psychology*. New York: Wiley.

Jones, E., & Linville, P. (1980). Polarized appraisals of out-group members. *Journal of Personality and Social Psychology, 38,* 689–702.

Jones, E., & Pittman, T. (1982). Toward a general theory of strategic self-presentation. In J. Suls (Ed.), *Psychological perspective on the self* (Vol. 1, pp. 231–262). Hillsdale, NJ: Erlbaum.

Jones, E., & Quattrone, G. (1980). The perception of variability within in-groups and out-groups: Implications for the law of small numbers. *Journal of Personality and Social Psychology, 38,* 141–152.

Kelley, H. H. (1967). Attribution theory in social psychology. In D. Levine (Ed.), *Nebraska Symposium on Motivation* (Vol. 15, pp. 192–240). Lincoln: Nebraska University Press.

Attribution and Social Interaction

PART ONE

Attribution and Person Perception

Speeding With Ned:
A Personal View of the
Correspondence Bias

Daniel T. Gilbert

Ned Jones was a brilliant psychologist, a wonderful human being, and a terrible driver. I discovered the last of these facts in 1982 when I was in graduate school and Ned was my advisor. One Saturday he had to make a long trip to some remote section of New Jersey and he invited me to keep him company on the drive. "We'll talk about your first-year project," he said. "Bring some jazz tapes." I didn't know any better. I thought he was serious. So I actually brought along the notes for my first-year project. I also brought along a tape of my hero, Keith Jarrett, whom Ned immediately dismissed as "too baroque." We quietly deposed my hero in favor of Ned's—the sublime Bill Evans— and listened to his music for the duration of the drive. At some point early in that drive I noticed two things. First, I noticed that Bill Evans was indeed a more subtle and articulate pianist than Keith Jarrett. Second, I noticed that we were traveling at about 90 miles per hour. Ned

Preparation of this chapter was supported by a Research Scientist Development Award from the National Institute of Mental Health (1-KO2-MH00939-01). I thank Joel Cooper, Art Miller, Maryann Opperman, and Lee Ross for their helpful comments.

must have seen me glancing nervously at the speedometer because he proudly announced that if he got another speeding ticket, he, his wife, and his insurance carrier were all going to part ways. At which point he nudged the car to 95.

Over the next decade of our friendship I came to learn that speeding was almost as much of a passion for Ned as was Bill Evans. Everywhere Ned drove, he drove too fast. But speeding, I came to learn, was not simply about going fast. Rather, it was a competitive sport in which a player attempted to move across a paved field as rapidly as possible without being detected by the opposing team, which, on this particular spring day, was the entire New Jersey State Troopers Association. Speeding is not about cars or roads. It is not really even about speed. It is about outsmarting other people who just happen to be police.

We talked. We sped. I think "Stella by Starlight" had just come on when I first spotted the police cruiser on the shoulder just a half mile ahead, idling happily beneath an antler of whirling, colored lights, a small foreign car captive before it. One moment Ned and I were chatting about this and that, listening to music, adjusting our visors against the afternoon sun, banking and listing into a curve, and the next moment our conversation abruptly ceased and our eyes were riveted to the scene at the shoulder. And as quickly as those flashing lights appeared in our field of vision, two things happened, one of them entirely predictable and one of them entirely unexpected. Every car on the turnpike predictably slowed down, and Ned unexpectedly sped up. Perhaps it was only in contrast to the suddenly legal crawl of nearby traffic, but I felt certain that we passed the cruiser at 100.

"That's Gary Peacock on drums," Ned said, scarcely nodding in time to the music. Could he have missed the one-act drama a quarter mile—now a half mile, now more—behind us? Of course not. He was just waiting for me to say something—waiting for me to offer him my incredulity like some exotic disease for which only he had the cure. I would come to learn in the following years that Ned taught his students in the same way that Bill Evans (never Bill, never just Evans) played his piano. Between the clever remark and the penetrating question were languid patches of silence that seemed casually, almost disinterestedly placed, but that were in fact carefully measured and impeccably timed. Conversation with Ned was a dance, a game, a jam.

"You went by that cop awfully fast," I said.

"Yep," Ned replied like a rimshot. More silence as he stared straight ahead. Perhaps there was another verse before the chorus.

"I can't believe you didn't slow down."

Ned smiled. "That's what everybody does. And it doesn't make sense." Ah. Here it was. The tempo changed, the dialogue hit the major seventh, and the melodic hook emerged from behind the drummer's fill. "The gut instinct, Danny Boy," (never Dan, never just Gilbert) "is to slow down when you see a cop giving someone a ticket. But cops aren't randomly distributed on a highway. They space themselves to cover the most territory, which means that when you see a cop giving a ticket you can be pretty sure that you have spotted the only cop on your particular section of highway, and you can be sure he's too busy to spot you back. So the odds of getting stopped just now were actually lower than they were earlier. I adjusted my speed accordingly." Ned looked satisfied. He stared out the driver's side window for a moment, and I let the pause linger. "People slow down as a reflex. They realize it's illogical, but they can't help it. They do it anyway." He shook his head. "It never ceases to amaze me."

We went on to talk about other things that afternoon—the Oakland Raiders ("No finesse"), JPSP ("too baroque"), and how to distinguish between good and bad gin ("One word, Danny Boy: Tanqueray"). And although I did not realize this at the time, we had also talked about my first-year project, because the thing that never ceased to amaze Ned had begun to amaze me a little bit too.

DRIVING THROUGH JONESLAND

Somewhere between the time that Ned became seriously devoted to Bill Evans and the time he became seriously devoted to speeding, he noticed something that never ceased to amaze him. In 1965, Ned and his student Keith Davis had tried to describe how ordinary people use behavior to infer the personal dispositions of the actor. Their theory was smart, well articulated, and not particularly counterintuitive. For example, it told us that if an actor does one thing rather than another, observers are likely to conclude that she desired the state of affairs to which her action uniquely led. It told us that when an actor's behavior is directly relevant to us as observers, we will be especially motivated to understand what makes him tick. It told us that when we are in the business of understanding what motivates people, their accidents, parapraxes, and other unintended actions don't really count. It told us that when people are forced to act as they do, we don't conclude that they were somehow predisposed toward that action. And so on. The theory was not meant to amaze. It was meant to formalize the rules that could enable the ordinary, mundane, and generally unamazing business of everyday person perception.

Ned Charts a Course

Although the theory's predictions were clearly too obvious to warrant a test, Ned liked to do experiments. So in 1967, he and Victor Harris tested the theoretically derived hypothesis that people will not draw dispositional inferences from actions that are mandated by the social situation—in other words, when people are in the business of understanding others, their constrained behaviors won't really count. Participants in their experiment read essays that supported or opposed Fidel Castro's regime, and some participants were told that the essayist had freely chosen to write the essay while others were told that the essayist had been ordered to write the essay by a debate coach. All participants were asked to estimate just how much the essayist personally supported or opposed Castro, and the timid prediction was that participants would draw *correspondent inferences* (i.e., they would conclude that the essayist's verbal behavior corresponded to the essayist's personal attitudes) when the essayist had chosen to write the essay, but not when the essayist had been forced to do so. The prediction was timid, the results were a foregone conclusion, and the experiment didn't work. Although participants made correspondent inferences about essayists whose behavior was freely enacted, they also made correspondent inferences (albeit much weaker ones) about essayists whose behavior was situationally constrained. Participants knew perfectly well that the essay's content had been dictated by the debate coach, and yet something about the actor's behavior elicited correspondent inferences. Rather than being annoyed by this experimental anomaly, Ned celebrated it as the *observer bias,* which he later renamed the *correspondence bias* (see Gilbert & Malone, 1995, for a review). Most of us know it by another name too. As Ned wrote (Jones, 1988), "This bias has also been referred to by Lee Ross as the fundamental attribution error, but I find that designation overly provocative and somewhat misleading. Furthermore, I'm angry that I didn't think of it first."

This small difference between two means did not intrigue Ned because it taught him something new; rather, it intrigued him because it seemed to be an example of something he had thought about for a long time, namely, that in everyday life people seem all too willing to take each other at face value and all too reluctant to search for alternative explanations for each other's behavior. Ned's early work on ingratiation (Jones, 1964) had explored how people convince others to like them, and he was fascinated by how easily and routinely this was accomplished. Why, he wondered, do we believe those who tell us that we have a wonderful child, a stylish haircut, or a winning personality when (a) it is so cheap and so tempting for others to say such things even when they don't mean them and (b) we tell fibs like this all the time ourselves? Magicians surely do not fall for the same sleights of hand they perpetrate, so why are people duped by the very ingratiation tactics they employ? Shouldn't observers chalk compliments up to the requirements of polite society and reserve judgment about what the flatterer really believes? It seemed to Ned that there was something about observing behavior that virtually compelled the observer to make correspondent inferences about the actor's personality—despite the observer's knowledge that such inferences might not be logically warranted—and he wondered what that something was.

Over the next 15 years or so, Ned's wondering led to a score of experiments in which he and his collaborators toyed with the effect that he and Harris had found (see Jones, 1979, 1990, for reviews). Such toying typically took two forms. The first involved challenging the effect—creating circumstances under which it would be likely to disappear and then showing that, in fact, it didn't. So, for example, he and Art Miller and Steve Hinkle showed that the effect occurred even when participants had the experience of being an arm-twisted essayist prior to reading the arm-twisted essay of another (Miller, Jones, & Hinkle, 1981; see also Jones & Harris, 1967, Experiment 2). He and I showed that it occurred even when participants did the arm twisting themselves (Gilbert & Jones, 1986). And so on. The second form of play involved ruling out local explanations of what Ned believed to be a ubiquitous phenomenon. So, for example, he and Mel Snyder showed that the experimenter-generated essays that Jones and Harris had used were not necessary to produce correspondence bias, which occurred even when the essays were written by ordinary college students (Snyder & Jones, 1974). He and I showed that the bias did not require that participants change their own attitudes or presume that the essayists' attitudes had been changed by the essay-writing task (Gilbert & Jones, 1986). In short, Ned's empirical work on correspondence bias was largely directed toward demonstrating the robustness and generality of the effect.

Ned was a great believer in the pedagogical value of mistakes, and he liked to point out when others were making them. But he also encouraged his students to point out to him his own, and he listened graciously and agreed occasionally. It is an homage to him that we can, in hindsight, say what was wrong with this work as well as what was so very right with it. The first problem is that, in the long run, the work was paradigm bound. Ned's beloved attitude-attribution paradigm was a fine way to bottle the phenomenon, and he chose to demonstrate the generality of the correspondence bias by ruling out a variety of alternative explanations within this paradigm rather than by demonstrating the same effect in a variety of other paradigms. Ultimately this may have been a tactical error because Ned became embroiled in a host of minor debates about whether this or that aspect of the experimental paradigm was a prerequisite for the effect. Indeed, a quick glance at the literature shows that most of the relevant research of the day was about the Jones and Harris experiment and was not about the correspondence bias itself. In some ways, Ned became too busy outmaneuvering critics to explore the more far-reaching implications of his amazing phenomenon. He should have been the one who taught us why the correspondence bias was such a vitally important effect, but he wasn't. The person who did that was Lee Ross (1977), who had the decided advantage of not being mired in the wet cement of the attitude-attribution paradigm and who was thus free to think more broadly about the phenomenon. The somewhat ironic denouement is that now, nearly 30 years later, most researchers probably agree that (a) the correspondence bias is a fairly robust and general phenomenon, and (b) the attitude-attribution paradigm is not the best way to bottle it.

The second mistake was not so much an error of commission as an error of omission. Ned showed us that the phenomenon was real, that it didn't go away quietly, and that its persistence resisted most artifactual explanations, but he did not tell us why it occurred in the first place. Of course, hindsight is dangerously sharp and we do well to remember that yesterday is not today. Ned's was not the era of process models, and the geist of his zeit called for social psychologists to invent same-level alternatives to reexplain results (e.g., the dissonance versus self-perception debate) rather than to invent lower-level models that predict them. Jones and Harris approvingly quoted Heider's (1958, p. 54) well-known maxim that behavior "tends to engulf the total field," and correctly noted that "this describes the results without really explaining them" (Jones & Harris, 1967, p. 22). Nonetheless, Ned did not explain the results himself, and privately he continued to bet on Heider's unit-formation notion as the one with the most staying power. Until the early 1980s, Ned seemed to feel that attempts to explain correspondence bias were premature, and that in the early stages of a relationship with an amazing thing one should simply play with it— tweak it, twist it, and see what pops out. This view may or may not be right, but surely it is not difficult to understand why Ned held it. After all, the amazing thing had itself just popped out of his attempt to demonstrate something much less amazing, so why shouldn't he expect that some lovely, parsimonious explanation would ultimately present itself if he kept his heart open and his eyes peeled?

As usual, Ned was right.

George Takes the Wheel

One Friday morning in 1982, Ned and I were speeding to Trenton to meet the departmental colloquium speaker, Bob Abelson, whose train from New Haven arrived at noon. Soon the three of us had retired for lunch to a chummy, neighborhood Italian restaurant that Ned told us was renowned for its stunning version of olives in Tanqueray sauce. As we waited for our drinks, Bob said, "I read George Quattrone's article in *JPSP* last month. A beautiful piece of work."

Ned nodded in agreement, glanced over to make sure I was paying attention, and without hesitation said, "Yep, he's the smartest student I've ever had."

Whether or not George was the smartest of Ned's students, he was certainly the person who changed the direction of Ned's work and moved him beyond demonstrations of robustness and generality to descriptions of the psychological mechanisms that actually produce the bias. Social psychology was at the zenith of its love affair with cognitive psychology (after the honeymoon but before the bickering), and Dick Nisbett and Lee Ross had just immortalized that relationship in their seminal book on human inference (Nisbett & Ross, 1980). One of the book's many contributions was that it brought the decade-old work of Amos Tversky and Danny Kahneman to the attention of mainstream social psychologists. That work suggested that ordinary people solve a large number of inferential problems by using a small number of judgmental heuristics, one of which they dubbed the *anchor–adjust heuristic* (see Tversky & Kahneman, 1974).

To understand Quattrone's contribution, one must understand the state of the art at the time. What did attribution theories of the early 1980s have to say about the psychological processes that enabled attributional judgments? Not much. Next to nothing, in fact. With a few exceptions, attribution theories simply articulated the formal inferential rules that a thinking system might use to move from observations of action to inferences about the underlying qualities of the actor. As Ned and his student Daniel McGillis had noted in 1976, attribution theories were rational baseline theories and were not intended as descriptions of the mental work that real, meaty, sweaty people did when they made inferences about each other. As geometry was to architecture, so attribution theories were to person perception. Experiments revealed that people's attributional inferences looked very much like the attributional inferences that a thinking system would generate if it was relying on formal attributional rules such as the calculus of noncommon effects, the covariation and discounting principles, and so on. But no one knew whether people were actually using those rules, and if they were, certainly no one knew how. In general, study participants seemed to understand when behavior should be taken as a fair indicator of the actor's personal dispositions and when it should be ascribed to the pressures of the social situation. The variables that should have affected judgments made by formal rules (e.g., the consistency of the behavior over time, the number of noncommon effects) seemed to affect the judgments made by ordinary people. But whether ordinary people were using those formal rules—and if so, how they were doing it—remained a mystery.

Quattrone set out to solve this mystery by borrowing an idea from Tversky and Kahneman, who had suggested that people do not typically wait until they have considered all the evidence before they generate an inference, but instead, they roughly estimate a problem's solution and then smooth out that rough estimate as they consider each new piece of information in turn. This heuristic displays nature's genius for compromise because it allows people to move toward accurate solutions while having somewhat less accurate solutions in hand as they do so, which is quite useful when one is carefully considering whether to wander away from the campfire and is suddenly interrupted by a bear. Quattrone was intrigued by this description of the process by which complex problems were solved, and he wondered whether people might solve "the attributional problem" in the same way. Whereas correspondence-inference theory suggested that people make correspondent inferences under some circumstances (e.g., when behavior is freely authored) and not under others (e.g., when behavior is constrained), Quattrone (1982) suggested that people actually make correspondence inferences under both circumstances and that they then go on to adjust those inferences as they consider the possibility that the behavior was situationally constrained.

Quattrone reasoned that if people do indeed anchor on dispositions and then adjust for situations, then perhaps under other circumstances they could be encouraged to anchor on situations and adjust for dispositions. In other words, perhaps people could begin the attributional task by first using behavior to estimate the situational pressures that were impinging on the actor, and then continue by adjusting those estimates as they considered the actor's dispositions. In his 1982 paper, Quattrone turned the well-worn attitude-attribution paradigm inside out with two moves. First, instead of telling participants that there had or had not been strong situational pressure on the essayist, he told participants that the essayist was already known to have a pro- or anti-something attitude. Second, instead of asking participants to estimate the strength of the essayist's dispositions, he asked them to estimate the strength of the situational pressures that had impinged on the essayist. In other words, rather than manipulating what participants knew about the situational pressures and then measuring what they thought about the essayist's dispositions, he manipulated what they knew about the essayist's dispositions and measured what they thought about the situational pressures. He did this by suggesting to participants that although the essays had been freely rendered by persons who were known to support the positions they advocated, there was reason to suspect that the person who commissioned the essays had applied subtle, nonverbal pressure on the essayists to defend the commissioner's own personal position. Participants were asked to read the essay and to estimate the commissioner's (and not the essayist's) position on the issue. And in this topsy-turvy version of the attitude-attribution paradigm participants did a topsy-turvy thing: They concluded that the essay reflected the commissioner's personal position even when they knew full well that the essayist's attitude was congruent with the position advocated in the essay. In other words, participants believed that the situation (the commissioner's subtle pressure) had caused the actor's behavior even though they knew that the actor was predisposed toward it.

Hey, Dad, Can I Drive?

It was 1984, and Ned and I were speeding through Toronto. Something about a rented car always made Ned drive faster than usual—as if some part of him believed that police officers the world over were on the lookout for his sleek, black Pontiac Bonneville 1000, and that behind the wheel of a rented rosy red Ford Fiesta he was invisible. He was wearing his trademark driving cap—the one that made him look like Mr. Toad from *The Wind in the Willows*—and when he finally became convinced that the radio would harvest nothing but "rock noise," he switched it off and began to talk to me about the correspondence bias. "It would be wonderful to show that you can really reverse the effect," he said. "George did it, but he cheated." Given Ned's dim view of cheaters and his high regard for George, I asked him to clarify. "What I mean is that he got people to attribute the essay to the situation, but in his case 'the situation' was another person's dispositions. His subjects did, in fact, attribute the behavior to dispositions—it was just the wrong person's dispositions. Somehow that doesn't seem to me like really *reversing* the correspondence bias." As the years passed, I would come to understand that Ned enjoyed pondering the mystery of the correspondence bias like he enjoyed guessing the killer's identity in a good whodunit, and as with an engrossing novel, part of him did not want the story to end. Right up until his death, he resisted the idea that anyone had actually achieved The Complete Solution.

If his resistance was understandable, his enthusiasm was contagious. His lifelong quest to understand the correspondence bias seemed to me thoroughly heroic, and as a graduate student, I never had the slightest doubt that joining that crusade was the most noble destiny a young soldier could hope for. I spent several years reading and thinking about the work that Ned, George and others had done, and in the end I found myself convinced of two things: First, I was convinced that Quattrone's theory was essentially right, and second, I was convinced that his experiment did little to show just how right his theory was. What was wrong with that experiment? In my view, the experiment was not flawed (as Ned thought) so much as irrelevant to Quattrone's beautiful idea. Quattrone had invented circumstances under which people would use

15

human behavior to generate inferences about the situations in which that behavior occurred. This seems remarkable if you have your head stuck inside the attitude-attribution paradigm because, on the face of it, such a finding seems to violate the maxim that people always use human behavior to generate inferences about the actor's dispositions. But who ever believed such a maxim in the first place? Indeed, social psychologists had known for quite some time that people draw situational inferences from behavior. Darley and Latane (1968), for example, had shown that bystanders use the behavior of other bystanders to determine the situational requirements of an emergency—and decades before that, Sherif (1935) had shown that people use the behavior of others to determine the physical nature of the stimuli to which they are responding. The fact that people look to the behavior of others to tell them what is happening in the world around them had been explored and exploited by everyone from Solomon Asch to Alan Funt. To my mind, it looked as though Quattrone had given participants the same essays that Ned had always used and had then given them a different task to perform (i.e., "I'll tell you about dispositions and you tell me about situations" instead of the other way around). So it did not strike me as particularly remarkable that under such circumstances subjects would . . . well, perform a different task. Moreover, I could not see (a) how participants' behavior in George's experiment demonstrated that they were anchoring and adjusting in either George's or Ned's experiments, and (b) if they were, why they were adjusting insufficiently. As far as I could see, George had demonstrated that people were capable of doing something other than drawing correspondent inferences about essayists and that they did this other something when you asked them to.

Now, the joy of having a brilliant mentor who had brilliant students before you is that you don't have to be very smart yourself to find an interesting problem and a partially assembled solution. Really, all you need is a little patience and a library card. I had both, and by 1988 my students and I had used them to develop a new theory and some new experiments that I thought would be congenial with both Ned's and George's thinking, but that might also provide The Complete Solution we had all lusted after in our hearts. Our theorizing comprised three arguments.[1] First, we argued that George was basically right—people begin the attributional task by assuming a correspondence between the actor's behavior and one of the attributional elements, which may be either the actor's dispositions (as in Ned's studies) or the actor's situation (as in George's study). One might additionally suppose that people are inclined to make this assumption about the element they most wish to understand, and that they will most wish to understand the element that they don't already understand or the element that they have been explicitly instructed to understand. Second, we argued that people may subsequently repudiate this assumption of correspondence as they consider the element that they were not trying to understand. Third, we argued that the initial assumption of correspondence constituted a qualitatively different kind of mental activity than the subsequent repudiation of that assumption. Specifically, we suggested that the first process (which we called *characterization*) was more automatic or less effortful than the second process (which, in an alliterative frenzy, we called *correction*).

Taken together, these three axioms solve several otherwise puzzling problems. For example, why had subjects tended to anchor on dispositions in Ned's experiments? Because in Ned's experiments the experimenter typically told participants all about the situation into which the essayist had been thrust, and typically instructed participants to diagnose the essayist's dispositions. If people do indeed characterize the element that they are most eager to understand and about which they already know the least, then the experimental instructions and the experimental task provide a rather compelling explanation for participants' choice of anchors in the attitude-attribution paradigm. In everyday life, I supposed, people are sometimes like Ned's participants in that they are interested in knowing about the enduring properties of

---

[1] Ned once told me that readers are not interested in the writer's intellectual odyssey and that they just want to know what the writer believes and not how he or she came to believe it. To that end, I present my current view of these issues rather than an accurate historical account of how I achieved it. This will spare the reader several pages of truly dull history, and it will spare me having to recall all those embarassing mistakes.

the actor, and they are sometimes like George's participants in that they are interested in knowing about the vagaries of the situation. These motivations must surely combine with what the person already knows to determine whether the person will characterize dispositions or situations—in other words, to determine what task the person will, in a sense, instruct herself to perform. The question of why participants tended to anchor on dispositions seemed to me rather easily answered by our theory.

The more puzzling question, to my mind, was why adjustment in either case should necessarily be insufficient. Tversky and Kahneman (1974) said that adjustment was often insufficient, but they hadn't said why, and I saw no a priori reason to assume that just because people sometimes start by assuming a correspondence between dispositions and actions that they should somehow be expected to finish with that assumption intact. People change their minds all the time, and if insufficient adjustment was to explain the correspondence bias, then something had to explain insufficient adjustment. For me, that something was the relative automaticity of the characterization (anchoring) and correction (adjustment) processes. One of the hallmarks of an effortless or automatic process is that its execution is *robust*—that is, it tends not to be impaired or truncated by the simultaneous performance of other tasks. (Most of us can recite the alphabet, but not the Fibonocci series, while sorting laundry.) My students and I reasoned that if characterization was indeed a heartier, less fragile, less effortful operation than correction, then across all experimental instances one would expect it to fail less often. In fact, we assumed that if people *did* characterize and then correct, and if characterization *was* less effortful than correction, then we should be able to impair the correction process by putting people under cognitive load (i.e., by requiring them to perform an attributional task and some other task concurrently). By our reckoning, such a manipulation should exacerbate the correspondence bias when people are characterizing dispositions (i.e., when they know about the actor's situation and are instructed to diagnose the actor's dispositions, as they did in Ned's studies) and should have the opposite effect when they are characterizing situations (i.e., when they know about the actor's dispositions and are instructed to diagnose the situation, as they did in George's studies).

Armed with a new theory, Brett Pelham, Doug Krull, and I set out to demonstrate these effects (Gilbert, Pelham, & Krull, 1988). We borrowed and modified Mel Snyder and Art Frankel's (1976) anxious-woman paradigm in which participants are shown a silent videotape of an anxious-looking woman who was ostensibly discussing with an off-camera stranger either a series of anxiety-provoking topics (such as her sexual fantasies) or a series of mundane topics (such as gardening). Our participants were instructed to diagnose the woman's dispositional anxiety and, under normal conditions, they did just what any reasonable attributer would do: They concluded that a woman who looked nervous while discussing sex was not nearly so anxious a person as was a woman who looks equally nervous while discussing gardening. In other words, one must be pretty high strung to wig over rutabagas. Another group of participants watched the same videotape while simultaneously attempting to memorize the topics that the anxious woman was discussing. We assumed that such participants would rehearse the topics ("Rutabagas, rutabagas, rutabagas") and that doing so would impose a cognitive load that would keep them from correcting their initial characterizations of the woman. In fact, loaded participants attributed the same amount of dispositional anxiety to the woman in both the anxious-topic and mundane-topic conditions—as if they had been unable to consider the attributional implications of the very information they were rehearsing. This study suggested to us that when people know about the actor's situation and are instructed to diagnose the actor's dispositions, they do indeed characterize before they correct, and that this situational correction is more easily impaired than is the dispositional characterization that precedes it.

With this encouraging result in hand, we set out to see whether George's effect behaved the same way Ned's effect did. In a follow-up to his dissertation (Krull, 1993), Doug Krull and Darin Erikson turned the anxious-woman paradigm inside-out, just as George had done with the attitude-attribution paradigm (Krull & Erikson, 1993, 1995). Their participants watched the anxious-woman videotape and were told that the woman was known either to be dispositionally anxious or dispositionally calm, and they were asked to determine which of several topics she was likely to be discussing. Under normal conditions, participants concluded that the dispositionally calm woman must be discussing juicier topics than was the dispositionally anxious woman. In other words, it takes more than rutabagas to fluster a mellow soul. But loaded participants concluded that both the dispositionally anxious and the dispositionally calm women were discussing equally juicy topics—as if they had assumed a correspondence between actor's behavior and the actor's situation, and had subsequently questioned that assumption only when they had the cognitive resources to do so.

In short, it seemed to us that we had The Complete Solution on paper, some good evidence in the bag, and that all we had to do now was auction the movie rights and hope that Richard Gere agreed to play several of us. In fact, it turned out that we had achieved a solution, but not The Complete Solution. In fact, it turned out that there was not and never had been a complete solution to be achieved.

ON BEYOND JONESLAND

I've told the story of the correspondence bias not from Ned's perspective (he did that quite nicely in his 1990 book) but rather, from his passenger's seat. Even so, that story is still too Jones-centric to be the whole story. Ned would have been the first to acknowledge that his was only part of a bigger picture, and he would have enjoyed having his students find out what that bigger picture was and then having them tell him about it.

Dear Ned

I haven't spoken with you since we hooked up in Chicago the month before you died. But I've thought many times about that last evening we spent together, about that wonderful dinner we had with our friends, how you tried to get me to eat thymus glands, and how you ran up the tab with all that wine and then hid in the men's room until I paid. And then, a month later, poof, you were gone. I always suspected you would check out when it was your turn to buy dinner. But this is not a dunning letter. Rather, I'm writing to share with you some thoughts about one of our mutual interests—the correspondence bias. I'm going to marinate you in a reasonable amount of chatter, so let me telegraph the punchline: There is no cause of correspondence bias. Now, now— let me drop the second shoe: There is no cause of correspondence bias because there are, in fact, four different kinds of correspondence biases, each with its own unique cause. The reason why people in the field don't agree about causes is that we are not, by and large, studying the same thing. Let me see if I can convince you.

First, People May Be Unaware of Situational Constraints

Think about what it would take for someone to avoid making correspondence-biased inferences. Surely the first thing they'd have to do is realize that situational forces are causing an actor's behavior, and they can only do that when they're aware that such forces exist in the first place. If they don't even know that a hostage is being threatened, a senator is being bribed, or a basketball player is being hindered, then they can't possibly do the inferential work that making an accurate attribution requires. My reading of the literature suggests that there are two discrete problems—the *invisibility problem* and the *construal problem*—that make it particularly difficult for observers to attain this basic information.

You often pointed out that the word *situation* typically refers to things that have little or no physical presence: One can't see, smell, taste, or hear audience pressure or social norms. If one can't see the situation then one may not know about the situation, and in that case one can't possibly take the situation into account when making an attribution. The best illustration of this kind of correspondence bias is the quiz-master study (Ross, Amabile, & Steinmetz, 1977). Participants were arbitrarily assigned to play the roles of contestant or quizmaster in a mock game-show. Quizmasters were allowed to generate a list of questions from their private store of arcane knowledge and, as expected, contestants typically failed to answer the questions. So what did observers conclude? They concluded that the quizmasters were genuinely brighter than the contestants. And why not? Observers couldn't hear or see a role-conferred advantage like they could hear and see a "dumb answer" and a "smart question." They surely realized that the quizmaster had the good fortune of asking all the questions and that the contestant had the bad fortune of having to stumble over them, but they probably did not consider the fact that even the dimmest bulb can come up with a handful of idiosyncratic tidbits that others are unlikely to carry around with them (e.g., "How many albums did Bill Evans release in 1964?"). They could have considered that fact, but they probably didn't. So really, I'm only saying what Heider was saying when he talked about the relative salience of behavior and situations: Situations are often invisible and you can't consider the effect of something if you don't even know it's there.

But there's more to say about this first cause because there is a more subtle version of the invisibility problem that I'll call *the construal problem*. Ever since Heider (1958) first compared human behavior to the physical motion of a boat on a lake, most of us have fallen into the flabby habit of talking about situational constraints as though that term described one thing. But, as you and I have agreed on many occasions (most of them speeding on the Garden State Parkway), there are two very different kinds of situational constraints. *Behavioral constraints* directly constrain an actor's behavior and are entirely independent of the actor's understanding of them. For example, the contestants in the quizmaster experiment had no choice but to give incorrect answers on many trials. Regardless of what they may have felt, wanted, thought, hoped, wished, or believed, the objective difficulty of the quizmasters' questions guaranteed that they would perform poorly. *Psychological constraints,* on the other hand, don't change an actor's behavior by changing her behavioral options so much as they change it by changing her understanding of those options. The constraint imposed by a debate coach's instructions, for instance, is quite different than the constraint imposed by a role-conferred advantage because, unlike a role-conferred advantage, instructions don't literally force the essayist's hand or make an anti-Castro speech impossible to write. Instead, a debate coach's instructions alter the payoffs associated with the behavioral options. When a debate coach assigns a debater to defend Castro, then saying "Yes, sir" and writing a pro-Castro speech is suddenly an easier, healthier alternative than is saying "Buzz off" and writing an anti-Castro speech, but the essayist is still technically free to do either. This is America, after all. Psychological constraints don't change behavioral options—they change the actor's motivation to enact the behavioral options.

Now here's why this distinction matters. When constraints are psychological, then the observer doesn't need to be aware of the actor's situation as it is objectively constituted, but rather, she needs to be aware of the situation as it is subjectively construed. Even if the observer can hear the debate coach's instructions, the critical question is whether the debater can hear them, and, if so, whether he hears them the same way the observer does. I mean, imagine that the coach asks for a pro-Castro essay, that the debater is a bit deaf and mistakenly believes the coach asked for an anti-Castro essay, but that the debater decides to write a pro-Castro essay anyway. He's just got to be pro-Castro, right? Surely a dispositional inference is warranted, even though the behavior is exactly what the situation-as-it-truly-was demanded because it is exactly the opposite of what the situation-as-the-essayist-sees-it demanded. Okay. So here's my point: If you think people have trouble recognizing the situation-as-it-is (the invisibility problem), then just imagine how much trouble they have recognizing the situation-as-the-actor-sees-it (the construal problem). In fact, people often adopt an egocentric point of view and assume that the situation they see is the situation that the actor sees too (Griffin & Ross, 1991; Keysar, 1994), perhaps because it is just so difficult to imagine what the situation would look like to someone who had different information about it than they do (Fischoff, 1975; Jacoby, Kelley, & Dywan, 1989).

Well, I've gone on quite a bit about this, and I really didn't mean to. It is painfully obvious that one must be aware of situational constraints if one is to avoid the correspondence bias, and it is equally obvious that attaining such awareness can at times be difficult (the invisibility problem), and at other times, very difficult (the construal problem). The first kind of correspondence bias, then, is caused by simple ignorance.

DANIEL T. GILBERT

Second, People May Have Unrealistic Expectations for Behavior

Even if one hears the debate coach's instructions (no invisibility problem here) and understands the essayist's take on those instructions (no
construal problem either), one must still have an idea of how a debate
coach's instructions generally affect a debater's essays. Are most debaters
so intimidated by their coaches that they obey their every command,
or do debaters tend to take such instructions as mild suggestions and
ignore them whenever they please? People make dispositional inferences
when the actor's behavior violates their normative expectations, so if
we have unrealistic expectations about how situations normally affect
behaviors (e.g., "A true American would never write a pro-Castro
speech"), then those expectations are going to be violated when they
shouldn't be. So how realistic are these normative expectations? Put
another way: How accurately do we estimate the power of particular
situations to evoke particular behaviors? Put yet another way: How accurately do we predict how the average person will behave?

Figuring out how powerful a situation is can be tricky, and people
use some ingenious but fallible methods. For example, when we try to
estimate a situation's power by imagining how the average person would
behave, we may assume they would behave as we assume we would
behave. (There's that egocentric assumption again.) That's what happened in that false consensus study in which an experimenter asked
participants whether they would march around wearing a signboard
that read "Eat at Joe's," and found that both consenters and refusers
considered their own choices to be typical of the population (Ross,
Greene, & House, 1977). Refusers personally experienced the experimenter's request as a weak situational force; they refused, they expected
others to refuse, and they drew dispositional inferences about people
who complied. Ditto for consenters. The problem, of course, is that
other people don't always act as we think we would act. Sometimes we
are unique, or at least in the minority. Furthermore, *we* don't always
act as we think we would act. Jim Sherman (1980) asked college students to predict whether they would comply with an experimenter's
request to write a counterattitudinal essay, and nearly three quarters
said they wouldn't. You know as well as I do that in decades of cognitive

24

dissonance studies, college students almost *never* refuse the experimenter's request. Now imagine that Sherman's participants were taking part in the attitude-attribution paradigm. They mispredict their own behavior ("I'd say no"), which leads to unrealistic expectations about how others will behave ("Most anyone would say no"), which leads to having those expectations violated ("That guy said yes"), which leads to—*voila!*—the correspondence bias.

Third, People May Misidentify Behavior

You'd think that the bias would evaporate when people are perfectly aware of the actor's situation and have perfectly realistic expectations for the actor's behavior in that situation. And you'd be wrong. In fact, rather than providing protection against correspondence bias, a perfect awareness of situational constraints can actually cause it.

As I argued above, people make dispositional inferences when an actor's behavior exceeds their expectations. Technically, of course, people don't compare their expectations to the actor's actual behavior, but rather, to their perceptions of that behavior, and perception ain't reality. Just as the sentence "I'm having a friend for dinner" means one thing when uttered by Martha Stewart and another when uttered by the head of the Donner party, so a mother's tears may appear more wrenching when shed at her daughter's funeral than at her daughter's wedding. In other words, behaviors can be ambiguous, and Yaacov Trope and his colleagues (Trope, 1986; Trope & Cohen, 1989; Trope, Cohen, & Maoz, 1988) have suggested that our perfect awareness of a situation can cause us to have an imperfect understanding of the ambiguous behaviors that unfold within it. It's interesting to imagine just how this can happen. For example, if a situational force (a debate coach's instructions) actually induces a certain kind of behavior (a pro-Castro speech), then the observer who is aware of the situation and who has a realistic estimate of its power should expect precisely that sort of behavior. However, the very awareness that enables the observer to have a realistic expectation for behavior may also cause the observer to have an unrealistic perception of behavior; in this case, the behavior may be seen as conforming more to situational demands than it actually does. The observer may be prepared to hear a pro-Castro speech, but that very expectation may cause her to hear an incredibly pro-Castro speech. As the model I sketched earlier suggests, that observer would then be struck by the mismatch between her expectations and her perception of "reality," and will draw a dispositional inference about the essayist. The irony, of course, is that the observer's perfect knowledge of the situation has befuddled her observation of the actor's behavior, which leads her to make an unwarranted dispositional inference about an actor whose situation she understands perfectly well, but whose behavior she has misconstrued.

What's more, this actually happens. Consider that experiment in which participants watched a silent film of a woman who was ostensibly being interviewed about politics or sex (Snyder & Frankel, 1976). Some were told about the interview topic prior to seeing the film and some were only told afterwards. When participants learned about the interview topic only after seeing the film, they took the woman's situation into account and concluded that she was less dispositionally anxious when discussing sex than when discussing politics. But those who learned about the interview topic before seeing the film drew precisely the opposite conclusion. Apparently, participants who knew that the woman was talking about sex expected her to be anxious, and they then went on to see more fidgeting and shuffling in her ambiguous behavior than was actually present. So even though these participants knew all about the woman's situation, knew all about the situation's power, and took all of this into account when making attributions, they were damned from the get go. They couldn't possibly make the right attribution because they were making attributions for the wrong behavior. The third type of correspondence bias is caused by misidentification of the actor's behavior.

Fourth, People May Not Correct Their Dispositional Inferences

Here's the point where you expect me to go on forever, and I'm going to surprise you. We both know what the fourth cause is because it's the one that you and George and I have been contemplating for a combined total of 60 years. In short, even if you know about situations and their power, and even if you have the behavior pegged correctly, there is still a tendency for those of us who are striving to understand dispositions to assume a correspondence between the behavior we see and the dispositions we are striving to understand—and we seem to correct that assumption only subsequently and effortfully. If we can't exert the effort then we can't make the correction, and we end up stung by the correspondence bias. If you want to read more about this, you know where to look (Gilbert, 1989).

So that's what I've been thinking about. When we first met 15 years ago, you told me you wished someone would solve the problem of correspondence bias. It seems to me that you've gotten your wish. The problem has been more than solved—it's actually been solved four times. So why do I have a funny feeling that you aren't going to buy it? Maybe because this analysis is right but not elegant. It isn't $E = MC^2$. In fact, it is a little bit like a 600-page murder mystery in which it turns out that everybody killed the damned butler. But on the other hand, it's a reasonable framework that brings a certain degree of order to an otherwise untidy set of issues, and science is about getting it right, not making it pretty. Don't you think?

As always,

D'boy

Much Ado About Everything

From Rousseau to Hobbes to Freud to Rogers, psychologists never seem to grow weary of talking about whether people are good or bad, smart or stupid, right or wrong. By focusing so intently on the causes of inferential error, the social psychology of the 1970s and 1980s gave rise to a minor but predictable backlash in which some critics argued that both the extent and the importance of inferential error had been vastly overplayed by laboratory science. Differing points of view often fuel discovery, but in this case, thesis and antithesis collided with a whimper instead of a bang. Rather than exploring together the meaning and consequences of inferential error, the two sides tacitly agreed to view each other as idiots. Critics often chose to vilify the workers rather than improve the work, and as a result, the criticized often dismissed the shrill chorus as incapable of serious dialogue. All of which was too bad, because a thoughtful and friendly debate about the nature of error exercises all the important intellectual muscles. Is the correspondence bias an error? In raw form this is a lot like asking if chimps can think or if fetuses are people: The answers depend entirely on what one means by words such as *think* and *people* and *error*. Consider two ways of thinking about error.

Errors as Logical Violations

If we take error to mean a violation of Aristotelian logic, or as a difference between one person's beliefs and the "objective reality" that most other sensible people subscribe to, then yes, the correspondence bias is an error. When actors are randomly assigned to be quizmasters or contestants, then the average intelligence of the actors should not differ by condition. And if observers on average believe otherwise, well then, observers on average are wrong. And we don't have to measure the intelligence of the actors to prove it. The interesting question is not whether, but why the observers are wrong. Are they wrong because the experimenter did not allow them to gather or use the information they needed to be right? If so, then their erroneous inferences merely provide support for the hypothesis that people make errors when they have been deprived of important information—not a terribly thrilling conclusion. Or are they wrong in spite of the fact that they had or had access to the information they needed, but did not recognize it as such, did not seek it, or did not use it? If so, then their erroneous inferences may tell a much more interesting story about people and how they think.

Often times when colleagues ask me if the correspondence bias is an error, they are really asking me if a particular experimenter gave a particular set of subjects a "fair chance" to do otherwise. Sometimes I say "yes" and sometimes I say "no" and never do I change anyone's mind because, as those who have pitched baseballs at milk bottles know, what the carney and the mark consider a fair chance are often worlds apart. *Fair chance* is another one of those terms that means what we want it to mean. Perhaps, then, we should not worry so much about whether participants were given a fair chance in a particular study, but rather, we should be concerned with how the chance they were given by the experimenter compares with the chances they are ordinarily given by nature. My guess is that experimenters can be less fair than nature: For example, explicitly instructing participants to diagnose dispositions may initiate a chain of mental events that ends with inferential error when, in the real world, people might never have had such a goal in the first place. But I would guess that there are just as many instances in which nature is not nearly so fair as we are: For example, experimenters routinely tell participants about the situational constraints on an actor's behavior ("There was this debate coach, see, and ..."), whereas in the real world, people must often dig for such information on their own.

Each of us can think of a dozen instances in which experimenters and nature are more or less fair than the other, and that sort of game could be played for years—and it should be, because it is interesting and important. But it is not new. It is the game that experimentalists have played ever since they decided to take behavior out the meadow and put it under the microscope. Anyone who believes that the world beneath the microscope is a perfect mirror of the world in the meadow ought to sit down and have a long, hard think. And anyone who believes the microscope can teach us nothing about the meadow should probably not even bother with that. Correspondence bias is a logical error, and the fact that people violate logic can be interesting and important in some cases and entirely trivial in others.

Errors as Trouble Makers

There is another way to think about errors, and that is in terms of their consequences. The pragmatist philosophers (Dewey, 1908; James, 1907) were keen on this way of thinking and suggested that inferential errors are simply inferences that don't do the work that the inference-maker wanted done. If we take *error* to mean something that leads to dire consequences, then the correspondence bias is an error on some occasions, but not on others (Swann, 1984). It is clear how believing that a person is smart or honest when he's not might have unfortunate repercussions in marriage, business, or bowling, but perhaps it is not equally clear how such logically incorrect beliefs can end up having no repercussions at all. Consider two circumstances under which correspondence-biased inferences will not be a problem for the observer, namely, the cases of *self-induced constraint* and *omnipresent constraint*.

First, many of the important situations that shape our lives are situations that we enter by choice or are drawn into by proclivity (Snyder & Ickes, 1985, p. 918). In other words, situational constraints are often self-induced, and such constraints often "push us" in the same direction as do our own dispositions. It will do the observer little harm—and even much good—to ignore the effects of self-induced constraints when making attributions. If, for example, a debater chose to serve a debate coach who was known to assign his debaters to defend the pro-Castro position, then an observer would be quite justified in ignoring the debate coach's instructions altogether and simply judging the debater on the basis of his essay. When people choose constraining situations, then those situations do not mask their dispositions so much as they provide evidence of them. A correspondence-biased inference, then, is not a trouble maker when constraints are self-induced. Second, situations may present omnipresent constraints—that is, the constraints on an actor's behavior may be enduring rather than temporary. This means that observers may never encounter circumstances under which their correspondence-biased inferences will be challenged. If an essayist were forced to write one pro-Castro essay every day for the rest of his natural life, we might be technically wrong to infer that he is personally pro-Castro, but that technically inaccurate inference would allow us to predict his future behavior quite perfectly. When the situational constraints on the behavior we observe are also the situational constraints on the behavior we wish to predict, then we might just as well ignore them. In addition, such enduring situations may create dispositions rather than merely causing behaviors (Higgins & Winter, 1993). It is not difficult to imagine that the poor debater who is doomed to write a pro-Castro essay every day for the rest of his life might eventually become pro-Castro, thus turning our inaccurate correspondence-biased inference into an accurate one. Once again, a correspondence-biased inference is not a troublemaker when constraints are omnipresent.

There is a useful way to think about the cases of self-induced con-

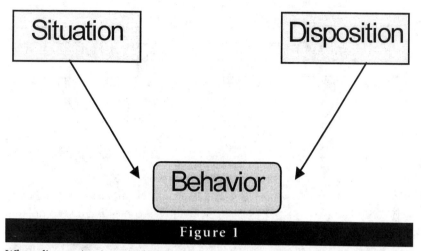

Figure 1

When discounting is a good idea.

straint and ominpresent constraint. Attribution theories tell us that if we wish to determine an actor's dispositions, we must first "subtract out" or "discount" or "remove" the effects that situations may be having on the actor's behavior. Under some circumstances this is sound advice. For example, when situations and dispositions are independent causes of behavior (see Figure 1), then one should indeed remove the effect of one cause in order to estimate properly the effect of the other. But dispositions and situations are not always independent. In fact, they often cause each other, and when this happens, then mentally removing the effect of the situation is precisely the *wrong* thing to do. As Figure 2 shows, the case of self-induced constraint is an instance in which a person's dispositions (Fred is authoritarian) exert a causal influence on the person's situation (Fred is in the military). Similarly, the case of omnipresent constraint is an instance in which a person's situation (Freda grew up in a military family) exerts a causal effect on the person's dispositions (Freda is authoritarian). In each of these cases, there is a strong correlation between the person's situation and the person's dispositions, which means that the situation does not hide the effects of dispositions so much as it provides evidence for them. In such instances, the effect of the situation should not be subtracted out of one's

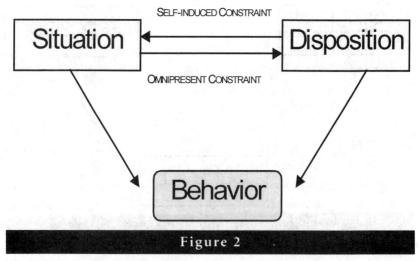

Figure 2

When discounting isn't such a good idea.

estimate of the actor's dispositions—rather, it should be added in! If, for example, the essayist chose to join a debate team whose coach was famous for assigning nothing but pro-Castro essays (self-induced constraint), or if the debater were forced to write such essays three times a day for the rest of his life (omnipresent constraint), then the debate coach's instructions would be good evidence of the essayist's pro-Castro attitude. The point here is simply this: Correspondence bias occurs when people fail to subtract out the effects of the situation; but there are instances in which that failure is a very good thing. The correspondence bias, then, is not always a troublemaker, and thus for the pragmatist, not always an error.

CODA

Ned loved his codas. He was a careful writer and he used the coda as an opportunity to jump out of the bog and onto the lily—out of data and out of the detail and up to some higher place, at which he would pause, adjust his bow tie, clear his throat, and then tell us something true. Those truths were never shocking or outrageous or unbelievable. They were not revelations. Ned's truths were elegant, simple, astute observations that were just so right—so perfectly on the money—that the moment you heard one you realized that you could have thought of it yourself , except that . . . well . . . you hadn't. When Ned gave you a birthday present it was never a card-shuffling machine or an electric corkscrew. It was a blue tie. Similarly, he did not give the world exotic intellectual gifts that will end up in the attic except when they are being trotted out for a history lesson. Instead, he gave us stuff we really needed. Ned was the master of telling us what we didn't quite know, and in a too short life, he hit that sweet note again and again and again.

There are people who change the world, there are people who don't, and then there are people like Ned who change it in such a way that you can hardly imagine what it would have been like without him. I hear people say about Aristotle, Einstein, and yes, Bill Evans, that their influence is so pervasive as to render them invisible. Ned Jones will be invisible soon too. His vision of social psychology so permeates our own that we can hardly tell we are looking through him anymore. Maybe that's inevitable and maybe that's good, but before he disappears altogether we should climb to a higher place, pause and clear our throats, and say this about him: If science is a race to get it right, then Ned drove us fast and far. We will all, for a long time to come, be speeding with Ned.

REFERENCES

Darley, J. M., & Latane, B. (1968). Bystander intervention in emergencies: Diffusion of responsibility. *Journal of Personality and Social Psychology, 8*, 377–383.

Dewey, J. (1908). What does pragmatism mean by the practical? *Journal of Philosophy, Psychology, and Scientific Methods, 5*, 85–99.

Fischoff, B. (1975). Hindsight ≠ foresight: The effects of outcome knowledge on judgments under uncertainty. *Journal of Experimental Psychology: Human Perception and Performance, 1*, 288–299.

Gilbert, D. T. (1989). Thinking lightly about others: Automatic components of the social inference process. In J. S. Uleman & J. A. Bargh (Eds.), *Unintended thought* (pp. 189–211). New York: Guilford.

Gilbert, D. T., & Jones, E. E. (1986). Perceiver-induced constraint: Interpretations of self-generated reality. *Journal of Personality and Social Psychology, 50,* 269–280.

Gilbert, D. T., & Malone, P. S. (1995). The correspondence bias. *Psychological Bulletin, 117,* 21–38.

Gilbert, D. T., Pelham, B. W., & Krull, D. S. (1988). On cognitive busyness: When person perceivers meet persons perceived. *Journal of Personality and Social Psychology, 54,* 733–740.

Griffin, D. W., & Ross, L. (1991). Subjective construal, social inference, and human misunderstanding. In M. Zanna (Ed.), *Advances in Experimental Social Psychology* (Vol. 24, pp. 319–356). New York: Academic Press.

Heider, F. (1958). *The psychology of interpersonal relations.* New York: Wiley.

Higgins, E. T., & Winter, L. (1993). The "acquisition principle": How beliefs about a behavior's prolonged circumstances influence correspondent inference. *Personality and Social Psychology Bulletin, 19,* 605–619.

Jacoby, L. L., Kelley, C. M., & Dywan, J. (1989). Memory attributions. In H. L. Roediger & F. I. M. Craik (Eds.), *Varieties of memory and consciousness: Essays in honor of Endel Tulving* (pp. 391–422). Hillsdale, NJ: Erlbaum.

James, W. (1907). *Pragmatism.* New York: Longmans-Green.

Jones, E. E. (1964). *Ingratiation.* New York: Appleton-Century-Crofts.

Jones, E. E. (1979). The rocky road from acts to dispositions. *American Psychologist, 34,* 107–117.

Jones, E. E. (1988). *Attributional anomalies during social interaction.* Paper presented at the Katz-Newcomb Lecture, University of Michigan, Ann Arbor.

Jones, E. E. (1990). *Interpersonal perception.* New York: Macmillan.

Jones, E. E., & Davis, K. E. (1965). From acts to dispositions: The attribution process in person perception. In L. Berkowitz (Ed.), *Advances in Experimental Social Psychology* (Vol. 2, pp. 219–266). New York: Academic Press.

Jones, E. E., & Harris, V. A. (1967). The attribution of attitudes. *Journal of Experimental Social Psychology, 3,* 1–24.

Jones, E. E., & McGillis, D., (1976). Correspondent inferences and the attribution cube: A comparative reappraisal. In J. H. Harvey, W. J. Ickes, & R. F. Kidd (Eds.), *New Directions in Attribution Research* (Vol. 1, pp. 389–420). Hillsdale, NJ: Erlbaum.

Keysar, B. (1994). The illusory transparency of intention: Perspective taking in text. *Cognitive Psychology, 26,* 165–208.

Krull, D. S. (1993). Does the grist change the mill? The effect of the perceiver's inferential goal on the process of social inference. *Personality and Social Psychology Bulletin, 19,* 340–348.

Krull, D. S., & Erikson, D. J. (1993). *How do people think dispositionally when they are situationally focused? The effortful processing of dispositional information.* Unpublished manuscript, University of Missouri.

Krull, D. S., & Erikson, D. J. (1995). On judging situations: The effortfull process of taking dispositional information into account. *Social Cognition, 13,* 417–438.

Miller, A. G., Jones, E. E., & Hinkle, S. (1981). A robust attribution error in the personality domain. *Journal of Experimental Social Psychology, 17,* 587–600.

Nisbett, R. E., & Ross, L. (1980). *Human inference: Strategies and shortcomings of social judgment.* Englewood Cliffs, NJ: Prentice-Hall.

Quattrone, G. A. (1982). Overattribution and unit formation: When behavior engulfs the person. *Journal of Personality and Social Psychology, 42,* 593–607.

Ross, L. (1977). The intuitive psychologist and his shortcomings. In L. Berkowitz (Ed.), *Advances in experimental social psychology* (Vol. 10, pp. 173–220). New York: Academic Press.

Ross, L., Amabile, T. M., & Steinmetz, J. L. (1977). Social roles, social control, and biases in social-perception processes. *Journal of Personality and Social Psychology, 35,* 485–494.

Ross, L., Greene, D., & House, P. (1977). The "false consensus effect": An egocentric bias in social perception and attribution processes. *Journal of Experimental Social Psychology, 13,* 279–301.

Sherif, M. (1935). A study of some social factors in perception. *Archives of Psychology, 27,* 1–60.

Sherman, S. J. (1980). On the self-erasing nature of errors of prediction. *Journal of Personality and Social Psychology, 39,* 211–221.

Snyder, M. L., & Frankel, A. (1976). Observer bias: A stringent test of behavior engulfing the field. *Journal of Personality and Social Psychology, 34,* 857–864.

Snyder, M. L., & Ickes, W. (1985). Personality and social behavior. In G. Lindzey & E. Aronson (Eds.), *The Handbook of Social Psychology* (3rd ed., Vol. 2, pp. 883–947). New York: Random House.

Snyder, M. L., & Jones, E. E. (1974). Attitude attribution when behavior is constrained. *Journal of Experimental Social Psychology, 10,* 585–600.

Swann, W. B., Jr. (1984). Quest for accuracy in person perception: A matter of pragmatics. *Psychological Review, 91,* 457–477.

Trope, Y. (1986). Identification and inferential processes in dispositional attribution. *Psychological Review, 93,* 239–257.

Trope, Y., & Cohen, O. (1989). Perceptual and inferential determinants of behavior-correspondent attributions. *Journal of Experimental Social Psychology, 25,* 142–158.

Trope, Y., Cohen, O., & Maoz, Y. (1988). The perceptual and inferential effects of situational inducements on dispositional attributions. *Journal of Personality and Social Psychology, 55,* 165–177.

Tversky, A., & Kahneman, D. (1974). Judgments under uncertainty: Heuristics and biases. *Science, 185,* 1124–1131.

Some Thoughts Prompted by "Speeding With Ned"

Arthur G. Miller

> *It is quite clear that such bias is not always the effect of some*
> *unique cause: There is not a single, fundamental antecedent to go*
> *with the fundamental error.*
> —*Jones, E. E. (1979).* The rocky road from acts to dispositions,
> American Psychologist, *34, p. 115.*

> *People who do crazy things are not necessarily crazy.*
> — "Aronson's first law," in Aronson, E. (1995).
> The Social Animal, *p. 9.*

As I indicate in the quotation from the "Rocky Road" essay, (Jones, 1979), Ned anticipated that the correspondence bias would ultimately be understood in terms of more than one process or theoretical model. Thus, Gilbert's contribution in articulating four mechanisms, and showing how they embrace diverse instances of correspondence bias, is a most fitting capstone to Ned's prediction.[1]

---

[1] Being invited to participate as a discussant to Dan Gilbert's chapter in this volume is a very special honor for me. I count two individuals, both now sadly departed—Ned Jones and Stanley Milgram—as the most significant influences in my life as a social psychologist. I remember sending Ned, in the spring of 1986, a copy of a book I had written about the obedience experiments of Stanley

The quotation from Aronson (1995) reflects the fact that for many social psychologists, the very essence of the discipline of social psychology can be seen as providing a situational correction for the pervasive phenomena of correspondence bias. The power of the situation, specifically as construed by the actor, is surely a fundamental premise on which social psychology is built (Ross & Nisbett, 1991). Consider the challenges in getting across the fact that most people can be influenced, in really not too unfathomable circumstances, to engage in evil behavior (Darley, 1992). I can see, for example, a meaningful connection between the correspondence bias and Hannah Arendt's thesis of the banality of evil. Arendt (1963) shocked the world in her report on Eichmann because she failed to deliver the so-called politically correct portrait, that is, she failed to voice the correspondence-bias account that everyone expected—that a person engaged in evil deeds must have a correspondent disposition to do so. Thus, the issue of the correspondence bias is so interesting and vital not only as a particular judgmental tendency or logical error, but also in its larger context as a reflection of an important feature of the social psychology of the lay perceiver against which the products of empirical social psychology can be contrasted.

In this response to Gilbert's chapter, I will first comment on each of the four pillars that Gilbert has identified and on which the correspondence bias (CB) appears to rest in its diverse appearances. Two apparent exceptions to the broad coverage of Gilbert's paper will then be addressed, as will a note on CB as a laboratory artifact. I conclude by speculating on future conceptualizations of CB in light of Gilbert's review.

FOUR REASONS FOR FOUR TYPES OF CB

People May Be Unaware of Situational Constraints

Ned and his students rather quickly ruled this particular factor out as an explanation of CB in the attitude-attribution paradigm, that is, that

---

Milgram. Ned, who was not particularly enthusiastic about the obedience studies, was nevertheless (and characteristically) gracious in a letter that he sent me on receiving it. My inscription on Ned's copy was something to the effect that, for me, Ned had always kept the fires of social psychology glowing. I can see his eyes rolling with that one, but I think he knew I meant it.

the CB was not simply an artifact of participants not realizing the constraint involved in the essay assignment. Gilbert's point is valuable, however, in reminding social psychologists that there are many forces that increase the likelihood of not appreciating the constraints operating on others. Consider, as one simple example, the nature of stereotyping. In Donald Campbell's (1967) seminal essay, he articulated four specific errors involved in stereotyping. One clearly relates to the current subject, the CB: "The third error involves the erroneous causal perception of invoking racial rather than environmental causes for group differences" (p. 825).

Stereotype-based expectancies, in evoking a powerful dispositional-causality mindset, are particularly forceful in blunting an awareness of situational constraints. Examples of this, of course, abound. We can think of Rodin and Langer's famous nursing-home studies (Langer & Rodin, 1976; Rodin & Langer, 1977) in which they demonstrated that situationally induced responsibility had powerful effects on the well-being of residents. This was a striking disconfirmation of the stereotype of the aged as intractably declining and dispositionally unresponsive, and of the power of a relatively small situational manipulation to evoke some remarkably strong effects. In a related study, Levy and Langer (1994) have recently shown that members of cultures that do not hold negative stereotypes of the aged (the Chinese hearing and American deaf) exhibit substantially less age-related deficits in memory—dramatic evidence of the benefits to be achieved by avoiding category-based stereotypes.

Not recognizing another's constraint can be the result of many factors, a number of these identified by Jones and Nisbett (1972) and many subsequent investigators. Clearly one factor relates to what might now be termed *motivated reasoning*. People may or may not wish to acknowledge another's constraints, depending on the conclusion that we wish to reach (see Pettigrew, 1979; Regan, Strauss, & Fazio, 1974). Anna Goldhahn and I are currently conducting a study in which we are examining the degree to which participants exposed to a constrained act of a liked or disliked target person will selectively display CB or a discounting effect, depending on their motives. I think it is important to also obtain perceiver accounts in these studies to gain some access to their construal of the constrained actor's situation.

Gilbert's emphasis on the importance of construal in terms of understanding the CB is of special note. Recognizing the situation-as-the-actor-sees-it (the construal problem) is, of course, what is commonly termed *empathy*, although that concept seems to have a vicarious emotional connotation as well. My favorite current example of construal comes from, of all places, the O. J. Simpson trial. Recall the judge's pivotal ruling in the preliminary trial during the summer of 1994, allowing evidence obtained by the officers in storming Simpson's house to be entered, even though violations of warrant procedures had been at issue. Her comment was a marvelous example of construal in terms of her perceiving the constraints on the officers:

> We have to judge the officers' conduct and the exigency if there was one, not based upon what we all know today, but based upon what the officers knew at the time ... We know now, obviously, that there was no dying person or injured person on the property at the Simpson estate at that time ... But the officers didn't know that at the time. ("Excerpts from ruling by Municipal Court Judge Kennedy-Powell," 1994)

Regardless of whether her ruling was accurate, the point is that it was driven by an explicit recognition that the situation, as interpreted by observers in hindsight, was far different from the situation facing the officers at the scene.

People May Have Unrealistic Expectations for Behavior

I can resonate most strongly to Gilbert's second pillar because it has been the focus of a number of my own studies (Miller, Ashton, & Mishal, 1990; Miller & Rorer, 1982). Glenn Reeder's important work is pertinent here also (Reeder, Fletcher, & Furman 1989). My colleagues and I have thought for some time that the most straightforward solution to the riddle of the CB in the attitude attribution paradigm (and the Ross, Amabile, & Steinmetz, 1977, quiz-game scenario also) rests on an analysis of the perceiver's task from the perceiver's point of view.

From this perspective, the constrained essay is endowed with diagnosticity regarding its author's true attitude.

I continue to hold to the view that the attitude-attribution paradigm (and many other paradigms as well) communicates to study participants the general idea that information that is given to them and subsequently connected to the key response measure is useful for that task, that is, that the target's attitude can in fact "get through." (See Kahneman & Tversky, 1982, for an elegant discussion of methodological issues relevant to this and related paradigms.) This perspective by no means guarantees that a CB will occur. The classic experiment here is by Ned himself (Jones, Worchel, Goethals, & Grumet, 1971). Using weak, ambivalent essays under constraint, Jones et al. demonstrated the "foot-dragging" effect. Participants attributed attitudes in opposition to the essay assignment under these conditions. The pitiful essays clearly suggested to perceivers that the writers were under enormous constraint, that is, they had been unlucky in the draw and asked to write on the side of the issue that was clearly against their personal belief.

My colleagues and I have shown that people have preexisting beliefs concerning the relationship between features of constrained behavior and the dispositions of the actors under such constraint, which is what we have termed *implicit theories of constraint* (Miller et al., 1990; Miller & Rorer, 1982). These schemas enable participants to assess the strength or extremity of the constrained essay, and to then infer the most likely attitude to have given rise to such an essay. It would thus be possible to use two essays, one pro and one anti, of a particular strength that would not elicit a significant CB effect. However, it is our experience that the typical essays used in this paradigm (including those written by participants themselves under assignment) are far stronger than participants expect to see from anyone whom they believe is not attitudinally predisposed to that position. This, in the short run, is why the paradigm typically produces a significant essay direction effect under no-choice conditions. The magnitude of this effect can be systematically varied—from a relatively large difference to no difference, simply by manipulating the perceived strength of the essay (Miller et al., 1990).

Gilbert states that "to the extent that people underestimate the power of situations—for example, when they think 'A true American would never write a pro-Castro speech'—then they will surely see behavior that is more extreme than they think it should have been and will then make correspondence biased inferences." This is virtually identical to our point of view stated above. We might reword it slightly (and more clumsily), as follows: To the extent that people underestimate the capability of most individuals to comply with a request to generate an essay on virtually any issue, regardless of their personal attitude on that subject, they are likely to construe anything other than a relatively weak, ambivalent essay as having been written by a person who basically believes in what he or she has written.

Even When People Are Aware of Situational Constraints and Do Correctly Estimate Their Power to Induce Behavior, They May Misidentify the Behavior Itself

Gilbert acknowledges the crucial role of the behavior, itself, *as perceived by the participant*, in driving CB. He suggests that simply in knowing the pro-Castro assignment, perceivers may engage in biased processing so as to confirm the expectancy. The result? The perception of an incredibly pro-Castro speech; that is, the perceiver will see more "pro-Castroness" in the essay than actually exists. Given this perceived behavioral extremity, "it is easy to understand why the observer would make a dispositional inference from it."

Gilbert's point here is compelling. It reminds me of a fascinating CB study by Ajzen, Dalto, and Blyth (1979), in which participants displayed the CB even when they did not see any essays, but simply were informed about the instructions assigning a position to the essay writer and were given an ambiguous biographical sketch about the writer. Ajzen et al.'s interpretation was that participants confirmed their hypothesis, which was induced by the constraining instructions, by means of a biased processing of the ambiguous biographical information. This is consistent with Gilbert's suggestion that when constrained behavior in fact is presented, it may be ultimately perceived as stronger simply because of the expectations generated by the constraint.

Given the Ideal Status in Terms of the Above-Listed Factors, Participants May Still Fail to Correct Their Dispositional Inferences

This, of course, relates to Gilbert's highly influential cognitive busyness studies—experiments that, I think, are the strongest evidence to date for the anchoring–insufficient adjustment account of CB (Gilbert & Hixon, 1991; Gilbert, Pelham, & Krull, 1988). The idea that the correction of an initially correspondent inference requires effort that the perceiver may be unable to muster is certainly persuasive and is supported by a wealth of data. This correction mechanism reminds me of Tetlock's (1985) accountability studies, in which the perceiver's inducement to engage in cognitive correction is also seen as relatively unlikely unless the circumstances warrant such systematic processing. Thus, the notion of the lazy, cost-efficient perceiver again makes its appearance.

I have another favorite example, which is pertinent to Gilbert's idea, that comes again from the archives. Early in Gordon Allport's (1954) pioneering book on prejudice, he spoke to the idea that a simplistic, undifferentiated group stereotype would, for reasons of economy, be the default value unless there were circumstances that made correction worthwhile. In a stunningly foresightful chapter titled "The Normality of Prejudgment," Allport wrote

> He may think that Italians are primitive, ignorant, and loud until he falls in love with an Italian girl of a cultured family. Then he finds it greatly to his self-interest to modify his previous generalization and act thereafter on the more correct assumption that there are many, many kinds of Italians. (p. 24)

The one issue which has puzzled me on the "busyness" studies is the presence of the CB effect in experiments where the perceiver would, on the surface, appear to be cognitively non-busy. Gilbert shows rather vividly that "loaded" perceivers produce exaggerated CB effects. But what about the many attitude-attribution studies in which the perceiver would, in effect, be in the status of a "cognitively non-busy" control group? The effects are still present and often very strong.

TWO ISSUES NEEDING ATTENTION

I would like to mention now two issues that, at this point at least, do not seem easily reconcilable with Gilbert's construction. One involves the perception not of the actor's dispositions, but of the actor's motives. Fein, Hilton, and Miller (1990) have shown that perceivers will avoid correspondent inferences if they are suspicious of the actor's motives (see also Fein, 1996; Hilton, Fein, & Miller, 1993). Similarly, evidence regarding the ubiquitousness of lying and the fact that we may be attuned to the possibility that someone is lying to us, also suggest occasions when correspondent inferences will be attenuated or at least made very tentatively (Saxe, 1991). Thus, one might ask, what do these apparent failures of CB tell us? Where do they fit in Gilbert's conceptualization? If they do not fit in, or are not supposed to, why not? The work on suspiciousness is particularly interesting, in my view, because it introduces an element of interpersonal relations that are known to be pervasive in many social settings—that is, mistrust, skepticism, suspicion—but likely do not to prevail in the laboratory (Kahneman & Tversky, 1982). Gilbert himself (with Malone) has criticized laboratory experiments: "Because no effort is made to select representative situations or subjects, such experiments cannot reveal the kinds of attributions people usually, normally, routinely, generally, or typically make" (1995, p. 28).

The second issue concerns the motives of the perceiver. What happens if, as is commonly the case, the perceiver happens to like, love, dislike, or perhaps hate the actor? There is some evidence suggesting that the CB is an attributional option that the perceiver is likely to take or reject depending on the self-serving status of the judgmental outcome. People want friends and (liked) relatives to be given dispositional credit for their successes and situational dispensation for their failures, and the converse for our enemies (Pettigrew, 1979; Regan, Strauss, & Fazio, 1974). This kind of problem does not appear to fit easily into Gilbert's conceptualization. However, given the current renaissance of motivated reasoning (Kunda, 1990), I think an integration of Gilbert's essentially "cool," cognitive perspectives with some of these more "heated" matters would be of great interest.

CB AS ARTIFACT?

One final thought. The distinction between viewing CB as a genuine attributional phenomenon and not as an artifact was, understandably, extremely important to Ned, and, I presume, many others. A major heading in chapter 6 of his book asks, "Is Correspondence Bias Merely an Artifact?" (Jones, 1990, p. 141). Of course, his answer was a resounding "no!" and I certainly agree, although I appear to have been relegated by some to the camp of the artifactualists, much to my dismay (Jones, 1990, p. 145). However, it seems to me that some of the mechanisms identified by Gilbert could, with a little pushing and shoving, be construed as artifactual accounts or, perhaps more accurately, what used to be termed *artifacts*

Consider the first mechanism, "unawareness of situational constraints." Missing the constraint involved in the essay assignment could well have produced the CB in Jones and Harris (1967). However, Snyder and Jones (1974) performed a study that demonstrated a powerful CB effect in participants who had just written essays under similarly constraining instructions. Thus, CB effects may occur even under conditions where observers are presumably very keenly sensitive to the target's constraint, although, of course, there are obviously many circumstances where this empathy would not prevail.

Gilbert also pays quite serious attention to the specific content of the constrained behavior (i.e., writing the essay) and how this is perceived by the participants in the context of his or her expectations. This, of course, is also a focus of Yaacov Trope's influential model of dispositional inference (1986). Interestingly, it had always seemed to me that Ned minimized the need to pay attention to the specific strength or extremity of the essay. For example, in his earlier and highly influential "Rocky Road" article he noted that "within wide limits, the quality, strength, or persuasiveness of the essay has little effect on observer attributions" (Jones, 1979, p. 110). Similarly, in his recent book *Interpersonal Perception,* he noted that "we have found, in general, that subjects are quite insensitive to variations in extremity of content or enthusiasm of delivery" (Jones, 1990, p. 142).

Yet Ned may well have been more flexible on this point than I had always thought. Gilbert's article prompted me to reexamine chapter 3 of Ned's book (Jones, 1990), where I notice that he went to considerable effort to lay out the essentials of Trope's (1986) two-stage model of dispositional inference (e.g., Figure 3-5, p. 71). This model is unequivocal in emphasizing the importance of the "raw" behavior and how it is initially identified by the perceiver. Ned saw Trope's model as revealing that "a number of fascinating things occur beyond a level of our awareness in the very production of information to begin the more elaborate processes that we refer to under the label of attribution" (p. 74).

Ned illustrates the use of Trope's model in explaining one of his favorite experiments, the Snyder and Frankel (1976) study on contextual influences on the perception of emotion. In this study, participants viewed silent videotapes of a college student (actually) talking about her experiences the previous summer. However, the observers were under the impression that she was either talking about something relatively uninteresting (politics) or provocative (her sexual experiences). Judgments of the student's dispositional anxiety were of primary inest. It was expected, via the discounting principle, that judgments of anxiety would be substantially higher in the politics condition, given that virtually anyone would presumably be anxious in the sexual-practices condition. The sexual topic thus should have been relatively nondiagnostic of the target's unique or dispositional anxiety. However, more anxiety was in fact attributed in the sex condition. Using Trope's (1986) model, Ned's explanation is that the situation (i.e., talking about sex) was essentially unambiguous and thus pulled very strongly for identifying the relatively ambiguous behavior (talking on tape, but with no sound) as consistent or correspondent with the situation. The behavior was thus initially identified as laden with anxiety. Subsequently, when asked to infer a disposition from that behavior, perceivers were unable to engage in a sufficient correction in line with a normatively prescribed discounting principle.

CONCLUSION

If memory serves correctly, my first encounter with the CB was not reading the now classic 1967 Jones and Harris study in the *Journal of*

Experimental Social Psychology but rather the observer part of the monograph on actor–observer differences in causal attribution by Jones and Nisbett (1972). Years later, I told Ned that I considered that essay to be the most influential paper in the history of attribution theory. Not surprisingly, he had other candidates for that sort of accolade. Nevertheless, as one of Ned's most prominent intellectual heirs, Dan Gilbert makes a contribution in the present volume that is, in my view, a fitting testimony to the uniquely seminal role that Ned played in developing this cornerstone of social psychology.

Gilbert surmises that Ned would have found his paper too busy, too complex, or things to that effect. I doubt it. Gilbert's contribution seems a major one. Ned, who joined his students in many experiments apparently seeking the one grand answer, would have been in accord with the realization that all four of the reasons for the phenomena of CB outlined by Gilbert are highly viable. I noted previously some possible exceptions to the inclusive coverage of Gilbert's review. Other ideas and research directions will, I am confident, also be stimulated by Gilbert's discussion. Perhaps paradoxically, it seems likely, on the basis of Gilbert's multiprocess view, that the general designation of CB may ultimately lose its heuristic value. Gilbert and Jones had, in 1986, come to the opinion that the rubric of the fundamental attribution error (to which I and many others had bonded so proudly!) had outgrown its usefulness or clarity: "it is not clear that these biased inferences are always erroneous ... or specific to observers" (Gilbert & Jones, 1986, p. 269). They recommended instead "the less value-laden and more descriptive term *correspondence bias*" (p. 269). It seems conceivable that CB will also, in turn, eventually be seen as overly descriptive and contingent on specific judgmental conditions. If there are different types of CB based on different underlying processes, the generic term itself may come to lack sufficient precision to be conceptually useful.

A case in point is a recent study by Robins, Spranca, and Mendelsohn (1996) who have questioned the robustness of the actor–observer effect. As noted previously, this classic distinction in attributional perspective was intimately linked, historically, to the CB formulation itself (Jones & Nisbett, 1972). Arguing (with data) that the so-called actor–

observer effect is highly dependent on the specific causal factor at issue, the target individual's history in a particular situation, and individual differences among attributors, Robins et al. (1996) noted that the "belief in a general actor–observer effect has persisted in the literature for more than two decades. We are now convinced by the accumulated evidence that the time has come to set this idea aside" (1996, p. 388).[2] The merit of this claim remains to be established. However, it reminds me of a strikingly different position, offered by a graduate student after reading Gilbert's article—that the paper "really brings everything together." Whether Gilbert's contribution will, in time, be viewed primarily as a needed synthesis or as setting the stage for social psychologists to become less interested in the concept of a highly generalizable attributional bias will be an interesting development that promises to be well worth tracking.

REFERENCES

Ajzen, I., Dalto, C. A., & Blyth, D. P. (1979). Consistency and bias in the attribution of attitudes. *Journal of Personality and Social Psychology, 37,* 1871–1876.

Allport, G. W. (1954). *The nature of prejudice.* Reading, MA: Addison-Wesley.

Arendt, H. (1963). *Eichmann in Jerusalem: A report on the banality of evil.* New York: Viking.

Aronson, E. (1995). *The social animal.* San Francisco: Freeman.

Campbell, D. T. (1967). Stereotypes and the perception of group differences. *American Psychologist, 22,* 817–829.

Darley, J. M. (1992). Social organization for the production of evil. *Psychological Inquiry, 3,* 199–218.

Excerpts from the ruling by Municipal Court Judge Kathleen Kennedy-Powell. (1994, July 8). *The New York Times,* p. A14.

Fein, S. (1996). Effects of suspicion on attributional thinking and the correspondence bias. *Journal of Personality and Social Psychology, 70,* 1164–1184.

---

[2]Robins et al. (1996) make several references to Gilbert and Malone's (1995) review of the CB literature, a review which is structurally similar to Gilbert's chapter in the present volume.

Fein, S., Hilton, J. L., & Miller, D. T. (1990). Suspicion of ulterior motivation and the correspondence bias. *Journal of Personality and Social Psychology, 58,* 753–764.

Gilbert, D. T., & Hixon, J. G. (1991). The trouble of thinking: Activation and applications of stereotypic beliefs. *Journal of Personality and Social Psychology, 60,* 509–517.

Gilbert, D. T., & Jones, E. E. (1986). Perceiver-induced constraint: Interpretations of self-generated reality. *Journal of Personality and Social Psychology, 50,* 269–280.

Gilbert, D. T., & Malone, P. S. (1995). The correspondence bias. *Psychological Bulletin, 117,* 21–38.

Gilbert, D. T., Pelham, B. W., & Krull, D. S. (1988). On cognitive busyness: When person perceivers meet person perceived. *Journal of Personality and Social Psychology, 54,* 733–740.

Hilton, J. L., Fein, S., & Miller, D. T. (1993). Suspicion and dispositional inference. *Personality and Social Psychology Bulletin, 19,* 501–512.

Jones, E. E. (1979). The rocky road from acts to dispositions. *American Psychologist, 34,* 107–117.

Jones, E. E. (1990). *Interpersonal perception.* New York: W. H. Freeman.

Jones, E. E., & Harris, V. A. (1967). The attribution of attitudes. *Journal of Experimental Social Psychology, 3,* 1–24.

Jones, E. E., & Nisbett, R. E. (1972). The actor and the observer: Divergent perceptions of the causes of behavior. In E. E. Jones, D. E. Kanouse, H. H. Kelley, R. E. Nisbett, S. Valins, & B. Weiner (Eds.), *Attribution: Perceiving the causes of behavior* (pp. 79–94). Morristown, NJ: General Learning Press.

Jones, E. E., Worchel, S., Goethals, G. R., & Grumet, J. (1971). Prior expectancy and behavioral extremity as determinants of attitude attribution. *Journal of Experimental Social Psychology, 7,* 59–80.

Kahneman, D., & Tversky, A. (1982). On the study of statistical intuitions. *Cognition, 11,* 123–141.

Kunda, Z. (1990). The case for motivated reasoning. *Psychological Bulletin, 108,* 480–498.

Langer, E. J., & Rodin, J. (1976). The effects of choice and enhanced personal responsibility for the aged: A field experiment in an institutional setting. *Journal of Personality and Social Psychology, 34,* 191–198.

Levy, B., & Langer, E. (1994). Aging free from negative stereotypes: Successful memory in China and among the American deaf. *Journal of Personality and Social Psychology, 66,* 989–997.

Miller, A. G., Ashton, W., & Mishal, M. (1990). Beliefs concerning the features of constrained behavior: A basis for the fundamental attribution error. *Journal of Personality and Social Psychology, 59,* 635–650.

Miller, A. G., & Rorer, L. (1982). Toward an understanding of the fundamental attribution error: Essay diagnosticity in the attitude attribution paradigm. *Journal of Research in Personality, 16,* 41–59.

Pettigrew, T. F. (1979). The ultimate attribution error: Extending Allport's cognitive analysis of prejudice. *Personality and Social Psychology Bulletin, 5,* 461–476.

Reeder, G. D., Fletcher, G. J. O., & Furman, K. (1989). The role of observers' expectations in attitude attribution. *Journal of Experimental Social Psychology, 25,* 168–188.

Regan, D. T., Strauss, E., & Fazio, R. (1974). Liking and the attribution process. *Journal of Experimental Social Psychology, 10,* 385–397.

Robins, R. W., Spranca, M. D., & Mendelsohn, G. A. (1996). The actor-observer effect revisited: Effects of individual differences and repeated social interactions on actor and observer attributions. *Journal of Personality and Social Psychology, 71,* 375–389.

Rodin, J., & Langer, E. J. (1977). Long-term effects of a control-relevant intervention with the institutionalized aged. *Journal of Personality and Social Psychology, 35,* 897–902.

Ross, L., Amabile, T., & Steinmetz, J. L. (1977). Social roles, social control, and biases in social-perception processes. *Journal of Personality and Social Psychology, 35,* 484–494.

Ross, L., & Nisbett, R. E. (1991). *The person and the situation: Perspectives of social psychology.* New York: McGraw-Hill.

Saxe, L. (1991). Lying: Thoughts of an applied social psychologist. *American Psychologist, 46,* 409–415.

Snyder, M. L., & Frankel, A. (1976). Observer bias: A stringent test of behavior engulfing the field. *Journal of Personality and Social Psychology, 34,* 857–864.

Snyder, M. L., & Jones, E. E. (1974). Attitude attribution when behavior is constrained. *Journal of Experimental Social Psychology, 10,* 585–600.

Tetlock, P. E. (1985). Accountability: A social check on the fundamental attribution error. *Social Psychology Quarterly, 48,* 227–236.

Trope, Y. (1986). Identification and inferential processes in dispositional attribution. *Psychological Review, 93,* 239–257.

Comment on Gilbert

Lee Ross

This commentary focuses not only on Dan Gilbert's provocative new analysis of the correspondence bias and its sources, but also on his account of the unique mentoring style and impact of the scientist honored in this volume. Accordingly, it is appropriate, perhaps, to begin by commenting on Ned Jones' role as a mentor and role model to some of us who were not his students. While talented young psychologists at Duke, and then Princeton, were speeding with Ned, a succession of Columbia students were emoting or smoking or, in my case, noshing with our mentor, Stan Schachter. We were struck, in those days, by how differently these two intellectual leaders approached the task of crafting a study. While Ned's students were learning to design straightforward no-frills experiments, Stan's students were learning how to stage complex experimental dramas using cover stories and manipulations that Ned would have rejected as needlessly complicated and overly "showy." Unlike Schachter who, in the Festinger tradition, wanted to create memorable vignettes, Jones seemingly wanted his readers to forget methodological particulars and remember only the basic phenomenon or functional relationship in question. A taste for two-by-two designs, a talent for well-turned phrases, and a willingness to tout the merits of their latest "best-ever" student seemed to be all that these two uniquely successful and influential mentors shared.

With the passage of time and a shift in the focal concerns of our field, another important similarity has become achingly apparent. Ned, like Stan (and most of the other giants of what surely will be remembered as experimental social psychology's golden age) focused on, or at least never lost sight of, specific recognizable, real-world phenomena. The exploration of cognitive, perceptual, or motivational processes in isolation from such phenomena (which constitutes a high proportion of what is published today in the leading journals) held little appeal for them, and won little respect from them. Regardless of whether we later opted for Stan's showiness or Ned's simplicity in the crafting of experiments, we continued to be inspired and sustained by their shared commitment to experiments that made contact with tasks, responses, and phenomena that comprise our everyday social experience.

So Ned Jones became, and remains, a second mentor for a great many of us. He taught us to love, and perhaps more importantly, to respect our discipline. He tirelessly promoted the careers of young psychologists in whom he saw glimmerings of talent, including many who had not been his students, often doing so in ways of which they were totally unaware. But most of all, Ned's own career offered a continuing seminar on how easy it is, if one looks to the real world for inspiration, to find research topics worth pursuing. As Gilbert so aptly noted, Ned asked good questions; most of those good questions arose from his uncanny ability to recognize provocative self-presentation and social perception phenomena. My commentary pursues the good questions. I begin by looking at the phenomenon that Ned termed the *correspondence bias* (but that much to his chagrin had characterized as *fundamental attribution error*). Then, I return to the main topic of Dan Gilbert's chapter: the underlying mechanisms and mediators of that phenomenon. I close by discussing two potential mechanisms that do not appear on Gilbert's list, that is the nature of attributional discourse and the individualist perspective or ideology that dominates our particular culture.

CORRESPONDENCE BIAS AND THE "FUNDAMENTAL" ATTRIBUTION ERROR

The rich and varied menu of phenomena that Ned offered tenure-hungry young investigators is familiar to most readers of this volume. To me and many others, however, the most important phenomenon that Ned identified was the tendency for social perceivers to make the inferential leap too readily from observed actions and outcomes to corresponding dispositions on the part of the relevant actors. As Gilbert observed, Ned personally didn't spend a lot of time, energy, or journal space trying to isolate the precise mechanisms underlying this correspondence bias. In fact, I think his research rarely focused on the sources underlying any of the other real-world phenomena that he identified and brought to the laboratory. He generally seemed content simply to illustrate, under controlled and relatively impoverished laboratory conditions, the real-world phenomena that he saw manifest in everyday social life. He did not ignore the question of underlying processes, but he pursued it mainly in discussion sections.

Ned's write-ups seemed to suggest that he presumed most significant social perception biases to be multiply determined, even overdetermined, and he usually offered his readers a satisfying list of straightforward social motives or familiar cognitive and perceptual processes in accounting for those biases. Jones and Nisbett's (1971) classic paper on the divergent causal perceptions of actors and observers offered a splendid example of this strategy. After presenting a persuasive mix of anecdotal evidence and illustrative experiments, the authors concluded with a tour-de-force analysis of possible informational and perceptual determinants. In fact, their analysis spoke to actor–observer differences in a way that served to illuminate the multiple underlying sources and potential moderators of the correspondence bias itself. The same analysis also prompted an important line of research, elegantly pursued first by Mike Storms (1973), and later by Taylor and Fiske (1975) and by McArthur and Post (1977). These investigators showed that it is possible, by manipulating perceptual or informational processes that normally distinguish actors' and observers' vantage points to make actors' attributions more observer-like (i.e., more susceptible to the correspondence bias) or to make observers' attributions more actor-like (i.e., less susceptible to that bias). The same point about the "non-fundamental" character of the dispositionism normally shown by observers was later driven home forcefully in a series of extremely clever experiments by George Quattrone (1982), then Ned's newest best-ever student. Ned took great pleasure in telling me about the underlying rationale, design, and result of these experiments (described in detail in Gilbert's chapter) as he complained about my characterization (Ross, 1977) of the relevant phenomenon as the fundamental attribution error.

My ultimately unfortunate use of the modifier *fundamental,* I should note in defense, certainly didn't come about because I thought the lay psychologist's readiness to make unwarranted dispositional attributions constituted a unitary or irreducible phenomenon. Then, and now, a variety of perceptual, cognitive, and motivational underpinnings were obvious, as was the possibility of demonstrating that the bias could be attenuated or reversed by manipulating those underpinnings in the laboratory or by identifying specific settings or judgments in which situational determinants of behavior would be more "available" or "representative" than dispositional ones. (The key findings in Lepper, Greene, and Nisbett's classic 1973 study on undermining intrinsic interest and Strickland's earlier 1958 opus on surveillance and trust had in fact depended on the salience and representativeness of external incentives or constraints that were irrelevant or superfluous causal factors.) Nor, for that matter, did I think the phenomenon to be inevitable or invariant, although I did venture to suggest it was ubiquitous and important.

At the time I first used the term (Ross, 1977) I was struggling to provide a context for my own empirical work on various, seemingly unconnected attributional biases and inferential shortcomings. In explaining how that work fit into the bigger picture I noted that perhaps the most important task of interpersonal attribution, and indeed of lay psychology, was that of distinguishing situational causes from personal ones, and thus of deciding what could be inferred about the actor as opposed to the situational pressures and constraints confronting that actor. Success in this task, it seemed, held the key to success in the three basic undertakings of lay psychology: that is, understanding, predicting, and controlling the behavior of those in our social world. What seemed to me implicit in the work of Kurt Lewin, and made explicit by Heider (1958) and by Ned's, was the systematic tendency for observers to err in this most basic or fundamental attribution task (hence my choice of the term *fundamental attribution error*).

It was also clear to me, as Gilbert noted, that recognizing the ubiquity and importance of this attribution error represented a central contribution of both theoretical and applied social psychology (see Nisbett & Ross, 1980; Ross, 1978; Ross & Nisbett, 1991). Indeed, appreciation of the role of this attribution error seemed to figure in everything from understanding why actors feel dissonance or draw inappropriate inferences about their attitudes when they act in the face of seeming small subtle social pressures, to recognizing the full significance of the Asch conformity paradigm (Ross, Bierbrauer, & Hoffman, 1976), the Milgram experiments (Ross, 1988), and other social psychology classics. Fully appreciating the power and subtlety of situational forces helps us not to blame victims, encourages us to look for channel factors in facilitating attitude and behavior change, and ties social psychology's central insights to Mischel's (1968) seminal work on the dispositionist bias that is manifest in lay personality theory and, arguably, in a lot of formal personality theory also.

I confess that I still don't use the term *correspondence bias* as frequently as Ned and students might think appropriate. (I generally prefer the umbrella term *lay dispositionism* to cover what I see as a broader multitude of sins.) But I remain deeply aware, as I was 2 decades ago, that the departure point for subsequent observation and speculation was Ned's seminal contribution, which (along with Hal Kelley's work) focused Lewin and Heider's message and launched attribution theory— thereby providing gainful employment, and tenure, to many of us who came together to celebrate the career of the man who, as Gilbert observed, pursued his job with such unwavering enthusiasm.

UNDERLYING MECHANISMS AND MEDIATORS

Dan Gilbert's first-person account of the continuing intellectual adventure on which he and George Quattrone embarked with Ned over the last few decades allows readers a rare "student's-eye" view of the dialogue between a talented mentor and a favorite junior associate. However, like Art Miller, I must confess to some surprise at learning of Ned's investment in the search for a single, irreducible, necessary, and sufficient cause for the correspondence bias.

Consider George Quattrone's (1982) suggestion, cited by Gilbert, that the social observer's seeming preference for dispositional attributions could be "reduced" to a special case of judgmental or inferential "anchoring" plus "inadequate adjustment" (a la Tversky & Kahneman, 1974). I know that Ned thought the work to be both clever and deep (which no one can deny); but I never imagined that he (or Quattrone) thought that this explanation might be either irreducible or the "whole story." Certainly, this anchoring/adjustment factor sometimes plays a role in producing unwarranted dispositional inferences; it sometimes even plays an important role. Quattrone's and Gilbert's successive experiments provided ingenious demonstrations of this role, and again showed that if one understands the sources of a phenomenon, one can heighten, attenuate, or even reverse it by manipulating those sources. But anchoring plus (inadequate) adjustment not only fails as a sufficient explanation for the wide variety of phenomena reflecting unwarranted lay dispositionism, it itself begs for reduction. Such an account obliges theorists and researchers to explore why (or in which particular contexts) observers begin their inferential labors by anchoring on a corresponding disposition rather than a corresponding feature of the situation and why (or in which particular contexts) the subsequent adjustment of dispositional inferences tends to be too small rather than too large or just right.

The wise if anticlimactic conclusion that Gilbert offers is that neither the inferential and judgmental shortcomings elucidated by Tversky and Kahneman (1974) nor the Heiderian perceptual biases cited in Ned's own accounts can do the whole job in accounting for the correspondence bias and related phenomena. Instead, he offers a neat and tidy list consisting of (a) erroneous behavioral expectations due to lack of information about (or failure to appreciate the impact of) situational constraints, (b) misidentification or misclassification of observed behavior, and (c) failure to correct initial dispositional inferences in light of what is known or could be readily inferred about the situation. This list, and the conceptual analysis it reflects, is a genuine intellectual contribution and a fine road map for future analysis and research. (The commentary provided in this volume by Arthur Miller elaborates this contribution and highlights its connection to existing research and theory, so I'll refrain from doing likewise.) However, as Gilbert seems to recognize quite well, his analysis constitutes a weigh station rather than the end of an intellectual journey. Each cause on the list once again begs to be explained in terms of more basic inferential shortcomings or processes, and each suggests a line of new experiments worth undertaking.

The journey of discovery and explication also promises to get a lot more complicated and messy. In particular, some more basic processes and biases may underlie more than one item in Gilbert's list. Consider, for example, Gilbert's suggestion that the attributor's failure to adequately take into account the subjective interpretations or construals of the actor, or more specifically the attributor's failure to take into account possible actor–observer differences in construal (see also Griffin & Ross, 1991; Ross & Ward, 1995). This failure may lead the observer to be ignorant of situational pressures and constraints felt by the actor, and at the same time to miscategorize and hence misattribute the behavior being observed. Indeed, this contributing cause of the correspondence bias can even be characterized as a failure of appropriate anchoring and adjustment. That is, upon observing an action that seems to violate one's expectations about how a "typical" individual would behave in a given situational context, the observer often would be well advised to "adjust" less drastically his or her assumptions of actor typicality, and to refrain from inferring prematurely the presence of extreme or unusual dispositions. Instead, the prudent observer would be well advised to revise his or her assumptions about the situation and of the observed response, that is, to assume that the situation and response, at least as they are construed and experienced by the relevant actor, differ from whatever that observer had perceived or imagined them to be. (This advice to the prudent observer–attributor is especially

LEE ROSS

relevant in cases where it is the extreme or seemingly deviant behavior of a group rather than an individual that is in question. In such cases the likelihood of extreme or deviant dispositions on the part of many different individuals is particularly unlikely.)

Thus, despite its neatness, I fear that Gilbert's scheme will continue to be challenged and made messier. The more basic determinants on Gilbert's list will inevitably prove themselves to be reducible and multiply determined, and newly recognized determinants will surely suggest new phenomena—all the while providing honest work in the profession that Ned found such an easy, inviting, and open road to intellectual adventure. The importance of Gilbert's invitation to venture beyond the narrow confines of the essay-writing paradigm becomes especially clear in this regard. The task of inferring opinions from words written or spoken in the face of particular situational pressures and constraints, may arise in part from sources unique to (or at least uniquely important in) that situation. It is equally clear that other settings for the correspondence bias, and other manifestations of lay dispositionism, may similarly reflect unique or uniquely important sources in addition to whatever sources apply more or less uniformly across different contexts or paradigms. These situation-specific or context-specific sources, moreover, are not best regarded as artifacts or confounds, just processes that are worth understanding and pursuing in their own right, especially because the processes in question invariably contribute to other noteworthy phenomena and inferential foibles worthy of investigation.

Heider's (1958, p. 54) provocative, but maddeningly vague, remark about behavior engulfing the field, and the related Heiderian suggestion that an act and actor form a more natural "unit" than an act and situation, offer another illustration. Such perceptual mechanisms, which so clearly figured in Ned's own thinking both about the correspondence bias and the actor–observer divergence, remain pertinent to an understanding of the relevant phenomena. But these mechanisms surely play a greater role in explaining the misattributions that occur when individuals see a frustrated mother slap her 2-year-old than those that occur when we read second-hand accounts of social actions and outcomes. (Indeed, in the latter case, the author of the account can readily ma-

60

nipulate the relative salience of actor, action, and situational context, and thus can exaggerate or counter any preexisting dispositionist tendencies on the part of the reader.) Heider's perceptual "explanation," like Quattrone's (1982) anchoring–adjustment explanation, is not wrong or even inadequate. It is merely incomplete and likely to be more pertinent in some attribution–misattribution contexts than in others.

Again, my point is not to challenge the inclusions and possible exclusions on Gilbert's provocative list. Nor, certainly, would I prefer a list of less reducible, more fundamental underlying processes. Gilbert's contribution will do very nicely as an inspiration and organization scheme for future research and conceptual analysis. To illustrate and pay tribute to the continuing generative power of Ned's work on the correspondence bias, I would like to conclude by discussing two factors of particular contemporary interest that are properly absent from Gilbert's list, but likely to influence all of the sources and processes on that list.

Attributional Discourse

In my very first discussion of the correspondence bias and related phenomena (Ross, 1977), I suggested that certain features of our language simultaneously reflect and contribute to our dispositionist tendencies. Consider how readily we can proceed linguistically from act to disposition: *brave* (or *generous*, or *altruistic*, or *cowardly*) deeds are done by actors who thereby manifest their *bravery* (or *generosity*, or *altruism*, or *cowardice*), and thereby earn the very same personal descriptors that we applied to their deeds. Now consider the awkwardness of characterizing a situation in similarly parallel terms. How would we characterize a situation that induces otherwise ordinary folks to show extraordinary bravery or cowardice? Ugly compound descriptors can be constructed (like bravery-*inducing* and cowardice-*precipitating*), but they hardly trip off the tongue, or sound any previously recognized alarm warning. What would warn the listener, reader, or even the first-hand observer to resist the temptation to infer a corresponding disposition on the part of the actor?

There are, of course, some situation descriptors that do exactly that job, and do it nicely. In the domain of task performance, guiding inferences about performers' ability, we have the simple terms *hard* and *easy*. Everyone knows how to adjust attributions upon hearing that the cross-country course, which Mary ran (slower than usual), was particularly hard, or that the test on which John got 90% (much above his average) was unusually easy. Indeed, the existence of such a simple and serviceable pair of descriptors serve to point out exactly what is missing in other response domains where equally consequential social inferences are made and communicated.

It's interesting to note, especially in light of Bob Zajonc's constant pleas not to overlook the domain of affect, that the linguistic possibilities and conventions regarding transient emotions are very different in this respect than those regarding stable traits or dispositions. That is, people readily can refer to frightening, infuriating, frustrating, amusing, or surprising situations, and thereby convey the message that the individual is feeling and expressing a degree of fear, fury, frustration, amusement, or surprise that is appropriate or typical, and in no way revealing of any particular, distinguishing personal disposition on the part of that individual.

Do these linguistic features merely reflect, or do they also contribute to the way people form expectations, code behavior, and adjust or fail to adjust our initial presumptions about actors and situations? Does the creation of new situational descriptors within specialized domains (*prisoner's dilemma, insufficient justification paradigm,* or even *Milgram situation*) protect social scientists, and could it protect laypeople, from making unwarranted inferences about actors who respond "normally" to such situations? I'm sure that Ned's former students could design unencumbered experiments and that Stan Schachter's former students could design complicated but memorable experimental dramas to answer at least the last and most researchable of these questions.

Attribution and Culture

Hazel Markus, Harry Triandis, and others have at last awakened our field to the role played by culture in determining phenomena that social scientists in our own particular corner of the world see as universal or as inevitable products of the very cognitive, perceptual, and motivational processes that define us as human. The correspondence bias is a particularly appropriate candidate for reconsideration in this light. Does our individualistic, Protestant-ethic culture, with its emphasis on individual responsibility and accountability (see Miller, 1984), and its moral injunctions to be consistent and true to our selves regardless of the obstacles or social pressures we face, predispose us to take behavior at face value? Would less individualistic cultures—ones that recognize and encourage attention to subtle social obligations and expectations— make observers less inclined to erroneously infer corresponding attitudes and dispositions on the part of a compliant actor? Indeed, do the languages of such cultures facilitate situationist insights? Finally, are other cultures more situationist (or charitable) than our own consistently, or only when it comes to making attributions about kinsmen, coworkers, close friends, and other in-group members? The zeitgeist has induced many investigators to undertake such research; and while the constraints of this chapter preclude discussion of specific studies and findings, it is appropriate to note here that the initial results from many laboratories do indeed suggest nontrivial cultural differences. (See Holloway, Kashiwagi, Hess, & Azuma, 1986; Kashima & Triandis, 1986; Markus & Kitayama, 1991; Miller, 1984; Morris & Peng, 1994; Sethi & Ross, 1996; Shweder & Bourne, 1984; Smith & Bond, 1993.)

Again, I offer these additional determinants not to suggest that Gilbert dilute or lengthen his elegant list, but rather to suggest that the correspondence bias (like the rest of the phenomena and questions Ned brought to the forefront) will keep social psychologists happily at work for many years to come. And as Gilbert's moving account of speeding with Ned made us recognize again, he would have fully recognized the value of such a gift, and welcomed no memorial more. In fact, I want to close with a coda of my own in tribute to another of Ned's mentoring contributions, a contribution that stood me in good stead when I got that latest rejection letter from the *Journal of Personality and Social Psychology*, which complained that my coauthors and I had focused too much on an "undeniably interesting phenomenon" and given too little attention to the really important task of explicating the "basic cognitive and motivational" mechanisms. Many of us who have contributed to this volume are no longer youngsters, and it gets more and more tempting all the time to bypass the frustrations of the journal review process. We are tempted to rely on review chapters, invited addresses, and books to tell the stories we want to tell in the way we want to tell them, often without doing the painstaking empirical work, or facing the rigors of the peer-review process. Ned Jones, perhaps more than any distinguished social psychologist of his generation, resisted that temptation. He continued to do careful, well-controlled laboratory experiments, to submit articles to our leading journals, and to challenge journal editors when he thought them misguided. For Ned's unique ability to retain his enthusiasm, not just for social psychology, but for doing it the old fashioned, "hard way," those of us following in his footsteps all owe him a final, special, debt of gratitude.

REFERENCES

Griffin, D. W., & Ross, L. (1991). Subjective construal, social inference, and human misunderstanding. In M. P. Zanna (Ed.), *Advances in experimental social psychology* (Vol. 24, 319–359). New York: Academic Press.

Heider, F. (1958). *The psychology of interpersonal relations.* New York: Wiley.

Holloway, S. D., Kashiwagi, K., Hess, R. D., & Azuma, H. (1986). Causal attributions by Japanese and American mothers and children about performance in mathematics. *International Journal of Psychology, 21,* 269–286.

Jones, E. E., & Nisbett, R. E. (1971). The actor and the observer: Divergent perceptions of the causes of behavior. In E. E. Jones, D. Kanouse, H. H. Kelley, R. E. Nisbett, S. Valins, & B. Weiner (Eds.), *Attribution: Perceiving the causes of behavior.* Morristown, PA: General Learning Press.

Kashima, Y., & Triandis, H. C. (1986). The self-serving bias in attributions as a coping strategy: A cross-cultural study. *Journal of Cross-Cultural Psychology, 17,* 83–98.

Lepper, M. R., Greene, D., & Nisbett, R. E. (1973). Undermining children's intrinsic interest with extrinsic reward: A test of the overjustification hypothesis. *Journal of Personality and Social Psychology, 28,* 129–137.

Markus, H., & Kitayama, S. (1991). Culture and self: Implications for cognition, emotion, and motivation. *Psychological Review, 98,* 224–253.

McArthur, L. Z., & Post, D. (1977). Figural emphasis and person perception. *Journal of Experimental Social Psychology, 13,* 520–535.

Miller, J. (1984). Culture and the development of everyday social explanation. *Journal of Personality and Social Psychology, 46,* 961–978.

Mischel, W. (1968). *Personality and assessment.* New York: Wiley.

Morris, M. W., & Peng, K. (1994). Culture and cause: American and Chinese attributions for social and physical events. *Journal of Personality and Social Psychology, 67,* 949–971.

Nisbett, R. E., & Ross, L. (1980). *Human inference: Strategies and shortcomings of social judgment.* Englewood Cliffs, NJ: Prentice-Hall.

Quattrone, G. H. (1982). Overattribution and unit formation: When behavior engulfs the person. *Journal of Personality and Social Psychology, 42,* 593–607.

Ross, L. (1977). The intuitive psychologist and his shortcomings. In L. Berkowitz (Ed.), Advances in experimental social psychology (Vol. 10). New York: Academic Press.

Ross, L. (1978). Afterthoughts on the intuitive psychologist. In L. Berkowitz (Ed.), *Cognitive theories in social psychology.* New York: Academic Press.

Ross, L. (1988). Situationist perspectives of the obedience experiments. *Contemporary Psychology, 33,* 101–104.

Ross, L., Bierbrauer, G., & Hoffman S. (1976). The role of attribution processes in conformity and dissent: Revisiting the Asch situation. *American Psychologist, 31,* 148–157.

Ross, L., & Nisbett, R. E. (1991). *The person and the situation.* New York: McGraw-Hill.

Ross, L., & Ward, A. (1995). Naive realism: Implications for social conflict and misunderstanding. In T. Brown, E. Reed, and E. Turiel (Eds.), *Values and knowledge.* Hillsdale, NJ: Erlbaum.

Sethi, S., & Ross, L. (1996). Correspondence bias in attributing the behavior of self, in-group, and out-group members: A cross cultural comparison. Unpublished manuscript, Stanford University.

Shweder, R., & Bourne, E. J. (1984). Does the concept of the person vary cross-culturally? In R. A. Shweder & R. A. Le Vine (Eds.), *Culture theory: Essays on mind, self, and emotion* (pp. 158–199). Cambridge, England: Cambridge University Press.

Smith, P. B., & Bond, M. H. (1993). *Social psychology across cultures: Analysis and perspectives.* New York: Harvester Wheatsheaf.

Storms, M. D. (1973). Videotape and the attribution process: Reversing actors' and obervers' point of view. *Journal of Personality and Social Psychology, 27,* 165–175.

Strickland, L. H. (1958). Surveillance and trust. *Journal of Personality, 26,* 200–215.

Taylor, S. E., & Fiske, S. T. (1975). Point of view and perceptions of causality. *Journal of Personality and Social Psychology, 32,* 439–445.

Tversky, A., & Kahneman, D. (1974). Judgment under uncertainty: Heuristics and biases. *Science, 185,* 1124–1131.

2

Dispositional Bias in Person Perception: A Hypothesis-Testing Perspective

Yaacov Trope

A common theme running through a great deal of Ned Jones's work is the conviction that the way people infer personal dispositions from behavior is a basic person-perception issue. Jones' research on ingratiation and inference from in-role and out-of-role behaviors (Jones, 1964) provided initial demonstrations of the principles underlying dispositional inference. Jones and Davis's (1965) seminal chapter "From Acts to Dispositions: The Attribution Process in Person Perception" integrated these initial findings within a comprehensive conceptual analysis of the dispositional inference process. In this and subsequent contributions, Jones and his colleagues sought to understand what determines whether perceivers will draw correspondent inferences, namely, whether they will believe that an actor actually possesses the attitudes or traits (s)he overtly displays (Jones, 1979, 1990; Jones & McGillis, 1976; Jones & Nisbett, 1971).

In the 3 decades since the publication of Jones and Davis' chapter, dispositional judgment has become one of the most active research areas in person perception (see reviews by Gilbert & Malone, 1995; Jones, 1990; Trope & Higgins, 1993). Much of this research has been inspired by Jones' work on the correspondence or dispositional bias, namely, perceivers' tendency to draw dispositional inferences from situationally constrained behavior (Jones, 1979, 1990; Jones & Nisbett, 1971). Jones' work has also been influential in recent developments of stage models of biased and unbiased dispositional judgment (see Gilbert, 1989, 1990; Hamilton, 1988; Hilton, Fein, & Miller, 1993; Ross & Olson, 1981; Trope, 1986). For example, the stages in Gilbert's (1989) model are related to the notion of anchoring and adjustment (see Jones, 1979). Specifically, the characterization stage, wherein perceivers make an initial dispositional attribution, parallels anchoring; the subsequent correction stage, wherein this initial judgment is corrected for situational constraints, parallels adjustment (see Gilbert, Pelham, & Krull, 1988). The stages I proposed (Trope, 1986) parallel the distinction between the dispositions actors display and the dispositions they actually possess in Jones' definition of correspondent inference. Specifically, in the first stage, called *identification*, perceivers represent the behavior episode in terms of behavior category ("Person A acted in a friendly manner"). In the second stage, called *inference*, they determine whether the actor possesses the corresponding disposition ("Is Person A a friendly person?").

The present chapter treats identification and inference as components of a hypothesis-testing process. It is argued that the behavior-correspondent disposition serves as a hypothesis about the target. It is assumed that both identification and inference are guided by perceivers' a priori models of the determinants of behavior (see Trope & Liberman, 1993). A major purpose of this chapter is to examine dispositional bias from a hypothesis-testing perspective. This perspective suggests that dispositional bias depends on (a) perceivers' a priori models of behavior and (b) how perceivers use these models to test dispositional hypotheses. *A priori models* are preexisting beliefs regarding the potential determinants of behavior in various domains such as aggressiveness, friendliness, or competitiveness (see Kelley, 1972; Reeder, 1993; Trope & Liberman, 1993). Perceivers' a priori models differ in the weight they assign to potential dispositional and situational determinants of behavior (see Dweck, Hong, & Chiu, 1993; Markus & Kitayama, 1991; Shoda & Mischel, 1993). These models are important because they constrain the inferences perceivers can draw from immediate behavior. For example, a perceiver's dispositional inferences from immediate behavior are unlikely to be attenuated by situational inducements if the perceiver assumes that this kind of behavior depends on personal dispositions rather than on situational inducements.

Even when perceivers believe situational inducements are important determinants of the behavior at hand, the hypothesis-testing process may produce dispositional bias through identification and inference errors. Initially, prior information about the target and the immediate situational context may activate a certain a priori model and inadvertently lead perceivers to identify behavior as an instance of a certain behavior category, even when it is not. Subsequently, in evaluating the hypothesis that the target possesses the corresponding disposition, perceivers may neglect situational constraints. For example, situational provocation will fail to attenuate inferences of dispositional hostility if (a) the provocation leads to misidentifying the target's reaction as hostile and (b) the provocation is disregarded in evaluating the hypothesis that the target is a hostile person.

Identification errors presumably stem from assimilative effects of contextual information on the representation of behavioral input (Higgins & King, 1981). Inference errors presumably stem from performing a *heuristic* (pseudodiagnostic) rather than an *analytic* (diagnostic) evaluation of the validity of the dispositional hypothesis suggested by the identification (Trope & Liberman, 1993). Specifically, diagnostic inference takes into account the extent to which the dispositional hypothesis is both a sufficient and necessary condition for the behavior. Situational inducements reduce the necessity of the hypothesized disposition, and thereby the confidence with which it is attributed to the target. In contrast, pseudodiagnostic inference gives little weight to the necessity of the hypothesized disposition. Therefore, situational inducements have little effect on the confidence with which this disposition is attributed to the target.

It is proposed that assimilative identification is less controllable than pseudodiagnostic inference. Motivational and cognitive resources should enable perceivers to engage in diagnostic inference, but may fail to eliminate assimilative identification. Hence, such resources may attenuate, but not entirely eliminate dispositional bias.

The first and second sections of this chapter describe perceivers' a priori models of behavior and the hypothesis-testing process as potential sources of dispositional bias. The third section presents research bearing on the assumption that inference biases are more controllable than identification biases. Finally, the fourth section discusses the implications of this research for the understanding and correction of dispositional bias.

PERCEIVERS' A PRIORI MODELS OF BEHAVIOR

A Priori Beliefs Regarding the Antecedents of Behavior

The various stages of inferring dispositions from behavior are presumably guided by perceivers' a priori models of behavior. These models are preexisting causal theories that specify how dispositional and situational factors combine to produce behavior in specific domains such as aggressiveness, friendliness, and helpfulness (see e.g., Dweck, Hong, & Chiu, 1993; Reeder, 1993; Shoda & Mischel, 1993; Trope, 1986; Trope & Liberman, 1993). Dispositions in these models are relatively stable personal characteristics such as personality traits, values, and abilities. They represent an enduring propensity to experience certain momentary states (feelings, wishes, and goals) in the presence of appropriate situational inducements. The models specify how situational inducements (incentives, demands, opportunities) actually elicit these internal states and how these states, in turn, are expressed in behavior. For example, perceivers' a priori model of aggressive behavior may specify the likelihood that situational provocation (e.g., being teased or criticized) will elicit aggressive feelings or wishes (e.g., anger, hostility) in aggressive and nonaggressive individuals and the likelihood that these feelings will be expressed in aggressive behavior (hitting or insulting somebody).

Situational inducements differ in how they are believed to affect behavior. Some situational inducements may affect behavior by eliciting

the corresponding internal state. We refer to such situational inducements as *intrinsic*. Other situational inducements may affect behavior
without eliciting the corresponding internal state. These situational inducements are *extrinsic* (see Trope, 1989a). For example, situational
provocation is intrinsic to aggressiveness because it may lead to aggressive behavior by eliciting aggression-related states in the actor. Similarly, task difficulty is intrinsic to achievement-oriented behavior because it may promote achievement endeavors by eliciting a wish to
excel. Social norms, role requirements, and commands are extrinsic to
aggressive or achievement-oriented behavior because they may induce
these behaviors without eliciting aggressive or achievement-oriented
wishes. Instead, extrinsic inducements may induce these and other
kinds of behavior by eliciting unrelated wishes to obey or secure some
social or material gains.

Implications of Perceivers' A Priori Models for Dispositional Bias

Perceivers' a priori models of the potential causes of behavior are important for the understanding of dispositional bias because they set
certain constraints on perceivers' inferences. Regardless of how perceivers process the information contained in an immediate behavior episode, the impact of this information will depend on perceivers' a priori
beliefs regarding potential dispositional and situational causes of such
behavior. Perceivers may use optimal strategies to draw inferences from
immediate behavior. Nevertheless, situational inducements will have little or no effect on their judgments if they believe that this kind of
behavior is fully determined by the corresponding personality trait. For
example, situational provocation or group pressure to act aggressively
will have little impact on inferences from an instance of aggressive behavior if this type of behavior is believed to be fully determined by the
actor's dispositional aggressiveness. The question, then, is what is the
weight of dispositional and situational factors as potential causes in
people's a priori models of behavior? Recent theoretical and empirical
work suggests that there is marked variation in these weights across

types of behavior, perceivers, and target persons. We now examine these three sources of variation.

Type of Behavior

Research by Reeder and his colleagues has found that people believe that certain types of behavior are unlikely to occur unless the target possesses the corresponding trait (Reeder, 1985, 1993; Reeder & Brewer, 1979; see also Trope, 1974; Trope & Burnstein, 1975). In these domains, traits are seen as necessary conditions for performing the corresponding behavior. For example, people assume that immoral dispositions are necessary for committing immoral behaviors and certain competencies are necessary for succeeding. People's a priori models in such cases simply assume that situational inducements are weak potential causes of behavior. Incompetent people are seen as unlikely to excel and moral people as unlikely to commit immoral acts regardless of situational incentives. In contrast, unsuccessful performance, moral or socially desirable behaviors are believed to depend on situational factors. A competent person may fail in the absence of incentives and an immoral person may act morally if appropriately rewarded.

Such a priori assumptions permit, and actually prescribe, correspondent dispositional inferences from successful performance and immoral behavior with little adjustment for situational inducements. Indeed, a number of studies have shown that situational inducements affect dispositional inferences from failure and moral behaviors, but not dispositional inferences from success or immoral behaviors (see Devine, Hirt, & Gehrke, 1990; Evett, Devine, Hirt, & Price, 1994; Reeder, 1993; Skowronski & Carlston, 1987). Moreover, a priori models have implications for the amount of behavioral evidence perceivers will need before concluding that the target possesses the corresponding disposition. If perceivers assume that situational inducements have little influence on successful or immoral behavior, then few instances of such behavior should enable perceivers to draw correspondent dispositional inferences. Research by Gidron, Koehler, and Tversky (1993) and Rothbard and Parke (1986) has actually found that perceivers need a relatively small number of successful performances, immoral acts, and socially undesirable behaviors to conclude that a target possesses the corresponding personality traits.

It is apparent from this research that perceivers' a priori models of behavior often justify insensitivity to situational inducements and behavior-sample size. Perceivers may draw confident correspondent inferences from a small amount of constrained behavior. But this may reflect a priori beliefs about the causes of such behavior rather than suboptimal inference rules.

Type of Perceiver

Within any given behavior domain, a priori models may vary depending on cultural, developmental, and individual difference factors. Western, individualistic cultures may generally tend to conceive of behavior as primarily determined by personality traits, whereas Eastern, collectivist cultures may conceive of behavior as primarily determined by social roles, norms, and group pressure (see Cousins, 1989; Markus & Kitiyama, 1991; Miller, 1984; Triandis, 1989). A considerable amount of research has also found developmental trends in children's models of behavior (see review by Rholes, Newman, & Ruble, 1990). It is only at a certain age (4–5 years) that children acquire the concept of traits as an invariant characteristic of people. At the initial stages of acquiring a trait concept, children may see the trait as the sole determinant of corresponding behavior. But at later stages they start giving more weight to situational contingencies.

Finally, Dweck and her colleagues' work suggests that as adults, perceivers differ in their conception of people as possessing invariant dispositions (see Dweck, Hong, & Chiu, 1993; Dweck & Leggett, 1988). In any given behavioral domain, some perceivers (entity theorists), more than others (incremental theorists), generally think that behavior is determined by stable and global personality traits rather than by immediate situational contingencies. According to Dweck, entity theorists, compared with incremental theorists, seek to assess others' personality and tend to rely on unreliable and small samples of behavior to draw inferences about corresponding personality traits. Incremental theorists explain immediate behavior in terms of situationally activated goals, strategies, and expectancies, whereas entity theorists see immediate behavior as reflecting others' essential qualities.

Type of Target

Perceivers may have different a priori models for different types of targets. Perceivers may believe that their own behavior is primarily determined by situational contingencies, whereas others' behavior is primarily determined by their personality traits (see Jones & Nisbett, 1971). Similarly, perceivers may think that personality traits are more influential in in-group behavior than in out-group behavior (Tajfel, 1982). Moreover, according to Shoda and Mischel (1993), perceivers may believe that different kinds of situational inducements elicit the same behavior in different individuals. For example, our stereotypes may lead us to believe that African Americans are motivated to perform well in athletic tasks, whereas Asian Americans are motivated to perform well in academic tasks. Perceivers may use, then, athletic challenges to assess achievement needs of African Americans, and academic challenges to assess achievement needs of Asian Americans. In general, situational inducements are unlikely to moderate inferences about individuals for whom these inducements are believed to be ineffective.

In sum, it is hard, if not impossible, to determine whether perceivers' a priori models are accurate. From the present perspective, what matters is their implications for processing the information contained in an immediate behavioral episode. Whether perceivers' a priori models are right or wrong in some objective sense, they may justify, and actually prescribe, assigning little weight to situational inducements in inferring a target's dispositions from immediate behavior. That is, situational information will have little effect on dispositional inferences not because perceivers do not know how to use situational information, but because they think this information is irrelevant.

THE PROCESS OF TESTING
DISPOSITIONAL HYPOTHESES

Dispositional bias depends not only on perceivers' a priori models of behavior, but also on the way these models are used to test dispositional hypotheses on the basis an immediate behavior episode. This section describes the identification and inference stages of hypothesis testing and how they may produce dispositional bias.

Stages of Dispositional Judgment

Based on Trope's (1986) two-stage mode, Trope and Liberman (1993) proposed that dispositional judgment proceeds in two stages. In the first, called *identification,* perceivers categorize the behavior episode in terms of one of their a priori models of behavior (e.g., "Bill reacted aggressively to provocation"). In the second stage, called *inference,* perceivers evaluate the hypothesis that the target actually possesses the behavior-correspondent disposition (e.g., "Is Bill an aggressive person?"). Often, perceivers start with some initial beliefs about the target's dispositions. In such cases, the inference stage involves revision of initial beliefs about the target in light of immediate behavioral evidence.

Diagnostic Inference

Under optimal processing conditions, perceivers' inferences from behavior follow the diagnostic rule. This rule systematically uses knowledge contained in the activated a priori model of behavior. Specifically, based on one's a priori beliefs regarding dispositional and situational determinants of the behavior at hand, diagnostic inference takes into account the probability of the behavior for people possessing the corresponding disposition (the sufficiency of the dispositional hypothesis) as well as the probability of the behavior for people who do not possess the corresponding disposition (the necessity of the hypothesis). Behavior is diagnostic to the extent that it is more probable for people possessing the corresponding disposition than for people who do not possess this disposition. Diagnostic behavior, in turn, leads to high levels of confidence that the target actually possesses the correspondent disposition.

Situational inducements may make behavior seem probable regardless of whether the target possesses the corresponding disposition. Situational inducements thus reduce the diagnostic value of behavior regarding the corresponding disposition, resulting in uncertain dispositional inferences. For example, strong provocation will reduce the diagnostic value of an aggressive response because such response will seem probable independent of whether the target person is dispositionally aggressive. An aggressive response to strong provocation will leave diagnostic perceivers uncertain as to whether the target is really an aggressive person. Diagnostic inferences thus produce situationally adjusted judgments. As argued earlier, however, this depends on the weight of situational inducements in the activated a priori model. If situational inducements are an important potential cause of behavior in the activated model, then strong situational inducement to produce the observed behavior will lead perceivers to assume that most people, not only those who possess the hypothesized disposition, would have behaved in the same way, thus rendering the identified behavior nondiagnostic regarding the corresponding disposition.

Processing Goals and Testing Hypotheses About the Situation

Behavior identification is not necessarily followed by evaluation of a hypothesis about the target dispositions. What perceivers do with behavior identification depends on their goals and what they already know about the target. When the goal is to form an impression of the target or to predict his or her future behavior, perceivers will use behavior identification to test hypotheses about the target's dispositions. The context of a person-perception experiment may, at least implicitly, activate impression formation goals and thus contribute to the prevalence of trait inferences (see Newman & Uleman, 1993; Uleman, 1987). However, perceivers may be unsure what the situation demands and may therefore be interested in assessing the situation rather than the target person. Perceivers may often want to assess the difficulty of a task, the norms of a group, and the requirements of a social role rather than the personal characteristics of a particular individual. In such cases, perceivers will use their behavior identifications and what they know about the target person to test hypotheses about the situation. From the present perspective, the same principles apply to inferences about persons and inferences about situations. In one case, perceivers use what they know about the behavior and the situation to draw inferences about the person, and in the other case, they use what they know about the behavior and the person to draw inferences about the situation.

More specifically, a diagnostic evaluation of the hypothesis that the situation has the behavior-correspondent property compares (a) the probability of the identified behavior given that the situation has that property and (b) the probability of the behavior given that the situation does not have that property. Behavior is diagnostic of the hypothesized situational property to the extent that the behavior is seen as more probable if the situation has the hypothesized property than if the situation does not have this property. The diagnostic value of behavior regarding situational properties depends on perceivers' prior knowledge about the target person. If the target is believed to possess the behavior-correspondent disposition, the behavior will seem probable regardless of whether the situation has the behavior-correspondent property. As a result, perceivers will draw weak situational inferences from the behavior. For example, an aggressive response will be nondiagnostic regarding situational provocation if the target is believed to be a very aggressive person because such person is likely to respond aggressively regardless of strength of provocation. Thus, in exactly the same way that diagnostic inference produces situationally adjusted dispositional judgments, diagnostic inference also produces dispositionally adjusted situational judgments.

Process Determinants of Dispositional Bias

Dispositional bias can be traced to misidentification of behavior and noncritical evaluation of the hypothesis that the target possesses the corresponding disposition. Below we discuss these two causes of dispositional bias.

Assimilative Identification

A common source of misidentification is assimilative encoding of the behavior input. Specifically, identification of behavior, like identification of any input, may be influenced by the context in which it is embedded (Higgins & Stangor, 1988; Trope, 1988). Context in this case includes the situation in which behavior occurred and prior information about the target. By activating a particular a priori model, contextual information sets expectations regarding the type of behavior the target will exhibit. These expectations, in turn, may implicitly bias the identification of what the target does. For example, situational provocation may activate perceivers' a priori model for aggression, which may specify aggressive behavior as the likely response to such situations. This expectancy may inadvertently lead perceivers to identify the target's behavior as aggressive, even when it is not. If, for instance, a target's response to an insult is silence, the insult will lead to the identification of the silent response as hostile, when this response could actually reflect inattention to the provocation or even an attempt to appease the provocateur. Thus, situational inducements may implicitly lead to identification of ambiguous behavior in terms of a particular behavior category. Perceivers are likely to identify ambiguous behavior as frightened in frightening situations, competitive in competitive situations, and friendly in friendly situations (see Trope, 1986).

Pseudodiagnostic Inference

My colleagues and I have argued that under optimal conditions perceivers perform a diagnostic evaluation of the hypothesis that the target possesses the behavior-correspondent disposition. Diagnostic evaluation is a relatively effortful procedure, requiring assessment of the probability of the behavior under the dispositional hypothesis and under alternative hypotheses. Pseudodiagnostic inference is a simpler heuristic rule for evaluating dispositional hypotheses (see Trope & Liberman, 1993, 1996). This heuristic focuses on the probability of behavior under the corresponding disposition (sufficiency). The probability of behavior under alternative hypotheses (necessity) is given little or no consideration. For example, an instance of aggressive behavior will be attributed to the target's dispositional aggressiveness to the extent that this behavior is seen as probable for someone who is dispositionally aggressive.

Pseudodiagnostic inference is an efficient heuristic. As discussed subsequently, perceivers are likely to rely on this heuristic under suboptimal processing conditions, when they are not particularly motivated to draw accurate inferences and when their cognitive resources are limited. Because pseudodiagnostic inference focuses on the behavior-correspondent disposition and ignores alternative possibilities, it can be performed rapidly and can be done without much conscious attention. After identifying behavior, perceivers can make a judgment merely on the basis of the probability of the behavior given this disposition. Moreover, the pseudodiagnostic heuristic is efficient because it is often correlated with the diagnostic rule. That is, when a behavior is probable for people possessing the corresponding disposition, it is often improbable for people who do not possess this disposition. Verbal or physical abuse is likely for aggressive persons, but is also unlikely for nonaggressive persons (see Trope & Liberman, 1993, 1996; Trope & Mackie, 1987).

Like any heuristic, however, the pseudodiagnostic rule may produce systematic bias. Specifically, in diagnostic inference, strong situational inducements to behave in a certain manner attenuate attribution of the corresponding disposition because the behavior seems probable regardless of whether the target possesses the corresponding disposition. However, because the pseudodiagnostic rule gives little weight to the probability of behavior for people who do not possess the hypothesized disposition, this rule is insensitive to situational inducements and results in situationally underadjusted inferences. For example, group pressure to be friendly will not attenuate pseudodiagnostic inferences of dispositional friendliness because the possibility that most people, not only dispositionally friendly persons, would have behaved in a friendly manner is given little consideration in pseudodiagnostic inference.

Thus, pseudodiagnostic perceivers underuse the knowledge contained in their own a priori models of behavior. Diagnostic perceivers take into account what they know about both dispositional and situational causes of behavior, whereas pseudodiagnostic perceivers take into account only what they know about dispositional causes of behavior. Identification errors (assimilative identification) result from overuse of reliance on a priori models to identify behavior, whereas inferential errors (pseudodiagnostic inference) result from underuse of these models in drawing dispositional inferences.

The Joint Effect of Identification and Inferential Errors on Dispositional Bias

Identification and inferential errors combine to determine the net effect of situational information on dispositional judgment. Figure 1 presents four types of such net effects, resulting from the presence or absence of an identification error (assimilative identification) and an inferential error (pseudodiagnostic inference). Suppose first that situational information does not produce an assimilative effect on behavior identification. Under these conditions, the effect of situational inducements on dispositional judgment will depend on how perceivers evaluate the behavior-correspondent dispositional hypothesis. If the hypothesis is evaluated diagnostically, situational inducements should produce a negative net effect on dispositional judgments (see Quadrant A in Figure 1). However, if the dispositional hypothesis is evaluated pseudodiagnostically, the situation will produce weak or null effect on a dispositional judgments (see Quadrant B). Thus, given accurate behavior identification, dispositional bias should depend on the quality of dispositional hypothesis evaluation. Heuristic (pseudodiagnostic) evalua-

Inference

		Diagnostic	Pseudo-diagnostic
Identification	Non-assimilative	A **Negative**	B **Null**
	Assimilative	C **Null**	D **Positive**

Figure 1

Figure shows the net effect of situational inducements on dispositional judgment as a function of identification and inference errors.

tion will produce dispositionally biased judgments, whereas analytic (diagnostic) evaluation will produce unbiased judgments.

Different kinds of judgment emerge when situational information produces assimilative effects on behavior identification. When inference is diagnostic, situational inducements have two opposite effects on dispositional judgment. On one hand, situational information leads to misidentifying behavior as an instance of a given disposition. On the other hand, situational information attenuates the diagnostic value of the behavior as evidence that the target actually possesses this disposition. The net effect of situational inducements is likely to be weak or null, and dispositional judgments will appear unadjusted for situational inducements (Quadrant C). For example, on one hand, situational provocation may lead to identifying a reaction as aggressive, even when it is not; but, on the other hand, provocation attenuates the diagnostic value of this reaction regarding dispositional aggressiveness. Situational provocation may therefore fail to reduce significantly attribution of behavior to dispositional aggressiveness.

This quadrant is important because the implicit processing of situational information (for identifying behavior) and its explicit processing (for adjusting the diagnostic value of behavior regarding the corresponding disposition) are in opposition. That is, the assimilative effect of situational information on behavior identification counteracts its effect on the diagnostic value of this behavior. As a result, the underlying adjustment of the diagnostic value of behavior will not be expressed in observed dispositional attributions. According to the present analysis, then, dispositional bias will be observed both in Quadrants B and C, but the underlying mechanism should be very different in these two cases. In Quadrant B, dispositional bias is due to an inferential error, namely, pseudodiagnostic evaluation of a dispositional hypothesis. In Quadrant C, dispositional bias is due to an identification error, namely, assimilative behavior identification.

Finally, Quadrant D represents cases where perceivers commit both identification and inferential errors. Here, perceivers misidentify behavior and then draw pseudodiagnostic inferences regarding the corresponding disposition. Situational information is used to identify what the actor does, but not to evaluate the hypothesis that (s)he actually possesses the corresponding disposition. For example, situational provocation will be used to identify a reaction as aggressive, but not to decide whether the target is really an aggressive person. Instead of attenuating attribution of behavior to dispositional aggressiveness, situational provocation will enhance attribution of behavior to dispositional aggressiveness. Quadrant D thus represents an extreme case of dispositional bias, a case where situational inducements produce positive net effects on dispositional judgments (adjustment reversals). Situational inducements to perform a behavior strengthen, rather than weaken, attribution of the corresponding disposition. For example, perceivers will attribute to targets greater friendliness in friendly situations, greater competitiveness in competitive situations, and greater anxiety in anxiety-provoking situations.

Determinants of Identification and Inferential Errors

The present distinction between identification and inferential errors allows for a broad range of attributional outcomes, dispositionally biased as well as unbiased. The question, then, is what determines the likelihood of committing these errors. The two-stage model (Trope, 1986; Trope & Liberman, 1993) suggests that assimilative identification is an implicit, largely automatic process that is performed with little conscious awareness. Whether situational information will produce an assimilative effect on behavior identification should depend on factors that determine context-driven categorization (see Higgins & King, 1981; Higgins & Stangor, 1988; Trope, 1989b). These include the *ambiguity* of behavioral input (the extent to which it has multiple meanings), the *applicability* of situational expectancies to this input (i.e., the match between situational expectancies and one of these meanings), *temporal order* (i.e., whether situational information precedes or follows behavioral information), and *time delay* (i.e., the time interval between situational information and behavioral information).

The process of evaluating dispositional hypotheses is more controllable. By default, perceivers may rely on the fast and easy pseudo-diagnostic heuristic. However, certain conditions may lead perceivers to engage in a more effortful diagnostic evaluation of a dispositional hypothesis. From a hypothesis-testing perspective, thinking about alternative hypotheses is crucial for diagnostic testing. In the present context, the alternative to the dispositional hypothesis is the possibility that the situation produced the behavior regardless of whether the target possesses the corresponding disposition. The likelihood that perceivers will evaluate their dispositional hypothesis against this alternative depends on three factors: (a) the perceptual salience of the situation, (b) perceivers' processing resources, and (c) their motivation to reach accurate conclusions.

Salience of the Situation

A number of attribution theorists have viewed low perceptual salience of situational inducements as a major cause of dispositional bias and actor–observer differences (Heider, 1958; Jones & Nisbett, 1971). Perceivers presumably focus on others' behavior because it is seen as figure against the situational background. A considerable amount of research has supported this proposal (see, e.g., Taylor & Fiske, 1978). From the present hypothesis-testing perspective, perceptual salience of the situation increases situational adjustment because it alerts perceivers to an alternative to their dispositional hypothesis, namely, the possibility that the behavior would occur without the target necessarily possessing the corresponding disposition.

Processing and Motivational Resources

A considerable amount of theoretical and empirical work has been devoted to the role of processing and motivational resources in producing dispositional bias. It has been argued that perceivers are less likely to adjust their inferences for situational inducements when they are distracted by competing cognitive tasks (see e.g., Gilbert, Pelham, & Krull, 1988) and when they have little incentive to draw accurate inferences about the target (see e.g., Tetlock, 1985). From the present perspective, this work can be interpreted to mean that distracted or poorly motivated perceivers focus on a dispositional hypothesis and disregard alternative situational hypotheses. Cognitive and motivational resources may thus influence the likelihood of engaging in diagnostic rather than pseudodiagnostic inferences. However, because assimilative identification is a relatively automatic process, it is less likely to be affected by cognitive and motivational resources.

RESEARCH ON IDENTIFICATION AND INFERENCE DETERMINANTS OF DISPOSITIONAL BIAS

Research bearing on the predictions contained in Figure 1 has focused on either identification or inference determinants of dispositional bias. The present section briefly summarizes this research (see Trope & Higgins, 1993, for a detailed review) and then turns to new research that integrates the two types of determinants of dispositional bias.

Identification Factors

Research on identification factors has investigated how ambiguity of behavior and the order of behavioral and situational information determine dispositional bias (see review by Trope & Liberman, 1993). Theoretically, situational information is more likely to produce assimilative identification when behavior is ambiguous and preceded by situational information than when behavior is unambiguous or followed by situational information. Because there was no distraction or time pressure in this research, participants could draw diagnostic inferences. That is, this research compared Quadrants A and C. For example, in a study by Trope, Cohen, and Alfieri (1991), participants heard an evaluator present an ambiguous or unambiguous evaluation of another person. The evaluator was said to be under situational demands to present either a positive or a negative evaluation. The evaluation was either unambiguously positive or ambiguous. Participants then judged both the favorability of the evaluation (behavior identification) and the evaluator's true attitude toward the evaluatee (dispositional judgment).

As expected, the demands produced assimilative identification of the ambiguous evaluation (i.e., the evaluation was seen as more favorable when a positive evaluation was requested), but not of the unambiguous evaluation. Theoretically, this assimilative identification of the ambiguous evaluation may offset diagnostic adjustment, thus reducing the likelihood of a negative net effect of situational demands on attitude attributions (see Quadrant A vs. C). Consistent with this prediction, demands to present a positive evaluation attenuated attribution of a positive attitude to the evaluator only when the evaluation was unambiguous. When the evaluation was ambiguous, the demands did not affect attitude attributions.

Moreover, we used a mediation analysis to decompose the overall effect of situational demands on attitude attribution into a positive indirect effect, via assimilative identification of the evaluation, and a negative direct effect, reflecting inferential adjustment for the demands. This analysis found that when the assimilative effect of demands was controlled for, the demands had a direct negative effect on attributions of the unambiguous as well as the ambiguous evaluations. This finding indicates that participants performed diagnostic adjustment for both ambiguous and unambiguous behaviors, thus the comparison between them indeed corresponded to Quadrants A and C.

Trope et al. (1991) also manipulated the order of situational and behavioral information. Participants' ratings of the favorability of the evaluation showed that situational demands produced assimilative identification only when the evaluation was ambiguous and was preceded by information about the demands. Theoretically, then, assimilative identification could not offset diagnostic adjustment when the evaluation was unambiguous or was followed by information about situational demands. Indeed, participants' attributions showed a negative effect of situational demands in these conditions (Quadrant C), but not in the condition where the evaluation was ambiguous and was preceded by information about situational demands (Quadrant A). These findings are consistent with the authors' assumption that behavior ambiguity and order of situational and behavioral information determine assimilative identification and, thereby, whether situational inducements will produce negative or null effects on dispositional judgment.

Inference Factors

Research on inferential causes of dispositional bias has used unambiguous behavioral information and manipulated cognitive and motivational resources. From the present perspective, the manipulation of these resources determines whether inferences will be made diagnostically or pseudodiagnostically. That is, this research compares Quadrants A and B. Gilbert and his colleagues (see Gilbert & Krull, 1988; Gilbert, Pelham, & Krull, 1988) studied the effect of cognitive resources by comparing a condition where participants were free to devote their full attention to the dispositional inference problem (no-load condition) and a condition where participants were distracted by a secondary task (load condition). These researchers found that situational inducements produced a negative effect on dispositional attributions of unambiguous behaviors in the no-load condition, but not in the load condition.

Tetlock (1985) investigated the impact of making participants accountable for their judgments on the dispositional bias. This research concerns the role of the motivation to make accurate attributions. As expected, Tetlock found that accountability reduced the dispositional bias in inferring a writer's attitude from his or her essay. Accountable participants were more sensitive to the situational constraints on a writer's behavior, specifically whether the writer had a choice of what position to advocate. Together, these findings are consistent with the assumption that reduced cognitive and motivational resources lead perceivers to evaluate dispositional hypotheses pseudodiagnostically rather than diagnostically, which, in turn, results in weak or null effects of situational inducements on dispositional judgments (see Quadrant B).

The Joint Effect of Identification and Inference Factors

It seems, then, that past research has compared either Quadrants A and C (e.g., Trope et al., 1991; Trope, Cohen, & Maoz, 1988) or Quadrants A and B (e.g., Gilbert, Pelham, & Krull, 1988). Recently, Trope and Alfieri (1997) sought to compare all four quadrants within the same study. This was done by varying both behavior ambiguity (and thus assimilative identification) and cognitive load (and thus diagnostic vs.

pseudodiagnostic evaluation). Participants heard an evaluator describing another person, John, to their boss who either liked or disliked John. The boss' opinion about John created a situational demand on the evaluator to present a positive or negative evaluation of John. The evaluation was either ambiguous or unambiguous, and the information was presented under cognitive load (keeping in memory an 8-digit number) or no cognitive load. Participants judged the favorability of the evaluation (behavior identification) and the evaluator's true attitude toward John (attitude attribution).

A mediation analysis was carried out on the behavior-identification and attitude-attribution data. This analysis decomposed the overall or net effect of situational demands on attitude attribution into a positive indirect effect, via assimilative identification of the evaluation, and a negative direct effect, reflecting inferential adjustment for the demands. As expected, the effect of situational demands on behavior identification increased with behavioral ambiguity. Moreover, this effect was independent of cognitive load. That is, situational demands affected behavior identification even when participants were under cognitive load. In contrast, the negative direct effect of situational demands on attitude attribution depended on cognitive load and was independent of behavioral ambiguity. Specifically, the direct effect was significant under no load and negligible under load. In sum, ambiguity determined how situational demands were used to identify the content of the evaluation, whereas cognitive load determined how demands were used to draw inferences about the evaluator's attitudes.

Reflecting these results, the overall (net) effects of situational demands on attitude attribution were consistent with Figure 1. First, the overall effect of situational demands was negative only when participants were under no load and behavior was unambiguous (Quadrant A). In this condition, participants used the situation for inferential adjustment but not for behavior identification. They committed neither an identification error nor an inferential error. Second, the overall effect of situational demands was nullified and even reversed when either participants were under load or the behavior was ambiguous (Quadrants B and C). Specifically, when participants were under cognitive load, they failed to use the situation for inferential adjustment (Quadrant B). When the behavior was ambiguous, they used the situation for behavior identification (Quadrant C). That is, they committed either an identification error or an inferential error. Finally, the overall effect was positive and highly significant when participants were under load and the behavior was ambiguous (Quadrant D). Here participants failed to use the situation for inferential adjustment, but used it for behavior identification. These individuals committed both an identification error and an inferential error.

Trope and Alfieri (1997) were thus able to obtain in a single experiment all three possible net effects of situational inducements— negative, null, and positive—in accordance with the predictions of Figure 1. This research demonstrates that to understand dispositional bias, it is necessary to take into account both factors that determine how behavior is identified and factors that determine how inferences are drawn from the identified behavior. In focusing on one set of factors, past research could account for part, but not the full range of effects of situational inducements on dispositional attribution. For example, ample cognitive and motivational resources may enable perceivers to use the situation in drawing inferences from behavior, but these resources may not prevent the more implicit use of the situation in identifying behavior. When behavior is unambiguous or is followed by situational information, ample cognitive and motivational resources may eliminate dispositional bias (Quadrant A) as Gilbert et al. (1988) have shown. However, when behavior is ambiguous and preceded by situational information, assimilative identification may produce dispositional bias regardless of cognitive and motivational resources (Quadrant C).

The Reversibility of Situational Effects

Suppose perceivers initially think an evaluator was expected to present a positive or negative evaluation, but then learn that the evaluator was unaware of these demands. The question is whether perceivers with ample cognitive and motivational resources can undo the judgmental effects of their invalid assumptions about the situation. From the present perspective, identification and inference processes differ in this respect. As argued here, the use of the situation in drawing dispositional inferences is a deliberate process. Hence, perceivers should be able to recompute the diagnostic value of behavior based on the new situational information. However, because the assimilative effect of situational information on behavior identification is largely implicit, it may be more difficult to reverse. Perceivers may see their initial behavior identifications as givens rather than seeing them as context derived and may, therefore, fail to change them when the original situational information is invalidated.

Trope and Alfieri's (1997) second experiment tested this analysis. Participants heard an evaluator describing another person, John, to their supervisor who either liked or disliked John. The description strongly implied, but did not actually state, that the evaluator knew the supervisor's opinion about John and thus was under demand to present a positive or negative evaluation. Before making their judgments, participants were told that this assumption was valid (validation condition), whereas others were told that this assumption was invalid, that the evaluator was actually unaware of the supervisor's opinions about John (invalidation condition). As before, the evaluation was either unambiguously positive or ambiguous, and participants judged the favorability of the evaluation (behavior identification) and the evaluator's true attitude toward John (attitude attribution).

As before, a mediation analysis decomposed the overall (net) effect of situational demands on attitude attribution into an indirect effect (via identification of the evaluation) and a direct effect (reflecting adjustment of attitude attribution for the demands). First, as expected, the effect of situational demands on behavior identification increased with behavior ambiguity. Importantly, this effect was independent of the validity of situational demands. That is, situational demands continued to affect behavior identification even when the demands were invalidated. Second, the direct effect of situational demands on attitude attribution (inferential adjustment) depended on the validity of situational demands, not on ambiguity of the behavior. The direct effect was significant when situational demands were validated, but it was negligible when these demands were invalidated.

The overall effects of situational demands on attitude attribution reflected these findings. First, the overall effect was negative when the demands were validated and behavior was unambiguous. In this condition, situational demands were used to adjust attitude inferences, but not to identify behavior. Second, the overall effect was nullified when either situational demands were invalidated or the behavior was ambiguous. Specifically, when situational demands were invalidated, participants apparently undid the initial inferential adjustment for their influence. When behavior was ambiguous, situational demands biased its identification, which, in turn, counteracted inferential adjustment. Finally, the overall effect of situational demands on attitude attribution was positive and highly significant when demands were invalidated and the behavior was ambiguous. Here, participants undid the initial inferential adjustment for situational demands, but not the biasing influence of these demands on behavior identification.

Together these results support the assumption that the use of the situation to identify behavior is less reversible than the use of the situation to draw inferences regarding the target's dispositions. Learning that one's assumptions about the situation were false can reverse inferential adjustment, but not assimilative identification. In general, the use of the situation to identify behavior seems to be an implicit, relatively uneffortful process, whereas the use of the situation to draw inferences regarding dispositional hypotheses seems a more explicit and effortful process. Motivational and cognitive resources and new information about the situation can affect how people use situational inducements for evaluating dispositional hypotheses, not so much how we use situational inducements to identify behavioral evidence for such hypotheses.

CONCLUSION AND IMPLICATIONS

The Origins of Dispositional Bias

The present hypothesis-testing perspective suggests that to understand dispositional bias we need to take into account perceivers' a priori models of behavior and how these models are used for processing the information contained in an immediate behavior episode.

A Priori Models of Behavior

Dispositional bias is likely to occur to the extent that perceivers think personal dispositions are the primary potential determinants of behavior. The role of situations and dispositions in perceivers' a priori models of behavior may vary across different types of perceivers, behaviors, and targets. Specifically, perceivers from Western (rather than Eastern) cultures, and perceivers who see traits as fixed entities (rather than as malleable qualities) are likely to see dispositions as the prime potential causes of behavior (see Dweck et al., 1993; Markus & Kitiyama, 1991). For certain types of behavior (e.g., extreme, immoral, successful, or extroverted behaviors), dispositional factors may be seen as primary potential causes. For other behaviors (e.g., moderate, moral, unsuccessful, or introverted behaviors), situational factors may be seen as primary (see Gidron, Koehler, & Tversky, 1993; Reeder, 1993). Finally, perceivers may have different models for different targets. For some targets (e.g., others, out-group members), dispositional factors may be seen as primary potential causes, whereas for other targets (e.g., self, in-group members), situational factors may be seen as primary.

The Hypothesis-Testing Process

Dispositional bias is likely to occur to the extent that perceivers misidentify behavior in terms of one of their a priori models and subsequently perform a heuristic (pseudodiagnostic) evaluation of the hypothesis that the target actually possesses the behavior-correspondent disposition. Situational inducements to perform a behavior may fail to attenuate and may even enhance attribution of the corresponding disposition to the extent that situational inducements (a) lead perceivers to identify behavior in terms of the activated behavior category (e.g., "John acted aggressively") and (b) are underused in pseudodiagnostic evaluation of the hypothesis that the target possesses the correspondent disposition (e.g., "John is an aggressive person").

It is assumed that assimilative identification is less controllable than pseudodiagnostic inference. Recent research by Trope and Alfieri (1997) found support for two implications of this assumption: First, cognitive resources enabled perceivers to use the situation in drawing inferences from behavior, but did not prevent assimilative effects of the situation on behavior identification. Second, perceivers were able to undo the effect of false situational information on inference, but not its effect on behavior identification.

From the present perspective, processing goals are an important determinant of dispositional bias because they determine what kind of hypotheses perceivers test. In a typical person-perception experiment, like in many real-life situations, perceivers observe what others do to form an impression about their personality (see Hilton & Darley, 1991). Given this goal, perceivers are likely to test a dispositional hypothesis, and pseudodiagnostic inference may favor confirmation of such a hypothesis. In other cases, perceivers may want to learn about the situation or the target's immediate goals. Perceivers may then test a hypothesis about the situation or the target's context-specific goals, preferences, and beliefs. In such cases, pseudodiagnostic inferences will favor confirmation of nondispositional hypotheses.

Debiasing

What are the implications of the present analysis regarding the feasibility of overcoming dispositional bias? Four origins of dispositional bias were proposed here: a priori models of behavior, processing goals, assimilative identification, and pseudodiagnostic inference. The present analysis suggests that it may be particularly difficult to eliminate the influence of a priori models of behavior and assimilative identification of immediate behavior. A priori conceptions of behavior as primarily caused by fixed personal dispositions may be rooted in ones' general world views (Dweck et al., 1993; Shoda & Mischel, 1993) and culture (Markus & Kitayama, 1991). They may therefore be resistant to change, and their influence on processing of an immediate behavior episode may be hard to annul. Similarly, given that assimilative identification is an implicit process, the process may be relatively hard to prevent or reverse by accuracy incentives or ample attentional resources, as the Trope and Alfieri (1997) research demonstrates.

Immediate processing goals and pseudodiagnostic inference may be relatively easier to change. Perceivers may generally believe that personality traits are the primary determinants of behavior. But in any given case, they can be motivated to test more circumscribed hypotheses about the target. Instead of trying to assess the target's personality, perceivers may be motivated to detect the target's immediate intentions, goals, and beliefs. Similarly, perceivers may adopt the goal of trying to find out something about the situation to which the target responded and thus test situational rather than dispositional hypotheses. Finally, with sufficient motivation to be accurate and adequate processing resources, perceivers may adopt careful, diagnostic inference rules, rather than pseudodiagnostic heuristics, and thus avoid drawing overconfident dispositional inferences from behavior.

Ned Jones' ideas provided the impetus for 3 decades of research on dispositional inference that established dispositional bias as one of the most pervasive phenomena in person perception. But right from the start Ned Jones' goal was to understand the cognitive mechanisms underlying dispositional bias and to uncover the conditions that limit its generality. He formulated the inferential logic of correspondent inference, proposed short-cut heuristics, and distinguished between actor and observer perspectives and in-group and out-group perceptions. The present two-stage, hypothesis-testing analysis was inspired by this goal and hopefully makes a step toward achieving it.

REFERENCES

Cousins, S. D. (1989). Culture and self-perception in Japan and the United States. *Journal of Personality and Social Psychology, 56,* 124–131.

Devine, P. G., Hirt, E. R., & Gehrke, E. M. (1990). Diagnostic and confirmatory strategies in trait hypothesis-testing. *Journal of Personality and Social Psychology, 58,* 952–963.

Dweck, C. S., Hong, Y., & Chiu, C. (1993). Implicit theories: Individual differences in the likelihood and meaning of dispositional inference. *Personality & Social Psychology Bulletin, 19,* 633–643.

Dweck, C. S., & Leggett, E. L. (1988). The social–cognitive approach to motivation and personality. *Psychological Review, 95,* 256–273.

Evett, S. R., Devine, P. G., Hirt, E. R., & Price, J. (1994). The role of the hypothesis and the evidence in the trait hypothesis testing process. *Journal of Experimental Social Psychology, 30,* 456–481.

Gidron, D., Koehler, D. J., & Tversky, A. (1993). Implicit quantification of personality traits. *Personality and Social Psychology Bulletin, 19,* 594–604.

Gilbert, D. T. (1989). Thinking lightly about others: Automatic components of the social inference process. In J. S. Uleman & J. A. Bargh (Eds.), *Unintended thought.* New York: Guilford.

Gilbert, D. T. (1990). How mental systems believe. *American Psychologist, 46,* 107–119.

Gilbert, D. T., & Krull, D. S. (1988). Seeing less and knowing more: The benefits of perceptual ignorance. *Journal of Personality and Social Psychology, 54,* 93–102.

Gilbert, D., & Malone, P. S. (1995). The correspondence bias. *Psychological Bulletin, 117,* 21–28.

Gilbert, D. T., Pelham, B. W., & Krull, D. S. (1988). On cognitive busyness: When person perceivers meet persons perceived. *Journal of Personality and Social Psychology, 54,* 733–740.

Hamilton, D. L. (1988). Causal attribution viewed from an information-processing perspective. In D. Bar-Tal & A. W. Kruglanski (Eds.), *The social psychology of knowledge* (pp. 359–385). Cambridge, England: Cambridge University Press.

Heider, F. (1958). *The psychology of interpersonal relations.* New York: Wiley.

Higgins, E. T., & King, G. (1981). Accessibility of social constructs: Information-processing consequences of individual and contextual variability. In N. Cantor & J. F. Kihlstrom (Eds.), *Personality, cognition and social interaction* (pp. 69–121). Hillsdale, NJ: Erlbaum.

Higgins, E. T., & Stangor, C. (1988). Context-driven social judgment and memory: When "behavior engulfs the field" in reconstructive memory. In D. Bar-Tal & A. Kruglanski (Eds.), *Social psychology of knowledge.* Cambridge, England: Cambridge University Press.

Hilton, J. L., & Darley, J. M. (1991). The effects of interaction goals on person perception. In M. P. Zanna (Ed.), *Advances in experimental social psychology* (Vol. 24, pp. 235–267). San Diego, CA: Academic Press.

Hilton, J. L., Fein, S., & Miller, D. T. (1993). Suspicion and dispositional inference. *Journal of Personality & Social Psychology, 19,* 501–512.

Jones, E. E. (1964). *Ingratiation: A Social Psychological Analysis.* New York: Appleton-Century-Crofts.

Jones, E. E. (1979). The rocky road from acts to dispositions. *American Psychologist, 34,* 107–117.

Jones, E. E. (1990). *Interpersonal perception.* New York: W. H. Freeman.

Jones, E. E., & Davis, K. E. (1965). From acts to dispositions: The attribution process in person perception. In L. Berkowitz (Ed.), *Advances in experimental social psychology* (Vol. 2, pp. 220–265). New York: Academic Press.

Jones, E. E., Davis, K. E., & Gergen, K. J. (1961). Role playing variations and their informational value for person perception. *Journal of Abnormal & Social Psychology, 63,* 302–110.

Jones, E. E., & McGillis, D. (1976). Correspondent inferences and the attribution cube: A comparative reappraisal. In J. H. Harvey, W. J. Ickes, & R. F. Kidd (Eds.), *New directions in attribution research* (Vol. 1, pp. 389–420). Hillsdale, NJ: Erlbaum.

Jones, E. E., & Nisbett, R. E. (1971). *The actor and the observer: Divergent perception of the causes of behavior.* Morristown, NJ: General Learning Press.

Kelley, H. H. (1972). Causal schemata and the attribution process. In E. E. Jones, D. E. Kanouse, H. H. Kelley, R. E. Nisbett, S. Valins, & B. Weiner (Eds.), *Attribution: Perceiving the causes of behavior* (pp. 151–174). Morristown, NJ: General Learning Press.

Markus, H., & Kitayama, S. (1991). Culture and the self: Implications for cognition, emotion, and motivation. *Psychological Review, 98,* 224–253.

Miller, J. G. (1984). Culture and the development of everyday social explanation. *Journal of Personality & Social Psychology, 46,* 961–978.

Newman, L. S., & Uleman, J. S. (1993). When are you what you did? Behavior identification and dispositional inference in person memory, attribution and social judgment. *Personality & Social Psychology Bulletin, 19,* 513–525.

Reeder, G. D. (1985). Implicit relations between dispositions and behaviors: Effects on dispositional attribution. In J. H. Harvey & G. Weary (Eds.), *Attribution: Basic issues and application* (pp. 87–116). New York: Academic Press.

Reeder, G. D. (1993). Trait-behavior relations and dispositional inference. *Personality and Social Psychology Bulletin, 19,* 586–593.

Reeder, G. D., & Brewer, M. B. (1979). A schematic model of dispositional attribution in interpersonal perception. *Psychological Review, 86,* 61–79.

Rholes, W. S., Newman, L. S., & Ruble, D. N. (1990). Understanding self and other: Developmental and motivational aspects of perceiving persons in terms of invariant dispositions. In E. T. Higgins & R. M. Sorrentino (Eds.), *Handbook of motivation and cognition* (Vol. 2, pp. 369–407). New York: Guilford.

Ross, M., & Olson, J. M. (1981). An expectancy-attribution model of the effects of placebos. *Psychological Review, 88,* 408–437.

Rothbart, M., & Parke, B. (1986). On the confirmability and disconfirmability of trait concepts. *Journal of Personality and Social Psychology, 50,* 131–142.

Shoda, Y., & Mischel, W. (1993). Cognitive social approach to dispositional inferences: What if the perceiver is a cognitive social theorist? *Personality and Social Psychology Bulletin, 19,* 574–595.

Skowronski, J. J., & Carlston, D. E. (1987). Social judgment and social memory: The role of cue diagnosticity in negativity, positivity, and extremity biases. *Journal of Personality and Social Psychology, 52,* 689–699.

Tajfel, H. (1982). *Social identity and intergroup relations.* Cambridge, England: Cambridge University Press.

Taylor, S. E., & Fiske, S. T. (1978). Salience, attention, and attribution: Top of the head phenomena. In L. Berkowitz (Ed.), *Advances in experimental social psychology* (Vol. 11, pp. 249–288). New York: Academic Press.

Tetlock, P. E. (1985). Accountability: A social check on the fundamental attribution error. *Social Psychology Quarterly, 48,* 227–236.

Triandis, H. C. (1989). The self and social behavior in differing cultural contexts. *Psychological Review, 96,* 506–520.

Trope, Y. (1974). Inferential processes in the forced-compliance situation: A bayesian analysis. *Journal of Experimental Social Psychology, 10,* 1–16.

Trope, Y. (1986). Identification and inferential processes in dispositional attribution. *Psychological Review, 93,* 239–257.

Trope, Y. (1988). The multiple roles of context in dispositional judgment. In J. N. Bassili (Ed.), *On-line cognition in person perception.* Hillsdale, NJ: Erlbaum.

Trope, Y. (1989a). Levels of inference in dispositional judgment. *Social Cognition, 7,* 296–314.

Trope, Y. (1989b). Perceptual and inferential effects of stereotypes. In D. Bar-Tal and A. Kruglanski (Eds.), *The Social Psychology of Knowledge.* Cambridge, England: Cambridge University Press.

Trope, Y., & Alfieri, T. (1997). Effortfulness and flexibility of dispositional judgment processes. *Journal of Personality & Social Psychology, 73,* 662–674.

Trope, Y., & Burnstein, E. (1975). Processing the information contained in another's behavior. *Journal of Experimental Social Psychology, 11,* 439–458.

Trope, Y., Cohen, O., & Alfieri, T. (1991). Behavior identification as a mediator of dispositional inference. *Journal of Personality and Social Psychology, 61,* 873–883.

Trope, Y., Cohen, O., & Maoz, I. (1988). The perceptual and inferential effects of situational inducements. *Journal of Personality and Social Psychology, 55,* 165–177.

Trope, Y., & Higgins, E. T. (1993). The what, how, and when of dispositional inference: New questions and answers. *Personality and Social Psychology Bulletin, 19,* 493–500.

Trope, Y., & Liberman, A. (1993). Trait conceptions in identification of behavior and inferences about persons. *Personality and Social Psychology Bulletin, 19,* 553–562.

Trope, Y., & Liberman, A. (1996). Social hypothesis-testing: Cognitive and motivational mechanisms. In E. T. Higgins & A. W. Kruglanski (Eds.), *Social psychology: Handbook of basic principles.* New York: Guilford Press.

Trope, Y., & Mackie, D. (1987). Sensitivity to alternatives in social hypothesis-testing. *Journal of Experimental Social Psychology, 23,* 445–459.

Uleman, J. S. (1987). Consciousness and control: The case of spontaneous trait inferences. *Personality and Social Psychology Bulletin, 13,* 337–354.

Dispositional and Attributional Inferences in Person Perception

David L. Hamilton

It has now been 30 years since the publication of Jones and Davis's (1965) classic paper "From Acts to Dispositions: The Attribution Process in Person Perception," which introduced correspondent-inference theory to social psychology. This chapter is often cited as the first of two papers (Kelley's, 1967, presentation of his covariation model being the other) that provided the catalyst for the flood of attribution research that appeared throughout the 1970s and that continues today (Smith, 1994).[1] It is a testament to the importance of correspondent-inference theory that the central question addressed in that chapter—how the perceiver goes from acts to dispositions in perceiving others—continues to be the focus of current theory and research, some 3 decades later (Hamilton, 1991; Trope & Higgins, 1993).

The work of Yaacov Trope (Trope, 1986; Trope & Liberman, 1993) has been among the important contributions to this inquiry in recent years. His chapter in this volume provides an excellent summary of his

Preparation of this comment was supported in part by NIMH Grant MH-40058.
[1]Both of these works, of course, developed ideas expressed earlier by Heider (1958).

model and the research evidence he has marshaled in support of it. In commenting on Trope's chapter, I briefly discuss three important conceptual models of the nature of dispositional inferences and how they are made. This provides a framework for understanding the unique contributions of Trope's model. I then examine the relationship between dispositional and attributional inferences. In essence, I argue that the two parts of the title of Jones and Davis's (1965) chapter—"from acts to dispositions" and "the attribution process in person perception"—may not be as intimately tied to each other as many have assumed.

THREE MODELS OF THE DISPOSITIONAL INFERENCE PROCESS

In this section I briefly review three prominent theoretical accounts of the dispositional inference process. The discussion highlights differences among the models with regard to several features, including the postulated stages (if any) in the theorized process, how and when information about situational context is used, and the spontaneous-versus-controlled nature of the process and its components.

Jones and Davis

Jones and Davis's (1965) chapter provided one of the first serious attempts to account for how dispositional inferences are made. In essence, the theory specified a number of factors that serve to promote or inhibit the perceiver in making such inferences.

Jones and Davis did not provide any specific description of the inference process itself. Rather, correspondent inference theory essentially proposed that a perceiver will make a correspondent inference from an observed behavior unless certain factors are present that would indicate that the behavior might have been situationally caused. For example, if the behavior is a highly normative behavior or a highly desirable behavior, then social norms about what is appropriate in a given situation could account for the behavior. Similarly, if the actor had little or no choice in performing the behavior, then that fact could explain the behavior. To the extent that these conditions prevail, the theory said that a dispositional inference would be less likely made. If these conditions are not present, then the behavior is assumed to reflect a correspondent disposition.

Although Jones and Davis never stated it explicitly, their analysis implies that the perceiver gives some consideration to possible situational constraints prior to making a correspondent inference; only if the extenuating circumstances are not present will the perceiver draw the correspondent inference. And there is the sense (again, implicit) that all of this involves a fairly deliberate, considered judgment process.

Gilbert

Jones and Davis's (1965) paper was published prior to the cognitive revolution in psychology, which brought an emphasis on information processing. Therefore contemporary readers cannot fault these authors for any lack of specification regarding stages or the nature of information processing that underlies correspondent inferences. More recent developments have led to newer conceptualizations that attempt to more explicitly describe the processes by which these inferences are made.

During the 1980s evidence began to accumulate suggesting that perceivers spontaneously infer trait characteristics as they encode behavioral information. This view was supported in particular by the work of Uleman and his colleagues (Newman & Uleman, 1989; Winter & Uleman, 1984; Winter, Uleman, & Cunniff, 1985), but findings reported by others were also compatible with this view (e.g., Carlston & Skowronski, 1994; Hamilton, 1988; Smith & Miller, 1983).[2] Thus, when a perceiver sees someone perform a helpful behavior, it is likely that he will spontaneously infer that the actor is a helpful person. These inferred traits would be correspondent to the manifest properties of the behavior; that is, a helpful behavior implies a helpful disposition. If this view is correct, then under many circumstances correspondent infer-

---

[2]Despite this evidence, debate continues in the literature regarding the extent to which spontaneous trait inferences are made as behavioral information is encoded. For alternative views, see Bassili (1989) and Uleman, Newman, and Moskowitz (1996).

ences are made spontaneously during the comprehension of the observed behavior, without consideration of situational forces that might preclude, qualify, or undermine such inferences.

Gilbert's (1989; Gilbert, Pelham, & Krull, 1988) work combined these findings on spontaneous trait inferences with the questions central to correspondent-inference theory. Gilbert argued that these dispositional inferences are made quickly and are made with relative ease, but that they may subsequently be corrected in light of relevant situational information. Moreover, whereas the dispositional inference (or, in his terms, *characterization*) is spontaneous, the correction process is more analytic, requires cognitive resources, and hence can be easily disrupted by competing task demands. Whereas correspondent-inference theory implied that possible situational constraints were considered prior to making a dispositional inference, in Gilbert's model that dispositional inference has primacy status; situational information is considered only after that inference has been made. Moreover, because it is resource demanding, the resulting correction may be an insufficient adjustment of the inference in light of the situational constraints.

Trope

Trope's (1986, this volume) model provides a more complex account of the process of how dispositional inferences are made and of how biases can enter into that process. In his two-stage model, the first step involves the *identification* of the observed behavior in disposition-relevant terms. This identification then serves as an hypothesis that is tested in the second, or *inference*, stage. Because people use less-than-optimal strategies in evaluating hypotheses, the result of this inference stage will often be biased in a confirmatory direction. In Trope's model the identification stage is essentially automatic, whereas the inference stage is resource demanding and therefore subject to constraints due to cognitive resource limitations.

It is important to recognize that biases can enter the process at either stage in Trope's model. This means, then, that an erroneous judgment of an actor's personality may be the consequence of bias that occurred either in the perceiver's initial identification of the actor's behavior or in the process of inferring dispositional properties from that behavior, or both. What factors contribute to these biases? Trope identifies two sources: (a) the perceiver's use (or nonuse) of information about the situational context and (b) the perceiver's knowledge or expectancies ("priors") about the actor's dispositional characteristics.

One of the important, and distinguishing, elements of Trope's analysis is that information about the situational context can influence what happens at both of these stages (in contrast to Gilbert's model, where situational factors are influential only after a dispositional inference has been made). Identification may be biased by assimilation of the perceiver's interpretation of the behavior in accordance with the situational context in which it occurred. Inference may be biased by insufficient adjustment of the identification-based hypothesis in light of other factors, including situational constraints. Trope calls this *pseudodiagnostic inference*. Thus, situational information can play an important role in either or both of these stages, and it is important to consider their combined influence on the ultimate judgment. This is perhaps the most novel aspect of Trope's model.

The other source of biasing influence that Trope cites is the perceiver's expectancies, which can include prior knowledge of the actor, stereotypes of the actor's group membership, and so forth. The role of these expectancies in social perception is a topic that has been extensively researched in recent years, and it will be a major focus of my discussion in this commentary.

THE IMPORTANT ROLE OF PERCEIVER EXPECTANCIES

Trope (this volume) characterizes his model as an *hypothesis-testing perspective* on dispositional bias in person perception. He discusses the hypothesis as arising in the identification of the meaning of the behavior in dispositional terms. Identifying the behavior as helpful generates the hypothesis that the actor is a helpful person. The hypothesis, then, is a product of the encoding process, an outcome of comprehending and construing behavior. This hypothesis is then tested in the inference stage, possibly biased by pseudodiagnostic inference.

Although the emphasis in Trope's discussion is on the hypothesis generated at the identification stage of his model, in many circumstances the perceiver will already have an hypothesis even before this stage. That is, the perceiver may have an expectancy or impression of the target person, based on prior knowledge. These expectancies, which Trope calls priors, are postulated to influence both the identification of the target person's behavior and the nature of inferences drawn from it. In general, the effect of prior expectancies is to moderate these processes; that is, expectancies influence the extent to which a behavior is given dispositional identification or the extent to which a corresponding dispositional property is inferred. Trope proposes that, at the identification stage, prior expectancies will have greater influence on the identification of ambiguous than of unambiguous behavior. At the inference stage expectancies can either enhance or attenuate the strength of the inference that is made.

In this section I argue that the inference process is more complex than this characterization.[3] In particular, I argue that consistency or inconsistency of the behavior with the perceiver's expectancies can have profound impact not simply on the strength of inference, but on the kinds of inference processes that unfold.

Consider an instance in which an actor makes a rude, caustic remark to another person, in public and without apparent provocation. The behavior is unambiguous, not easily open to alternative interpretation; it is clearly a rude, nasty comment. (Thus, in Trope's analysis, prior expectancies would not be expected to influence the identification of the behavior.) The present argument is that the relationship between behavior and expectancies can invoke qualitatively different inference processes.

Consider first the case in which the perceiver already thinks of the target individual as a mean and nasty person. In this case, the person's rude behavior is entirely consistent with expectancy, and the inference

---

[3]Jones and McGillis (1976) also considered the role of expectancies and differentiated between target-based and category-based expectancies (see also Weisz & Jones, 1993). As in Trope's case, this difference presumably influences the strength of the dispositional inference made by the perceiver.

process is quite straightforward. The behavior itself is easily interpreted as being rude or nasty, and the step from nasty behavior to nasty person is an easy inference. This part is simple.

In contrast, things get more complicated, though perhaps more interesting, when the perceiver's prior impression is that the target individual is a kind and friendly person. Now the behavior is clearly inconsistent with expectancy, and consequently a different set of processes is likely to be invoked. To develop this point, several fundamental differences in the way expectancy-consistent and expectancy-inconsistent information is processed, all of which are well documented in the literature, must be recognized:

1. Several studies have shown that people spend more time processing items of information that are inconsistent with expectancies than they do when processing expectancy-consistent information (Bargh & Thein, 1985; Hemsley & Marmurek, 1982; Stern, Marrs, Millar, & Cole, 1984). So at minimum, there is a quantitative difference in the way these two kinds of information are processed. The differences, however, are not merely quantitative.

2. When perceivers encounter an expectancy-inconsistent item of information, they spontaneously retrieve from memory other information they have already processed about the target person. However, this spontaneous retrieval of prior information does not occur when they encounter expectancy-consistent information (Sherman & Hamilton, 1994).

3. This extended processing time and retrieval of relevant information from memory reflect the perceiver's attempts to understand the expectancy-inconsistent behavior. That is, when the behavior does not fit with the perceiver's impression of the actor, the perceiver tries to explain why that behavior occurred, tries to make sense of why this kind and friendly person made such a rude remark. In other words, the inconsistent information spontaneously triggers attributional thinking (Clary & Tesser, 1983; Hamilton, 1988; Hastie, 1984; Schoeneman, van Uchelen, Stonebrink, & Check, 1986). Again, however, this process does not spontaneously occur in the course of processing expectancy-consistent behavior.

This evidence indicates that, when perceivers encounter behavioral information that is inconsistent with their expectancies or impressions, it sets off processes that are qualitatively different from those that routinely occur in processing behaviors that easily fit with those expectancies. And more specifically, attributional analysis—the analysis of causation—is at the heart of those differences.

All of this may seem quite plausible in light of the research findings I have cited. However, there are some important implications of this view for understanding inference processes in person perception, implications that generally are not recognized by the models I summarized previously.

First, although both dispositional inferences and attributions are inferences based on the behavioral information, there are basic differences in the processing of expectancy-consistent and expectancy-inconsistent behaviors. When the behavior fits nicely with expectancy, the inference process is more spontaneous and less analytic, more automatic and less controlled, more heuristic and less systematic than when the behavior violates an existing expectancy. None of the models I have referred to seem to adequately capture that fundamental difference.

Second, none of these models recognize the impact of expectancies on the nature of the inference they induce. Given an expectancy-consistent behavior, perceivers tend to make simple, spontaneous, non-analytic dispositional inferences—moving from acts to dispositions, making correspondent inferences. In doing so, however, the perceiver is *not* engaging in an analysis of *why* the friendly actor was so kind, or *why* the mean person behaved in a nasty manner. When behavior conforms to expectancy, there's no reason to ponder why it happened and the prior expectancy is confirmed and strengthened. In other words, the process of making these correspondent inferences does not seem to involve much attributional thinking.

In contrast, attributional thinking is most likely to occur precisely under those conditions when correspondent inferences are least likely to be made, specifically, when the behavior violates the operative expectancy. If this is so, then perhaps correspondent inferences are, in this important sense, fundamentally different from attributional inferences. They are likely to be made under quite different conditions and involve different kinds of processes. This analysis suggests that perhaps correspondent-inference theory was an important theory of how people make dispositional inferences, but not really a theory of how people make causal attributions.

Third, when a dispositional inference is made, it is likely to become a part of the perceiver's impression of the actor. The actor behaves in a friendly manner, so the perceiver infers that he's a friendly person. The trait characterization is a summary of the behavioral information that was obtained. However, there is an important consequence of having made this dispositional inference that relates directly to attributional judgments. Specifically, if the perceiver were later to wonder (or were to be asked) why the kind actor acted so friendly, or why the mean person behaved in a nasty manner, the perceiver now has a readily available explanation. That is, the dispositional inference made earlier, without any causal analysis, now becomes an easily accessible "explanation" for the actor's behavior. So a correspondent inference, though not involving attributional thought in its origin, can itself become an attribution (either for the same behavior or for other, similar behaviors).

Fourth, notice that the processes discussed here would bias perceivers in favor of person, as opposed to situational, attributions—a bias that is well documented in the literature (for reviews, see Jones, 1979, 1990; Nisbett & Ross, 1980; Ross, 1977). However, when the perceiver has clear expectancies about the actor, the mechanisms that produce this bias can be quite different from those that have been advanced by others.

EXPECTANCIES, DISPOSITIONAL INFERENCES, AND ATTRIBUTIONS

Most previous analyses of the tendency toward person attributions have not adequately considered the role of perceiver expectancies in this process. This is unfortunate because it is likely that perceivers have some kind of prior expectancy about most actors they encounter in most situations. The present analysis is specifically concerned with the role of perceiver expectancies in this context and has several interesting features.

Given the presence of relevant expectancies, most behavioral information learned about an actor will be either consistent or inconsistent with those expectancies. There are at least two reasons to expect that most of these behaviors will be perceived as consistent with the expectancy. First, if the perceiver's expectancy about the target person has some degree of validity, then that person's behavior will generally conform to the expectancy. Suppose the perceiver believes that Mark is an intelligent person. If Mark is indeed intelligent, then he will say and do intelligent things with regularity (and will do stupid things only rarely). Second, if the behavior in question is ambiguous and hence open to alternative interpretation, it is likely that the expectancy would influence the perceiver's construal of the behavior, with the consequence that the behavior would be assimilated to the operative expectancy (Trope, 1986). Thus, even behavior that does not objectively confirm an expectancy can be interpreted in an expectancy-consistent manner. Taken together, these considerations suggest that, from the perceiver's perspective, expectancy-consistent behavior should be the rule.

As I developed in the previous section, the common response to these expectancy-consistent behaviors is a correspondent inference (in essence confirming the prior expectancy). This dispositional inference is not attributional in nature, but is simply in the service of summarizing behavioral information at a more abstract level. However, as noted earlier, when the attributional question is posed—why did the actor do that?—the inferred disposition provides a ready-made heuristic answer, and obviously would produce a person (internal) attribution. Thus, the way perceivers process the most commonly occurring type of information (behaviors perceived as consistent with expectancy) biases them toward person, rather than situational, attributions.

In contrast, expectancy-inconsistent behavior is the exception to the rule. As noted previously, if the behavior is inconsistent with expectancy, then the attribution process will be activated. This, however, is not simple, heuristic processing but is more likely to be systematic, analytic thinking about the likely explanation for an unexpected event. Given its out-of-character nature, the behavior will often be attributed to external, situational forces (Crocker, Hannah, & Weber, 1983; Hamilton, 1988). However, this will not always be the case; the attributional analysis may also identify personal causes for the behavior (for a useful discussion of possible outcomes in this case, see Vonk, 1994). Thus, compared with the case for expectancy-consistent behaviors, the processing of expectancy-inconsistent information is likely to (a) immediately involve attributional (causal) thinking, (b) be more analytic in nature, and (c) result in attributions to either person or situation (depending on the perceiver's analysis and weighting of the relevant information).

In sum, these considerations, taken together, indicate that perceiver expectancies have effects on processing of behavioral information that are more likely to result in person than in situational attributions.

CORRESPONDENCE BIAS AND FUNDAMENTAL ATTRIBUTION ERROR?

The tendency of perceivers to view behavior in terms of its personological implications for understanding the actor is pervasive and well documented (Jones, 1979, 1990; Nisbett & Ross, 1980; Ross, 1977). People see the behaviors of individuals as reflecting their trait characteristics.

This tendency has been referred to by two different terms—*correspondence bias* and *fundamental attribution error*—which are used almost interchangeably in the literature. The choice of terms seems to be one of personal preference, reflecting perhaps one's professional or ideological roots, for example, whether you (or your mentors) were trained at Princeton or Stanford. Or perhaps the choice reflects a preference for one term over the other. *Correspondence bias*, for example, has an Eastern-establishment quality to it—a cautious, reserved means of characterizing the phenomenon, the kind of term that would be used by someone who enjoys wearing bow ties. In contrast, *fundamental attribution error* might be seen as reflecting a loose, free-wheeling California approach. The bias might not be fundamental, it might not be an attribution, and it might not be an error (how would anybody ever prove any of them?), but *fundamental attribution error* sure sounds a lot sexier than *correspondence bias!* Whatever the reasons for one's choice of terminology, most people seem to accept the use of these two terms as referring to the same thing.

I would like to suggest another possibility, one that has intriguing implications. Namely, I propose that we need both of these terms. We need both terms because there are two distinct processes that they can refer to. I propose that *correspondence bias* be used to refer to a bias toward dispositional *inferences* to a greater extent than warranted by the information at hand, whereas *fundamental attribution error* should be used to refer to a bias toward dispositional *attributions* in understanding the causes of behavior, even in the face of compelling situational causes. I now develop this distinction.

The ease with which perceivers make dispositional inferences from behavioral information clearly has been the focus of a great deal of theory and empirical inquiry in recent years. Indeed, this is the focus of Trope's chapter (this volume), and recently an entire issue of the *Personality and Social Psychology Bulletin* was devoted to this topic (Trope & Higgins, 1993). All of the theorists I discussed earlier recognize perceivers' inclination to assume (infer) that behaviors of actors reflect dispositional properties. As I have argued, this process does not necessarily include any consideration of the causes for the behavior on which the dispositional inference is based, hence it need not be attributional in nature. Because these dispositional inferences are correspondent inferences (i.e., corresponding to the manifest properties of the behavior), it seems reasonable that the tendency to make such inferences in a biased manner be called the *correspondence bias*.

Although dispositional inferences can occur without consideration of causal relations, it is obvious that they may also result from such attributional analysis. Moreover, there is abundant evidence (for review, see Jones, 1990; Ross, 1977) that when perceivers do engage in attributional thinking, they are predisposed toward person over situation attributions. In these cases, then, a dispositional characteristic is attributed to the person as an explanation for the observed behavior. Because this underlying process is inherently attributional in nature, the term *fundamental attribution error* seems uniquely appropriate to capture this bias in favor of person explanations.

CONCLUSION

The enduring interest in the question of how and when perceivers move from acts to dispositions attests to the insight of Jones and Davis's (1965) seminal analysis of correspondent inferences. More recent analyses have extended and refined the understanding of this process. This commentary has focused on the important, and insufficiently explored, role of perceiver expectancies in this process and, in particular, on their influence in activating qualitatively different inference processes. This analysis highlights the need to theoretically distinguish between dispositional inferences and causal attributions.

REFERENCES

Bargh, J. A., & Thein, R. D. (1985). Individual construct accessibility, person memory, and the recall-judgment link: The case of information overload. *Journal of Personality and Social Psychology, 49,* 1129–1146.

Bassilli, J. N. (1989). Traits as action categories versus traits as person attributes in social cognition. In J. N. Bassilli (Ed.), *On-line cognition in person perception* (pp. 61–89). Hillsdale, NJ: Erlbaum.

Carlston, D. E., & Skowronski, J. J. (1994). Savings in the relearning of trait information as evidence for spontaneous inference generation. *Journal of Personality and Social Psychology, 66,* 840–856.

Clary, E. G., & Tesser, A. (1983). Reactions to unexpected events: The naïve scientist and interpretive activity. *Personality and Social Psychology Bulletin, 9,* 609–620.

Crocker, J., Hannah, D. B., & Weber, R. (1983). Person memory and causal attributions. *Journal of Personality and Social Psychology, 44,* 55–66.

Gilbert, D. T. (1989). Thinking lightly about others: Automatic components of the social inference process. In J. S. Uleman & J. A. Bargh (Eds.), *Unintended thought* (pp. 189–211). New York: Guilford.

Gilbert, D. T., Pelham, B. W., & Krull, D. S. (1988). On cognitive busyness: When person perceivers meet persons perceived. *Journal of Personality and Social Psychology, 54,* 733–740.

Hamilton, D. L. (1988). Causal attribution viewed from an information processing perspective. In D. Bar-Tal & A. W. Kruglanski (Eds.), *The social psychology of knowledge* (pp. 359–385). Cambridge, England: Cambridge University Press.

Hamilton, D. L. (1991). Interpersonal perception: On charting the terrain. *Psychological Inquiry, 2,* 383–388.

Hastie, R. (1984). Causes and effects of causal attributions. *Journal of Personality and Social Psychology, 46,* 44–56.

Heider, F. (1958). *The psychology of interpersonal relations.* New York: Wiley.

Hemsley, G. D., & Marmurek, H. H. C. (1982). Person memory: The processing of consistent and inconsistent person information. *Personality and Social Psychology Bulletin, 8,* 433–438.

Jones, E. E. (1979). The rocky road from acts to dispositions. *American Psychologist, 34,* 107–117.

Jones, E. E. (1990). Interpersonal perception. New York: W. H. Freeman.

Jones, E. E., & Davis, K. E. (1965). From acts to dispositions: The attribution process in person perception. In L. Berkowitz (Ed.), *Advances in experimental social psychology* (Vol. 2, pp. 220–265). New York: Academic Press.

Jones, E. E., & McGillis, D. (1976). Correspondent inferences and the attribution cube: A comparative reappraisal. In J. H. Harvey, W. J. Ickes, & R. F. Kidd (Eds.), *New directions in attribution research* (Vol. 1, pp. 389–420). Hillsdale, NJ: Erlbaum.

Kelley, H. H. (1967). Attribution theory in social psychology. In D. Levine (Ed.), *Nebraska symposium on motivation* (Vol. 15, pp. 192–241). Lincoln: University of Nebraska Press.

Neuman, L. S., & Uleman, J. S. (1989). Spontaneous trait inferences. In J. S. Uleman & J. A. Bargh (Eds.), *Unintended thought* (pp. 155–188). New York: Guilford.

Nisbett, R. E., & Ross, L. (1980). *Human inference: Strategies and shortcomings of social judgment.* Englewood Cliffs, NJ: Prentice-Hall.

Ross, L. (1977). The intuitive psychologist and his shortcomings: Distortions in the attribution process. In L. Berkowitz (Ed.), *Advances in experimental social psychology* (Vol. 10, pp. 173–220). New York: Academic Press.

Schoeneman, T. J., van Uchelen, C., Stonebrink, S., & Cheek, P. R. (1986). Expectancy, outcome, and event type: Effects on retrospective reports of attributional activity. *Personality and Social Psychology Bulletin, 12,* 353–362.

Sherman, J. W., & Hamilton, D. L. (1994). On the formation of interitem associative links in person memory. *Journal of Experimental Social Psychology, 30,* 203–217.

Smith, E. R. (1994). Social cognition contributions to attribution theory and research. In P. G. Devine, D. L. Hamilton, & T. M. Ostrom (Eds.), *Social cognition: Impact on social psychology* (pp. 77–108). San Diego: Academic Press.

Smith, E. R., & Miller, F. D. (1983). Mediation among attributional inferences and comprehension processes: Initial findings and a general method. *Journal of Personality and Social Psychology, 44,* 492–505.

Stern, L. D., Marrs, S., Millar, M. G., & Cole, E. (1984). Processing time and the recall of inconsistent and consistent behaviors of individuals and groups. *Journal of Personality and Social Psychology, 47,* 253–262.

Trope, Y. (1986). Identification and inferential processes in dispositional attribution. *Psychological Review, 93,* 239–257.

Trope, Y., & Higgins, E. T. (1993). The what, how, and when of dispositional inference: New questions and answers. *Personality and Social Psychology Bulletin, 19,* 493–500.

Trope, Y., & Liberman, A. (1993). Trait conceptions in identification of behavior and inferences about persons. *Personality and Social Psychology Bulletin, 19,* 553–562.

Uleman, J. S., Newman, L. S., & Moskowitz, G. B. (1996). People as flexible interpreters: Evidence and issues from spontaneous trait inferences. In M. P. Zanna (Ed.), *Advances in experimental social psychology* (Vol. 28, pp. 211–279). San Diego: Academic Press.

Vonk, R. (1994). Trait inferences, impression formation, and person memory: Strategies in processing inconsistent information about persons. In W. Stroebe & M. Hewstone (Eds.), *European review of social psychology* (Vol. 5, pp. 111–149). Chichester, England: Wiley.

Weisz, C., & Jones, E. E. (1993). Expectancy disconfirmation and dispositional inference: Latent strength of target-based and category-based expectancies. *Personality and Social Psychology Bulletin, 19,* 563–573.

Winter, L., & Uleman, J. S. (1984). When are social judgments made? Evidence for the spontaneousness of trait inferences. *Journal of Personality and Social Psychology, 47,* 237–252.

Winter, L., Uleman, J. S., & Cunniff, C. (1985). How automatic are social judgments? *Journal of Personality and Social Psychology, 49,* 904–917.

Parallel Processing in Person Perception: Implications for Two-Stage Models of Attribution

Ziva Kunda

Ned Jones considered Yaacov Trope's (1986) model of identification and inferential processes in attribution to be the most important development in attribution research since Jones and McGillis (1976). And it is easy to see why. With this model, Trope ushered in a new era in theorizing about attribution in a manner that was informed and enriched by recent developments in cognitive psychology without losing sight of the original goals of attribution theory: to make sense of the judgments of real people in real-life situations.

One of the most important aspects of Trope's model is the recognition that person perception involves two different kinds of processes: an automatic one, which occurs immediately and spontaneously and is not readily disrupted even when cognitive resources are limited, and a more controlled process, which involves more elaborate inference and therefore requires more cognitive resources. In Trope's model, the identification of behavior (e.g., "this act is hostile") is done automatically,

Preparation of this comment was supported by grants from the Social Sciences and Humanities Research Council of Canada and by the Natural Sciences and Engineering Research Council of Canada.

whereas the dispositional inference (e.g., "this person is hostile"), which occurs subsequently, requires more controlled processes. Another influential model, developed by Dan Gilbert and his associates (Gilbert, Pelham, & Krull, 1988), draws the line between automatic and controlled processes somewhat differently. Gilbert's model assumes that both the identification of the behavior and the dispositional characterization of the person occur relatively automatically. In this model, controlled processes are required to correct the automatic dispositional inference so as to take account of the situation (e.g., "he was provoked, so maybe he's not that hostile").

Does the dispositional characterization of people occur automatically, as Gilbert proposes, or does it require controlled processes, as Trope proposes? I would like to suggest that both models are correct to some extent because dispositional characterization may be based on automatic processes sometimes and on controlled processes at other times. I will go further, and suggest that the same may be true for the identification of behavior and for recognition of the impact of the situation on behavior identification and on dispositional attributions. I suggest that the key to understanding the impact of a given piece of information lies in the patterns of associations between that piece of information and other relevant information rather than in the classification of the information into categories like behavior or situation.

In developing these ideas I am building on an important recent development in thinking about the nature of cognitive processes. Over the last decade there has been a major shift in theorizing about cognitive processes. Rather than viewing them as occurring serially, most current theories of cognition now view cognitive processes as occurring in parallel and as mutually constraining each other (Holyoak & Spellman, 1993). In person perception, parallel constraint satisfaction models imply that the implications of each piece of information relevant to one's impressions of the person can be activated simultaneously. Each piece of information could influence the meaning of other pieces of information, as well as their implications for one's impressions of the person. As a social psychologist I find these parallel-constraint-satisfaction models particularly attractive because of their affinity with the Gestalt approach to person perception (Asch, 1946). Indeed, they provide formal tools for exploring the Gestalt notion that person perception involves the integration of multiple sources of information into a coherent impression (Read & Miller, 1993). As Ned reminded social psychologists, these Gestalt ideas greatly influenced Heider's pioneering work on attribution (Jones, 1990).

Models that incorporate parallel processing are not as different from the serial stage models proposed by Gilbert and by Trope as one might think, however, because they too make a distinction between early, spontaneous, automatic processes and more controlled ones that may or may not occur subsequently (Kintsch, 1988). I will next briefly describe a parallel-processing model of impression formation that Paul Thagard and I have developed to explain how stereotypes and individuating information may be integrated to form a coherent impression of a person, and then discuss the implications of this kind of model for dispositional attribution (Kunda & Thagard, 1996).

The parallel-constraint satisfaction theory of impression formation (Kunda & Thagard, 1996) assumes that stereotypes, traits, and behaviors as well as any aspect of the situation can be represented as interconnected nodes in a spreading activation network. The nodes can have positive, excitatory connections or negative, inhibitory ones. I describe this model by working through an example of how one aspect of context—stereotype—can automatically affect both behavioral identification and dispositional characterization of the actor. Consider the classic demonstration that the same pushing behavior is identified as a violent push when performed by a Black person, but as a jovial shove when performed by a White person (Sagar & Schofield, 1980).

Figure 1 shows part of the knowledge net that would come into play when one observes a Black person or a White person pushing someone. The boxes depict the nodes representing the behavior (pushed someone), some of its possible interpretations (violent push and jovial shove), and the stereotyped categories (Black and White). The lines connecting these nodes indicate the nature of the connections among them. Bold lines indicate excitatory connections, and thin lines indicate

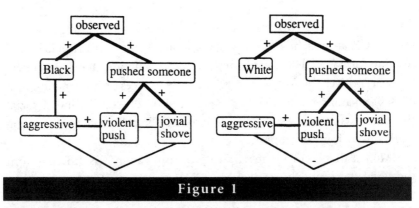

Figure 1

Stereotypes affect the meaning of behavior. *Violent push* and *aggressive* are activated more strongly in the network on the left than in the network on the right. From "Forming Impressions From Stereotypes, Traits, and Behavior: A Parallel Constraint-Satisfaction Theory," by Z. Kunda and P. Thagard, 1996, *Psychological Review, 103*, p. 286.

inhibitory connections. Each of the constructs depicted also has many additional associates that are not portrayed in the figure. The pieces of information that have been observed directly, in this case the behavior (pushed someone) and the stereotyped category (Black or White), are connected to a node that is termed *observed* to indicate its special status and to distinguish it from inferred knowledge. The possible interpretations of the behavior and the traits associated with the stereotype are not themselves observed, but become activated or deactivated through their associations with the observed information. These associations reflect perceivers' prior beliefs. In Trope's model prior beliefs are represented as probabilities (e.g., the probability of hitting after being insulted). It seems plausible that in many cases the strength of associations may indeed be based on such probabilities, although some kinds of information (e.g., the actor is Black) may trigger some associations (e.g., aggression) that the perceiver does not consider probable (Devine, 1989).

In this example, *aggressive* has a positive, excitatory link with *violent push* and a negative, inhibitory link with *jovial shove*. Therefore, when *aggressive* is activated, it will increase the activation of *violent push* and decrease the activation of *jovial shove*. *Jovial shove* will be further deactivated because it also has a negative link with *violent push*, so that the more *violent push* is activated, the more *jovial shove* is deactivated. Note also that as *violent push* becomes more activated, it further activates *aggressive*.

The model assumes that impression formation occurs through parallel satisfaction of all the constraints imposed by the observed information. Put differently, the associates of the observed information are activated and deactivated simultaneously, and jointly constrain the impression of the target.

In the above example, when one observes that a Black person pushed someone, *pushed someone* activates both *violent push* and *jovial shove*. At the same time, *Black* activates *aggressive*, which, in turn, activates *violent push* and deactivates *jovial shove*. In contrast, when the person is White, *aggressive* does not get activated by *White*. Therefore, both *violent push* and *aggressive* end up with more activation when the same pushing behavior is performed by a Black person than when it is performed by a White person.

Using this parallel-constraint-satisfaction model can account for most of the phenomena emerging from the literature on how stereotypes and individuating information determine each other's meaning and on how they are combined to form impressions of individuals (Kunda & Thagard, 1996). These include several phenomena that are problematic for more traditional, serial models (Brewer, 1988; Fiske & Neuberg, 1990). For example, the serial models assume that one stereotype dominates impressions at a time, and have trouble explaining how novel combinations of stereotypes can jointly influence impressions (e.g., what does one make of a Black, female, American astronaut?). In contrast, in the parallel-processing model multiple stereotypes are integrated just like any other sources of information, through the constraints imposed by the knowledge associated with them.

There are two important aspects of this model that I would like to call attention to. First, unlike other models of stereotyping (Brewer, 1988; Fiske & Neuberg, 1990) this model does not give stereotypes any special status. The important thing is not whether a given piece of information comes from a stereotype or a behavior, but how this information is associated with other pieces of information. This is an advantage because the distinction between stereotypes and individuating information is often problematic. For example, traits are typically considered to be individuating information. Yet many trait terms, such as *friendly*, *intellectual*, or *athletic*, are indistinguishable from stereotypes. And it is unclear when an attribute of a person (e.g. well dressed) will serve to trigger a stereotype (upper middle class) and when it will function as individuating information. The parallel-processing model avoids this problematic distinction by assuming that the impact of each piece of information depends entirely on its pattern of associations with other information, regardless of whether it constitutes a stereotype, a trait, or any other kind of information. I suggest that the same would apply to situational versus behavioral information—the impact of each piece of information would depend entirely on how it is associated with other pieces of information, regardless of whether it represents an aspect of the person, the behavior, or the situation.

The second important aspect of this model is that the processes I have described all occur automatically. In the "pushing" example I discussed, therefore, both the identification of behavior and the characterization of the actor occur automatically. However, there are some phenomena in the stereotyping literature that cannot be accounted for with this automatic-parallel-constraint-satisfaction model because they do seem to involve more controlled processes. And just as surely, attribution judgments often involve controlled processes. The challenge is to identify the conditions that trigger these controlled processes. I do not believe that a simple mapping of automatic and controlled processes onto the kinds of judgments they involve (behavior identification vs. dispositional characterization) as Trope suggests or onto the kind of information they are based on (person information vs. situational information) as Gilbert suggests will suffice.

There is no question that in many cases the impact of situations on behavioral identifications that Trope discusses can be captured by the kind of automatic parallel-constraint-satisfaction model that I have described. But I also suggest that some identifications can require inference (e.g., was this mild put down, delivered with a smile, meant to be taken as an insult or as a compliment?). Thus identifications may either occur automatically or require controlled inference, and the same is true for dispositional judgments. Sometimes a person engaging in a trait-related behavior may be automatically assumed to possess that trait, and sometimes dispositional characterization will require inference. Consistent with this view, both Ned's and Gilbert's more rebellious students have been able to show that the predominance of dispositions over situations can be reversed under certain conditions (Krull, 1993; Quattrone, 1982).

What determines whether controlled processes will come into play? I do not yet have a clear answer to that question. Neither, for that matter do cognitive psychologists dealing with text comprehension, whose models tend to focus either on low-level automatic processes (Kintsch, 1988) or on high-level controlled processes (Graesser, Singer, & Trabasso, 1994), with little discussion of how the two kinds of processes may work together. I consider spelling out these interactions in greater detail to be a major challenge for future theorizing. Although there is not yet a full understanding of how automatic and controlled processes interact with each other, I can point to some likely candidates for triggering controlled processes: (a) The nature of the judgment task. Some tasks explicitly require causal reasoning. This is the case for attribution judgments that require participants to determine why a behavior took place, as when they are asked to assess the extent to which different causal factors produced a behavior (e.g., Deaux & Emswiller, 1974). Controlled processes may also be triggered by task instructions that explicitly ask participants to identify causal relations among different pieces of information (e.g., Asch & Zukier, 1984). (b) The nature of information. Controlled processes may be triggered when people have trouble understanding the information they have observed (Kintsch, 1988), or when they are surprised by it (Kunda, Miller, & Claire, 1990; Wong & Weiner, 1981). This will occur if two or more of the observed pieces of information have strongly conflicting implications, as when a behavior seems particularly unlikely, given one's knowledge of the person and the situation. (c) Motivation. People may engage in controlled processes when they are particularly motivated to reach a thorough understanding of a person or a behavior (Brewer, 1988; Fiske & Neuberg, 1990).

I have not focused here on the nature of controlled processes once they are triggered. Trope's most recent development of his model provide some exciting ideas about the inferential rules and heuristics that may govern these processes. A particularly attractive aspect of his model is the notion that the first, automatic stage produces a hypothesis that is then tested in the next, controlled stage, a testing process that can be biased and incomplete. I would add that the hypothesis need not concern the actor's dispositions. Instead, sometimes one may generate hypotheses about the nature of the behavior or the situation. And sometimes, satisfied with the products of the automatic processes, one may generate no hypotheses at all. Another promising avenue for exploring controlled processes comes from work that applies parallel-constraint-satisfaction models to higher level processes of inference and explanation (Read & Marcus-Newhall, 1993; Thagard, 1989). In these models, one may choose among several possible inferences about a person as a function of how well each inference can explain the wealth of relevant information. For example, when trying to determine whether a behavior was caused by the person's trait or by the situation, one will prefer the attribution that explains more of the available facts. In these models inferences are constrained by the explanatory relations among hypotheses and evidence and by the logical relations among competing hypotheses.

The argument that the impact of a given piece of information on judgment depends not on the kind of information it belongs to but on its pattern of associations with other pieces of information entails a breakdown of traditional distinctions. I have argued that understanding impression formation does not require making distinctions between stereotypes and individuating information, or giving either type of information special status (Kunda & Thagard, 1996). What about the distinction between dispositions and situations? This distinction has been enormously fruitful. It lies at the core of Ned's notion of correspondent inference (Jones & Davis, 1965), and has led to the very important insight that people underestimate the power of situations and overestimate the power of dispositions in governing behavior.

However, framing this understanding of the task of the social perceiver entirely in terms of an attempt to disentangle situational and dispositions variables misses a great deal of what the social perceiver is trying to accomplish. Ned was a great believer in the need to maintain an interest in what he termed the *social embeddedness* of judgment, and the social purposes that it serves (Jones, 1993).

Consider the following example: When my 3-year-old rises from the dinner table, throws his food on the floor, and punches his father, what am I to make of this? Here are some hypotheses that I may entertain: The child is mischievous, impulsive, aggressive, or disturbed (all of which reflect stable internal dispositions); the child is suffering from lack of attention, lack of explicit rules, lack of clear disciplinary practice, or exposure to a bad role model (all of which reflect situational variables); or the child is bored, exhausted, or coming down with an ear infection (all of which reflect temporary internal variables). This is not trivial speculation; my understanding of the behavior will determine my reactions. Do I enjoy my child's free spirit, rush him to the family doctor, or take him to a psychiatrist? Do I put him to bed, give him a time out, or invite him to play snakes and ladders? Simply characterizing these many possible inferences in terms of person or situation variables will not suffice to describe my understanding of the event or to predict my reaction to it. And there may be more meaningful ways of grouping these attributions. They can be organized into whether they make me feel good about my child or myself, whether they allow me to blame my spouse, and whether they imply remedial action on my part, to name but a few examples.

Recently Mischel and Shoda (1995) have reconceptualized personality as a unique pattern of associations among a plethora of cognitive and affective units that jointly and simultaneously drive ones construal of situations and thereby determine one's behavior. This reconceptualization allows Mischel and Shoda to shed new light on classic controversies concerning the stability of trait-related behavior and to make novel predictions about the organization of behavior. I suggest that much like people seem to have idiosyncratic profiles of behaviors in diverse situations (Mischel & Shoda, 1995), they may also have idiosyncratic explanatory, attributional profiles. This suggestion is consistent with the recent focus of some personality theorists on people's unique construals of their social worlds (Cantor & Kihlstrom, 1987). Thus reconceptualizing the nature of social judgment as based on parallel satisfaction of the constraints imposed by diverse units of social information may shed new light on issues that have been of concern to attribution theorists and may also open up new areas of investigation.

REFERENCES

Asch, S. E. (1946). Forming impressions of personality. *Journal of Abnormal and Social Psychology, 41,* 303–314.

Asch, S. E., & Zukier, H. (1984). Thinking about persons. *Journal of Personality and Social Psychology, 46,* 1230–1240.

Brewer, M. B. (1988). A dual process model of impression formation. In T. K. Srull & R. S. Wyer (Eds.), *Advances in social cognition* (pp. 1–36). Hillsdale, NJ: Erlbaum.

Cantor, N., & Kihlstrom, J. F. (1987). *Personality and social intelligence.* Englewood Cliffs, NJ: Prentice-Hall.

Deaux, K., & Emswiller, T. (1974). Explanations of successful performance on sex-linked tasks: What is skill for the male is luck for the female. *Journal of Personality and Social Psychology, 29*(1), 80–85.

Devine, P. G. (1989). Stereotypes and prejudice: Their automatic and controlled components. *Journal of Personality and Social Psychology, 56,* 5–18.

Fiske, S. T., & Neuberg, S. L. (1990). A continuum of impression formation, from category-based to individuating processes: Influences of information and motivation on attention and interpretation. In M. Zanna (Eds.), *Advances in Experimental Social Psychology* (pp. 1–74).

Gilbert, D. T., Pelham, B. W., & Krull, D. S. (1988). On cognitive busyness: When person perceivers meet persons perceived. *Journal of Personality and Social Psychology, 54,* 733–740.

Graesser, A. C., Singer, M., & Trabasso, T. (1994). Constructing inferences during narrative text comprehension. *Psychological Review, 101,* 371–395.

Holyoak, K. J., & Spellman, B. A. (1993). Thinking. *Annual Review of Psychology, 44,* 265–315.

Jones, E. E. (1990). *Interpersonal perception*. New York: W. H. Freeman and Company.

Jones, E. E. (1993). Afterword: An avuncular view. *Personality and Social Psychology Bulletin, 19,* 657–661.

Jones, E. E., & Davis, K. E. (1965). From acts to dispositions: The attribution process in person perception. In L. Berkowitz (Ed.), *Advances in experimental social psychology* (pp. 219–266). New York: Academic Press.

Jones, E. E., & McGillis, D. (1976). Correspondent inference and the attribution cube: A comparative reappraisal. In S. H. Harvey, W. J. Ickes, & R. F. Kidd (Eds.), *New directions in attribution research* (pp. 389–420). Hillsdale, NJ: Erlbaum.

Kintsch, W. (1988). The role of knowledge in discourse comprehension: A construction-integration model. *Psychological Review, 95,* 163–182.

Krull, D. S. (1993). Does the grist change the mill? The effect of the perceiver's inferential goal on the process of social inference. *Personality and Social Psychology Bulletin, 19,* 340–348.

Kunda, Z., Miller, D. T., & Claire, T. (1990). Combining social concepts: The role of causal reasoning. *Cognitive Science, 14,* 551–577.

Kunda, Z., & Thagard, P. (1996). Forming impressions from stereotypes, traits, and behaviors: A parallel constraint satisfaction theory. *Psychological Review, 103,* 284–308.

Mischel, W., & Shoda, Y. (1995). A cognitive-affective system theory of personality: Reconceptualizing situations, dispositions, dynamics, and the invariance in personality structure. *Psychological Review, 102,* 246–268.

Quattrone, G. A. (1982). Overattribution and unit formation: When behavior engulfs the person. *Journal of Personality and Social Psychology, 42,* 593–607.

Read, S. J., & Marcus-Newhall, A. (1993). Explanatory coherence in social explanations: A parallel distributed processing account. *Journal of Personality and Social Psychology, 65,* 429–447.

Read, S. J., & Miller, L. C. (1993). Rapist or "regular guy": Explanatory coherence in the construction of mental models of others. *Personality and Social Psychology Bulletin, 19,* 526–541.

Sagar, H. A., & Schofield, J. W. (1980). Racial and behavioral cues in black and white children's perceptions of ambiguously aggressive acts. *Journal of Personality and Social Psychology, 39,* 590–598.

Thagard, P. (1989). Explanatory coherence. *The Behavioral and Brain Sciences, 12,* 435–467.

Trope, Y. (1986). Identification and inferential processes in dispositional attribution. *Psychological Review, 93,* 239–257.

Wong, P., & Weiner, B. (1981). When people ask "why" questions, and the heuristics of attributional search. *Journal of Personality and Social Psychology, 40,* 650–663.

3

Interaction Goals and Person Perception

James L. Hilton

I was a second-year graduate student at Princeton when John Darley suggested that I take a look at a chapter Ned Jones had written in the late 1950s with John Thibaut titled "Interaction Goals as Bases of Inference in Interpersonal Perception." More than any other article, this one changed the way I thought about person perception. At the time, it seemed like every graduate seminar became an arena in which motivational and cognitive explanations were pitted against each other. Everyone had their champion, but progress was hard to come by. For every explanation of one flavor there was an alternative explanation of the other flavor. In the midst of this maelstrom emerged an article, written 25 years earlier, that made sense. Perception is not about cognition or motivation. It is about cognition and motivation. It was, I believe, one of Ned's best contributions because it framed the problem of person perception as one that involves the interaction between motivation and cognition rather than as a question of which has suprem-

I am grateful to Steve Fein, William von Hippel, and John Darley for commenting on a draft of this chapter. I am also grateful for the many hours of conversation and guidance that I received from Ned while I was a graduate student at Princeton. His presence is sorely missed.

acy. The paragraphs that follow are about this interaction. But more than that, they are about the enormous influence Ned had on the field.

A HISTORY OF GOAL-DIRECTED
SOCIAL INTERACTION

The importance of the goal-directed nature of social interaction is, of course, not terribly new. As Fiske (1992, 1993) has pointed out, there is a pragmatic tradition that dates back at least as far as William James (1890). Put simply, this approach begins with the assumption that people's perceptions emerge as a function of what we do and why we do it. Or, if one prefers, a pragmatic approach assumes that perceptual processes serve specific goals.

Although James may have argued forcefully for the primacy of function, the roles that goals and motivation have been afforded in perception theories have seen considerable waxing and waning over the last half century. The "new-look" theorists of the 1940s and 1950s, for example, placed motivation at the very center of perception. They were intrigued by findings that seemed to implicate the roles that personality and motivation played in determining what perceivers saw: participants in word-recognition experiments were slow to recognize threatening words (Bruner & Postman, 1947); poor children appeared to overestimate the size of coins (Bruner & Goodman, 1947); and participants with different personalities emerged from the same situations with very different perceptions (Frenkel-Brunswik, 1949). Although many of these studies were later criticized on methodological grounds (for a review, cf. Erdelyi, 1974), the new-look theorists took them as evidence of the functional nature of perception. They saw perception as emerging in the service of the needs and goals of the perceiver.

By the end of the 1950s, a similar concern with the functional nature of perception became evident in the social psychological literature. Jones and Thibaut (1958), for example, argued that the interaction goals of perceivers determine how information about interactants' dispositions, motivations, and the situation more generally will be used by the perceiver. Different goals lead to different perceptual sets. When perceivers seek to determine what has caused their partners to behave in a particular way, for example, they are said to be in a *causal-genetic set*. When they seek to know what motivates others to approach or avoid their partners, they are said to be in a *value-maintenance set*. And, when perceivers strive to discover the norms and social sanctions that apply to the interaction, they are said to be in a *situation-matching set*. Thus, the importance that any particular piece of information has for a perceiver depends on the perceiver's goals at the time the information is encountered.

Similarly, in his work on cognitive tuning Zajonc (1960) argued that a perceiver's openness to new information depends on the communication goals of the perceiver. He found that when study participants were instructed to transmit information, they tended to form more unified impressions and to be less open to subsequent information. In contrast, when participants were instructed to receive information, they tended to remain open to new information and to hold beliefs more tentatively. In other words, Zajonc, like Jones and Thibaut, argued that how information is processed depends on the perceivers' goals at the time the information is encountered.

Despite the attention that the goal-directed nature of social perception received during this early period, by the mid 1970s the emphasis was to be found elsewhere. Motivational constructs were banished in favor of more purely cognitive explanations. In the impression-formation literature, for example, Asch (1946) argued passionately for a less passionate approach to person perception. He suggested that it was time to look at aspects of perception that did not focus so exclusively on the needs of the perceiver. In contrast to the new-look theorists, Asch believed in the primacy of cognition, noting that things must be perceived before they can be feared. Consistent with this belief, he developed an impression-formation paradigm that required study participants to have no motivation beyond the goal of comprehension. Participants were simply presented with lists of traits and were asked to form an impression of a person described by those traits.

Using this paradigm, Asch found that participants had no difficulty forming impressions and that by varying the content and order of the traits, he could change the impressions they formed in predictable, and often dramatic, ways. Impressions of a person described as intelligent and cold, for example, tended to be much more positive than impressions of a person described as cold and intelligent. Findings like these from studies in which informational factors were manipulated while motivational constructs were either ignored or held constant were consistent with a growing sense that the important factors involved in perception were primarily cognitive.

The movement away from motivated perception was even more explicit in the attribution literature. Consider the following quotation from the introduction to Jones et al.'s (1972) *Attribution: Perceiving the Causes of Behavior:*

> A central thematic concern throughout the book is an analysis of the assumptions and expectations the attributor brings to his task of causal understanding. These assumptions and expectations shape the attribution process by filling gaps in information, relating behavioral data to comparative standards, and effecting shifts in attention or emphasis. Because attributions go beyond the information given, the attributor's causal interpretations may be accurate or in error, functional or dysfunctional. Analysis of the attribution process takes on special practical importance because people frequently draw erroneous inferences about the causes of social events and act in accordance with these inferences. (pp. ix–x)

Notice that here, priority is given to expectations rather than to motivations. Expectations, fueled by a very general motivation to perceive the world veridically, shape perception. Moreover, it is the expectations that perceivers bring to a situation that give rise both to veridical and erroneous perceptions. Indeed, following the publication of the Jones et al. (1972) book, consensual agreement rapidly emerged that motivational explanations would be invoked only as a last resort. It is worth keeping in mind, however, that the preference for cognitive explanations of bias emerged not so much because anyone thought that motivations were not important, but rather as an experiment to see how far purely cognitive explanations could be pushed (see also Nisbett & Ross, 1980).

The commitment to invoke motivational explanations only as a last resort meant that when perceivers were found in error, the search for the source of the error would begin with purely cognitive elements. For example, although an apparently self-serving bias to take credit for success and place blame for failure could be explained motivationally, it could also be explained in terms of an actor's expectations regarding success and failure, assuming that most people spend most of their time engaging in behaviors that are more likely to succeed than to fail (Miller & Ross, 1975). Similarly, defensiveness could be explained motivationally, but it too could be explained in terms of a person's expectations. The fact that a person might resist a diagnosis of cancer, for example, could reflect motivated denial, but it could also reflect the fact that most aches and pains signal minor, rather than major, illness (Ditto, Jemmott, & Darley, 1988). As cognitive explanations of this sort multiplied, the concern with the goal-directed nature of perception retreated. By the end of the 1970s there was little patience for motivational ghosts in the machine.

Several things happened that led to the rediscovery of the goal-directed nature of social perception. First, a number of programs of research emerged that demonstrated the efficacy of including goal-based considerations in understanding person-perception processes. These programs included work on outcome dependency (e.g., Berscheid, Graziano, Monson, & Dermer, 1976; Fiske, Neuberg, Beattie, & Milberg, 1987; Neuberg & Fiske, 1987; Omoto & Borgida, 1988), accountability (e.g., Tetlock, 1983; Tetlock & Kim, 1987), and person memory (e.g., Hamilton & Katz, 1975; Hamilton, Katz, & Leirer, 1980; Srull, 1983; Wyer & Gordon, 1982). Importantly, one of the things that these programs of research had in common was that they all circumvented the motivation-versus-cognition debate by focusing on the effects that goals have on cognitive processes. How, for example, does the dependent nature of the interaction shape one's attention allocation strategies (Fiske & Neuberg, 1990)? How do the goals of forming an impression based on a list of traits versus memorizing a list of traits affect what is remembered (Srull, 1983; Wyer & Gordon, 1982)? Or, how does the goal of accuracy affect a person's reliance on heuristic processing (Fiske & Neuberg, 1990; Hilton & Darley, 1991)?

Second, and related, the field began to find the distinction between *cognitive* and *motivational* fairly unsatisfying, at least when it was regarded as an either–or distinction. Social perception almost always seems to involve an interaction between cognition and motivation. Indeed, what the recent crop of approaches to person perception take as their common starting point is the unpacking of this interaction. Specifically, they all assume that motivations shape cognitive processes and vice versa. The goal to form an accurate impression, for example, surely shapes how one allocates one's attention. How one allocates one's attention is, in turn, certain to shape one's future goals.

Though not explicitly concerned with social perception, Markus' work on the structure and nature of the self provides an excellent example of this shift in strategy. After all, her work on schematicity (Markus, 1977) is clearly more cognitive than motivational. The primary goal in those studies was to find whether there exists a cognitive structure that could be identified as "the self." In contrast, her more recent work on future selves (Markus & Nurius, 1986) gives primacy to motivation. The goal there is to find a way to measure the cognitive representation of an individual's hopes and wishes for the self and to then show how this cognitive representation in turn serves motivational purposes. From this perspective, the distinction between cognitive and motivational becomes less antagonistic.

The third thing that happened was that the field grew tired of generating purely cognitive counterexplanations for phenomena that looked motivational. Here I think work by Kunda (1990) and Ditto et al. (1988) provide excellent examples. In each case, there are multiple studies using different manipulations that all show the same motivated effect (e.g., denial of the significance of health-threatening symptoms). Although it may be possible to generate a different cognitive account of the results for each individual study (e.g., participants do not accept the diagnosis because the symptom is new and seemingly benign in all other respects), it is not terribly satisfying to do so from the perspective of parsimony. In short, I think the field began to tire of a game that became too easy from the perspective of hindsight and that began to add less and less to understanding of many social-perceptual phenomena.

CONCEPTUALIZING INTERACTANTS' GOALS

This brings the discussion to the current resurgence of interest in goal-based approaches to social perception and a potential problem. Specifically, one of the problems that emerges when one starts to take seriously the notion that social perception is primarily a goal-directed enterprise is that, at some level, perceivers have as many goals as they have interactions. If a person is stopped for speeding, for example, she may have the goal of avoiding a speeding ticket. Similarly, if a person is at a restaurant, he may have the goal of enjoying a well-prepared meal. Indeed, at a sufficiently concrete level, it is clear that perceivers often have multiple goals for an interaction. A person in a restaurant may not only have the goal of enjoying a well-prepared meal, he may also have the goal of enjoying the company of his dining partners.

Although it is possible to describe goals at this very concrete level, as a strategy for understanding social interaction and perception, descriptions like these are problematic because they require that each interaction be described separately. One question that emerges, then, is how to partition the goals perceivers and targets bring to social interaction in ways that preserve the insights that the goal concept brings to social perception without reducing social perception to a case-by-case analysis.

To date, investigators have taken a variety of complementary approaches to this problem. Neuberg and his colleagues (Neuberg, 1994; Neuberg, Judice, Virdin, & Carrillo, 1993), for example, propose classifying interactions according to the self-presentation goals of the perceiver. Neuberg et al. (1993) found, for example, that when perceivers are concerned with getting their interaction partners to like them, they are less likely to elicit behavioral information that confirms a negative expectancy and more likely to elicit behavioral information that disconfirms the expectancy than when they have no particular goal for the interaction.

In a somewhat different vein, Snyder (1992) and his colleagues (Copeland, 1994; Snyder & Haugen, 1994; Snyder & Miene, 1994) have advocated examining interactions from a functional perspective. According to their analyses, the critical factors that influence social interactions are the goals perceivers pursue and the needs they seek to fulfill. Snyder and Haugen (1994), for example, found that when perceivers are concerned with acquiring stable and predictable social impressions, they are more likely to elicit behavioral information that confirms the expectations they held prior to the interaction.

My own approach to this problem has been to work within the framework of an interaction goals model proposed by Hilton and Darley (1991; Hilton, Darley, & Fleming, 1989). At a very general level, this model simply assumes that prior to engaging in interaction, participants evaluate the interaction based on the information that they have about the situation (e.g., norms and resources), their fellow interactants (i.e., expectancy information), and the goals that they have for the interaction (e.g., evaluate a fellow interactant's suitability for a job, obtain a loan, enjoy the interaction, etc.). Based on this evaluation, participants choose specific interaction tactics and these tactics, in turn, shape the unfolding of the interaction. A perceiver who expects someone to be hostile, for example, may choose to compete when the interaction involves playing a game, and to ingratiate (Jones, 1964) when the interaction involves applying for a loan.

At a more specific level, Hilton and Darley (1991) posit that interaction goals can be seen as varying in the extent to which they lead to an explicit concern with finding out what one's fellow interactants are like. Evaluating someone's qualifications for employment, for example, is a task that typically places a premium on determining what the applicant is like. In contrast, cashing a check at a bank is a task that requires customers to interact with members of the bank's staff, but it places relatively little emphasis on discovering what the members of the staff are really like. When perceivers find themselves explicitly trying to figure out what the person is like, they are in an *assessment set.* When perceivers are in assessment sets, they weigh possibilities carefully, attempt to look at people from a variety of perspectives, and are concerned with arriving at correct impressions. In contrast, when perceivers are only incidentally concerned with finding out what the person is like, they are in an *action set.* When perceivers are in action sets, they are busily working toward some fairly specific goal that is only incidentally related to impression formation (Hilton & Darley, 1991).

Consistent with this analysis, Hilton and Shapiro (1991) have found that when participants are told to play a competitive game with a partner whom they do or do not expect to be hostile, results differ as a function of whether participants were asked to play the game to win or to play the game to learn about their partner. Those who have winning as their goal fall prey to the confirmation bias. They emerge from the interaction with their belief in the hostility of their partner intact. In contrast, participants who play the game in order to learn more about their partner show no effects of the expectancy. They emerge from the interaction believing that their partner is no more hostile than the average person.

Although my colleagues and I have found the distinction between assessment and accuracy sets useful for predicting when expectancies are likely to have their greatest impact, the distinction is rather crude as a way of classifying goals. Life's goals are reduced to two categories, and the classification tends to draw attention to a rather narrow concern with what happens in the head of the perceiver vis-à-vis a fairly explicit goal to perceive versus to act. In order to explore goals more fully I briefly present another way of classifying perceivers' and targets' goals in the remainder of the chapter. This new classification scheme is orthogonal to the distinction between assessment sets and accuracy sets and I present it more as a rough and ready guide than as a formal taxonomy of goals.

Explicit Goals

To begin, one can talk about perceivers' goals that are held at a fairly explicit level. Often perceivers can (or could if you asked them to) articulate their perceptual goals. Sometimes, for example, people care about the veridicality of their perceptions and try hard to form accurate impressions. Other times, however, people care more about how they come across than about what others are like. Still other times people may have no perceptual goal. (For example, "I do not care to know what my waiter has been doing and thinking recently, I just want to order some coffee.") In situations like these, there is a very good chance that if an individual were stopped on the street and asked what she was doing, she would explain her actions in goal-based terms.

Explicit goals of this sort are the kinds of goals that have received the most attention in recent years (e.g., Fiske, 1993; Hilton & Darley, 1991; Neuberg, 1994; Snyder, 1992), and there is now considerable evidence to suggest that explicit, intentional goals affect perceptions. Manipulations of outcome dependency (Berscheid et al., 1976), accountability (Tetlock, 1983; Tetlock & Kim, 1987), cognitive tuning (Zajonc, 1960), and memory instructions (Hamilton & Katz, 1975) have all been found to influence the way perceivers think about and, to a lesser extent (see Neuberg et al., 1993), behave toward their fellow interactants. Perceivers who are dependent on their partners, for example, pay more attention to their partner, form more favorable impressions, and remember more about the interaction than do perceivers who are not dependent on their partners (Berscheid et al., 1976; Neuberg & Fiske, 1987). Similarly, when study participants are instructed to form an impression, they remember more of a target's behavior than when they are simply told to remember the behavior (Hamilton, Katz, & Leirer, 1980; Srull, 1981, 1983; Wyer, Bodenhausen, & Srull, 1984; Wyer & Gordon, 1982).

In situations like these, it is reasonable to assume that people can articulate their goals, and may, quite accurately, be able to articulate the strategies they will invoke to achieve these goals. If participants are asked what they plan to do following a manipulation of accountability, for example, it is quite likely that they will respond that they plan to process everything very carefully and to avoid making quick, potentially erroneous decisions. So at one level, it is possible to talk about goals that are, at least implicitly, possible to articulate, held consciously, and acted on intentionally. The metaphor here is the motivated strategist (Fiske, 1993). Perceivers allocate resources to the perceptual task at hand as a function of their explicit goals for the interaction.

"Nonconscious" Goals

At another level, it is possible to talk about goals that are less consciously held, or at least less consciously executed. Consider the debate that surrounds the proposition that stereotypes operate automatically. According to Devine's (1989) account, stereotypes are automatically activated whenever a member of a stereotyped group is encountered. She has found, for example, that high- and low-prejudiced study participants often have the same initial reactions to members of a stereotyped group, but that low-prejudiced participants subsequently engage in controlled thinking in which they reject their initial reactions. In other words, at the core of Devine's argument is the notion that high-prejudiced and low-prejudiced people share the same stereotype—the same attributes come to mind when they encounter a member of the stereotyped group—but low-prejudiced people actively resist the contents of their stereotypes.

Although Devine's results suggest that stereotypes are activated automatically, Gilbert and Hixon (1991) have called this finding into question by demonstrating that stereotype activation can be prevented by increasing the cognitive demands that are on the perceiver at the time the member of the stereotyped group is encountered. Specifically, they found that White participants who were cognitively busy at the time they encountered an Asian American failed to activate their Asian American stereotype. This finding suggests that stereotypes require conscious attention and effort to be activated. In other words, Gilbert and Hixon's results suggest that stereotypes are not automatic.

But what does a debate about automaticity have to do with the current thesis? Recently Spencer and Fein (1994) have complicated the debate by noting that participants in Gilbert and Hixon's research had no particular reason to engage in stereotypic processing. In other words, stereotyping was irrelevant to their goals at the time. In an effort to determine whether cognitively busy participants in Gilbert and Hixon's experiments could have activated their stereotypes had they been more motivated to do so, Spencer and Fein (1994) replicated Gilbert and Hixon's experiments and added a manipulation of threat to self-esteem. They predicted that because the motivation to stereotype is enhanced when people experience a threat to their self-esteem, participants who were both cognitively busy and threatened would activate their stereotypes. Consistent with this prediction, they found that although cognitively busy subjects who had not been threatened showed no evidence of stereotype activation, cognitively busy subjects who had experienced a threat to their self-esteem did show evidence of activation of the Asian American stereotype. In follow-up research, Fein and Spencer (1994) demonstrated that stereotypes concerning African Americans also were not activated when participants were cognitively busy, unless they had experienced a threat to their self-esteem.

How is it that stereotypes can be activated automatically, but only when the perceiver is motivated to do so? The solution to this seeming inconsistency lies in the conditional nature of automaticity. Put simply, automaticity is not a unitary construct (Bargh, 1989). Different types of automaticity require different levels of processing on the part of the perceiver, and it seems likely that stereotype activation is at the level of *goal-dependent automaticity*. Before a stereotype is activated automatically, perceivers must have a goal (e.g., denigration or impression formation) that triggers the automatic processing.

The converse of this proposition is also true and can be found in Fiske and Neuberg's (1990) continuum model of impression formation. According to their model, the attention-allocation strategy that perceivers typically use gives priority to category-based information. When sufficiently motivated, however, perceivers switch their attention and begin a more effortful processing of individuating information. In other words, their model explicitly assumes that the attention-allocation strategies that perceivers automatically use can be overridden by intentional action on the part of the perceiver.

So, again, a second category of goals consists of goals that invoke or interact with automatic or unintended processes. One of the interesting things about these goals is that they have the potential to lead perceivers in unexpected ways. Consider, for example, Ross and Ellard's (1986) winnowing manipulation (or Jones' inclusion–exclusion set manipulation). In their study, participants were told to evaluate 12 applicants for a job. Half were told that there were two slots available. The other half were told that there were six slots available. The results showed that this manipulation of availability strongly influenced the participants' perceptions of the candidates. When positions were relatively plentiful, the participants formed favorable impressions of the candidates. When the positions were scarce, they formed considerably more negative impressions of the same candidates. Moreover, when the participants were later told that the hiring constraints had been lifted, their initial impressions and recommendations persisted. Presumably, in situations like this a goal (e.g., including versus excluding people as a function of availability) triggers a set of processes over which the perceiver has relatively little control or awareness. Thus, when circumstances change the perceiver fails to make the appropriate accommodations.

Implicit Goals

The third category of goals consists of goals that are implicit, and rarely examined. These goals often serve as the backdrop against which conversation and social interaction take place. Consider a recent study by Yzerbyt, Schadron, Leyens, and Rocher (1994) in which participants were given the opportunity to make stereotypic judgments about an individual. Although none of the participants received any individuating information about the person, half of them were led to believe that, outside of their awareness, they had been exposed to individuating information. The results showed that participants who thought they had been exposed to individuating information subsequently made more stereotypic judgments. Yzerbyt et al. suggested that this result emerges because perceivers strive to obey a set of social rules that specify the conditions under which people are entitled to judge others. Put simply, people are entitled to make strong (and, in the absence of any real information, potentially stereotypic) judgments only when we feel that we know something about the person. Yzerbyt et al. maintained that implicit rules of this sort shape all social interactions.

Conversational goals and conventions provide similar examples of the ways in which what one says and how one thinks are often dependent on not only what one is asked, but also how one is asked something. Indeed, Schwarz (1994) has recently analyzed a variety of errors from precisely this vantage. At the core of his analysis is the proposition that research in social cognition has tended to proceed in relative ignorance of the conversational context that surrounds study participants. He maintained that many of the errors that researchers observe may tell us more about the goals that we implicitly communicate to study participants through procedures than about participants' reasoning abilities.

For example, both the correspondence-bias literature and the base-rate literature suggest that people often use irrelevant information when making social judgments. In the correspondence-bias literature, participants routinely estimate that a person's true attitude is in line with the position the person expresses in an essay, even when it is made clear that the position was assigned by the experimenter (cf. Jones, 1990). Similarly, in the base-rate literature participants routinely use nondiagnostic information about individuals and ignore the diagnostic information available from the base rates (e.g., Kahneman & Tversky, 1973; Nisbett & Borgida, 1975).

But why do participants use irrelevant information? One possibility is that it is easier to process information about individuals than it is to process information about situations or base rates. In other words, people lack either the capacity or motivation to process abstract information (cf. Nisbett & Ross, 1980). The possibility that Schwarz (1994) raised, however, is that participants fully recognize the irrelevance of the information but fail to recognize that the experimenter sees its irrelevance. In other words, Schwarz suggested that participants use the irrelevant information because, in the logic of conversation, they are justified in assuming that if the experimenter presents the information, it must be important. In support of this notion, Schwarz, Strack, Hilton, and Naderer (1991) have found that when participants were encouraged to abandon the logic of conversation (e.g., they are told that the information is provided by a computer rather than by another person) they make greater use of base-rate information. Similarly, when participants were asked whether there is anything to be learned from an essay that is written under conditions of constraint, they correctly conclude that there is not (Miller, Schmidt, Meyer, & Colella, 1984).

Similarly, consider a study that Steve Fein and I once ran but never published on the base-rate fallacy. For reasons that are not relevant here, we were interested in trying to make the base-rate problem—the familiar lawyer–engineer problem (discussed subsequently; Kahneman & Tversky, 1973)—come and go as a function of the kind of individuating information that was available to participants. No matter what we did, however, participants insisted on ignoring the base rate. Then we discovered Clark's given-new contract and the proposition that in everyday conversation questions pertain to new information rather than to old assumed information (Clark & Haviland, 1977; Clark & Lucy, 1975) and our participants' responses began to make sense. Let me explain.

In the typical lawyer–engineer problem, participants are told about a group that consists of 70 lawyers and 30 engineers (or vice versa). They are then told some individuating information about one of the members of the group (e.g., "Fred is a member of the group and he is very smart") and are asked to state what the probability is that the individual is a lawyer or an engineer. What routinely happens is that participants ignore the base rate and spit back the individuating information. (In the example given, this would be 50%, assuming that both lawyers and engineers are thought to be equally smart.) Although this pattern clearly constitutes an error on the part of the participants, when we began to look at what the problem asks from the perspective of conversational norms, we discovered that there is a sense in which participants do exactly what they are asked to do. Specifically, the way the base-rate problem is traditionally framed, the base-rate information is the given information and the individuating information is the new information. So, when participants are asked what they think, they respond on the basis of the new information. After all, in everyday conversation that is what people do. People do not normally waste time telling someone something they already know. If someone asks a person which hotel burned down, he implicitly communicates his belief that the listener is already aware that there was a fire and that it was a hotel that burned. The new information that the asker desires is which hotel burned. If the listener responded "it was the hotel that burned" the asker would think the person very strange indeed.

When Steve Fein and I reframed the base-rate problem in a way that did not violate the given-new contract, we found that participants were quite willing and able to use the base-rate information. For example, when participants were told of the existence of two groups, one consisting of a group of 70 lawyers and 30 engineers (Group A) and the other consisting of a group of 30 lawyers and 70 engineers (Group B) and then learned information about a particular group member that included, as part of the new information, the group to which the person belonged (e.g., "Fred is a member of Group A and is very smart"), they were quite willing to use the base-rate information. Indeed, when Fein and I framed the problem this way, it was difficult to get the participants to pay attention to any of the individuating information.

At the time, Fein and I did not pursue this line of research. We did not run the necessary controls, for example, to make sure that the presence of two groups did not simply increase the salience of the base-rate information. We did not pursue the findings because we believe that in many situations people do ignore base-rate information for precisely the reasons Kahneman and Tversky (1973) lay out, and there did not seem much point in publishing what, at the time, struck us as a largely methodological note that would lead to the wrong conclusion. Viewed from a different perspective, however, I think that these results highlight again the role that conversational norms play in setting the interaction–perception agenda. Put simply, they highlight the ways in which what one says and how one thinks depends not only on what one is asked, but also how one is asked.

Reciprocal Goals

Finally, there is the reciprocal nature of goals. That is, not only do the perceivers' goals matter, but so too do targets' both directly, in the sense that their goals shape the interaction (e.g., Hilton & Darley, 1985; Swann & Ely, 1984) and indirectly through perceivers' assumptions about target's goals.

Jones and Pittman's (1982) attributional analysis of self-presentation clearly implies the importance of this latter perspective. After all, self-presentation works only to the extent that the presenter is able to shape the appropriate attributions in the mind of the audience. Similarly, the work that Steve Fein and I have done on suspicion (Fein & Hilton, 1994; Hilton, Fein, & Miller, 1993) suggests that perceivers readily consider the motivations of the people with whom they interact. Consider, for example, the problem that confronts members of many stereotyped groups. It is often noted that negative parts of the stereotypes are often extremely difficult to disconfirm. A number of reasons for this have been put forward (e.g., the confirmation bias, illusory correlations, etc.), but one of the most important, and often overlooked reasons, has to do with the public nature of stereotypes and assumptions that perceivers make about the interaction goals of the members of the stereotyped group.

Imagine, for example, that a colleague tells you about a student who strikes her as being particularly lazy. But then imagine that you watch this student over the course of several days, and you notice that the student always seems to be working quite hard. What are you likely to conclude about your colleague's impression? Quite likely that she was wrong. Now imagine a bigot who thinks that most African Americans are lazy. What happens when the bigot is confronted with a particularly hard working African American male? Does the bigot decide that he was wrong? Probably not for a variety of reasons, but one of the most important reasons is that the bigot is very likely to decide that the African American is working very hard in order to disconfirm the stereotype. That is, the bigot is likely to question the interaction goals of the African American in a way that leads him to be suspicious of the man's motives for working so hard. On the one hand, the African American could be working hard because he is a hard worker; he is driven to it by his dispositional nature. On the other hand, he could be working hard simply to dispel the stereotype. (For a similar analysis

143

JAMES L. HILTON

of the dilemma that confronts those who are visually impaired, see Jones et al., 1984.)

Notice that what separates the bigot's dilemma from the earlier example is that the bigot is keenly aware that the interaction goals of the target may lead the target to misrepresent, or strategically manage his behavior. More generally, the negative and public nature of stereotypes ensures that when perceivers are confronted with stereotype inconsistent behavior, they will question the interaction goals of the target and become suspicious of his or her motives. As a consequence, perceivers may subsequently refrain from taking disconfirming behavior at face value.

To examine this problem, Steve Fein and I had study participants read about a college student who had applied for a fellowship that would allow him to study abroad (Fein & Hilton, 1993). Participants first read that the important parts of the selection process consisted of the candidate's (named "Patrick") letters of reference and his performance during an interview with a member of the selection committee. All of the participants then learned that most of the student's letters were quite good. However, one third of the participants read that one of the letters contained some potentially damning information. Specifically, they learned that one of the letters indicated that the candidate might not be ideally suited for the fellowship because he appeared to be weak concerning culture and the arts. The author of the letter then backtracked and went on to say that perhaps a semester abroad would be a good thing because it would help broaden the candidate. Participants in this condition were told further that, because of the confidentiality of letters of recommendation, Patrick was unaware of the contents of the letter (expectancy-unaware condition). Another third of the participants read the same damaging letter, but were told that "due to the Freedom of Information Act," the candidate was able to get access to his letters, and that he had read them the day before his interview (expectancy-aware condition). The final third of the participants were in the control condition. These individuals read the letter with the damaging material removed and were also told that Patrick had not seen the contents of the letter (control condition).

All of the participants next read an excerpt from the interview that included Patrick's answer to the question, "What activities do you enjoy when you're not doing schoolwork?" In answering this question, Patrick behaved in a way that was designed to be inconsistent with the expectation that he was weak in the arts. He mentioned a number of cultured activities, including his enjoyment of museums, plays, and concerts. He also mentioned by name an opera and a Shakespearean play that were in town.

We predicted that participants who both knew of the negative expectancy about the student's cultural interests and also knew that the student was aware that the interviewer would have this expectancy would be the most hesitant to take the student's expectancy-disconfirming response at face value. Supporting this prediction, although Patrick's response was sufficient to eliminate the effects of the expectancy in the unaware condition, it did not eliminate those effects in the expectancy-aware condition. Participants in the expectancy-aware condition rated Patrick's true attitude toward theater, opera, and art significantly more negatively than did the participants in any of the other conditions.

What these results suggest is that when perceivers begin to question the interaction goals of the target and become suspicious, they become overly cautious in accepting expectancy-disconfirming behavior. At a more general level, the results highlight the reciprocal nature of social perception and interaction. Perceivers and targets often find themselves in situations that require them to second guess the goals and strategies that their partners are likely to use or infer.

This recursive nature is perhaps most evident in the attributional ambiguity literature. Consider a study by Snyder, Kleck, Strenta, and Mentzer (1979) in which participants were given an opportunity to sit near a member of a stigmatized group. Half of the participants in the study were given an opportunity to avoid the person under attributionally unambiguous conditions. These participants were escorted to a room that contained a person in a wheelchair, numerous empty seats, and two television sets showing the same program. If these participants chose to sit away from the person in the wheelchair, it would appear to that person that they were avoiding him or her. The other half of the participants were given an opportunity to avoid the person under attributionally ambiguous conditions. These people were escorted to the same room, but the televisions were showing different programs. Thus, if they chose to sit away from the person in the wheelchair, it could always be argued that they chose their seat based on their preference for one of the television programs. Consistent with predictions, Snyder et al. found that when the meaning of the participant's behavior would be clear to the person in the wheelchair, they chose to sit close. In contrast, when the meaning would be ambiguous, they chose to sit away from the person in the wheelchair.

Similarly, consider the analysis that Crocker and Major (1989; Crocker, Voelkl, Testa, & Major, 1991; Major & Crocker, 1993) have performed on the relationship between self-esteem and attributional ambiguity for members of stigmatized groups. According to Crocker and Major, members of stigmatized groups find themselves confronted with a dilemma whenever they receive performance feedback from a person who is aware of their group membership. For example, although negative feedback could be attributed to a poor performance, it could also be attributed to the prejudices of the evaluator. Similarly, although positive feedback could be attributed to a good performance, it could also be attributed to a desire on the part of the evaluator to avoid appearing prejudiced. Crocker and Major argued that this ambiguity leads to a variety of effects. Ambiguity can, for example, serve as a buffer against negative feedback (Crocker et al., 1991) while undermining self-esteem following positive feedback (Crocker et al., 1991). For the present purposes though, the important thing that the ambiguity highlights is the reciprocal nature of social perception. To reiterate, studies like these suggest that perceivers and targets constantly adjust their behaviors based on the inferences that they make concerning their fellow interactants' goals, beliefs, and aspirations.

SUMMARY

In virtually all social interactions, individuals bring with them goals— detailed or general, explicit or implicit—that often have profound effects on the individuals' behaviors and inferences. Despite the rather obvious nature of this observation, the position that the goal concept has occupied in social theories of perception has varied considerably. In this chapter, I have focused on research that suggests that it is not only possible to analyze social perception from the perspective of perceivers' and targets' goals, but that it is, in fact, necessary to do so to understand a variety of social-perceptual phenomena. I have also highlighted some of the ways in which the field is beginning to move beyond simple demonstrations of the importance of the goal concept to a richer understanding of the dynamic roles that goals play in social interaction and social perception. The four categories of goals outlined in this chapter were presented in this spirit. It is not yet clear, of course, whether the categories that I chose will prove to be ones that carve social interaction at its critical joints. What is clear, though, is that goals are back—and I think Ned would be happy about that.

REFERENCES

Asch, S. E. (1946). Forming impressions of personality. *Journal of Abnormal and Social Psychology, 41*, 258–290.

Bargh, J. A. (1989). Conditional automaticity: Varieties of automatic influence in social perception and cognition. In J. S. Uleman & J. A. Bargh (Eds.), *Unintended thought.* New York: Guilford Press.

Berscheid, E., Graziano, W., Monson, T., & Dermer, M. (1976). Outcome dependency, attention, attribution, and attraction. *Journal of Personality and Social Psychology, 34*, 978–989.

Bruner, J. S., & Goodman, C. C. (1947). Value and need as organizing factors in perception. *Journal of Abnormal and Social Psychology, 42*, 33–44.

Bruner, J. S., & Postman, L. (1947). Emotional selectivity in perception and reaction. *Journal of Social Psychology, 27*, 203–208.

Clark, H. H., & Haviland, S. E. (1977). Comprehension and the given-new contract. In R. O. Freedle (Ed.), *Discourse, production, and comprehension* (pp. 1–40). Norwood, NJ: Ablex.

Clark, H. H., & Lucy, P. (1975). Understanding what is meant from what is said: A study in conversationally conveyed requests. *Journal of Verbal Learning and Verbal Behavior, 14*, 56–72.

Copeland, J. (1994). Prophecies of power: Motivational implications of social power for behavioral confirmation. *Journal of Personality and Social Psychology, 67,* 264–277.

Crocker, J., & Major, B. (1989). Social stigma and self-esteem: The self-protective properties of stigma. *Psychological Review, 96,* 608–630.

Crocker, J., Voelkl, K., Testa, M., & Major, B. (1991). Social stigma: The affective consequences of attributional ambiguity. *Journal of Personality and Social Psychology, 54,* 840–846.

Devine, P. G. (1989). Stereotypes and prejudice: Their automatic and controlled components. *Journal of Personality and Social Psychology, 56,* 5–18.

Ditto, P. H., Jemmott, J. B., & Darley, J. M. (1988). Appraising the threat of illness: A mental representational approach. *Health Psychology, 7,* 183–201.

Erdelyi, M. H. (1974). A new look at the new look: Perceptual defense and vigilance. *Psychological Review, 81,* 1–25.

Fein, S., & Hilton, J. L. (1993). [Base-rate fallacy and the given-now contract]. Unpublished raw data.

Fein, S., & Hilton, J. L. (1994). Judging others in the shadow of suspicion. *Motivation and Emotion, 18,* 167–198.

Fein, S., & Spencer, S. J. (1994). *Self-affirmation processes in stereotyping and prejudice.* Paper presented at the annual meeting of the Person Memory Interest Group, Lake Tahoe, CA.

Fiske, S. T. (1992). Thinking is for doing: Portraits of social cognition from daguerreotype to laserphoto. *Journal of Personality and Social Psychology, 63,* 877–889.

Fiske, S. T. (1993). Social cognition and social perception. *Annual Review of Psychology, 44,* pp. 155–194.

Fiske, S. T., & Neuberg, S. L. (1990). A continuum of impression formation, from category-based to individuating processes: Influences of information and motivation on attention and interpretation. In M. P. Zanna (Ed.), *Advances in experimental social psychology* (Vol. 23, pp. 1–74). San Diego, CA: Academic Press.

Fiske, S. T., Neuberg, S. L., Beattie, A. E., & Milberg, S. J. (1987). Category-based and attribute-based reactions to others: Some informational conditions of stereotyping and individuating processes. *Journal of Experimental Social Psychology, 23,* 399–427.

148

Frenkel-Brunswik, E. (1949). Intolerance of ambiguity as an emotional and perceptual personality variable. *Journal of Personality, 18,* 108–143.

Gilbert, D. T., & Hixon, J. G. (1991). The trouble of thinking: Activation and application of stereotypic beliefs. *Journal of Personality and Social Psychology, 60,* 509–517.

Hamilton, D. L., & Katz, L. B. (1975). *A process oriented approach to the study of impressions.* Paper presented at the meeting of the American Psychological Association, Chicago.

Hamilton, D. L., Katz, L. B., & Leirer, V. O. (1980). Organizational processes in impression formation. In R. Hastie, T. M. Ostrom, E. B. Ebbesen, R. S. Wyer, D. L. Hamilton, & D. E. Carlston (Eds.), *Person memory: The cognitive basis of social perception* (pp. 121–153). Hillsdale, NJ: Erlbaum.

Hilton, J. L., & Darley, J. M. (1985). Constructing other persons: A limit on the effect. *Journal of Experimental Social Psychology, 21,* 1–18.

Hilton, J. L., & Darley, J. M. (1991). The effects of interaction goals on person perception. In M. P. Zanna (Ed.), *Advances in experimental social psychology* (Vol. 24, pp. 235–267). Orlando: Academic Press.

Hilton, J. L., Darley, J. M., & Fleming, J. H. (1989). Self-fulfilling prophecies and self-defeating behavior. In R. Curtis (Ed.), *Self-defeating behaviors: Experimental research and practical implications* (pp. 41–65). New York: Plenum.

Hilton, J. L., Fein, S., & Miller, D. T. (1993). Suspicion and dispositional inference. *Personality and Social Psychology Bulletin, 19,* 501–512.

Hilton, J. L., & Shapiro, J. (1991). [Interaction goals and expectations of hostility]. Unpublished raw data.

James, W. (1890). *The principles of psychology.* New York: Henry Holt & Co.

Jones, E. E. (1964). *Ingratiation.* New York: Appleton-Century-Crofts.

Jones, E. E. (1990). *Interpersonal perception.* New York: Freeman.

Jones, E. E., Farina, A., Hastorf, H. H., Markus, H., Miller, D. T., Scott, R. A. (1984). *Social stigma: The psychology of marked relationships.* New York: Freeman.

Jones, E. E., Kanouse, D. E., Kelley, H. H., Nisbett, R. E., Valins, S., & Weiner, B. (Eds.). (1972). *Attribution: Perceiving the causes of behavior.* Morristown, NJ: General Learning Press.

Jones, E. E., & Pittman, T. S. (1982). Toward a general theory of strategic self-presentation. In J. Suls (Ed.), *Psychological perspectives on the self* (pp. 231–262). Hillsdale, NJ: Erlbaum.

Jones, E. E., & Thibaut, J. (1958). Interaction goals as bases of inference in interpersonal perception. In R. Tagiuri & L. Petrullo (Eds.), *Person perception and interpersonal behavior*. Stanford, CA: Stanford University Press.

Kahneman, D., & Tversky, A. (1973). On the psychology of prediction. *Psychological Review, 80*, 237–251.

Kunda, Z. (1990). The case for motivated reasoning. *Psychological Bulletin, 108*, 480–498.

Major, B., & Crocker, J. (1993). Social stigma: The consequences of attributional ambiguity. In D. M. Mackie & D. L. Hamilton (Eds.), *Affect, cognition, and stereotyping: Interactive processes in group perception* (pp. 345–370). San Diego, CA: Academic Press.

Markus, H. (1977). Self-schemata and processing information about the self. *Journal of Personality and Social Psychology, 35*, 63–78.

Markus, H., & Nurius, P. (1986). Possible selves. *American Psychologist, 41*, 954–969.

Miller, A. G., Schmidt, D., Meyer, C., & Colella, A. (1984). The perceived value of constrained behavior: Pressures toward biased inference in the attitude attribution paradigm. *Social Psychology Quarterly, 47*, 160–171.

Miller, D. T., & Ross, M. (1975). Self-serving biases in the attribution of causality: Fact or fiction? *Psychological Bulletin, 82*, 213–225.

Neuberg, S. L. (1994). Expectancy-confirmation processes in stereotype-tinged social encounters: The moderating role of social goals. In M. P. Zanna and J. M. Olson (Eds.), *The Psychology of Prejudice: The Ontario Symposium* (Vol. 7, pp. 103–130). Hillsdale, NJ: Lawrence Erlbaum.

Neuberg, S. L., & Fiske, S. T. (1987). Motivational influences on impression formation: Outcome dependency, accuracy-driven attention, and individuating processes. *Journal of Personality and Social Psychology, 53*, 431–441.

Neuberg, S. L., Judice, T. N., Virdin, L. M., & Carrillo, M. (1993). Perceiver self-presentational goals as moderators of expectancy influences: Ingratiation and the disconfirmation of negative expectancies. *Journal of Personality and Social Psychology, 64*, 409–420.

Nisbett, R. E., & Borgida, E. (1975). Attribution and the psychology of prediction. *Journal of Personality and Social Psychology, 32*, 932–943.

Nisbett, R. E., & Ross, L. (1980). *Human inference: Strategies and shortcomings of social judgment.* Englewood Cliffs, NJ: Prentice-Hall.

Omoto, A. M., & Borgida, E. (1988). Guess who might be coming to dinner?: Personal involvement and racial stereotyping. *Journal of Experimental Social Psychology, 24,* 571–593.

Ross, M., & Ellard, J. H. (1986). On winnowing: The impact of scarcity on allocators' evaluations of candidates for a resource. *Journal of Experimental Social Psychology, 22,* 374–388.

Schwarz, N. (1994). Judgment in a social context: Biases, shortcomings, and the logic of conversation. In M. P. Zanna (Ed.), *Advances in experimental social psychology* (Vol. 26, pp. 123–162). Orlando, FL: Academic Press.

Schwarz, N., Strack, F., Hilton, D. J., & Naderer, G. (1991). Judgmental biases and the logic of conversation: The contextual relevance of irrelevant information. *Social Cognition, 9,* 67–84.

Snyder, M. (1992). Motivational foundation of behavioral confirmation. In M. P. Zanna (Ed.), *Advances in experimental social psychology* (Vol. 25, pp. 67–114). Orlando, FL: Academic Press.

Snyder, M., & Haugen, J. A. (1994). Why does behavioral confirmation occur? A functional perspective on the role of the perceiver. *Journal of Experimental Social Psychology, 30,* 218–246.

Snyder, M., & Meine, P. (1994). On the functions of stereotyping and prejudice. In M. P. Zanna (Ed.), *The psychology of prejudice: The Ontario Symposium* (Vol. 7, pp. 33–54). Hillsdale, NJ: Erlbaum.

Snyder, M. L., Kleck, R. E., Strenta, A., & Mentzer, S. J. (1979). Avoidance of the handicapped: An attributional ambiguity analysis. *Journal of Personality and Social Psychology, 37,* 2297–2306.

Spencer, S. J., & Fein, S. (1994). *The Effect of self-image threats on stereotyping.* Paper presented at the 65th Annual Meeting of the Eastern Psychological Association, Providence, RI.

Srull, T. K. (1981). Person memory: Some tests of associative storage and retrieval models. *Journal of Experimental Psychology: Human Learning and Memory, 7,* 440–463.

Srull, T. K. (1983). Organizational and retrieval processes in person memory: An examination of processing objectives, presentation format, and the possible role of self-generated retrieval cues. *Journal of Personality and Social Psychology, 44*, 1157–1170.

Swann, W. B., Jr., & Ely, R. M. (1984). The battle of wills: Self-verification versus behavioral confirmation. *Journal of Personality and Social Psychology, 46*, 1287–1302.

Tetlock, P. E. (1983). Accountability and complexity of thought. *Journal of Personality and Social Psychology, 45*, 74–83.

Tetlock, P. E., & Kim, J. I. (1987). Accountability and judgment processes in a personality prediction task. *Journal of Personality and Social Psychology, 52*, 700–709.

Wyer, R. S., Bodenhausen, G. V., & Srull, T. K. (1984). The cognitive representation of persons and groups and its effect on recall and recognition memory. *Journal of Experimental Social Psychology, 20*, 445–469.

Wyer, R. S., & Gordon, S. E. (1982). The recall of information about persons and groups. *Journal of Experimental Social Psychology, 18*, 128–164.

Yzerbyt, V. Y., Schadron, G., Leyens, J., & Rocher, S. (1994). Social judgeability: The impact of meta-informational cues on the use of stereotypes. *Journal of Personality and Social Psychology, 66*, 48–55.

Zajonc, R. B. (1960). The process of cognitive tuning in communication. *Journal of Abnormal and Social Psychology, 61*, 159–167.

Goal Taxonomies, Then and Now

Susan T. Fiske

People, and probably all of the higher animals, gear their information-seeking activities to the possibilities for acting in their environment.

—*Jones and Gerard, 1967, pp. 120–121*

A s a scientist, Ned Jones was brilliant, a social psychology god in the pantheon of great and original minds. His elegantly simple message was that people perceive other people in the service of social interaction, and he knew it both intellectually and personally. In writing a centennial history of social cognition, I was struck again and again by how persistently Jones, ubiquitous in that literature, advocated for the primacy of the social in social perception, regardless of current fashions.

Jones' acute awareness of the importance of people's social-interaction goals nicely motivates James Hilton's chapter for this volume. Like Jones

The writing of this chapter was supported by National Science Foundation Grant SBR 9421480.

and like Hilton, I share an appreciation of the importance of goals (Fiske, 1992, 1993). The question of the moment, exemplified by both Jones and Hilton, is how to sort interaction goals—or whether sorting is a good idea at all:

> It is quite possible to surface after a brief immersion in the literature on "social perception" with the impression that people, when they are with other people, are preoccupied with the cognitive task of assessing each other's fundamental nature. This is essential, so the argument is likely to run, because [goal-] appropriate and adjustive reactions depend on accurate perceptions of the characteristics of the other persons in our social environments . . . The question thus arises: accurate in what respect? with regard to which set of characteristics? (Jones & Thibaut, 1958, p. 151)

This comment has aged gracefully, being as true today as it was 40 years ago. The rest of the chapter, "Interaction Goals as Bases of Inference in Interpersonal Perception," analyzes how social context guides social perception, the core theme in Jones' work that the rest of the field only now appreciates. Hilton ably reviews the reasons for the field's renewed appreciation of interaction goals.

Jones and Thibaut in their chapter, Hilton in his, and some of the rest of us in the field, quickly get into the taxonomy business. The question now is how to sort interaction goals or whether sorting is a good idea. Indeed, Jones and Thibaut proposed three separate taxonomies in one chapter. It is clearly an appealing enterprise. As Hilton notes, without a taxonomy, each interaction carries its own unique goals, so one quickly wishes for a more systematic approach. But which taxonomy? And what makes a taxonomy more or less useful? The taxonomies proposed by Jones, Hilton, and myself, and our collaborators illustrate some critical issues in choosing taxonomies. This commentary begins by sampling taxonomies—those with multiple factors and those that are dichotomous. Then I turn to how to evaluate taxonomies.

SAMPLING TAXONOMIES

Taxonomies With Multiple Factors

Jones and Thibaut (1958), established three different taxonomies in delineating the consequences of interaction goals on interpersonal perception. The first taxonomy explores formal classes of interaction, investigating the effect of outcome dependency on cognition. The second one, a taxonomy of substance, explores what type of information perceivers will be seeking, processing, and responding to. Their third and final taxonomy relates to intermediate goals, and is very similar to a taxonomy my colleagues and I created from themes within the personality literature.

Formal Classes of Interaction

According to Jones and Thibaut (1958), formal classes of interactions include those interactions that are noncontingent, asymmetrically contingent, and reciprocally contingent, that is, respectively, the two actors are independent, or only one depends on the other, or each depends on the other for outcomes that matter to them. In other words, interactions can be classified according to outcome dependency, reflecting Thibaut and Kelley's (1959; Kelley & Thibaut, 1978) definition of social relationships in terms of the interdependence structures between people. Outcome dependency shapes social perception and interaction because "the more contingent A's behavior on B's behavior, the greater the need for inferences concerning B's motives and personality" (Jones & Thibaut, 1958, p. 177). This insight underlies work in my laboratory on power dynamics and social information seeking. In contingent relationships, people demonstrably attend to the most informative things about the powerful person, and they make more dispositional inferences about that person while also being sensitive to information that disconfirms prior expectancies (Erber & Fiske, 1984; Goodwin & Fiske, 1996; Neuberg & Fiske, 1987; Ruscher & Fiske, 1990). Classifying interactions by relative contingency clearly buys some insights about social perception.

Taxonomy of Substance

As Hilton notes, the taxonomy of substance promoted by Jones and Thibaut focuses on how different goals lead to different perceptual sets and different processing of information available about the target person. This taxonomy includes a causal-genetic (i.e., attributional) orientation, a value-maintenance (i.e., liking) orientation, and a situation-matching (i.e., norm) orientation. Given these three sets—attribution, liking, and norms—Jones and Thibaut then proceeded to focus on the value-maintenance (liking) set, paving the way for Jones's enduring interest in ingratiation. And no wonder. Value maintenance, being liked, is central to human social survival.

Elsewhere, Stevens and Fiske (1995) argued that basic interaction goals all revolve around the survival value of being liked and included. To survive physically, people need to survive socially, that is, to maintain their value to the group. Stevens and Fiske reviewed basic motives that are thematic within the personality literature, in terms of this social survival perspective. People survive socially if (a) they are motivated to belong to the group. Belonging in turn is facilitated by two more cognitive and two more motivational goals. People in groups need to (b) understand and gain shared meaning, simply in order to predict and coordinate with others and to (c) be effective and control some outcomes, to be most adaptive in the group. On the more explicitly motivational side, people need to (d) maintain their self-esteem, which Leary, Tambor, Terdal, & Downs (1995) argued is a barometer of social standing. Finally, people need to (e) trust the world to be a benevolent place (otherwise, the effort to adapt is doomed). These core goals—belonging, understanding, controlling, self-enhancing, and trusting—recur in countless analyses of personality over the decades, and they can expand the rather limited types of interaction goals currently examined in social cognition research, which tend to be confined to understanding and controlling (see Fiske, 1993; Pittman, 1998, for reviews).

Intermediate Interaction Goals

Jones and Thibaut (1958) described intermediate interaction goals as facilitating personal-goal attainment. A striking resemblance links the

Stevens–Fiske social-survival goals and this third Jones–Thibaut taxonomy. Assuming that the value-maintenance orientation approximates the Stevens–Fiske emphasis on belonging, for social survival, the other four motives are closely analogous to those of Thibaut and Jones: Their *gaining cognitive clarity* fits our *need for understanding and shared meaning*. Their *accomplishing external outcomes* fits our *need for control*. Their *securing motivational and value support* fits our *self-esteem maintenance*. And their *maximizing beneficent social response* may fit our *trusting the world to be benevolent*. If independent theoretical convergence points toward truth, then it is reassuring indeed to come upon roughly the same five basic motives, not only in personality psychology, but also in Jones and Thibaut's wise heads from social psychology. Of course, theoretical convergence can simply reflect shared scholarly delusion, but if this array of motives proves usefully distinct in research, progress will be served.

The three separate Jones–Thibaut taxonomies label themselves respectively in terms of form, substance, and interaction, and the Stevens–Fiske also is labelled in terms of interaction. Hilton presents quite a different analysis, focusing instead on a "rough-and-ready" classification, which seems predicated on the type of consciousness associated with goals. Hilton (this volume) describes four types of goals: explicit and reportable, nonconscious and at least conditionally automatic, implicit and essentially background rules for social interaction, and recursive or responsive to the goals of the other person. Jones would certainly endorse the importance of the socially recursive goal, which Hilton's own research so nicely illustrates. These categories perhaps lie along a dimension of accessibility to individual consciousness, from fully accessible (explicit), to inaccessible except through a separate person (recursive).

Dichotomous Taxonomies: Closed Versus Open Mental Systems

Of course, these taxonomies are not the only possible breakdowns of goals. As reviewed elsewhere, several theorists have posited a basic antinomy (Jones & Gerard, 1967, p. 227) between goals that tend toward accuracy (openness to change) and those that tend toward parsimony (preserving a preexisting view). Kruglanski (1990) focused on motivations for avoiding or seeking closure; Fiske and Neuberg (1990) described the tension between goals for accuracy or an immediate decision; Stangor and Ford (1992) identified expectancy-confirming versus accuracy-oriented goals; Gollwitzer (1990) described deliberative versus action-oriented mindsets; Hilton and Darley (1991) distinguished an assessment set and an action set; and Snyder (1991) described goals of getting to know the other's stable dispositions versus getting along with the particular other. In a distinction less familiar to some American readers, Lewicka (1988) contrasted the subjective perspective of the actor and the objective perspective of the observer. Although these theories are by no means identical, they all do posit two different types of goals for social perception, one tending toward openness and accuracy and the other toward parsimony and prior expectancies.

HOW TO EVALUATE TAXONOMIES

Given this daunting array of goal taxonomies, a reader has to wonder where they take the field, and where could they take the field, in the best-case scenario. Certainly, all the taxonomies serve a didactic purpose. The desperate teacher and the frantic reviewer each need ways to carve up the literature, and all of these do that.

More importantly, such taxonomies of goals are most useful if they are principled; all of the dichotomous classification schemes are based on broader theories of the social perceiver. Likewise, the Jones–Thibaut (1958) taxonomy of form, based on contingency, certainly ties into Thibaut and Kelley's interdependence theory, as well as Jones subsequent analyses of motivations for impression management (e.g., Jones & Pittman, 1982). The Jones–Thibaut taxonomy of substance (causal, liking, and norm oriented), as well as their five intermediate interaction goals, have had less theoretical payoff so far. The same may prove true of Hilton's rough-and-ready scheme, although broader theoretical possibility is implicit, arrayed in terms of goals' accessibility to individual consciousness. The Stevens–Fiske taxonomy is intended to be read in the theoretical context of minimal social-survival needs; its theoretical payoff also remains to be seen.

The other evaluative criterion for taxonomies is ultimately empirical. By this token, the dichotomies have been more successful than the multicategory taxonomies, perhaps because of social psychology's propensity for experimental designs in powers of 2.

Taxonomy however is not important for its own sake. Although the history of science teaches that researchers must first describe nature and then explain it, psychology has long ago seen that laundry lists of motives do not create useful theories of personality just as major recent laundry lists of errors and biases (Fiske & Taylor, 1991) did not create useful theories of social cognition. What is important is the clear role of goals, and taxonomies can encourage thinking about varieties of goals and their common causes and impacts.

FINAL COMMENT

In renewed enthusiasm for goals, it is likely that more and more social psychologists will describe their approaches in goal-relevant new vocabularies. As a cautionary note, it may be helpful to distinguish among approaches that are (a) functional, that is, related to natural, required, or expected activity; (b) pragmatic, that is, determining meaning by effectiveness; and (c) purposeful, which is equivalent to goal-oriented or intentional. Ned Jones, the master of linguistic precision, would want social psychologists to choose their words carefully, at the same time that he would applaud the renewed interest in goals, confirming his own abiding loyalty to the social perceiver in actual interaction.

REFERENCES

Erber, R., & Fiske, S. T. (1984). Outcome dependency and attention to inconsistent information. *Journal of Personality and Social Psychology, 47*, 709–726.

Fiske, S. T. (1992). Thinking is for doing: Portraits of social cognition from daguerreotype to laserphoto. *Journal of Personality and Social Psychology, 63*, 877–889.

Fiske, S. T. (1993). Social cognition and social perception. In M. R. Rosenzweig & L. W. Porter (Eds.), *Annual review of psychology* (Vol. 44, pp. 155–194). Palo Alto, CA: Annual Reviews, Inc.

Fiske, S. T., & Neuberg, S. L. (1990). A continuum model of impression formation, from category-based to individuating processes: Influence of information and motivation on attention and interpretation. In M. P. Zanna (Ed.), *Advances in experimental social psychology* (Vol. 23, pp. 1–74). San Diego, CA: Academic Press.

Fiske, S. T., & Taylor, S. E. (1991). *Social cognition* (2nd ed.). New York: Mc-Graw-Hill.

Gollwitzer, P. M. (1990). Action phases and mind-sets. In E. T. Higgins & R. M. Sorrentino (Eds.), *Handbook of motivation and cognition: Foundations of social behavior* (Vol. 2, pp. 53–92). New York/London: Guilford Press.

Goodwin, S. A., & Fiske, S. T. (1996). Judge not, unless . . . Standards for social judgment and ethical decision-making. In D. M. Messick & A. Tenbrunsel (Eds.), *Codes of conduct: Behavioral research and business ethics* (pp. 117–142). New York: Russell Sage.

Hilton, J. L., & Darley, J. M. (1991). The effects of interaction goals on person perception. In M. P. Zanna (Ed.), *Advances in experimental social psychology* (Vol. 24, pp. 235–267). San Diego, CA: Academic Press.

Jones, E. E., & Gerard, H. B. (1967). *Foundations of social psychology.* New York: Wiley.

Jones, E. E., & Pittman, T. S. (1982). Toward a general theory of strategic self-presentation. In J. Suls (Ed.), *Psychological perspectives on the self* (pp. 231–262). Hillsdale NJ: Erlbaum.

Jones, E. E., & Thibaut, J. W. (1958). Interaction goals as bases of inference in interpersonal perception. In R. Tagiuri & L. Petrullo (Eds.), *Person perception and interpersonal behavior* (pp. 151–178). Stanford, CA: Stanford University Press.

Kelley, H. H., & Thibaut, J. W. (1978). *Interpersonal relations: A theory of interdependence.* New York: Wiley.

Kruglanski, A. W. (1990). Motivations for judging and knowing: Implications for causal attribution. In E. T. Higgins & R. M. Sorrentino (Eds.), *Handbook of motivation and cognition: Foundations of social behavior* (Vol. 2, pp. 333–368). New York/London: Guilford Press.

Leary, M. R., Tambor, E. S., Terdal, S. K., & Downs, D. L. (1995). Self-esteem as an interpersonal monitor: The sociometer hypothesis. *Journal of Personality and Social Psychology, 68,* 518–530.

Lewicka, M. (1988). On objective and subjective anchoring of cognitive acts: How behavioral valence modifies reasoning schemata. In W. J. Baker, L. P. Mos, H. V. Rappard, & H. J. Stam (Eds.), *Recent trends in theoretical psychology* (pp. 285–301). New York: Springer.

Neuberg, S. L., & Fiske, S. T. (1987). Motivational influences on impression formation: Outcome dependency, accuracy-driven attention, and individuating processes. *Journal of Personality and Social Psychology, 53,* 431–444.

Pittman, T. S. (1998). Motivation. In D. T. Gilbert, S. T. Fiske, & G. Lindzey (Eds.), *The handbook of social psychology* (4th ed., Vol. 1, pp. 549–590). New York: McGraw-Hill.

Ruscher, J. B., & Fiske, S. T. (1990). Interpersonal competition can cause individuating processes. *Journal of Personality and Social Psychology, 58,* 832–843.

Snyder, M. (1991). Motivational foundations of behavioral confirmation. In M. P. Zanna (Ed.), *Advances in Experimental Social Psychology* (Vol. 25, pp. 67–114). San Diego, CA: Academic Press.

Stangor, C., & Ford, T. E. (1992). Accuracy and expectancy-confirming processing orientations and the development of stereotypes and prejudice. In W. Stroebe & M. Hewstone (Eds.), *European review of social psychology* (Vol. 3, pp. 57–89). New York: Wiley.

Stevens, L. E., & Fiske, S. T. (1995). Motivation and cognition in social life: A social survival perspective. *Social Cognition, 13,* 189–214.

Thibaut, J. W., & Kelley, H. H. (1959). *The social psychology of groups.* New York: Wiley.

Interaction Goals: Their Structure and Function

Mark Snyder

For all who participated in the conference held at Princeton University in March of 1995 to honor the legacy of Ned Jones, it was a time for reminiscing, for thinking back over the course of our personal and professional histories with him. In that spirit of reminiscence, I found that reading James Hilton's chapter "Interaction Goals and Person Perception" (this volume) and preparing this commentary on it took me back to a time, some 25 years ago when I was a young graduate student just starting out at Stanford University. I entered graduate school knowing that I was interested in the subject matter of social psychology, but having had almost no coursework at all in its theories and methods. Partially as a result of that state of affairs, I decided that I should sit in on a basic survey course in social psychology. As it happened, the text in that course was the big red book—the classic Jones and Gerard (1967) *Foundations of Social Psychology* textbook— which I found to be a truly wonderful book, exciting and challenging in the breadth and depth of its ideas. Moreover, it seemed to confirm

This comment was prepared with the support of grants from the National Science Foundation and from the National Institute of Mental Health.

that I actually had made the right decision by gravitating toward social psychology.

I then gravitated toward Ned's other writings, especially the Jones and Thibaut (1958) paper "Interaction Goals as Bases of Inference in Interpersonal Perception." I was (and continue to be) very taken with its ideas about interaction goals. The perspective on interaction goals articulated in the Jones and Thibaut paper continues to inform contemporary researchers, inspiring them with its enduring intellectual vitality. Its essential claim is that people, in their attempts to understand the world and in their attempts to deal with others are pursuing a variety of goals—such goals as striving to maintain cognitive clarity, to get support for their values, to boost their self-esteem, and (as Jones and Thibaut described it) to maximize beneficent social responses (in other words, to get good outcomes in their lives). In his paper "Interaction Goals and Person Perception" prepared for this volume, James Hilton has done an excellent job of capturing the high points of some several decades of research and theorizing on the problem of interaction goals. He has provided a sampling of several of the currently active and exciting programs of research that carry on in the intellectual tradition defined by Jones and Thibaut in their classic paper, research programs that are guided by diverse theoretical perspectives and that use diverse investigative strategies, but that nevertheless reflect the spirit of the interaction goals formulation.

Of particular importance, Hilton has emphasized the pendulum shifts that have occurred between preferences for relatively cognitive explanations and for relatively motivational explanations of individual and social psychological phenomena, and the noteworthy creativity of proponents of either perspective in interpreting evidence offered in support of the other perspective as actually quite compatible with their own preferred point of view. If one stands back and takes the long view, it becomes readily apparent that there has always been in psychology (at least within social and personality psychology) a general agreement on the goal-directed, goal-seeking, goal-setting nature of how people function both as individuals and as social beings, with such themes pervading theoretical formulations of many forms. This has been true throughout it all, no matter which was the currently preferred explanation, no matter which perspective was on the upswing and which was on the downswing.

In the rest of this commentary, I touch first on how psychology is the study of movement, of how individuals move and are moved through their lives. Next, I suggest that any serious taxonomy of goals must use the functional properties of goals in the classification process. Finally, I call on goal theorists to begin exploring the antecedents of interaction goals, their inculcation and integration into the lives of individuals moving and being moved.

PEOPLE MOVING AND BEING MOVED

An emphasis on goals should be an integral part of psychological theorizing. I don't see how there could be a social psychology or a personality psychology that is not fundamentally motivational in nature. Think of what the term *motivation* means. If it is traced to its etymological roots, it comes back to the word *move* and the idea of people somehow being moved to action. Now, think about what social psychology is all about. So much of social psychology is about how people move through their lives, focusing on how they are, in fact, moved through their lives by the social contexts in which they operate and by the influences of the other people who form their social networks and who provide normative and prescriptive guidelines and constraints for their beliefs, attitudes, behaviors, and relationships. Think too about the defining features of the psychology of personality as the study of the individual. It too is fundamentally concerned with how people move through their lives, emphasizing as it does such themes as how people are moved by dispositions that they carry with them in a relatively enduring sense, including their concepts of self and identity, their values and attitude, and their traits and dispositions.

From this perspective on the concerns of personality and social psychology, a perspective that focuses on how people move and are moved through their lives, it seems that personality and social psychology are fundamentally motivational in their defining and characteristic orientations. I think that this has been true even in those periods of time when intellectual historians would characterize these fields as being dominated by concerns with cognition. So many of the treatments of cognitive phenomena and processes offered by personality and social psychologists represent rather motivational views of cognition. The very notion, which underlies so much cognitive and attributional theorizing in social psychology and personality, that people engage in cognitive activity in the service of gaining stable and predictable images of the world, images that they can and do use to help guide them through their lives, is ultimately a motivational idea. That is, this notion places cognitive activity in a clearly and explicitly goal-directed context, one that emphasizes that, as it has been characterized in pragmatic terms, "thinking is for doing" (Fiske, 1992).

FUNCTIONAL GOALS AND TAXONOMIES

Largely in recognition of this essentially motivational characterization, many use the term *functional* or *functionalist* in umbrella-like fashion to embrace those approaches that focus on the functions or purposes served by what people think, feel, and do, as well as by how these functional purposes are related to the agendas that people set for their lives, and that have effects on their functioning in diverse domains. A guiding theme of this functional approach is the attempt to understand what people are trying to do in their lives, how they are trying to do it, and why they are trying to do it. Analyses of function have been applied to phenomena and processes as diverse as attribution and person perception, attitudes and persuasion, social interaction and interpersonal relationships, altruism and prosocial behavior, and activism and social participation (for further perspectives on functionally oriented approaches to personality and social psychology, see Cantor, 1994; Snyder, 1993).

Clearly, the concept of interaction goals is a central building block in the functionalist approach, as it would surely be in any broadly based motivational perspective on individual and social behavior. Quite rightly, Hilton in his essay has challenged proponents of the interaction-goals approach to develop a taxonomy of these interaction goals. To be useful, such a taxonomy would need to partition interaction goals into meaningful units, and offer the means of classifying them into these categories. Hilton offers one such taxonomic approach. It is a most promising one, I believe, in its focus on the categories of the relatively explicit goals, the less conscious and perhaps more automatic ones, the ones that are implicit and rarely explained, but can still be articulated, and the more recursive goals that link the motivational concerns of both parties to an interaction in a relationship of mutual interplay and reciprocal influence. The empirical literature on social perception and interpersonal behavior is generous in the many illustrative (and persuasive) examples it provides for each of these categories of interaction goals.

What I find particularly appealing about Hilton's approach to classifying goals is that there seems to be a functionalist quality to this classification. To be sure, similar to most classification schemes, his is a structural one. But his classification scheme is oriented toward the functional properties of the goals. Each category of goals is defined by how such goals work, how such goals operate to influence how people think, perceive the world, and conduct their interactions with other people. Quite possibly, such a functionally oriented classification system has the potential to bridge the gap between structural considerations of what goals are and functional considerations of how goals work.

THE ORIGINS AND ANTECEDENTS OF GOAL SETTING

I also expect to see continuing concern with the functional significance of goals, with attention increasingly focused on the mechanisms and processes by which individuals choose and define goals for themselves, how they set their agendas for individual and social action, how they actively and purposefully pursue those motivational agendas, and the consequences of such activities for understanding the worlds in which people function. The matter of mechanism is, of course, a critical one.

It's one thing for people to identify, define, and classify the goals that pervade our lives, but, it's quite another thing to figure out exactly how goals work to guide and direct thought, feelings, and actions. Perhaps too, and ideally so, personality and social psychologists will see greater integration and coordination of the pursuit of structural and functional considerations, with the eventual emergence of theories that, at one and the same time, speak to both the structure and function of interaction goals specifically and motivational operations more generally.

On the assumption that attempts to chart the structural organization and the functional significance of interaction goals will continue, then social psychologists should ask ourselves what else should be prominent on the agenda for psychological inquiry in this domain. There are, no doubt, many answers to this question, but one answer that repeatedly comes to my mind is the need to chart the origins and antecedents of interaction goals. All too often, psychologists find ourselves looking at relatively fully formed products. After all, the college students who are so omnipresent in psychological laboratories, whether one regards them as late adolescents or as young adults, have spent a long time traveling on the socialization highway by the time they have the opportunity to participate in research efforts and provide the data used to build theories. No doubt, some (if not much) of their socialization has concerned the very interaction goals that they pursue, both in laboratories and in their lives beyond the social psychologist's research-based transactions with them. As such, socialization processes provide one important source of context for understanding the agendas that individuals pursue in their lives. Of course, there are other contexts also, and there are corresponding benefits to recognizing their importance—ethological, biological, cultural, developmental, and historical contexts—all of which can and do provide contexts for the phenomena that psychologists study and for the theories that we build. But the time has come to get serious about mapping out those contexts, so that psychologists can and will have theories and research strategies that are as serious about the antecedents of psychological phenomena and processes as they are about the phenomena and processes themselves.

CONLUDING COMMENTS

Just as considerations of interaction goals have had a distinguished past, and just as an impressive amount of attention is currently being devoted to them, so too can we expect that discussions of interaction goals will continue well into the future and will be central features of theorizing and research in the psychological sciences. Looking to that future, I think that researchers will see further articulation and specification of the structural organization of interaction goals. Whether the categories offered by Hilton will prove, as he put it in his concluding observations on his taxonomic efforts, "to be ones that carve social interaction at critical joints" (p. 147) remains to be seen. But surely his efforts will be integral to ensuing considerations of the structural organization of interaction goals.

In closing, let me note that this commentary on the structure and function of interaction goals was prepared as part of a tribute to the memory of Ned Jones and his contributions to psychology. To be sure, interaction goals are an essential part of that legacy, as are his many, many other theoretical and empirical contributions to psychology. But an equally important and a most cherished part of that legacy, I firmly believe, is the vast and cohesive collegial network and community of scholars that Ned worked so hard to foster and to cement together. It is a network and a community that has played a defining role in the emergence and development of so many areas of psychology as it is known today. And it is a network and a community that will help to ensure the continuing vitality and generativity of psychology in times yet to come.

REFERENCES

Cantor, N. E. (1994). Life task problem solving: Situational affordances and personal needs. *Personality and Social Psychology Bulletin, 20,* 235–243.

Fiske, S. T. (1992). Thinking is for doing: Portraits of social cognition from daguerreotype to laserphoto. *Journal of Personality and Social Psychology, 63,* 877–889.

Jones, E. E., & Gerard, H. B. (1967). *Foundations of social psychology.* New York: Wiley.

Jones, E. E., & Thibaut, J. (1958). Interaction goals as bases of inference in interpersonal perception. In R. Taguiri & L. Petrullo (Eds.), *Person perception and interpersonal behavior.* Stanford, CA: Stanford University Press.

Snyder, M. (1993). Basic research and practical problems: The promise of a "functional" personality and social psychology. *Personality and Social Psychology Bulletin, 19,* 251–264.

Essence and Accident

Richard E. Nisbett

Dan Gilbert expressed the opinion that the most important accomplishment of social psychology is its discovery of the *correspondence bias*—the tendency to assume that actors have stable dispositions that correspond to their behavior. Of course this concept was central to Ned's work and therefore places the center of Ned's work at the center of social psychology; no surprise to attendees at this conference.

What I would like to do in this commentary is to try to place the correspondence bias notion in broader historical, scientific, and cultural context. The result of this effort, I believe, is to make it clear that the importance of the correspondence bias concept is even greater than usually assumed by social psychologists and that the concept is going to be "the gift that keeps on giving": It is going to continue to generate interesting research for the foreseeable future.

The correspondence bias occurs primarily because the observer is not sufficiently attentive to the constraints and opportunities that confront the actor, that is, not sufficiently cognizant of the context in which behavior occurs, and hence takes the behavior of the actor at face value. The consequence is that the observer attributes dispositions to the actor that would explain the behavior and that the observer believes can be used to predict future behavior. I make no attempt to summarize the very large body of literature on the correspondence bias because this has just recently been done in an excellent review by Gilbert and Malone (1995).

In this chapter, I touch briefly on the Aristotelian approach to knowledge, in particular its emphasis on locating causality within the essence of an object. I then discuss some of the early demonstrations and theorizing about the correspondence bias and its extension into the actor–observer difference and the out-group homogeneity effect. Next, I shift focus toward the recent work that suggests that the correspondence bias is culturally bound, found more in Western, independent-oriented cultures and less in Eastern, interdependent, collectivist cultures. Two explanations are explored to explain this cultural difference. The first explanation examines the notion that individuals in these different societies do live in very different worlds with concomitant different lay theories regarding the laws governing daily life and social interaction. The second explanation suggests that individuals within the separate cultures are focused on and attend to different features of their social worlds.

THE ESSENCE OF THE CORRESPONDENCE BIAS

The very first important theoretical treatment of the correspondence bias placed the concept in a much broader historical and theoretical context than social psychologists generally recognize. Kurt Lewin, in an essay published in 1935, characterized Aristotle's physics as being exclusively object-focused in the same way that he believed psychology—both lay and professional—to be. In Aristotelian physics, the most important activity for the scientist was to discover the properties of the object—its essence—and to make sure that its accidental properties were ignored for purposes of understanding and predicting its behavior. The *essence* of an object is made up of those properties without which the object would not be itself. Those properties in turn could be identified by knowing the critical categories that describe the object. *Accidental properties* are those that do not define the object or change one's understanding of its fundamental nature. Aristotle (though Lewin does not focus on this) made it clear that his ontology included social objects. Thus one would not regard the property *musical* as being part of one's human essence. If that property were absent, one would still be fully human. The presence of a moral sense or of a need for human society, however, seem defining of a human. Someone lacking such qualities might be held to lack a human essence.

Lewin's concern in that early essay was to establish the error of focusing exclusively on properties of the object. This error led Aristotle to explain that a rock falls when dropped because it has the property of gravity, whereas a piece of wood floats when placed in water because it has the property of levity. Lewin observed that it was not until the work of Galileo that it was recognized that the behavior of physical objects can only be understood by considering both the properties of the object and the field within which the object operates. Thus correct explanation always invokes relational notions, not the purely categorical ones that describe the object.

The social psychology that Lewin offered was one that he intended to be Galilean rather than Aristotelian—that is, it was to be a field theory that would emphasize the relation between the actor and the social context. This view has now become dogma in social psychology and remains the principal way in which a social psychological view is likely to differ from a lay view. Lay physics, incidentally, appears to differ from current scientific physics in just the way that lay psychology differs from scientific psychology; that is, lay physics remains more nearly Aristotelian than Galilean (Champagne, Klopfer, & Anderson, 1980; McCloskey, 1983). Untutored laypeople (and for that matter, many tutored ones) believe that forces can impart properties to objects, and these properties can then direct their behavior. Thus one can propel an object by some sort of transfer of energy, but the object will slow down after that initial acceleration because the property of impetus dissipates over time. The layperson does not understand that objects would continue in motion eternally were it not for aspects of the field that bring it to a halt, and that the impetus ascribed to the object conflates the inertia of the object with the friction of the field.

Much of the most interesting and important social psychology of the last few decades has fleshed out Lewin's field-theory notions and justified his hunch that lay psychology is Aristotelian at base. The most important theoretical work on this topic following Lewin's was that of Fritz Heider (1958) with his famous dictum that "behavior engulfs the field." This statement has been taken by many to mean that Heider agreed with Lewin that people are Aristotelians when explaining behavior and that he was proposing a Gestalt theory explanation for this: Behavior tends to be more salient than the context in which it occurs and hence people are inclined to infer that dispositions of the actor explain the actor's behavior.

FROM INFERENTIAL DESCRIPTION TO INFERENTIAL BIAS

Ned's initial work on the question of correspondence (Jones & Davis, 1965) did not focus on the notion of bias in the sense of error. Indeed, at the time Ned began his work the very notion of an inferential bias in the sense of a predilection to erroneous judgment did not have much legitimacy in psychology. The job of the social scientist was just to report the facts, ma'am. To speak about error-producing bias would be to arrogate to the psychologist the role of the philosopher, if in fact even the philosopher had a right to speak of cognitive error.

Instead, the problem that Ned thought he was working on was the question of the determinants of a correspondent inference—that is, an inference that a state or trait exists corresponding to an observed behavior. This early work showed, for example, that when people say things that it is not in their interest to say (e.g., when an applicant for a job as a submariner says that he is not very sociable) others make *correspondent inferences*, that is, they assume that a trait corresponding to the behavior really exists.

However, it was not too long before this work began to show anomalies, the most famous of which was the phenomenon shown in the Jones and Harris (1967) experiment. In that demonstration, study participants were asked to read an essay allegedly (and in later versions actually) written by a fellow student. The essay either supported or opposed a position on some topic such as the legalization of marijuana. The essay was, in one variation, written at the request of a political science instructor, in another variation at the request of a debate coach, and so on. The manipulation was the degree of choice the actor had in writing the essay. In one condition, actors allegedly were given their choice as to what position to take. In the other condition, actors were required to take a particular position. Participants were more likely to make a correspondent inference in the first condition than in the second, thus establishing perceived choice as an important factor underlying correspondent inference. Much more interesting, however, was how little difference choice actually made to participants' attitude ascriptions. Or to put that another way, it was surprising how inclined participants were to make correspondent inferences under circumstances where it would seem sensible to make no correspondent inference at all.

Jones and his students pursued this phenomenon through a range of possible alternative explanations, including the possibility that participants didn't understand just how strong the pressure would be in actual essay-writing situations to take the position required by the authority, the possibility that the essays seemed so well written that participants would assume that only someone with real conviction could have produced the essay, and so on. Nothing erased the implications of the original Jones and Harris (1967) data that people are inappropriately susceptible to a correspondence bias. Of course, many subsequent demonstrations have shown the extent to which people are insufficiently sensitive to the situational factors that prompt behavior of a given kind and consequently infer traits where there are none.

Actors and Observers

It was while the follow-up work to the Jones and Harris study was being done that I met Ned, under circumstances that will produce nostalgia in people of a certain age and astonishment and envy in those who are younger. Hal Kelley, who had just written his classic paper on attribution processes, wanted to spend several weeks talking to Ned

Jones, who had just written, with Keith Davis, his classic paper on the same topic. They thought it might be a good idea to include some students working with Stanley Schachter, who also seemed to be working on matters having to do with causal attribution. (I suspect, though I don't know for sure, that Hal asked Schachter himself first. I do know for sure that Stan would not have accepted the invitation because this would have meant foregoing a large part of his lengthy stay at his beloved summer cottage at Amagansett.) Stu Valins and I were the students, actually the new PhDs, chosen. Bernie Weiner and David Kanouse, then assistant professors at UCLA, joined the conference. And now the nostalgia or astonishment, as the case may be: Hal wrote a brief proposal to the National Science Foundation (NSF) asking for support for a 6-week conference to chat about attribution, which entailed putting up three visitors from the East Coast for 6 weeks. It's a little hard to imagine ready approval of such a thing these days.

The conference was all one could possibly hope for. It became clearer and clearer that the topic of causal attribution was not going to be a flash in the pan, but was going to become a very important research area, which indeed it did and remained so for approximately the next decade. At the very end of the conference, attendees decided to do a book showing what could be done with the topic. I wanted to do a chapter on self-perception and another chapter with Stu Valins on psychopathology. When Ned said he had been thinking about doing a chapter on differences in causal attributions for self and other, I immediately said I had too. Maybe I had. Certainly I quickly came to believe I had. In any case, we were off and running on the paper (Jones & Nisbett, 1972) that argued that actors are situationists, being inclined to believe that their behavior is the result of rational responses to the context in which their behavior occurs, while observers are trait theorists, being inclined to attribute the actor's behavior to stable dispositions such as traits and abilities. Ned and I listed a large number of factors that might produce this difference, but the one I at least preferred calls on Heider's Gestalt perceptual notions: Correspondent inferences are easier when it is the actor who is focal, as it is for the observer, than when it is the situation that is focal, as it is for the actor.

Though Ned and I referred to these different tendencies as biases, we used the term *bias* in the sense of general tendency or preference, and our only real normative analysis of these different attribution tendencies came at the end of the paper where we simply noted that the actor is sometimes wrong and the observer is sometimes wrong.

This all changed when I told Lee Ross what I was up to with Ned. He said that this was all very interesting, but Ned and I were framing things incorrectly. Both the actor and the observer are overly inclined to make correspondent inferences. It's just that the actor, for some mix of reasons identified by Lewin, Heider, Icheiser, and Jones and me, is less susceptible to the error. As a result of Ross's famous (1977) essay, this became known as the *fundamental attribution error*. Aside from making an important theoretical point, the essay was a major contributor to the change in the philosophy of science of social psychology. Social psychologists began to talk of judgment and reasoning in normative terms: Error joined the more neutral concept of bias in analyses of human inferential tendencies. The climate favored this because it was just at this time that Kahneman and Tversky, following Ward Edward's initial work on "man as an intuitive Bayesian," were beginning to compare human judgment in general to normative standards of statistics and logic.

Correspondence Bias in Perceptions of Groups

The next step in Ned's explorations of the topic of correspondence bias came in his work, with George Quattrone and Patty Linville (Linville & Jones, 1980; Quattrone & Jones, 1980), showing that people see less variability in the behavior of out-groups than in-groups. This demonstration makes sense in terms of one of the explanations that Ned and I drew on for the actor–observer effect: Actors have more information about their own behavior than they do about that of others and thus trait inferences that are logically allowable for others are blocked for themselves. The same applies for groups. ("I know too much about members of my group for me to make stereotypic judgments about them, that is, to infer a narrow range of behavioral preferences. But the evidence allows me to make stereotypic judgments about members of other groups, that is, to assume that their attributes are universal and chronically exhibited.") Put in essence and accident terms, these tendencies result in an interesting paradox: "I believe that members of outgroups have stronger, clearer essences than members of my in-groups or even than I myself have."

The final step in the correspondence bias line of notions is what has come to be called, by scholars in history and ethnography and other humanistic studies, the *essentialization of the other*, that is, the assumption that members of other groups are fundamentally and irreducibly, and possibly biologically, different from members of one's own group. In support of the notion that the attributes of out-groups may be biologized, the cognitive anthropologist Lawrence Hirschfeld (1996) has shown that children begin to perceive race as unchangeable almost as soon as they perceive gender as unchangeable. And there is little doubt that European nobles perceived peasants literally as a different order of being, in some cases until well into the 20th century. In the late 19th and early 20th centuries, some pseudoscientists encouraged the notions that human "racial" groups (in some cases defined down to the preposterous level of sub-subtypes of alleged European races) were of fundamentally different kinds. This had a receptive enough audience to suggest that there was a fertile ground for this kind of naturalizing of out-group essence. On the other hand, I am not sure that biologizing out-group differences is such an important aspect of out-group stereotyping or prejudice. There is good reason to believe that classical Greeks and Romans regarded physical differences among human groups as being due to environmental factors—to accidents. Thus, Egyptians and others from southern regions were dark because of exposure to the sun rather than because of any inborn characteristics. And in any case, it is well known that people are capable of powerful stereotypes and great hatred of out-groups whose appearance is identical to that of their in-group.

Explanations for the Correspondence Bias

In our book *Human Inference*, Lee Ross and I (Ross & Nisbett, 1991) emphasized perceptual reasons as the important ones for the correspondence bias. To the extent that this is correct, the error should be universal, occurring among all human groups. In contrast, Gilbert and Malone (1995), believe that the lay-theoretical account is the primary explanation of the correspondence bias. They argue that it does not necessarily follow from the behavior-engulfing-the-field notion that dis- positional inferences should be made just by virtue of witnessing the behavior and overlooking the situational factors that caused it. But Hei- der (1958) gave the reason to expect this: There is a perceptual *unit formation* between the actor and the actor's behavior. The "glue" for this unit formation could be, at least in part, presumed dispositions of the actor that might in principle explain the behavior. Gilbert and Ma- lone also noted, however, that direct manipulations of the salience of the actor seem to have little effect on study participants' tendencies to make dispositional inferences. This seems a direct violation of the per- ceptual explanation for the correspondence bias. On the other hand, although it appears to be the case that manipulations of actor salience have little effect on trait ascriptions, the literature shows that manip- ulations of salience affect participants' preferences for dispositional ver- sus situational explanations of behavior. Gilbert and Malone dismissed these findings on linguistic and technical grounds that are debatable in my view. Moreover, it is important to note that manipulations of the salience of the situation repeatedly have been shown to affect partici- pants' willingness to make dispositional inferences. For example, when the salience of the low incentive is increased in dissonance experiments, participants infer stronger attitudes in line with behavior (e.g., Zanna, Lepper, & Abelson, 1973) and when the salience of the high incentive is increased in overjustification experiments, participants infer stronger attitudes contrary to the behavior (e.g., M. Ross, 1975).

CULTURAL DIFFERENCES AND THE CORRESPONDENCE BIAS

Regardless of the role of lay theory in producing the correspondence bias in mainstream American culture, it should be clear that, to the extent that lay theory is important, members of various cultural groups would be expected to show the correspondence bias to different degrees. This is so because cultures might be expected to differ in their theories about the causes of behavior. And indeed there do appear to be cultural differences in susceptibility to the correspondence bias. For example, Shweder and Bourne (1982) asked Hindu Indians and Americans to describe people they knew. The Indians were more likely to describe behavior in a particular social relationship, occurring at a particular time and place. Americans were more likely to describe behavior at a high level of decontextualized generality, referring to presumed traits and personal dispositions. Similarly, Cousins (1989) found that, when describing themselves, Japanese people are unwilling to ascribe traits of high levels of generality whereas Americans readily do so. This pattern is reversed when participants are asked to describe themselves in specific contexts, in relation to specific people. Under these conditions, Japanese people are quite willing to ascribe dispositions to themselves.

Joan Miller (1984) conducted a study with Hindu Indians and Americans in which she showed that intuitions about causality for human behavior differ with respect to the degree that they show an inclination toward the correspondence bias. Her work indicated that Indians are less susceptible to the fundamental attribution error than are Americans. She asked participants to explain behavior by acquaintances and coded the explanations for the degree to which they referred to presumed dispositions of the actor versus more contextual or situational causes. The explanations of Indians emphasized situational factors, including social context and role constraints, whereas Americans were more likely to invoke generalized dispositions. The different patterns of explanation did not occur because the two groups selected different kinds of behavior to explain. When Americans were given Indian-generated behaviors to explain, they did so in an American fashion, not an Indian fashion. That these differences reflect different theories in the two cultures is indicated by a developmental aspect of Miller's study. American and Indian children start out making similar types of attributions and diverge increasingly over the course of development.

Michael Morris and Kaiping Peng (Morris, 1993; Morris, Nisbett, &

Peng, 1995; Morris & Peng, 1994) have extended these demonstrations by examining public representations of well-known events. At about the same time, a Chinese graduate student at the University of Iowa murdered his adviser, some classmates, and bystanders, and a disgruntled Irish-American postal employee in Detroit murdered his supervisor, some colleagues, and bystanders. Morris and Peng (1994) observed that Chinese newspapers tended to explain both murders in contextual terms whereas American newspapers tended to explain both murders in dispositional terms. Formal coding of the explanations showed that this impression was correct. They then asked both Chinese and American graduate students to explain the same events after reading brief descriptions of them generated from newspaper accounts. Again, the Chinese participants preferred contextual explanations more than the American subjects while the American subjects preferred dispositional explanations more than Chinese subjects.

Other work by Morris and Peng (1994) indicates that these different intuitions about causality for behavior are sufficiently strong that they extend even to the understanding of animal behavior. They asked participants to observe animated cartoons showing the behavior of a group of fish in relation to a single fish. In one vignette, for example, the individual fish moves away from the group; in another the individual moves toward the group and swims away with it. Participants were asked to explain whether the behavior of the individual fish was best explained as being due to external or to internal causes. Chinese participants were more likely to prefer external causes; Americans were more likely to prefer internal causes. This demonstration suggests that causal intuitions about behavior differ between the two cultures at a deep level.

Finally, Lee, Hallahan, and Herzog (1996) have shown that newspaper accounts of sports events in Hong Kong newspapers emphasize situational causes for outcomes, but newspaper accounts of sports events in the United States are more likely to emphasize dispositional causes.

Thus there are several demonstrations of similar points. The Asians studied explain social events with respect to the context in which behavior occurs and are relatively unwilling to invoke general dispositions. The Westerners (Americans in all studies to date) rush in where Asians fear to tread and explain behavior in terms of broad traits and preferences. Why might this be? As Ross and Nisbett (1991) speculated, there appear to be two possibilities for these cultural differences: a theory-based explanation and an attention-based explanation.

Different Worlds and Different Theories

Differences in cultural theories might arise from the fact that Asians live in a world where behavior is in fact likely to be caused by factors external to the individual, as compared with Europeans and Americans who have more freedom about how to behave. Asians subordinate their preferences and coordinate their behaviors with those of the group, following prescribed roles and seeking to maintain harmony (Hsu, 1981; Markus & Kitayama, 1991; Triandis, 1995) in a pattern variously called *collectivist* or *interdependent*. In contrast, American life leaves the individual relatively free from social obligations and constraints and is full of choices—from whether to have chocolate or cherry mocha fudge to what sort of school to attend to whom to marry—a pattern variously called *individualist* or *independent*. Relatively few aspects of Asian life involve so much choice, and indeed Asian informants sometimes confide to me that they find themselves annoyed at the requirement that they constantly make what they regard as trivial choices—among a myriad of salad dressings or ways to have their eggs prepared or their hair cut. As Chiu (1972) put it, "Chinese are situation-centered. They are obliged to be sensitive to their environment. Americans are individual-centered. They expect their environment to be sensitive to them" (p. 36).

Consistent with the notion that individualistic, independent Americans experience choice more routinely than do collectivist, interdependent Asians, Heine and Lehman (1996) have found that the same operations that cause Americans to show "spreading apart of alternatives" in the free-choice-dissonance paradigm have no effect on the evaluations of Japanese people. They explain this by noting that Americans constantly have the experience of making choices and come to care a great deal about their competence as decision makers. Difficult decisions such as those engineered by experimenters in free-choice studies make Americans uncomfortable, and they can feel better about themselves by amplifying the difference in the value of the alternatives and hence feeling more confident about their competence as decision makers (Steele, 1988). Because choices are less frequent for Japanese people and because their sense of self is less bound up with feeling themselves to be competent decision makers, at least for trivial matters, Japanese people do not show the dissonance-reduction effects.

Similarly, Iwao (1996) has shown that Americans and Japanese people differ greatly in their preferred responses to the discovery that they disagree with someone else's opinion regarding an important matter. Americans are uncomfortable with the discrepancy and reported that they would try to reduce it in various ways including trying to change the other person's opinion, or at least trying to change the subject and avoid discussion of it. For Japanese people, on the other hand, who constantly have to deal with others in situations where consensus and harmony is valued, the discrepancy seems not to be as troublesome. They were more likely to report preferring to express public agreement with the other person's opinion while leaving their own views intact. Needless to say, Americans find this alternative dishonest. Americans place a strong value on consistency between attitudes and behaviors and between expressed attitudes and privately held attitudes—a luxury they are allowed because they do not normally operate in situations with social constraints sufficiently strong as to require frequent discrepancies in these respects. So the basic reactions to attitudinal imbalance in Heider's sense seem to be quite different in the two cultures, with Japanese being relatively content to accept imbalanced relations.

The same cultural differences in the importance of attitude–behavior consistency may mean that Asians are less likely to experience dissonance when placed in a situation where they are required to engage in some behavior that does not follow from their attitudes. And indeed, there is evidence that this is the case. For example, Choi (1992) attempted to replicate with Korean study participants the classic Festinger and Carlsmith (1959) experiment in which participants were offered a small or a large amount of money for giving a counterattitudinal opinion and found that incentive had no effects on subsequent attitudes. Such a failure is consistent with the notion that Asians are accustomed to acting in ways that follow from social role and situational context and not from private belief. Hence counterattitudinal behavior may produce less discomfort for Asians.

Thus there is some evidence from the social psychological literature that is consistent with the ethnographic record suggesting that Asians live in societies where tradition and role expectations and the need for harmony are far greater than is typical for Americans, and where there are fewer choices to make and less of a requirement that behaviors are in accord with attitudes. This characterization suggests that Asians would understand their own and others' behavior as being more directed from the outside, and less an expression of free will, than would Americans. It is therefore natural that Asians would be less susceptible to the correspondence bias. The differences derive from theory, by this account, and the differences in theory derive from the life circumstances of Asians and Americans. Life is situationally determined for Asians to a greater degree than for Americans so Asians are situationists. Life is a function of choices, preferences, and dispositions for Americans to a greater degree than for Asians so Americans are dispositionists.

But note that the evidence just presented about dissonance and balance effects indicates that the different theoretical views about causality separating Americans and Asians also entail very important social and cognitive process differences. Content and process are bound up together in fact. Because Americans believe in broad dispositions and believe their choices and other behaviors are guided by them, they are subject to dissonance- and inconsistency-reduction processes that are not required for Asians, or at least are not required for the same sort of relatively trivial discrepancies that motivate Americans to engage in these processes. The belief that choices are important and decisions reflect on one's competence results in an eagerness to alter the attitudinal terrain after choosing one object over another. The belief that one's behavior is a function of one's attitudes and preferences may set one up for the requirement to change one's attitudes after engaging in behavior that would seem to contradict one's attitudes. In contrast, the belief that suppression of one's personal preferences and beliefs is sometimes necessary for harmony and polite discourse may make one highly accepting both of states of attitudinal imbalance and of expressing opinions one does not hold. If something like this account of cultural differences is correct, then it makes little sense to distinguish sharply between social ontology and cognitive process.

Differences in Attention and Perception

Differences in social theory, and differences in cognitive processes driven by such differences, should produce still other important differences, notably in the domain of attention. If I believe certain things about social causality and I engage in certain cognitive processes as a consequence of those beliefs, it is natural that my attention will be directed toward aspects of the environment that make sense given those beliefs and cognitive processes. Thus if Asians are inclined to believe their behavior must be coordinated with the social context, and Americans are inclined to believe their behavior is caused by their dispositions, it is reasonable to assume the attention of the two groups will be differently directed. Asians could be expected to attend more to the external environment and to relations between a particular salient object and the environment. Americans could be expected to attend more to the object in isolation from the environment and to focus relatively more on their own preferences, attitudes, dispositions, and choices. If the two groups are differentially attuned in this way, Asians could be expected to focus their attention on the global field and Americans could be expected to focus their attention more on individual objects and on the self.

There is a fair amount of evidence, some going back a good bit in time, providing support for these expectations. Abel and Hsu (1949) showed that when responding to Rorschach cards, Asian-born Chinese people were more likely to give whole-card responses that were based on the entire gestalt of the figure on the card, while American-born Chinese people were more likely to give part responses, focusing on smaller individual components of the whole.

Other research suggesting that Asians and Americans direct their attention differently was conducted by Peng and Nisbett (1998). They presented Chinese and American study participants (all of whom were undergraduate students) with a bifurcated computer monitor screen: On one side was displayed one of two arbitrary figures (e.g., a schematic medal or a schematic light bulb). Immediately following, on the other side of the screen, one of a pair of different arbitrary symbols was displayed. The participant's task was to guess, after a series of ten presentations, what the degree of covariation was between figures on the left and figures on the right. The actual covariation was set at one of three levels. One level was a random degree of association, meaning that the probability of a given picture on the right was independent of the symbol on the left. The other two levels of association corresponded to Pearson correlation coefficients of about .40 and about .60 respectively. Participants were also asked how confident they were about their guess. Finally, they were presented with one of the two symbols on the left and asked to predict which symbol would come up on the right.

Chinese participants reported higher levels of association than American participants and were more confident about their guesses about covariation. The Chinese participants' confidence about their guesses was also better calibrated, that is, the higher the actual correlation the higher the confidence about covariation judgments for the Chinese participants. This was much less true for American participants. Finally, Americans seem to have made their covariation judgments largely on the basis of initial observations rather than on the basis of continued monitoring of the covariation. When participants were presented with a symbol on the left and asked to predict what would come up on the right, American participants' judgments were overwhelmingly the same as the initial pairing they had seen. Chinese participants' guesses, in contrast, reflected accurate judgments about covariation rather than use of this simple and often erroneous heuristic.

In order to show that the Peng and Nisbett (1998) results were not due simply to the Chinese participants taking the task more seriously, the nature of the task was changed in a way that was expected to affect the performance of the two groups differently. Participants were given control of presentation of stimuli on the left. They were allowed to choose the interval between stimulus presentations on the left and which stimulus to present. What appeared on the right was random, so that the correlations that participants saw were centered around, but not always equal to, zero. It was anticipated that injecting the element of illusory control into the procedure in this way would prompt Americans to attend more to the display, causing them to see more covariation and be more confident than when they lacked control. This was the case.

Differential Attention and Categorization

Another implication of the differential-attention hypothesis is that Americans should be more concerned with the category membership of the object. Indeed, this point is central to Aristotle's essence theory of the behavior of physical and social objects, by considering the category membership of the object people can know its properties, which can then be used to predict its behavior. For Asians, on the other hand, categories should be less important because it is always the relation between the object and the environment that is determinative of behavior, not the object's properties alone. This contention about the relative unimportance of categories in the East has been made by the British intellectual historians Joseph Needham (1962) and G. E. R. Lloyd (1990) and the Japanese philosopher Hajime Nakamura (1964/1985). These scholars have also argued that Asians in general are more attuned to the field in which the object is located than are Westerners, as reflected by the fact that action at a distance (e.g., a correct appreciation of the effect of the moon on the tides) was understood by Chinese scientists 1,500 years before it was understood by Western scientists.

Two lines of evidence support the hypothesis that Asians are less concerned with category membership than are Westerners. Work by Chiu (1972), showed that Chinese people, when asked to group objects, do so relationally rather than categorically. When shown a man, a woman, and a baby and asked to group the two that belong together, American participants placed the man and the woman together on the grounds that both are adults. Chinese participants were more likely to place the woman with the baby on the grounds that the woman nurses the baby. Categories, of course, should be more important to the individual who is focusing on the object, while relations between objects should be more salient to the individual who is responding to the entire field.

More recent research, by Choi, Nisbett, and Smith (in press), indicated that categories are used for purposes of induction more by Americans than by Koreans. Osherson, Smith, Wilkie, Lopez, and Shafir (1990) showed that people make use of categories for inductive inferences both about particular objects that are members of the category and about the category as a whole. Participants were shown two arguments and asked to indicate which they thought was more convincing with respect to a given conclusion. For example, they were given the following arguments, and asked to judge which was the better one:

1. Lions use norepinephrine as a neurotransmitter.
    Giraffes use norepinephrine as a neurotransmitter.
    _____
    Rabbits use norepinephrine as a neurotransmitter.

2. Lions use norepinephrine as a neurotransmitter.
    Tigers use norepinephrine as a neurotransmitter.
    _____
    Rabbits use norepinephrine as a neurotransmitter.

To the extent that participants are tacitly attending to the category *mammal,* they should prefer the first argument because lions and giraffes do a better job of covering the mammal category than do lions and tigers. This greater coverage or diversity encourages generalization more. Osherson et al. (1990) also found that greater numbers of exemplars within a category increased willingness to generalize, whereas adding an exemplar outside the category decreased willingness to generalize.

If categories are less salient to Asians, they might be less likely to differentiate between arguments on the basis of diversity, number of cases within a category, or introduction of a case outside the target category. And indeed this was what Choi and his colleagues (in press) found, unless categories were made salient by asking participants to generalize to *mammals* rather than just to an individual mammal. When categories were made salient in this way, Koreans were just as responsive to diversity, number, and category inclusion as were Americans.

There was a set of in press reversals of these findings (Choi et al., in press). When the category was a social one, namely different types of professions, and the attribute in question was behavioral, namely preferences such as between jazz and classical music, Koreans were actually more influenced by categories in their inductions about individual cases than were Americans. Continuing the symmetry, when the category was mentioned, Americans made as much use of it as did Koreans. To extrapolate more than is quite justified at this point, it would appear that categories are less important to Koreans, unless those categories refer to social events, which might be expected to be more important to Asians than to Westerners.

Field Dependence and Independence

If it is different cultural features related to interdependence versus independence that explain these perceptual differences, there is no reason to assume that the terms *Asian* and *Western* are the appropriate ones to describe the sorts of ontological, cognitive process, and attentional differences I have been describing. And in fact there is good evidence that there are cognitive differences of this sort associated with interdependence versus independence differences unrelated to geographical origins. Witkin and his colleagues (e.g., Witkin & Berry, 1975; Witkin, Dyk, Faterson, Goodenough, & Karp, 1962; Witkin & Goodenough, 1977; Witkin et al., 1974) had a large program examining what they called *psychological differentiation,* or the ability to distinguish various aspects of the visual field from one another. Differentiation or field independence was measured in a variety of ways, including the ability to detect a figure embedded in a larger, more complex one and the ability to turn a rod into an upright position when one is being thrown off by the orientation of a surrounding frame. All of these tasks require the ability to ignore the whole or to differentiate between a particular object and other nearby objects in order to see the object in itself or in order to form a new relationship between the object and other objects.

Dershowitz (1971) studied the field dependence of Orthodox Jewish boys, assimilated Jewish boys, and White Protestant boys. Dershowitz argued that the socialization of the Orthodox boys was of a sort designed to produce obedience and conformity, with the mother playing a dominant role in demanding proper behavior in everyday life settings and the father being heavily involved in spiritual and religious development. Using several different tests of field dependence, Dershowitz found that his Orthodox participants were more field dependent than his Protestant participants, with the assimilated Jewish boys falling between the two groups. Other studies found similar differences, even when Jewish and non-Jewish subjects were matched on verbal ability (Adevai, Silverman, & McGough, 1970; Meizlik, 1973). In addition, Witkin et al. (1974) found that boys from communities emphasizing conformity in Holland, Italy, and Mexico, were more field dependent than boys from communities in the same countries where socialization practices were more likely to emphasize independence and initiative. Witkin and Goodenough (1977) also found that field dependence measured by their various cognitive tests was related to U.S. participants' differential tendencies to attend to social information obtained from observing other people's behavior, for example, attending to an experimenter's face while solving a problem in her presence.

Other contrasts on related cognitive dimensions within the Western world might be expected to show differences between cultures. Triandis and his colleagues (1986) and Hofstede (1991) have shown that many Hispanic groups are highly collectively oriented or interdependent. Thus we might expect that, though Western, they show more "Eastern" cognitive patterns than Anglo-Americans. This hypothesis has been examined with the spontaneous trait inference paradigm of Winter and Uleman (1984), who found that when Anglo-American participants read sentences about the behavior of a person and are subsequently asked to recall them, they recall the sentence better when primed with a trait word that describes the behavior. Indeed, a trait word is a better prime than one of the words that was part of the predicate of the original sentence. Newman (1993), however, has found that his Hispanic participants were less likely to make spontaneous trait inferences than his Anglo-American participants, a finding replicated by Zarate and Uleman (1994). In addition, Newman (1991) found that Hispanic participants were more likely to predict behavior from situational information than were his Anglo-American participants. Finally, Duff, Newman, and Wolsko (1995) found that the tendency to make spontaneous trait inferences was associated with individual differences in orientation toward *idiocentrism*, that is, the preference for individualist beliefs and values, among U.S. participants.

Origins of Cultural Differences

Why might cultures differ in orientations toward other people and the field versus the self and isolated objects? Several theorists have proposed that economies prompt different social orientations and resultant cognitive styles along lines that resemble the ones discussed here. Barry, Child, and Bacon (1959); Witkin and Berry (1975); and Berry (1967; Berry & Annis, 1974) have proposed that agriculturalists emphasize obedience, hierarchy, and harmonious relationships because these are useful attributes for pursuing that particular kind of economy. Hunters, on the other hand, have little need for complex cooperative social arrangements and benefit from individual initiative and independence. Witkin and Berry (1975) and Berry and Annis (1974) showed that the two different economies were indeed associated with different cognitive styles, the hunters being less field dependent than the agriculturalists. The relevance of differentiation theory, and the various findings related to it, is that Asians are in general still agriculturalists, or at least have been so until recent times. Europeans are not of course hunters (though much of Europe was based on hunting and herding economies to a greater degree and to a later point than Asia), but with every generation fewer and fewer people in the West are agriculturalists. Instead, Europeans have been industrial, and are now postindustrial, people. Berry (1981) has argued that industrial societies are more nearly like hunting societies than agricultural societies in their requirements for independence, self-reliance, and individual initiative as attributes helpful for the critical, creative, and achievement-oriented of the modern world.

Summary of Cultural Differences

Thus there is substantial evidence that reasoning about the social world is different in fundamental ways. Interdependent people seem to emphasize contextual explanations for events whereas independent people emphasize dispositional ones. Interdependent people take note of relationships whereas independent ones emphasize categories. And interdependent people have difficulty in differentiating the object from the field whereas independent ones are capable of focusing on the object and disentangling it from the field. All of these findings are consistent with the view that the correspondence bias is less common among interdependent people.

Note also that there are now two good explanations of why cultures might differ in their susceptibility to the correspondence bias: differences in theory and differences in attention. But it should be clear that these alternatives are going to turn out to be inseparable. The theoretical differences derive from living in different worlds, but these different worlds require focusing on different things. The member of the interdependent society must attend to the social world—to the field and to the relation of the self to the field as a whole. In contrast, the member of the independent society is allowed to attend to a discrete portion of the field, ignoring its relations to other portions of the field, and to attend to the relation of the self to that discrete portion. These differential attentional foci will in turn be reflected in beliefs about causality for particular physical and social events. Indeed there is a wealth of evidence that attentional focus is to a very substantial extent a determinant of causal attributions (Storms, 1973).

CONCLUSION

It appears as if phenomena such as a strong belief in essence and a susceptibility to the correspondence bias are going to turn out to be more culture-bound than social psychologists would have guessed. Societies that preach independence are more industrially based and provide multitudes of choices and decisions, and draw attention toward the isolated individual, independent of the field and its forces, as the causal agent. The processes associated with more agricultural, interdependent, and collectivist societies, on the other hand, integrate the individual in the field of social roles and constraints and, therefore, appropriate causality to the forces in that field. Some social psychologists may be inclined to use this fact as one more indication that members of the field are condemned to studying historical accidents. Others will feel that the cultural differences bring the field closer to an understanding of the essence of what it means to be human. If one can ever be allowed to make a correspondent inference without fear of contradiction it is that, based on observation of many aspects of his behavior, Ned would have been firmly on the side of essence.

REFERENCES

Abel, T. M., & Hsu, F. I. (1949). Some aspects of personality of Chinese as revealed by the Rorschach Test. *Journal of Projective Techniques, 13*, 285–301.

Adevai, G., Silverman, A. J., & McGough, W. E. (1970). Ethnic differences in perceptual testing. *International Journal of Social Psychiatry, 16*, 237–239.

Barry, H., Child, I., & Bacon, M. (1959). Relation of child training to subsistence economy. *American Anthropologist, 61*, 51–63.

Berry, J. W. (1967). Independence and conformity in subsistence-level societies. *Journal of Personality and Social Psychology, 7*, 415–418.

Berry, J. W. (1981). Developmental issues in the comparative study of psychological differentiation. In R. H. Munroe, R. L. Munroe, & B. B. Whiting (Eds.), *Handbook of cross-cultural human development* (pp. 475–499). New York: Garland Press.

Berry, J. W., & Annis, R. C. (1974). Ecology, culture and differentiation. *International Journal of Psychology, 9*, 173–193.

Champagne, A. B., Klopfer, L. E., & Anderson, J. H. (1980). Factors influencing the learning of classical mechanics. *American Journal of Physics, 48*, 1074–1079.

Choi, I. (1992). *Cognitive consequences of forced compliance* [in Korean]. Unpublished Bachelor's thesis, Seoul National University.

Choi, I., Nisbett, R. E., & Smith, E. E. (in press). Culture, category salience, and inductive reasoning. *Cognition.*

Chiu, L-H. (1972). A cross-cultural comparison of cognitive styles in Chinese and American Children. *International Journal of Psychology, 8,* 235–242.

Cousins, S. D. (1989). Culture and self-perception in Japan and the United States. *Journal of Personality and Social Psychology, 56,* 124–131.

Dershowitz, Z. (1971). Jewish subcultural patterns and psychological differentiation. *International Journal of Psychology, 6,* 223–231.

Duff, K. J., Newman, L. S., & Wolsko, C. (1995, May). *Culture and spontaneous trait inference.* Paper presented at the Annual Meeting of the Midwestern Psychological Association, Chicago.

Festinger, L., & Carlsmith, J. M. (1959). Cognitive consequences of forced compliance. *Journal of Abnormal and Social Psychology, 58,* 203–210.

Gilbert, D. T., & Malone, P. S. (1995). The correspondence bias. *Psychological Bulletin, 117,* 21–38.

Heider, F. (1958). *The psychology of interpersonal relations.* New York: Wiley.

Heine, S., & Lehman, D. R. (1996). *Culture, dissonance, and self-affirmation.* Unpublished manuscript, University of British Vancouver.

Hirschfeld, L. (1996). *Race in the making: Cognition, culture, and the child's construction of human kinds.* Cambridge, MA: MIT Press.

Hofstede, G. (1991). *Cultures and organizations: Software of the mind.* London: McGraw-Hill.

Hsu, F. (1981). *American and Chinese: Passage to differences.* Honolulu: University of Hawaii Press.

Iwao, S. (1996). *Social psychological models of social behavior: Is it not time for West to meet East?* Unpublished manuscript, Institute for Communication Research, Keio University.

Jones, E. E., & Davis, K. E. (1965). From acts to dispositions: The attribution process in person perception. In L. Berkowitz (Ed.), *Advances in experimental social psychology* (Vol. 2, pp. 220–266). San Diego, CA: Academic Press.

Jones, E. E., & Harris, V. A. (1967). The attribution of attitudes. *Journal of Experimental Social Psychology, 3,* 1–24.

Jones, E. E., & Nisbett, R. E. (1972). The actor and the observer: Divergent perceptions of the causes of behavior. In E. E. Jones, D. E. Kanouse, H. H. Kelley, R. E. Nisbett, S. Valins, & B. Weiner (Eds.), *Attribution: Perceiving the causes of behavior* (pp. 79–94). Morristown, NJ: General Learning Press.

Lee, F., Hallahan, M., &, Herzog, T. (1996). Explaining real life events: How culture and domain shape attributions. *Personality and Social Psychology Bulletin, 22,* 732–741.

Lewin, K. (1935). The conflict between Aristotelian and Galilean modes of thought in contemporary psychology. *Journal of General Psychology, 5,* 141–177.

Linville, P. W., & Jones, E. E. (1980). Polarized appraisals of out-group members. *Journal of Personality and Social Psychology, 38,* 689–703.

Lloyd, G. E. R. (1990). *Demystifying mentalities.* New York: Cambridge University Press.

Markus, H. R., & Kitayama, S. (1991). Cultural variation in the self-concept. Culture and self: Implications for cognition, emotion and motivation. *Psychological Review, 98,* 224–253.

McCloskey, M. (1983). Intuitive physics. *Scientific American, 24,* 122–130.

Meizlik, F. (1973). *Study of the effect of sex and cultural variables on field independence/dependence in a Jewish sub-culture.* Unpublished master's thesis. City University of New York.

Miller, J. G. (1984). Culture and the development of everyday social explanation. *Journal of Personality and Social Psychology, 46,* 961–978.

Morris, M. W. (1993). *Culture and cause: American and Chinese understandings of physical and social causality.* Unpublished doctoral dissertation, University of Michigan.

Morris, M. W., Nisbett, R. E., & Peng, K. (1995). Causal attribution across domains and cultures. In D. Sperber, D. Premack, & A. J. Premack (Eds.), *Causal cognition.* Oxford, England: Clarendon Press.

Morris, M. W., & Peng, K. (1994). Culture and cause: American and Chinese attributions for social and physical events. *Journal of Personality and Social Psychology, 67,* 949–971.

Nakamura, H. (1964/1985). *Ways of thinking of Eastern peoples.* (Philip P. Wiener, Ed.). Honolulu: University of Hawaii Press.

Needham, J. (1962). *Science and civilisation in China.* New York: Cambridge University Press.

Newman, L. S. (1991). Why are traits inferred spontaneously? A developmental approach. *Social Cognition, 9,* 221–253.

Newman, L. S. (1993). How individualists interpret behavior: Idiocentrism and spontaneous trait inference. *Social Cognition, 11,* 243–269.

Osherson, D. N., Smith, E. E., Wilkie, O., Lopez, A., & Shafir, E. (1990). Category-based induction. *Psychological Review, 97,* 185–200.

Peng, K., & Nisbett, R. E. (1998). *Cultural differences in the detection of co-variation.* Unpublished manuscript, University of Michigan.

Quattrone, G. A., & Jones, E. E. (1980). The perception of variability within in-groups and out-groups: Implications for the law of small numbers. *Journal of Personality and Social Psychology, 38,* 141–152.

Ross, L. (1977). The intuitive psychologist and his shortcomings. In L. Berkowitz (Ed.), *Advances in Experimental social psychology* (Vol. 10). New York: Academic Press.

Ross, L., & Nisbett, R. E. (1991). *The person and the situation: Perspectives of social psychology.* New York: McGraw-Hill.

Ross, M. (1975). Salience of reward and intrinsic motivation. *Journal of Personality and Social Psychology, 32,* 245–254.

Shweder, R. A., & Bourne, E. J. (1982). Does the concept of person vary cross-culturally? In A. J. Marsella & G. M. White (Eds.), *Cultural conceptions of mental health and therapy* (pp. 130–204). London: Reidel.

Steele, C. M. (1988). The psychology of self-affirmation: Sustaining the integrity of the self. In L. Berkowitz (Ed.), *Advances in Experimental Social Psychology (Vol. 21).* Orlando, FL: Academic Press.

Storms, M. D. (1973). Videotape and the attribution process: Reversing actors' and observers' points of view. *Journal of Personality and Social Psychology, 27,* 165–175.

Triandis, H. C. (1995). *Individualism and collectivism.* Boulder, CO: Westview Press.

Triandis, H. C., Bontempo, R., Betancourt, H., Bond, M., Leung, K., Brenes, A., Georgas, J., Hui, C. H., Marin, G., Setiadi, B., Sinha, J. B. P., Verna, J., Spangenberg, J., Touzard, H., & Montmollin, G. (1986). The measurement of etic aspects of individualism and collectivism across cultures. *Australian Journal of Psychology, 38,* 257–267.

Winter, L., & Uleman, J. S. (1984). When are social judgments made? Evidence for the spontaneousness of trait inferences. *Journal of Personality and Social Psychology, 47,* 237–252.

Witkin, H. A., & Berry, J. W. (1975). Psychological differentiation in cross-cultural perspective. *Journal of Cross Cultural Psychology, 6,* 4–87.

Witkin, H. A., Dyk, R. B., Faterson, H. F., Goodenough, D. R., & Karp, S. A. (1962). *Psychological differentiation.* New York: John Wiley.

Witkin, H. A., & Goodenough, D. R. (1977). Field dependence and interpersonal behavior. *Psychological Bulletin, 84,* 661–689.

Witkin, H. A., Price-Williams, D., Bertini, M., Christiansen, B., Oltman, P. K., Ramirez, M., & Van Meel, J. (1974). Social conformity and psychological differentiation. *International Journal of Psychology, 9,* 11–29.

Zanna, M. P., Lepper, M. R., & Abelson, R. P. (1973). Attentional mechanisms in children's devaluation of a forbidden activity in a forced-compliance situation. *Journal of Personality and Social Psychology, 28,* 355–359.

Zarate, M. A., & Uleman, J. S. (1994). *Lexical decision evidence that Anglos do, and Chicanos do not make spontaneous trait inferences.* Unpublished manuscript, University of Texas at El Paso.

PART TWO

The Self

4

The Interface Between Intrapsychic and Interpersonal Processes: Cognition, Emotion, and Self as Adaptations to Other People

Roy F. Baumeister

M y mentor, Edward E. Jones, spent much of his career and achieved great recognition for his work on two main issues. One was an interpersonal one: ingratiation. The other was an intrapsychic one: motivated attribution. He also had a great deal of success studying the interface between these two, such as in his studies of how interpersonal patterns of self-presentation and ingratiation depend on the attributional processes that occur inside the individual. The interface between interpersonal concerns and intrapsychic processes—where inside meets outside—is a fertile one, and one can continue to mine it for new insights. To do so is to honor Jones by emulating his example.

The central argument of this chapter is that intrapsychic processes, such as attribution and emotion, are often driven by interpersonal motives. It is not only or always the other way around. One reason for the expansion of research interest in attribution and social cognition is the widespread assumption that social behavior follows from these intrapsychic processes, and undoubtedly there are many causal patterns of

The author gratefully acknowledges National Institute of Mental Health Grants MH 51482 and 43826, both of which contributed to the preparation of this chapter.

that nature. But probably the reverse is more common and more fundamental: The intrapsychic patterns of responses are adaptations to the interpersonal environment. In other words, although interpersonal behavior may often follow from attributions, it may also be true that the need to cope with and succeed in the interpersonal world causes people to make attributions in certain patterns.

To illustrate the contrast, it is useful to consider the definition of *ingratiation* used by E. Jones (1964) and E. Jones and Wortman (1973): Ingratiation is "a class of strategic behaviors, illicitly designed to influence a particular other person concerning the attractiveness of one's personal qualities" (E. Jones & Wortman, 1973, p. 1). Although this definition is quite serviceable and I have used it in my undergraduate lectures for years, something about it always bothered me. It is quite dreadfully cold, in the sense that it lacks all feeling, emotion, and desire. In this phrasing, the goal of ingratiation is not to get them to like you but to get them to regard you as having likable traits.

Thus, in this view, the interpersonal actions, such as ingratiation, derive from a fundamental motivation that is based on concern with the self. The interpersonal processes are designed to construct a particular image of self. Jones and Wortman (1973) went on to point out that ingratiation serves to enhance power, because if a person likes you, he or she will be reluctant to withhold rewards or thwart your endeavors, because to do so would cause him or her to suffer. Thus, they said, success at ingratiation will increase one's chances of securing and keeping material rewards.

Undoubtedly these arguments are correct. Yet perhaps they omit another key aspect of the process. Many people seek the liking of others without having material rewards in mind. Indeed, considerable evidence suggests that happiness and well-being depend on being liked at least as much as on material rewards (for reviews, see Argyle, 1987; Baumeister, 1991; Campbell, 1981; Myers, 1992). The interpersonal bond may often be the fundamental or ultimate need. Perhaps even the private concern with self-esteem is derived from a more basic and fundamental need to be accepted and liked by others.

I address these ideas among others in this chapter. I proceed as follows. I first examine the interface between interpersonal and intra-psychic processes to develop the view that the interpersonal processes are often the basic, fundamentally motivating ones, so that the intra-psychic processes (cognition, emotion, and self-conception) are deriv-ative. Following that I briefly consider another interpersonal motive, namely power. The next section will then take a close look at some patterns of motivated cognition (specifically, self-deception) to examine the balance between intrapsychic and interpersonal processes. Following that, the role of the self as an interpersonal tool is considered.

BELONGINGNESS AND INTRAPSYCHIC PROCESSES

There is ample evidence in the work of Jones and many others that people have strong, pervasive concerns with maintaining favorable im-ages of themselves as well as with getting along with other people. The chicken-or-egg question remains, however: Which one comes first? Much of Jones's thinking reflects the view that concern with self-evaluation is the most fundamental concern (see, e.g., his theory about self-handicapping: E. Jones & Berglas, 1978). Interpersonal activities are aimed toward that end.

Yet one could just as well argue the opposite—namely, that the most basic motivation is for maintaining interpersonal relations, and concern with self-esteem is merely an adaptation to help one achieve that interpersonal end. On an a priori basis, one would argue that a basic motivation would presumably be something deeply instilled in human nature, presumably by evolutionary processes. The survival and reproductive benefits would therefore have to be quite strong and clear (e.g., Buss, 1991). And so one might well ask which motive has the clearer advantages for survival and reproduction: self-esteem or inter-personal connectedness?

The benefits of self-esteem are rather scarce and marginal, despite the currently popular view in American pop culture that raising self-esteem can solve most personal and social problems (for critiques, see Colvin & Block, 1994; Dawes, 1994). Thinking well of oneself does not lead in any direct or obvious way to better chances for living longer, avoiding danger, or reproducing. High self-esteem may have some small advantages for boosting the confidence that helps one persist in the face of failure (e.g., Shrauger & Sorman, 1977). On the other hand, that same confidence can make people take dangerous and costly risks, leading to poorer outcomes, in some circumstances (Baumeister, Heatherton, & Tice, 1993). In short, the drive for high self-esteem does not seem a strong candidate for a fundamental motivation, given its mixed and small contribution to survival and reproduction.

In contrast, interpersonal belongingness seems likely to have clear and strong advantages for both survival and reproduction. In the primeval forest, groups afforded safety against predators and enemies (Bowlby, 1969, 1973). Some degree of affiliation is necessary to conceive children, and lasting relationships between sexual partners would increase the offspring's chances of surviving to the point at which they would reproduce (Buss, 1991; Shaver, Hazan, & Bradshaw, 1988). Groups can also accumulate and pass along information, and they can maximize efficiency by the division of labor. Indeed, some theorists have proposed that small groups are the single most important evolutionary adaptation of human beings (Barchas, 1986). Thus, the drive to form and maintain social bonds is very plausible as a basic motivation because of strong and multiple evolutionary advantages.

This is not to argue that evolutionary perspectives should be the sole or main criteria for evaluating psychological theories. It is quite clear that cultural socialization and immediate, situational influences are capable of exerting considerable effects on motivational patterns. My point is only that if something is to be proposed as a fundamental human motivation, an evolutionary argument ought to be at least plausible.

Overall, then, it seems far more plausible to suggest that people are programmed by nature and evolution to desire good interpersonal connections than to maintain high self-esteem. This is not to deny that people are often preoccupied with maintaining self-esteem, for clearly they are. It suggests, however, that attempts to explain interpersonal patterns as directed toward serving self-esteem may be overly reductionistic. The concern with interpersonal relations is probably more fundamental than the concern with self-appraisal.

Let me propose, therefore, that people have a fundamental, pervasive, and powerful motivation to form and maintain at least a minimum number of attachments. This "need to belong" might well be one of the central organizing principles in human behavior (Baumeister & Leary, 1995). If so, then cognition, emotion, and other intrapsychic processes may be adaptations that have developed to serve this basic interpersonal need.

I hasten to add that I am not proposing that the need to belong is the only human motive or even the only interpersonal motive. There is no theoretical need to reduce all of human striving to a single motivational construct, and indeed efforts to make such reductions seem doomed to failure. The hypothesis here is merely that the need to belong is one of the main and most powerful motives. Is it plausible, then, that the wide assortment of intrapsychic processes that social psychologists have demonstrated is in substantial part a reflection of adaptations to serve the need to belong?

Cognition

It is surprisingly easy to understand cognitive processes as designed to further interpersonal ends. The very fact that people think so much about other people—reflected in the existence of the field of social cognition, which has no rival in size or scope among other foci of cognitive processes, presumably because people think more about other people than about anything else—may well be indicative of this fundamental preoccupation with interpersonal relations.

Of course, the hypothesis of a need to belong requires more proof than the mere fact that people are prone to think about people. In particular, it seems essential to show that people think about actual and potential relationship partners in special ways and at greater length than they think about others.

Ample evidence supports that view. Close relationships operate as natural cognitive categories, in the sense that people spontaneously organize incoming information in terms of those relationships (Sedikides,

Olsen, & Reis, 1993). People do not necessarily store incoming information on a person-by-person basis when the information pertains to strangers, but they do store it on that basis when the information pertains to people they know and care about, such as in-group members (Ostrom, Carpenter, Sedikides, & Li, 1993; Pryor & Ostrom, 1981). Thus, information about relationship partners is processed in special ways.

One of the main thrusts of cognitive and attribution research in the 1970s was to show that information pertaining to the self was processed in special ways and was subject to particular patterns of bias (e.g., E. Jones, Rock, Shaver, Goethals, & Ward, 1968; E. Jones & Nisbett, 1971; Rogers, Kuiper, & Kirker, 1977). Subsequent work, beginning perhaps with Brenner's (1976) demonstration that the next-in-line encoding deficit occurs for one's dating partner as well as for oneself, has shown that close relationship partners receive similar cognitive treatment (e.g., Brown, 1986; Fincham, Beach, & Baucom, 1987; Linville & Jones, 1980; Perloff & Fetzer, 1986). Indeed, there is some evidence that people tend to confuse information about themselves with information about their relationship partners, thereby cognitively blurring the distinction between self and partner (Aron, Aron, Tudor, & Nelson, 1991).

The work by Anderson (1991) on attribution theory is especially important for understanding the interpersonal bases for cognitive patterns. Anderson tested the major attribution theories in the context of spontaneous attributional activity to learn whether people's spontaneous thoughts follow the attributional principles that had been demonstrated in laboratory studies with specially tailored measures. In other words, hundreds of studies had shown that people would make certain patterns of attributions when the questions were put to them in carefully structured questionnaires, but would the same patterns show up in unstructured responses? Anderson found that the insights of Jones and other attribution theorists were well supported, for indeed the spontaneous attributions exhibited most of the patterns that social psychologists had proposed. However, Anderson found one further dimension that had not been anticipated in the major attribution theories but that emerged repeatedly in spontaneous attributional comments: interpersonalness (e.g., inferring that someone did something because she is married). In fact, interpersonalness was the single biggest and most common category of attribution in Anderson's study.

The implication is that social psychologists had largely been doing a sound and correct job of mapping out the major dimensions of attribution theory, except that collectively they had missed the single biggest dimension. One possible reason for this oversight is a broad and reasonable assumption that informational and intrapsychic needs would be the main factors shaping attributional activity. It seems likely, however, that a fundamental concern with interpersonal relationships is also a powerful factor behind attributions.

Emotion

Like cognitive processes, emotional patterns can be understood as adaptations to serve interpersonal ends. It is clear that many emotions operate as signals to initiate, interrupt, or guide behavior (e.g., Frijda, 1986; Simon, 1967). Many of the behavioral patterns that activate emotion are interpersonal. Thus, emotions can be regarded as an inner signal system to help the individual regulate his or her behavior so as to form and maintain good relationships with others.

There are ample links between the formation of social bonds and positive emotion. Almost all occasions in which bonds are formed or solidified bring positive affect: joining an organization, becoming engaged, having a child, and the like. Falling in love is perhaps the prototype of an emotion helping to solidify an interpersonal bond (e.g., Shaver et al., 1988; Sternberg, 1986).

Negative affect, meanwhile, is strongly linked to threats, disruptions, or damage to interpersonal relationships. The majority of cases of anxiety can be understood as anticipatory responses that signal the danger of social rejection or exclusion (Baumeister & Tice, 1990). Depression is often linked to feeling that one is not accepted or included by others (Tambor & Leary, 1993). Jealousy is generally a response to perceived threats to interpersonal bonds, and it involves feeling that one is being abandoned or excluded (Pines & Aronson, 1983). Some degree of sexual jealousy appears to be cross-culturally universal (Reiss, 1986).

Even some emotions that are commonly regarded as private, intra-psychic patterns have strong interpersonal aspects. Guilt, in particular, seems to operate in multiple ways to improve and stabilize close relationships (Baumeister, Stillwell, & Heatherton, 1994). Guilt is tied to transgressions against significant others (W. H. Jones, Kugler, & Adams, 1995), and indeed guilt appears to be more interpersonal (and more tied to close relationships) than many other forms of negative affect—such as fear, which is often felt toward strangers (Baumeister, Reis, & Delespaul, 1995).

Summary

There is a broad assortment of evidence supporting the view that people have a fundamental need to belong, and it has not been my purpose to summarize all of it here (see Baumeister & Leary, 1995, for review). Instead, the purpose of this section has been the rather modest one of suggesting that some major intrapsychic patterns can be understood as serving interpersonal ends. Consistent with that view, it appears that both cognitive and emotional processes are highly sensitive to interpersonal circumstances, such as the formation or dissolution of close relationships. People reserve special ways of thinking for relationship partners, and emotional states go up and down in response to good and bad interpersonal changes.

Once again, I am not proposing that all cognition or emotion conform to this pattern. It would be recklessly reductionistic to propose that interpersonal belongingness is the sole determinant of emotional states, for example. But I am asserting that no theory of cognition or emotion can be adequate without covering these interpersonal functions. For example, early theories of guilt (e.g., Mosher, 1965) now seem foolish and absurd because of their failure to appreciate or explain the interpersonal and relationship functions that recent evidence has confirmed.

WHAT ABOUT POWER?

At the conference on which this volume is based, some of the most insightful responses to my comments on belongingness had to do with power. Jones's own work often referred to power. For example, he explained ingratiation as a means of enhancing one's power (E. Jones & Wortman, 1973). Likewise, E. Jones and Pittman (1982) provided a classic analysis of how to use self-presentation to manipulate other people in ways that will clearly enhance one's power.

It appears to me that one can make a case about power that would be parallel to the one I have made for belongingness. That is, power is not just a means to serve intrapsychic ends, such as enhancing self-esteem or gaining information. Rather, power is an interpersonal reality that is often sought as an end in itself. If one wishes to consider an evolutionary perspective, it is not hard to construct an argument that some motivations to seek power are innately prepared, insofar as power undoubtedly has both survival and reproductive benefits. And if one does not like evolutionary theorizing, then it still seems plausible that the potential benefits of power are so common and palpable that people would generally be motivated to pursue it.

Meanwhile, there is ample evidence that cognitive processes change in response to power, at least in the form of interpersonal dependency (Erber & Fiske, 1984). More broadly, one could plausibly propose that cognitive processes and emotional responses have developed in part as means of helping people adapt to power relationships.

Are there other variables as well, beyond power and belongingness? Social psychology has not developed good conceptual or empirical techniques for ascertaining when a certain list is exhaustive, and so any answer must be somewhat speculative. In that spirit, however, I wish to offer the impression that power and belongingness would jointly offer a conceptual foundation for a theory of interpersonal relations that could probably account for the majority of interpersonal interactions. Undoubtedly there are other factors and motives, but these others are probably less common and more restricted in scope than power and belongingness.

INTERPERSONAL CIRCUMSTANCES AND SELF-DECEPTION

For a close look at the interplay between intrapsychic and interpersonal processes, I have chosen the topic of self-deception. For years, the topic of self-deception languished in theoretical limbo, because researchers could not imagine how to satisfy the seeming requirement that the same person both know and not know a particular piece of information (i.e., the same person would be the deceiver and the deceived; see Sartre, 1953; also Gur & Sackeim, 1979). Yet the fact of self-deception seems so clear from everyday life that it was hard to deny it simply because researchers could not agree on an operational definition. Eventually, however, work by Jones and many others gradually suggested a way in which the paradox could be circumvented. Self-deception begins with systematic bias in attributional and other cognitive activity: People process information in biased ways, leading to preferred conclusions. In self-handicapping, for example, people manage to sustain inflated but gratifying views of themselves by discrediting in advance any information that might disconfirm them (E. Jones & Berglas, 1978).

For present purposes, the issue is not whether such biases occur—clearly they do—but rather what they have to do with interpersonal circumstances. If interpersonal processes are merely means toward intrapsychic ends, such as sustaining self-esteem, then how the information bears on the self should be the decisive factor in how it is processed. In contrast, if interpersonal concerns are truly fundamental, then they might well dictate some patterns of information processing regardless of, or even contrary to, self-interest.

One relevant set of findings shows that people seem to extend various self-serving biases to their close relationships. That is, it is well-known that people make a broad variety of errors and distortions in information processing that help them maintain favorable views of themselves (e.g., Greenwald, 1980; Taylor & Brown, 1988). As noted earlier, some of these biases and distortions are also made to favor positive views of relationship partners (Brown, 1986; Fincham et al., 1987; Perloff & Fetzer, 1986). Thus, the self is not as unique or special as once thought.

Even more important, some of the biases have recently been shown to apply to the relationship. That is, people engage in self-serving biases and other self-deceptive maneuvers so as to preserve positive views of their close relationships. For example, most happy couples report minimal conflict in their relationships. But when a sample of such couples was given an experimental manipulation telling them that a certain amount of conflict was a sign of a good, healthy relationship, suddenly they started reporting a great deal more conflict than previously (Murray & Holmes, 1993, 1994). Thus, they reconstrued information in a seemingly opposite fashion so as to draw the conclusion that depicted their relationship in the most positive light, just as people tend to interpret ambiguous information in ways that will be most flattering to the self (Dunning, Meyerowitz, & Holzberg, 1989).

My own dissertation, under Jones's direction, provided another form of evidence that interpersonal circumstances often intrude into self-deceptive processes (Baumeister & Jones, 1978). In that first study, individuals were randomly assigned to receive either a flattering or an unflattering personality evaluation, and they were also randomly assigned to either a private or a public condition—that is, either they were told that the evaluation was thoroughly confidential, or they were told that other people including an interaction partner had seen it. If the impact of the information on the self-concept had been people's only concern, then subsequent self-ratings should have been about the same regardless of whether the information was public or private, because the implications of the information about the self would be the same in both cases. In fact, however, people described themselves quite differently after the evaluations depending on whether the information was public or private. An important subsequent study by Greenberg and Pyszczynski (1985) showed that even confidential self-ratings changed in different ways depending on whether an identical evaluation had been public or private.

The implication of these studies is that the impact of feedback on the self-concept depends on the interpersonal status of the feedback. Identical information elicits different responses depending on whether other people know about it. This means, in turn, that the concern with self-esteem and self-appraisal is not the only motivation operating in such circumstances. Even when implications for self-appraisal are precisely the same, people respond differently depending on the interpersonal impact, which suggests that interpersonal concerns exist independently of the private concern with maintaining a certain opinion of oneself.

The impact of interpersonal circumstances on self-deception was made even more explicitly in a recent study. One popular and easy form of self-deception is simply to ignore unpleasant or unflattering feedback. Baumeister and Cairns (1992) operationalized this strategy by measuring how much time people spent reading unfavorable as opposed to favorable personality feedback. As in earlier work, we also varied whether the feedback was public or private. When it was private and confidential, people followed the standard self-deceptive strategy of skipping rapidly through unflattering information as opposed to lingering over pleasant, flattering information. When the information was public, however—that is, when an interaction partner was supposedly receiving the same information to read, as a way of learning about them—the tendency to ignore unflattering information was eliminated. In fact, it was reversed: People (especially repressors) spent more time reading the bad feedback than the flattering, favorable feedback. The reason was apparently that people wanted to know the details of the bad impression someone had of them.

Thus, disagreeable information can be safely dismissed and ignored only when it is known only to the self. When others know about it, it gains *social reality*, in the term of Wicklund and Gollwitzer (1982). The broader implication is that interpersonal circumstances exert a decisive influence over how information about the self is processed, even when the implications of that information for the self-concept are identical.

The view that other people may serve as a check on certain self-deceptive processes received support from another recent study (see Baumeister & Ilko, 1995). In this study, participants were instructed to write about the greatest success experience they had had in the past 2 years. Half of them were told that they would drop off their response anonymously, and no one would ever read it. The others were told that they would read their response aloud in front of a group of other students. The stories were then collected and coded for the degree to which people thanked others or acknowledged receiving help from other people, as opposed to claiming all the credit for themselves.

The stories they wrote turned out to depend heavily on whether the authors expected to read them aloud or not. When they did expect their accounts to be public, people modestly and generously shared the credit for their successes by thanking others for help and support. In their private accounts, however, there were very few signs of help from others. The implication is that the gratitude displayed in such public accounts is often quite shallow—possibly a concession to public norms of modesty, or an effort to humor others, or again a reflection of how the presence of other people provides a reality check that prevents certain self-flattering excesses (Baumeister & Ilko, 1995).

It would be a rash oversimplification to propose that interpersonal contacts and circumstances always elicit more accurate and balanced processing of information. Indeed, some patterns of attributional distortion seem to occur more commonly in public settings. Weary (1980) showed that people made more defensive, self-serving attributions for their outcomes when an observer and the experimenter had monitored their performance than when no one had been watching.

For present purposes, the key point is that how people process information about the self depends heavily on the interpersonal circumstances. The next decade will face the inviting theoretical challenge of resolving how self-flattering distortions are affected by the presence or interest of other people. In some ways people become more self-serving, in other ways less so, when other people are watching—all of which suggests that there are some subtle moderators that need to be identified and analyzed. In any case, however, it is no longer satisfactory to conceptualize self-deception entirely in terms of a person's private processing of information in relation to his or her self-concept. The psychological presence of other people must be accorded an important role in future theories about how people seek to fool and flatter themselves.

SELF AS INTERPERSONAL TOOL

Thus far I have proposed that the interface between interpersonal and intrapsychic processes may yield further insights if researchers considered intrapsychic processes as adaptations to interpersonal circumstances. This is to a substantial extent a reversal of the prevailing approach, which tends to assume that intrapsychic processes have causal primacy and that interpersonal events follow from them.

Perhaps the most striking theoretical challenge of the view I am espousing is to understand the self as a response to interpersonal events. A great many studies have documented that the way people interact with others is substantially dependent on efforts to maintain or enhance self-esteem, for example. How can that be turned around? After all, if self-esteem is the most fundamental motive, then no further explanations are needed for all the self-serving patterns that have been shown. But if people are originally and basically concerned with interpersonal ties such as belongingness, then where does self-esteem fit in?

One provocative answer has been provided by Leary, Tambor, Terdal, and Downs (1995). In this view, self-esteem functions as a measure of one's interpersonal status. The studies by Leary et al. found that self-esteem rises and falls with changes in interpersonal belongingness; for example, romantic or occupational rejections lower self-esteem. The researchers labeled self-esteem a *sociometer*, by which they meant an internal gauge designed to help people monitor their belongingness and know when to take steps to increase or strengthen their social ties. Self-esteem thus can be understood as an intrapsychic adaptation to the need for interpersonal connections.

Another way of understanding the interpersonal roots of self-esteem is to consider that self-esteem is based on almost exactly the same criteria that are used by groups to include or exclude individuals. Self-esteem is largely a matter of perceiving oneself as an attractive, competent, likable, and morally virtuous person (see the compilation in Baumeister, 1993). In parallel fashion, groups tend to reject or exclude individuals who are unattractive or unappealing, who lack the competence to contribute to group tasks, who are unpleasant or disagreeable or who in other ways make poor interaction partners, and who break the group's rules by dishonest or immoral actions. Self-esteem may thus function as an appraisal of how desirable a group member or relationship partner one is likely to be.

I hasten to add that this is not the only or the definitive view of self-esteem. Still, there does seem to be something fundamentally correct about it. At present, the links between self-esteem and social inclusion or attachment are being studied in diverse ways in many laboratories, and it is safe to say that a clearer and more definitive view of the interpersonal operation of self-esteem will be available in a few years.

The familiar correlation between self-esteem and anxiety is readily understandable in this connection. People with low self-esteem tend to show higher levels of anxiety than others (see Janis & Field, 1959). Anxiety, meanwhile, tends to be largely a response to actual or feared social exclusion (Baumeister & Tice, 1990). Low self-esteem is literally an appraisal that one has a relative lack of the traits that make one a desirable group member, and so it does carry the implication that one is more likely to experience rejection, exclusion, ostracism, and other forms of social failure. Presumably a history of experiences of social rejection may contribute to such a low level of self-regard.

There is a further twist to this analysis. After all, if self-esteem is an adaptation to interpersonal relationship status, then why would people seek to boost their self-esteem without necessarily increasing their social belongingness? As I have already indicated, abundant evidence suggests that people distort the feedback they receive in ways that flatter and enhance their views of themselves, without necessarily producing any corresponding improvement in their social ties. Would this pattern not be maladaptive?

In my view, the widespread tendency to seek self-esteem enhancement directly does indeed represent a somewhat maladaptive but all too understandable pattern. Because of the importance of maintaining good social ties, people are quite concerned with self-esteem as the internal measure of their eligibility for belongingness. Increases and drops in self-esteem carry strong emotional consequences, and so people become preoccupied with self-esteem for its own sake. The salience and emotional potency of the meter—self-esteem—are sufficient to make people address their efforts to the meter itself rather than to the underlying issues of relatedness. Efforts to boost self-esteem artificially can be compared to trying to twist the needle on a car's gas gauge or odometer: They may make the car look better to the driver even though they leave the underlying problems unresolved.

For example, consider someone who is vulnerable to social rejection because of being incompetent or dislikable. Anyone who appraises himself or herself as incompetent or dislikable might well have low self-esteem. If someone responds to this view by trying to improve his competence or likability, he might actually increase his chances of forming good social ties and eventually end up with higher self-esteem too. In contrast, someone who responds by simply trying to raise her opinion of herself may boost self-esteem without addressing the underlying interpersonal problem. In the short run, she will feel better—indeed, she is likely to feel better more rapidly than the person who sought to improve his competence, which takes more time. It may generally be easier and quicker to convince oneself that one is competent than actually to become more competent.

The preoccupation with boosting self-esteem can thus be compared to a kind of drug abuse. Drugs make people feel good by deceiving the natural mechanisms of the body. The human organism is well equipped to generate feelings of pleasure when certain favorable conditions are achieved. Drugs enable the person to feel similar pleasure without actually achieving those conditions. Boosting self-esteem directly is similar. In essence, one boosts self-esteem by convincing oneself that one is a desirable partner, without having to go through the effort of actually becoming a more desirable partner. One deceives the inner meter just as a drug might do, to enable oneself to feel good.

The drug abuse analogy brings up another seeming paradox of self-esteem, namely its role in interpersonal violence. There is a long tradition of regarding violence as the result of low self-esteem, which has occasionally led theorists to make the somewhat plausible but empirically doubtful conclusion that violence is a way of making friends (e.g., Toch, 1993). The evidence however shows that low self-esteem does not produce violence; rather, violence results from high but threatened self-esteem (see Baumeister, Smart, & Boden, 1996, for review). Yet this pattern again shows the interpersonal roots of self-esteem even in a sphere that is as fundamentally antisocial as violence. What actually happens most of the time is some variation on the following theme. A person (or group, or nation) holds a highly favorable, possibly inflated view of his (or, less often, her) worth, which is then disputed by someone else. Instead of accepting the negative feedback and revising his self-esteem in a downward direction, the person lashes out at the other person, as if hurting the other will somehow refute the other's criticism. Violence is thus an interpersonal, communicative act designed to preserve a highly favorable view of self. One can go on merrily thinking oneself a superior being, as long as all contrary views are suppressed by violent rebuttal and intimidation.

The more arduous task of making oneself into a desirable relationship partner is however something one cannot fully avoid. This raises the broader issue of what the self is for, in the sense of its basic functions. Although multiple functions and other roots of selfhood can be enumerated, it is clear that one vital function of the self is to attract and maintain interpersonal relationships. To some extent, people must make themselves sufficiently attractive, competent, likable, and moral so as to enable them to sustain at least a minimum number of relationships with others.

At some level, I think most people realize this. The vast self-improvement industry provides useful evidence. In the 1960s, American society embraced Maslowian notions of self-actualization to the extent that people believed it was desirable to improve oneself for the sake of achieving spiritual fulfillments and peak experiences (see Maslow, 1968). If one examines the actual behavior of seekers of self-improvement, however, these are far less geared toward cultivating spiritual experiences than toward improving one's eligibility for groups and relationships. For example, the most widespread form of self-improvement in today's America, and the one on which the greatest amounts of money are spent, is almost certainly dieting. Yet people do not so much diet for the sake of spiritual fulfillments or peak experiences or even for the alleged health benefits of dieting (which research continues to question); they diet to become more attractive. Likewise, people take courses, adopt hobbies, exercise, and do many other things mainly for the sake of making them more appealing to potential romantic partners, employers, universities, and other social groups.

In the final analysis, then, the self is an interpersonal tool. More precisely, it is an instrument that people fashion and modify to improve their chances for being included by other people in desirable social groups, ranging from multinational corporations to marital dyads. The self does not exist in a vacuum, independent of social ties, nor does it develop out of itself alone. It is a remarkably sensitive and powerful adaptation to the unstable but terribly important world of interpersonal relations.

CONCLUSION

Ned Jones was one of the most creative researchers ever to examine the interface between interpersonal and intrapsychic processes. One way to honor his memory is to look for insights where he looked at that same interface. I have suggested that there may be a great deal more to learn from examining that interface, to add to and build on to the insights that Jones and his colleagues contributed over the course of his illustrious career.

My suggestion has been that social and personality psychologists may benefit by reversing the causal assumptions that have dominated thinking in recent decades. More specifically, it may be useful and instructive to consider intrapsychic processes as adaptations to interpersonal circumstances and needs. The inner realities of emotion, attribution, cognition, and self may in many cases reflect attempts by the individual to satisfy fundamentally social needs. In plainer terms, people may have come to think and feel in particular ways because these help people to have more satisfying relationships with others.

REFERENCES

Anderson, C. A. (1991). How people think about causes: Examination of the typical phenomenal organization of attributions for success and failure. *Social Cognition, 9,* 295–329.

Argyle, M. (1987). *The psychology of happiness.* London: Methuen.

Aron, A., Aron, E. N., Tudor, M., & Nelson, G. (1991). Close relationships as including other in the self. *Journal of Personality and Social Psychology, 60,* 241–253.

Barchas, P. (1986). A sociophysiological orientation to small groups. In E. Lawler (Ed.), *Advances in group processes* (Vol. 3, pp. 209–246). Greenwich, CT: JAI Press.

Baumeister, R. F. (1991). *Meanings of life.* New York: Guilford Press.

Baumeister, R. F. (1993). (Ed.). *Self-esteem: The puzzle of low self-regard.* New York: Plenum Press.

Baumeister, R. F., & Cairns, K. J. (1992). Repression and self-presentation: When audiences interfere with self-deceptive strategies. *Journal of Personality and Social Psychology, 62,* 851–862.

Baumeister, R. F., Heatherton, T. F., & Tice, D. M. (1993). When ego threats lead to self-regulation failure: Negative consequences of high self-esteem. *Journal of Personality and Social Psychology, 64,* 141–156.

Baumeister, R. F., & Ilko, S. A. (1995). Shallow gratitude: Public and private acknowledgment of external help in accounts of success. *Basic and Applied Social Psychology, 16,* 191–209.

Baumeister, R. F., & Jones, E. E. (1978). When self-presentation is constrained by the target's knowledge: Consistency and compensation. *Journal of Personality and Social Psychology, 36,* 608–618.

Baumeister, R. F., & Leary, M. R. (1995). The need to belong: Desire for interpersonal attachments as a fundamental human motivation. *Psychological Bulletin, 117,* 497–529.

Baumeister, R. F., Reis, H. T., & Delespaul, P. A. E. G. (1995). Subjective and experiential correlates of guilt in everyday life. *Personality and Social Psychology Bulletin, 21,* 1256–1268.

Baumeister, R. F., Smart, L., & Boden, J. M. (1996). Relation of threatened egotism to violence and aggression: The dark side of high self-esteem. *Psychological Review, 103,* 5–33.

Baumeister, R. F., Stillwell, A. M., & Heatherton, T. F. (1994). Guilt: An interpersonal approach. *Psychological Bulletin, 115,* 243–267.

Baumeister, R. F., & Tice, D. M. (1990). Anxiety and social exclusion. *Journal of Social and Clinical Psychology, 9,* 165–195.

Bowlby, J. (1969). *Attachment and loss. Vol. 1: Attachment.* New York: Basic Books.

Bowlby, J. (1973). *Attachment and loss. Vol. 2: Separation anxiety and anger.* New York: Basic Books.

Brenner, M. W. (1976). *Memory and interpersonal relations.* Doctoral dissertation, University of Michigan, Ann Arbor, MI.

Brown, J. D. (1986). Evaluations of self and others: Self-enhancement biases in social judgments. *Social Cognition, 4,* 353–376.

Buss, D. M. (1991). Evolutionary personality psychology. *Annual Review of Psychology, 42,* 459–491.

Campbell, A. (1981). *The sense of well-being in America.* New York: McGraw-Hill.

Colvin, C. R., & Block, J. (1994). Do positive illusions foster mental health? An examination of the Taylor and Brown formulation. *Psychological Bulletin, 116,* 3–20.

Dawes, R. M. (1994). *House of cards: Psychology and psychotherapy built on myth.* New York: Free Press.

Dunning, D., Meyerowitz, J. A., & Holzberg, A. (1989). Ambiguity and self-evaluation: The role of idiosyncratic trait definitions in self-serving assessments of ability. *Journal of Personality and Social Psychology, 57,* 1082–1090.

Erber, F., & Fiske, S. T. (1984). Outcome dependency and attention to inconsistent information. *Journal of Personality and Social Psychology, 47,* 709–726.

Fincham, F. D., Beach, S. R., & Baucom, D. H. (1987). Attribution processes in distressed and nondistressed couples: 4. Self-partner attribution differences. *Journal of Personality and Social Psychology, 52,* 739–748.

Frijda, N. H. (1986). *The emotions.* Cambridge, England: Cambridge University Press.

Greenberg, J., & Pyszczynski, J. (1985). Compensatory self-inflation: A response to the threat to self-regard of public failure. *Journal of Personality and Social Psychology, 49,* 273–280.

Greenwald, A. G. (1980). The totalitarian ego: Fabrication and revision of personal history. *American Psychologist, 35,* 603–618.

Gur, R. C., & Sackeim, H. A. (1979). Self-deception: A concept in search of a phenomenon. *Journal of Personality and Social Psychology, 37,* 147–169.

Janis, I. L., & Field, P. (1959). Sex differences and personality factors related to persuasibility. In C. Hovland & I. Janis (Eds.), *Personality and persuasibility* (pp. 55–68, 300–302). New Haven, CT: Yale University Press.

Jones, E. E. (1964). *Ingratiation.* New York: Irvington.

Jones, E. E., & Berglas, S. C. (1978). Control of attributions about the self through self-handicapping strategies: The appeal of alcohol and the role of underachievement. *Personality and Social Psychology Bulletin, 4,* 200–206.

Jones, E. E., & Nisbett, R. E. (1971). *The actor and the observer: Divergent perceptions of the causes of behavior.* Morristown, NJ: General Learning Press.

Jones, E. E., & Pittman, T. S. (1982). Toward a general theory of strategic self-presentation. In J. Suls (Ed.), *Psychological perspectives on the self* (Vol. 1, pp. 231–262). Hillsdale, NJ: Erlbaum.

Jones, E. E., Rock, L., Shaver, K. G., Goethals, G. R., & Ward, L. M. (1968). Pattern of performance and ability attribution: An unexpected primacy effect. *Journal of Personality and Social Psychology, 10,* 317–340.

Jones, E. E., & Wortman, C. (1973). *Ingratiation: An attributional approach.* Morristown, NJ: General Learning Press.

Jones, W. H., Kugler, K., & Adams, P. (1995). You always hurt the one you love: Guilt and transgressions against relationship partners. In J. P. Tangney & K. W. Fischer (Eds.), *Self-conscious emotions: The psychology of shame, guilt, embarrassment, and pride* (pp. 301–321). New York: Guilford Press.

Leary, M. R., Tambor, E. S., Terdal, S. K., & Downs, D. L. (1995). Self-esteem as an interpersonal monitor: The sociometer hypothesis. *Journal of Personality and Social Psychology, 68,* 518–530.

Linville, P. W., & Jones, E. E. (1980). Polarized appraisals of out-group members. *Journal of Personality and Social Psychology, 38,* 689–703.

Maslow, A. H. (1968). *Toward a psychology of being.* New York: Van Nostrand.

Mosher, D. L. (1965). Interaction of fear and guilt in inhibiting unacceptable behavior. *Journal of Consulting Psychology, 29,* 161–167.

Murray, S. L., & Holmes, J. G. (1993). Seeing virtues in faults: Negativity and the transformation of interpersonal narratives in close relationships. *Journal of Personality and Social Psychology, 65,* 707–722.

Murray, S. L., & Holmes, J. G. (1994). Storytelling in close relationships: The construction of confidence. *Personality and Social Psychology Bulletin, 20,* 650–663.

Myers, D. (1992). *The pursuit of happiness.* New York: Morrow.

Ostrom, T. M., Carpenter, S. L., Sedikides, C., & Li, F. (1993). Differential processing of in-group and out-group information. *Journal of Personality and Social Psychology, 64,* 21–34.

Perloff, L. S., & Fetzer, B. K. (1986). Self-other judgments and perceived vulnerability to victimization. *Journal of Personality and Social Psychology, 50,* 502–510.

Pines, M., & Aronson, E. (1983). Antecedents, correlates, and consequences of sexual jealousy. *Journal of Personality, 51,* 108–135.

Pryor, J. M., & Ostrom, T. M. (1981). The cognitive organization of social life: A converging-operations approach. *Journal of Personality and Social Psychology, 41,* 628–641.

Reiss, I. L. (1986). A sociological journey into sexuality. *Journal of Marriage and the Family, 48,* 233–242.

Rogers, T. B., Kuiper, N. A., & Kirker, W. S. (1977). Self-reference and the encoding of personal information. *Journal of Personality and Social Psychology, 35,* 677–688.

Sartre, J.-P. (1953). *The existential psychoanalysis* (H. E. Barnes, Trans.). New York: Philosophical Library.

Sedikides, C., Olsen, N., & Reis, H. T. (1993). Relationships as natural categories. *Journal of Personality and Social Psychology, 64,* 71–82.

Shaver, P., Hazan, C., & Bradshaw, D. (1988). Love as attachment: The integration of three behavioral systems. In R. J. Sternberg & M. L. Barnes (Eds.), *The psychology of love* (pp. 68–99). New Haven, CT: Yale University Press.

Shrauger, J. S., & Sorman, P. B. (1977). Self-evaluations, initial success and failure, and improvement as determinants of persistence. *Journal of Consulting and Clinical Psychology, 45,* 784–795.

Simon, H. A. (1967). Motivational and emotional controls of cognition. *Psychological Review, 74,* 29–39.

Sternberg, R. J. (1986). A triangular theory of love. *Psychological Review, 93,* 119–135.

Tambor, E. S., & Leary, M. R. (1993). *Perceived exclusion as a common factor in social anxiety, loneliness, jealousy, depression, and low self-esteem.* Manuscript submitted for publication, Wake Forest University.

Taylor, S. E., & Brown, J. D. (1988). Illusion and well-being: A social psychological perspective on mental health. *Psychological Bulletin, 103,* 193–210.

Toch, H. (1993). *Violent men: An inquiry into the psychology of violence.* Washington, DC: American Psychological Association. (Original work published in 1969)

Weary, G. (1980). Examination of affect and egotism as mediators of bias in causal attributions. *Journal of Personality and Social Psychology, 38,* 348–357.

Wicklund, R. A., & Gollwitzer, P. M. (1982). *Symbolic self-completion.* Hillsdale, NJ: Erlbaum.

Belongingness, Power, and Interpersonal Effectiveness

George R. Goethals

My happy task in this volume is to comment on Roy Baumeister's chapter (see chapter 4) on the interface between intrapsychic and interpersonal processes. Clearly, Baumeister has emerged as one of the most distinguished of Ned Jones's many students. His chapter is typically thorough, intriguing, scholarly, and well-written. My commentary will attempt to summarize the highlights of Baumeister's argument, discuss how Ned might have reacted to them, and then offer my own thoughts on Baumeister's position.

BAUMEISTER'S ARGUMENT

The gist of Baumeister's argument is that intrapsychic processes are often driven by interpersonal processes, not the other way around. More specifically, he contends that a need simply to be liked, a need for interpersonal connections and belongingness, are primary drives, much more fundamental than a drive for self-esteem. Interpersonal behavior is undertaken for its own sake, not to serve self-esteem needs. Baumeister points out that emotions, such as love and guilt, function not as a form of self-regulation, but serve as an inner signal system enabling the individual to regulate interpersonal behavior in the interest of establishing good relationships. Baumeister further suggests that Ned considered ingratiation as deriving from a desire to construct a particular self-image, such that he viewed an intrapsychic process, self-construction, driving an interpersonal process, ingratiation. Finally, Baumeister suggests that Ned might have been closer to the target if he had seen ingratiating behaviors as designed to elicit liking for its own sake, and to satisfy the need for belongingness, rather than get others to perceive positive traits, for reasons such as enhancing power or confirming a particular image of self.

JONES'S LIKELY RESPONSE TO BAUMEISTER'S ARGUMENT

As Baumeister notes, Ned Jones did work very productively at the interface between intrapsychic and interpersonal processes and was fascinated by the interplay between them. It is difficult to say whether he would have agreed with Baumeister's critique of his approach to ingratiation, or his assertion of the primacy of a belongingness drive. It does seem important to try to examine Ned's analyses of what ingratiation fundamentally was, that is, his views on self-esteem and the self-concept, and on what were the most fundamental interpersonal and intrapsychic issues, and how he would have reacted to Baumeister's suggestion that interpersonal processes are basic and intrapsychic processes are derivative.

Personal and Theoretical Confluence: Ingratiation and Self-Handicapping

In meditating on Ned's likely responses to the argument offered by Baumeister, it is useful to consider the autobiographical nature of both his writing and his theoretical concerns. Ned was very concerned about power and strategic interaction generally, and I think concerned about the fragility of the self-concept. A more basic concern with interpersonal competence or efficacy tied these interests together. These themes seem clear in both his writing and his behavior.[1]

Ned was concerned with the ambiguity of behavior, of how the same behavior could have different strategic purposes. For example, a well-timed barb could be mean-spirited or it could be playful, part of the dance of ingratiation. In a discussion of using flattery or "other-enhancement" as a tactic of ingratiation, Ned wrote,

> Other-enhancement may paradoxically be expressed by apparent deflation of the other, as evidenced in the phenomenon of the friendly insult. Masculine small talk, especially, is frequently peppered with barbs, derogation, and sarcasm. The recipient of a friendly insult is given notice that he (a) has the attention of the communicator and (b) has the strength and good nature to survive such an attack. He may also infer from the tone and the context that the insulting comment is actually inapplicable to him, for if it were true it would never have been offered. Friendly insults serve another purpose as well: They provide a contrasting backdrop for the expression of occasional (but nevertheless highly important) positive comments. Such comments from one who is known for his caustic wit and malicious sense of humor are all the more significant to the recipient. (Jones, 1964, p. 33)

This passage always gave me courage to interpret Ned's barbs as really backhanded signs of positive regard. It also seemed to describe Ned himself with uncanny accuracy. While I generally think of Ned on the giving end of the barbs described in the passage above, I've also wondered about how Ned himself may have struggled to deal with

---

[1]In terms of his interest in power, and also games and strategy, I will never forget my first meeting with Ned. It was in September 1966, late in the morning, and I dropped in on Ned in his office at Duke University. He was to be my adviser during that first year of graduate study. It was great fun finally to meet him, and we chatted amiably until around noon. At that point he suggested we go to lunch. Embarrassed, I mumbled that I didn't have any money. Ned said that he would treat and that "that'll put me one-up on you." I didn't realize how diagnostic that remark was of Ned's interaction style, at least as I encountered it over the years.

sarcastic remarks from powerful others, especially during those times when he doubted his own competence and effectiveness. Quite striking is Ned's description of the person who is most likely to self-handicap, the individual who experiences noncontingent success:

> To the extent that individuals have passed through a history of noncontingent reward, they may have a strong sense of being impostors or pretenders. They do not deserve their rewards because they did not really do anything to earn them. They were just lucky, they happened to be in the right place at the right time ... any of these subjective hypotheses are consistent with the underlying fear that (a) successful performance cannot be repeated or sustained and (b) impostors must eventually pay for their inequitable current receipts. (Berglas & Jones, 1978, p. 407)

Maybe Ned did have deep concerns about self-worth and future performance—at least during the time he wrote on self-handicapping, the period his family called "the dark years"—that subtly interacted with his concerns about the nuances of banter and gamesmanship. But the latter concerns had considerable continuity in Ned's life and work. Baumeister cites Ned's theory of self-handicapping as suggesting that Ned felt that self-evaluation "is the most fundamental concern." However, I would argue that for Ned the strategic elements of ingratiation and interpersonal effectiveness were generally more basic. Moreover, concerns with interpersonal competence, such as those discussed by White (1963) and Bandura (1977), were of key importance to Ned. Neither self-evaluation nor belongingness were as fundamental and central than the motivation to possess control over one's environment, a motive well served by power. These concerns can be seen to underlie a great deal of what he researched, what he wrote and talked about, and what preoccupied him across both time and modality.

THEORETICAL FOUNDATION OF INGRATIATION

Beyond making inferences from passages in Ned's research that may be autobiographically based, we can ask more directly how he described the underpinning of ingratiation. Two items seem relevant. One is the key word *illicitly* in the definition of ingratiation. Ned thought of ingratiation as a highly strategic, largely self-conscious kind of behavior that was quite instrumental in its desired effects. It was the "illegitimate and seamy side of interpersonal communication" (Jones, 1964, p. 3). Second, in his important *Science* article on conformity as a tactic of ingratiation (Jones, 1965), Ned spelled out with great clarity the view that ingratiation stemmed from the desire of lower power people to reduce the power differential in a relationship. Thus it seems clear that Ned believed that the class of behaviors he called ingratiation is fundamentally designed to get liking from others that is useful extrinsically, not liking that satisfies basic needs for belongingness and affection. Professionally Ned was not interested in liking for liking's sake. He was interested in its utility. He may have given liking for liking's sake greater acknowledgment personally, but that idea was not in his writing.[2] However, Ned's focus may have been too narrow. Baumeister may be correct in asserting that these same behaviors, or other kinds of ingratiating behavior, may simply be performed to get other people to like you.

SUMMING UP NED'S LIKELY REACTION TO BAUMEISTER

Where does this leave us in speculating about how Ned might have reacted to Baumeister's arguments? First, despite the concern with protecting self-esteem that is, as Baumeister points out, at the heart of the work on self-handicapping, it seems clear to me that Ned would have felt very comfortable with Baumeister's basic premise that interpersonal processes have some priority in their relation to intrapsychic processes. However, Ned probably would have disagreed about which interpersonal considerations are most important. Baumeister's emphasis is on

---

[2]In regard to the belongingness idea, I recall vividly asking Ned to read a paper I had written on "friendship theory" during my first year in graduate school. The paper made, rather clumsily, arguments similar to Roy's about the importance of the need for intimacy in driving social interaction. Ned's reaction was that he had no reaction. I took the hint and forgot about friendship theory.

belongingness. I think Ned would have emphasized power, or more generally interpersonal effectiveness. In sum, Ned would have applauded Baumeister's take on the interface between intrapsychic and interpersonal processes, but I'll bet he would also have taken delight in using his "caustic wit and malicious sense of humor" in expressing his disagreement about the importance of belongingness. Thus Baumeister is correct in asserting a fundamental difference between his own emphasis and Ned's.

Cataloging of Motivations: The Primacy of Power and Belongingness

As noted earlier, Ned was concerned with interpersonal agency and power. I found it particularly interesting to see how Baumeister handled the role of power in the context of interpersonal relations. As Baumeister notes, Ned's emphasis on power rather than belongingness was discussed fully at the conference honoring Ned's legacy in 1995. Baumeister proposes that perhaps both belongingness and power have a special status, being interpersonal realities often sought as ends in themselves, because of their survival and reproductive benefits. He goes on to suggest that the two motives could offer the foundation for a very useful theory of interpersonal relations. Here again, he emphasizes that the self or self-concept is derivative from interpersonal considerations.

Maslow (1970) and Murray (1938) attempted many years ago to catalog human motivations. Murray's list of 20 needs includes affiliation, and Maslow included belongingness as the need people seek to address after physiological and safety needs are met. Baumeister is in good company in suggesting the importance of belongingness. Neither Murray nor Maslow spoke directly of power, though one of Murray's followers, McClelland (1975), addressed the importance of power motivation and its interplay with the needs for achievement and affiliation.

Although power does not figure as prominently as belongingness in these approaches to basic human motivation, Leary's (1957) approach to interpersonal behavior and Brown's (1965) approach to social relationships emphasize the very basic importance of concerns with both power and belongingness. Leary provided evidence for friendliness versus hostility on the one hand and dominance versus submission on the other as the two fundamental dimensions of interpersonal behavior. That is, interpersonal behavior is largely defined by the way it addresses belongingness and power. More recently, Big Five researchers have linked the dominance and friendliness categories of interpersonal behavior to the basic personality dimensions of extraversion and agreeableness, respectively (Trapnell & Wiggins, 1990). Similarly, Brown argued that status and solidarity, which are really the same as power and liking, are the key dimensions of interpersonal relationships. For example, relationships can be marked by equal power and high degrees of solidarity, and so forth. Clearly, the two motives put forth by Baumeister are critical in human interaction.

The Self as Interpersonal Tool and Energizer

After arguing for the priority of interpersonal processes, Baumeister (see chapter 4) returns to the question of the self. Having relegated it to secondary importance, he asks, "What does it do anyway?" What is the function of the self? His answer is an elegant one—the self as interpersonal tool. For example, self-esteem can function as a way of measuring one's desirability as a group member or partner and thereby guide one's interpersonal behavior. This formulation is reminiscent of the earlier work on the matching hypothesis in interpersonal attraction that proposed that people target their romantic overtures toward others of similar attractiveness and social desirability, both out of concern with rejection from more attractive others and out of concern with equity (Berscheid, 1985; Berscheid, Dion, Walster, & Walster, 1971). Baumeister's approach is broader and considers how self-esteem can direct interpersonal behavior more generally to satisfy belongingness needs.

It seems to me that one key function of the self and self-esteem that can be accommodated to Baumeister's approach is the idea that high self-esteem is an energizer, something that provides the courage and the energy to develop richly rewarding interpersonal connections. Baumeister and his colleagues in fact argue that high self-esteem, essentially because of its energizing qualities, can sometimes lead people to take costly risks and suffer poorer outcomes (Baumeister, Heatherton, & Tice, 1993). Although they have been ingenious in devising an experimental paradigm in which self-esteem is indeed self-defeating, in general self-esteem would seem to serve as an important and effective source of energy. In addition, as Baumeister suggests, self-esteem can provide useful guidance in negotiating interpersonal interaction.

CONCLUSION

Baumeister has written an elegant and scholarly chapter on the primacy of interpersonal processes. I think Ned Jones would strongly agree with the importance Baumeister attaches to interpersonal processes and the way they can drive intrapsychic processes. Ned's self-handicapping work seems to be a good example of a domain in which he believed self-esteem concerns actually drive interpersonal behavior, but on the whole he generally saw interpersonal processes as extremely fundamental. Ned was clearly convinced of the prominence of power considerations in interpersonal behavior. He felt that people wanted power, because it could significantly improve one's effectiveness and outcomes in interpersonal behavior. Although very concerned with aspects of interpersonal attraction, I think Ned would have given power primacy as a fundamental need over belongingness.

One might see Baumeister's and Ned's work as complimentary, together describing two fundamental, ubiquitous motivations—power and belongingness. In their work, separate and together, the self emerges not as an isolated, bounded entity, but as part of the main, the social world. As Tetlock and Manstead (1985) pointed out, pitting intrapsychic motives against impression management concerns has not always led to fruitful theorizing. Rather, the self is best represented as both a compass and a barometer, navigating the self through the interpersonal world and marking one's standing within that world. Ned was, throughout his career, concerned with the interface between the intrapsychic and the interpersonal, and Baumeister, with his provocative essay, will continue to explore the intellectual landscape that Ned first traversed.

REFERENCES

Bandura, A. (1977). Self-efficacy: Toward a unifying theory of behavior change. *Psychological Review, 84,* 191–215.

Baumeister, R. F., Heatherton, T. F., & Tice, D. M. (1993). When ego threats lead to self-regulation failure: Negative consequences of high self-esteem. *Journal of Personality and Social Psychology, 64,* 141–165.

Berglas, S., & Jones, E. E. (1978). Drug choice as a self-handicapping strategy in response to noncontingent success. *Journal of Personality and Social Psychology, 36,* 405–417.

Berscheid, E. (1985). Interpersonal attraction. In G. Lindzey & E. Aronson (Eds.), *The handbook of social psychology.* (3rd ed., Vol. 2, pp. 413–484). New York: Random House.

Berscheid, E., Dion, K., Walster, E., & Walster, G. W. (1971). Physical attractiveness and dating choice: A test of the matching hypothesis. *Journal of Experimental Social Psychology, 7,* 173–189.

Brown, R. (1965). *Social psychology.* New York: Free Press.

Jones, E. E. (1964). *Ingratiation: A social psychological analysis.* New York: Appleton-Century-Crofts.

Jones, E. E. (1965). Conformity as a tactic of ingratiation. *Science, 149,* 144–150.

Leary, T. (1957). *Interpersonal diagnosis of behavior.* New York: Ronald.

Maslow, A. H. (1970). *Motivation and personality* (2nd ed.). New York: Harper.

McClelland, D. C. (1975). *Power: The inner experience.* New York: Irvington.

Murray, H. A. (1938). *Explorations in personality.* New York: Oxford.

Tetlock, P. E., & Manstead, A. S. R. (1985). Impression markets versus intrapsychic explanations in social psychology: A useful dichotomy? *Psychological Review, 92,* 59–77.

Trapnell, P. D., & Wiggins, J. S. (1990). Extension of the interpersonal adjective scales to include the Big Five dimensions of personality. *Journal of Personality and Social Psychology, 59,* 781–790.

White, R. W. (1963). Sense of interpersonal competence: Two case studies and some reflections on origins. In R. W. White (Ed.), *The study of lives.* New York: Atherton.

Intrapsychic and Interpersonal Processes: Cognition, Emotion, and Self as Adaptations to Other People or to Reality?

Thane S. Pittman

Roy Baumeister (chapter 4) has suggested that we view attributional motivation as stemming not from a concern with self-esteem and self-concept, but from a "need to belong." I would like to begin my discussion by changing this dichotomy before addressing its advantages and drawbacks. I then discuss Baumeister's important identification of emotion in interpersonal interaction and the work that Ned and I did on this theme.

First, if one looks for a fundamental intrapersonal motive to contrast with the need to belong, I think that self-esteem is clearly the wrong foil. I agree that concern with self-esteem is not a good candidate for a primary motive. The self is not something we are born with, rather it is something that develops, perhaps around the age of 18 months (Harter, 1983), as the result of experience. Concerns with self-esteem likewise are the result of other processes. So I would like to substitute something else that could more sensibly be used as an alternative to Baumeister's interesting suggestions. In so doing, I refer to a chapter Ned Jones and I wrote on strategic self-presentation (Jones & Pittman, 1982). In that chapter, we argued that the underlying motive, at least for strategic self-presentation, is a concern with gaining effective influence over the social environment: "In all cases we conceive of the underlying goal as the augmentation or protection of the strategist's power to influence and control his social environment" (pp. 248–250). This goal might be a specific outcome, or it could be a more generalized desire to be in a reasonably good position to have some interpersonal influence should a specific goal arise later, a notion we called a *power bank.*

I would argue, further, that this is a manifestation of a more general motive to have effective commerce with the environment, both the social and the nonsocial environment, so that the fundamental underlying intrapersonal motive that I would choose for contrast with Baumeister's suggested need for belonging is the drive to gain adequate understanding, prediction, and potential for control (see Pittman, 1997). That, I think, can be put forward as the individual's underlying reason for attributional activity (Pittman & D'Agostino, 1985)—a view that is compatible with the basic tenets of traditional attribution theory as originally described by Jones and Davis (1965) and by Kelley (1967).

Taking this approach, I like the suggestion that self-esteem be viewed as a sort of readout or result of the person's progress on his or her major life tasks, but self-esteem can just as well be thought of as an indicator of the person's evaluation of how he or she is doing in the struggle to make sense out of and operate effectively in a difficult and perhaps fundamentally chaotic world. We feel on top of that world when things are going our way—when expectations are confirmed; when we feel competent, effective, and powerful; when we are feeling the flow that comes with the full exercise of our capabilities. But we feel much less on top of the world when things either social or nonsocial are not making sense, spinning out of control, or seem to be out of our realm of understanding and influence. Many of the events about which we are concerned are, of course, interpersonal, but interpersonal events are only one aspect of our existence. We can experience positive and negative emotion, and feel good or bad about ourselves, as the result of nonsocial as well as social experiences. In this view, concern with others, with getting along and with being accepted, is just one manifestation of the general struggle to make sense out of and operate

236

effectively in a complex, puzzling, and only imperfectly understandable world. It is not at all clear that assuming there is a special social motive for belongingness is necessary.

This view of self-esteem is also, I think, compatible with the way Ned and I (Jones & Pittman, 1982) were thinking about the connections between the phenomenal self and self-presentation. We saw self-representation as being both influenced by and exerting some restraining influence on self-presentation, but we did not see self-esteem as the major source of self-presentational motivation. However, Baumeister's (this volume) more explicit identification of a sort of intermediary rather than primary role for self-esteem is a contribution that goes well beyond our thinking and that is clearly on the mark. So, against this fundamental concern with achieving effective commerce with the social and nonsocial environment, one can contrast the suggestion that there is a fundamental need to belong.

NEED TO BELONG?

A reasonable case could be made for the view that nature has selected an effectance motive that is likely to explain all of the results that Baumeister describes, and more, in a rather neat and parsimonious way. In this view, the drive for effective commerce with the environment applies to such basic problems as the acquisition of food and shelter and the development and exercise of competence, as well as to the problems of influence, acceptance, and belonging posed by social interactions. Because our lives are so intertwined with those of others, it is no surprise that we spend a great deal of time and energy thinking about, working on, and assessing how we are doing in our social relations.

However, having said that, I also think that it is pretty clear that we have evolved, and we probably would be foolish to ignore the fact that to some extent human characteristics have been shaped by species history. It is clear that some motives that are obviously built-in, such as the sex drive, have an inherently social referent (Kenrick, 1994), and other candidates for built-in social motives, such as altruism (Batson, 1987) and aggression (Berkowitz, 1965), have already been proposed.

In that light, I think it is entirely reasonable to entertain the possibility that some interpersonal motives are part of the basic human set of inclinations and concerns. Perhaps more important, whether one sees concern for effective social interaction as primary, or as learned or derived from other motives, there is no denying the central role in each person's life of the effects of the evaluations and feelings of others on one's own sense of well-being. And there is certainly a rich and long-standing precedent in social psychology for thinking that something like a need to belong is part of human nature. I need only to mention a term like *affiliation* for social psychologists to retrieve a rich history of relevant social psychological theory and research.

However, to be useful, adding the assumption that a need to belong is a fundamental aspect of human nature should offer new insights, challenge old understandings, and pose new questions. Whether assuming a fundamental need to belong will prove to have these benefits is still, of course, an open question. It is not entirely clear that anything is to be gained by raising this concern about others to the status of built-in fundamental motive from our current implicit assumption that social concerns arise because we find ourselves having to operate in a social milieu. Certainly, none of the data cited by Baumeister here and elsewhere (Baumeister & Leary, 1995) demands that *need to belong* be granted such status, and the utility of such an assumption remains to be demonstrated.

One reason that I have reservations about adding a need to belong to a list of basic human motives comes from a sense that we could be an awful lot better than we are at handling interpersonal interactions. If natural selection had led us to excel in working in small groups, wouldn't we expect to be much better at that than we are? For example, we apparently learn at a relatively young age to take the perspective of others, as Piaget demonstrated. However, although we are capable of engaging in this fundamental relational activity, it seems we often fail to do so. As Ned pointed out in his early theorizing about the attribution process (Jones & Davis, 1965), two variables in particular can interfere with and distort perspective taking. When another's behavior has *hedonic relevance* (i.e., affects what happens to the perceiver for good or ill), or when it is seen to have an element of *personalism* (i.e., is actually intended by the actor to have an effect on the perceiver), attributional distortions are likely to occur. Particularly when another's behavior has negative hedonic relevance with personalism, perspective taking goes out the window in favor of attributions of evil and mental deficiency. This is a truly bad habit for an organism supposedly innately programmed to work well with others. There is no shortage of evidence showing that we are not optimally inclined to get along in small groups. Entire professions depend on our apparent natural tendency to be fairly poor at managing our interpersonal interactions in the home and in the workplace. Is this the best that natural selection can do?

On the positive side, I do think that if we try taking the view that Baumeister has suggested, we might be able to generate some interesting new ideas. For instance, if we take the view that humans are naturally inclined to create small-group or close relations, then phenomena such as the *out-group homogeneity effect* (our tendency to see members of out-groups as relatively homogeneous, while viewing members of our own groups as relatively individualized and differentiated; cf. Linville & Jones, 1980) could be understood as byproducts of these natural attempts to create small group coalitions. Here I think there is potential for some interesting new ideas to be developed.

EMOTION AND INTERPERSONAL MOTIVATION

I would like to finish by picking up on Baumeister's identification of emotion in interpersonal interaction as an important theme and by revisiting some of the work that Ned and I did together (Jones & Pittman, 1982) to remind us that Ned was quite aware of and interested in the important role of emotion in affecting actions.

First, to recap the argument, the underlying goal of the self-presenter was described to be a desire to augment and maintain the power to influence others and thereby to control the social environment. The general strategy toward that end that we discussed was that self-presenters achieve the ability to influence by affecting the thoughts and feelings that others have toward them. And we identified five particular versions of that general influence strategy.

239

I have included a simplified summary of Ned and my argument (see Table 1; Jones & Pittman, 1982) to emphasize that we saw the self-presenter as being concerned with both the thoughts and feelings of others. The table shows that our analysis specifies that certain cognitive appraisals either be accompanied by or lead to particular kinds of emotional reactions that would in turn be likely to motivate the target person in desired ways.

For example, the ingratiation strategy is to create both the attribution of likability, which all by itself is "cold" as Baumeister has noted and the emotion of affection, which is the warm part of the intended reaction. It is the warmth we feel when others like us that makes the ingratiation strategy so effective.

Similarly, we suggested that the other strategies had particular kinds of desired thoughts and feelings. The list of emotions includes affection, fear, respect, guilt, and nurturance. We believe that those feelings could exert powerful influences on interpersonal behavior. We did not, however, go beyond that assumption, given the scope of the chapter that we were writing. But the existence of that list of emotions does raise some interesting questions about human nature. Clearly, at least some of those emotions are unique to interactions with others. They imply

Table 1

Attributions and Emotions Sought Through Strategic Self-Presentation

Strategy	Attribution sought	Emotion to be aroused
Ingratiation	Likable	Affection
Intimidation	Dangerous	Fear
Self-promotion	Competent	Respect
Exemplification	Worthy	Guilt
Supplication	Helpless	Nurturance

NOTE: From "Toward a General Theory of Strategic Self-Presentation," by E. E. Jones and T. S. Pittman, in *Psychological Perspectives on the Self*, J. Suls (Ed.), 1982, Hillsdale, NJ: Erlbaum. Copyright 1982 by Erlbaum. Adapted with permission.

a set of important human reactions to others that Baumeister's analysis has usefully brought to our attention with his suggestion that a concern with social interaction may be a basic part of the human makeup. Some of the most interesting and novel aspects of assuming a fundamental need to belong may lie in helping us to understand why we experience the particular set of emotions that seem to be characteristic of human nature. It remains to be seen whether the specification of a need to belong as a fundamental human motive will have any unique and useful implications for our understanding of human social interaction, but perhaps an analysis of emotion is a good place to begin.

REFERENCES

Batson, C. D. (1987). Prosocial motivation: Is it ever truly altruistic? In L. Berkowitz (Ed.), *Advances in experimental social psychology* (Vol. 20, pp. 65–122). San Diego, CA: Academic Press.

Baumeister, R. F., & Leary, M. R. (1995). The need to belong: Desire for interpersonal attachments as a fundamental human motivation. *Psychological Bulletin, 117,* 497–529.

Berkowitz, L. (1965). The concept of aggressive drive: Some additional considerations. In L. Berkowitz (Ed.), *Advances in experimental social psychology* (Vol. 2, pp. 301–329). San Diego, CA: Academic Press.

Harter, S. (1983). Developmental perspective on the self-system. In E. M. Hetherington (Ed.), *Handbook of child psychology, Vol. 4: Socialization, personality, and social development* (pp. 275–386). New York: Wiley.

Jones, E. E., & Davis, K. E. (1965). From acts to dispositions: The attribution process in person perception. In L. Berkowitz (Ed.), *Advances in experimental social psychology* (Vol. 2, pp. 220–266). San Diego, CA: Academic Press.

Jones, E. E., & Pittman, T. S. (1982). Toward a general theory of strategic self-presentation. In J. Suls (Ed.), *Psychological perspectives on the self* (Vol. 1, 231–262). Hillsdale, NJ: Erlbaum.

Kelley, H. H. (1967). Attribution theory in social psychology. *Nebraska Symposium on Motivation, 15,* 192–240.

Kenrick, D. T. (1994). Evolutionary social psychology: From sexual selection to social cognition. In M. Zanna (Ed.), *Advances in experimental social psychology* (Vol. 26, pp. 75–162). San Diego, CA: Academic Press.

Linville, P. W., & Jones, E. E. (1980). Polarized appraisals of out-group members. *Journal of Personality and Social Psychology, 38,* 689–703.

Pittman, T. S. (1997). Motivation. In D. Gilbert, S. Fiske, & G. Lindsay (Eds.), *Handbook of social psychology* (4th ed). Boston: McGraw-Hill.

Pittman, T. S., & D'Agostino, P. R. (1985). Motivation and attribution: The effects of control deprivation on subsequent information processing. In G. Weary & J. Harvey (Eds.), *Attribution: Basic issues and applications* (pp. 117–151). San Diego, CA: Academic Press.

5

From Expectancies to Worldviews: Regulatory Focus in Socialization and Cognition

E. Tory Higgins

"Socialization" refers to the adoption and internalization by individuals of values, beliefs, and ways of perceiving the world that are shared by a group. When internalization is effective the individual ends up wanting to behave as others want and expect him to behave...[The] fascination stems from the fact that most of society's codes and values become part of the very fabric of an individual's personality during the process of socialization.
—Jones and Gerard, 1967, pp. 76–77

[If] highly valued or need-satisfying objects are actually present in the environment, it is to the perceiver's advantage to locate them as soon as possible and with the least expenditure of effort.
—Jones and Gerard, 1967, p. 231

Appropriately, most of the papers presented at the conference honoring Ned Jones were given by students, colleagues, and close friends of Ned. But, it should be noted that there are many social personality psychologists who, like me, do not fall into these categories. Yet to us as well, Ned was and is a valued role model who shaped and continues to shape our scholarly lives. I was struck years ago by just how great was Ned's influence when I re-read his classic textbook with Hal Gerard (Jones & Gerard, 1967). I had forgotten how much I had learned from that book (*Foundations of Social Psychology*) about the role of cognition and development in social behavior. Although I did not know Ned very well personally, I could not resist telephoning him to thank him for his contributions to my thinking. Perhaps, there are other social personality psychologists who have not read Jones and Gerard's (1967) book for several years (or, heaven forbid, have never read it). I urge them to do so! In this chapter, I discuss one central issue from *Foundations of Social Psychology:* the existence of self-regulatory systems associated with distinct worldviews. I also explore how these systems allow socialization effects to be produced in the laboratory setting. I hope that it will inspire the reader to go back to the book to rediscover other fascinating issues that deserve further attention.

SOCIAL REGULATION AND SELF-REGULATION

How do the significant others in a person's life influence the values and beliefs the person acquires, and how do these values and beliefs in turn affect the person's responses to the world? That is, how does social regulation affect self-regulation? It could be argued that this is *the* fundamental question in the social science of psychology. Certainly this question is at the heart of the work of Freud, Lewin, Murray, Vygotsky, Mead, and other founders of personality and social psychology. Indeed, Jones and Gerard (1967) in their classic review of the "foundations of social psychology" devoted almost a third of their topical chapters to this basic question.

In addressing how social regulation affects self-regulation, Jones and Gerard (1967) took the classic approach that has continued to dominate the field. This approach begins with the recognition that the human child cannot survive without caretakers providing food, protection, shelter, and so forth. That is, self-regulatory mechanisms arise from "the child's dependence on others for rewards and relief from pain" (Jones & Gerard, 1967, p. 78). Because of the child's dependence, socialization agents have a pervasive influence on the beliefs and values that the child acquires. Children are motivated to behave as others want and expect them to behave, to adjust to the standards of their significant others. In attempting to adjust to other's expectations for them, they view themselves as social objects. Over time, the child's interactions with the social environment create a "cognition of the self" that links personal beliefs and values, relates "acts to each other and to underlying dispositions," and has clear implications for behavior (Jones & Gerard, 1967, pp. 182–183).

The classic approach next links the internalization of beliefs and values to mechanisms that influence self-regulation and responses to the world. The basic argument is that both beliefs and values "establish expectancies," and such expectancies produce a preparedness to respond to objects relevant to them. That is, belief-relevant and value-relevant knowledge becomes highly accessible (Jones & Gerard, 1967, pp. 230–231). High knowledge accessibility in turn sensitizes a person to knowledge-related stimuli and increases the likelihood that knowledge-related stimuli will be noticed, responded to, and remembered.

This classic approach to understanding how social regulation affects self-regulation and responses to the world has yielded significant advances in personality and social psychology. For example, this approach underlies the historical contributions of Kelly (1955) and Bruner (1957) to person perception, as well as more recent work on the emotional and motivational effects of chronic accessibility (for reviews, see Fazio, 1986; Higgins, 1996a, 1996b). There is a limitation of this approach that needs to be considered, however. The beliefs and values that are internalized and become chronically accessible are conceptualized as specific, relatively distinct mental elements, such as the personal constructs of Kelly (1955), the accessible categories of Bruner (1957) and Higgins and King (1981), and the "attitude object-evaluation" units of Fazio (1986). In addition, expectancies themselves are typically conceptualized as specific, relatively distinct mental elements (see Olson, Roese, & Zanna, 1996).

Given the specificity and distinctiveness of beliefs and values, as well as the expectancies they establish, how do general ways of responding to the world develop? How do psychologists account for the fascinating phenomena, noted by Jones and Gerard (1967), that society's codes and values become part of the very fabric of an individual's personality during the process of socialization? Simply put, how do we get from specific expectancies to general worldviews?

This chapter proposes one possible solution to this problem—the existence of distinct regulatory systems associated with distinct worldviews. This proposed solution, moreover, is capable of resolving another problem raised by Jones and Gerard (1967, p. 77). Jones and Gerard suggested that socialization effects are as difficult to study as they are fascinating to consider because they arise from long and complicated learning histories. Given this, it is unreasonable to suppose that the same kinds of effects could be produced in brief laboratory studies. Another purpose of this chapter is to suggest how the proposed solution of regulatory systems associated with distinct worldviews permits the kinds of effects resulting from socialization to be produced in brief laboratory studies.

DISTINCT REGULATORY SYSTEMS AND THEIR INTERNALIZATION DURING SOCIALIZATION

I propose that different systems of regulating pains and pleasure can be distinguished in terms of the variable of *regulatory focus*. In his classic book *Learning Theory and Behavior*, Mowrer (1960) distinguished between two positive or pleasurable psychological situations, the presence of positive outcomes and the absence of negative outcomes, and between two negative or painful psychological situations, the absence of positive outcomes and the presence of negative outcomes. Mowrer (1960) and others (e.g., Higgins, 1987; Roseman, 1984; Stein & Jewett, 1982) related these distinct psychological situations to distinct emotions. These distinct emotions are organized in Exhibit 1 as a function of the valence of the experience and the regulatory focus of the experience.

It is clear from Exhibit 1 that two distinct systems for regulating pain and pleasure can be distinguished in terms of the variable of reg-

Exhibit 1		
Types of Psychological Situations and Emotions as a Function of Regulatory Focus and Overall Valence of Experience		
Regulatory focus	Positive valence	Negative valence
Positive outcome focus	Presence of positive Happy; satisfied	Absence of positive Sad; dissatisfied
Negative outcome focus	Absence of negative Calm; relieved	Presence of negative Tense; nervous

ulatory focus. First, there is a *positive outcome* regulatory focus that involves maximizing the presence of positive outcomes (pleasure) and minimizing the absence of positive outcomes (pain). Second, there is a *negative outcome* regulatory focus that involves maximizing the absence of negative outcomes (pleasure) and minimizing the presence of negative outcomes (pain). (I should note that since this chapter was initially written the label *promotion focus* has replaced the label *positive outcome focus*, and the label *prevention focus* has replaced the label *negative outcome focus*. To avoid confusion in reading the comments to this chapter, however, I have retained the earlier labels.)

As noted earlier, the classic approach to understanding how social regulation affects self-regulation recognizes that self-regulatory mechanisms arise from children's dependence on others. It does not explicitly distinguish, however, between the presence of positive outcomes (e.g., food or rewards) and the absence of negative outcomes (e.g., protection or relief from pain). But these types of dependency needs are distinguishable with respect to the distinct regulatory systems. In terms of Bowlby's (1969, 1973) classic account of people's fundamental survival needs, the positive outcome focus system would be responsive to people's nurturance needs and the negative outcome focus system would be responsive to people's security needs. Both systems for regulating pain and pleasure would be adaptive and thus all people would possess both systems. Nevertheless, different socialization experiences could make one system predominate in self-regulation.

SELF-DISCREPANCY THEORY

Self-discrepancy theory (see Higgins, 1989, 1991) postulates that the psychological significance of matches (i.e., congruencies) and mismatches (i.e., discrepancies) between individuals' actual self (or self-concept) and their desired selves derives from distinct developmental histories of caretaker–child interactions. Parents (as the usual caretakers) who hope or wish that there child will possess certain valued attributes orient to their child in terms of positive outcomes. When the child matches their hopes, wishes, or aspirations, the parent responds so as to produce positive outcomes for the child (e.g., hugging or kissing). When the child is discrepant from their hopes or wishes, the parent responds so as to remove positive outcomes for the child (e.g., love withdrawal).

To control their parents' responses to them, these children over time construct an ideal self representing their parents' hopes or wishes for them that they can use as a self-regulatory guide. In this way, the specific form of social regulation that these children experience in their interactions with their parents produces a specific form of self-regulation. According to self-discrepancy theory, such children begin to self-regulate in terms of an ideal self-guide that orients them toward positive outcomes—to maximize the presence of positive outcomes (as a type of positive event) and to minimize the absence of positive outcomes (as a type of negative event). As predicted by self-discrepancy theory, there is considerable evidence that discrepancies between the actual self and the ideal self are uniquely related to suffering from absence of positive emotions; that is, dejection-related emotions (see Higgins, 1987).

In contrast, parents who believe that it is their child's duty, obligation, or responsibility to possess certain valued attributes orient to their child in terms of negative outcomes. When the child behaves in a manner that mismatches their demands or prescriptions, the parent responds so as to produce negative outcomes for the child (e.g., sanctions or punishment). When the child behaves in a manner that matches their demands or prescriptions, the parent responds so as to remove the threat of negative outcomes for the child (e.g., comfort or reassurance).

To control their parents' responses to them, these children over time construct an ought self representing their parents' demands and prescriptions for them, which they use as a self-regulatory guide. Again, the specific form of social regulation that these children experience produces a specific form of self-regulation. Such children begin to self-regulate in terms of an ought self-guide that orients them toward negative outcomes—to maximize the absence of negative outcomes (as a type of positive event) and to minimize the presence of negative outcomes (as a type of negative event). As predicted by self-discrepancy theory, research has shown that discrepancies between the actual self and the ought self are uniquely related to suffering from the presence of negative outcomes, that is, agitation-related emotions (see Higgins, 1987).

I now consider the socialization process more generally from the perspective of self-discrepancy theory (see Higgins, 1989, 1991). To begin with, children learn that a caretaker responds to them in a certain manner when they behave in a particular way. In relation to that significant other, then, they develop specific expectancies relating certain behaviors to particular responses. When the children's mental representational capacity develops sufficiently, they begin to infer and represent the fact that the significant other's responses to them are mediated by the significant other's desires for them. They begin to understand that the significant other hopes or demands that they be a specific type of person and not simply behave in particular ways. Thus, over time children acquire specific beliefs and values that involve expectancies about a significant other's hopes or demands for them and how the significant other will respond to them when these hopes or demands are or are not fulfilled. These specific expectancies, then, form the basis for the children's self-regulation.

As a model of how social regulation affects self-regulation, this part of self-discrepancy theory is clearly compatible with the classic approach. But self-discrepancy theory proposes that socialization has an impact beyond the acquisition of specific beliefs, expectancies, and goals. Self-discrepancy theory also proposes that a nurturant mode of caretaker–child interaction with ideal self-guides generally involves a positive outcome focus, and a security mode of caretaker–child interaction with ought self-guides generally involves a negative outcome focus. Moreover, these two types of regulatory focus become general ways of orienting to the world that are independent of specific beliefs, expectancies, or goals. Each regulatory focus becomes a general viewpoint on how the world works. That is, the world becomes a world of nurturance issues involving the presence or absence of positive outcomes or a world of security issues involving the absence or presence of negative outcomes.

In sum, different modes of interaction between children and their significant others emphasize different types of regulatory focus, which in turn become general orientations to the world. By emphasizing either nurturance and a positive outcome focus or security and a negative outcome focus, caretakers' social regulation communicates to the child a particular viewpoint on the world. By learning to adapt their self-regulation to fit this viewpoint, children acquire a shared reality with their caretakers concerning the nature of the world. In this way, the child can move from specific expectancies to general worldviews, and society's values can become part of the very fabric of an individual's personality during socialization. Indeed, society's beliefs and values not only function as specific self-regulatory guides, but they also become a general shared reality about what is the essential nature of the world, how the world basically works. As a personality variable, one can now think of different individuals becoming strongly nurturance oriented or security oriented because of their socialization. And these personalities, these general worldviews, have consequence for how individuals respond to the world. I now consider some of these consequences.

REGULATORY FOCUS AS A PERSONALITY VARIABLE INFLUENCING COGNITION

As mentioned earlier, general worldviews should influence how one responds to the world (e.g., Kelly, 1955). Events that are relevant to a person's regulatory focus should be remembered better than events that are irrelevant. And this should be true not only for events in which perceivers themselves are involved (i.e., autobiographical memory) but also for events in which others are involved (i.e., biographical memory). Chronic self-discrepancies, then, should influence memory for events as a function of their regulatory focus. Thus, Higgins and Tykocinski (1992) predicted that when people read descriptions of events in another person's life, those events that reflected the presence or absence of positive outcomes would be remembered better by persons who possessed predominantly an actual/ideal discrepancy than by persons who possessed predominantly an actual/ought discrepancy, whereas the reverse would be true for those events that reflected the absence or presence of negative outcomes.

This prediction was tested by selecting individuals who either were relatively high in actual/ideal(own) discrepancy and relatively low in actual/ought(own) discrepancy (i.e., predominant actual/ideal[own] discrepancy persons) or were relatively high in actual/ought(own) discrepancy and relatively low in actual/ideal(own) discrepancy (i.e., predominant actual/ought[own] discrepancy persons). A few weeks after the selection procedure, all participants were given the same essay to read about several days in the life of a target person. Ten minutes after reading the essay (following a nonverbal filler task), these participants were asked to reproduce the essay word for word.

In the essay, the different types of psychological situations described earlier were represented by different events that the target person experienced. The target person's experiences were circumstantial and not personality related. The different types of psychological situations were represented in each day of the target person's life as follows:

1. The presence of positive outcomes—positive outcome focus, positive overall valence (e.g., "I found a 20 dollar bill on the pavement of Canal street near the paint store.")
2. The absence of positive outcomes—positive outcome focus, negative overall valence (e.g., "I've been wanting to see this movie at the 8th Street Theatre for some time, so this evening I went there straight after school to find out that it's not showing anymore.")

3. The presence of negative outcomes—negative outcome focus, negative overall valence (e.g., "I was stuck in the subway for 35 minutes with at least 15 sweating passengers breathing down my neck.")
4. The absence of negative outcomes—negative outcome focus, positive overall valence (e.g., "This is usually my worst school day. Awful schedule, class after class with no break. But today is election day—no school!").

By using these materials, one could test whether a chronic pattern of self-beliefs representing a distinct psychological situation (i.e., type of predominant self-discrepancy) produces sensitivity to events reflecting that psychological situation, despite there being no overlap between the pattern and the events in either their specific content or topic.

Because self-discrepancies can influence mood (see Higgins, 1987, 1989) and mood can influence memory (see Gilligan & Bower, 1984; Isen, 1984), this study was designed both to control and to check for any possible effects of mood on memory. Previous studies of self-discrepancies have found that exposure to trait-related input can prime self-discrepancies and change individuals' moods (see Higgins, 1989). The essay used as input in the present study minimized such priming by including events that did not concern the target person's traits. Rather, the events were clearly circumstantial factors such as finding money by chance or getting stuck in a crowded subway. In addition to attempting to control for mood in this way, study participants' mood was also measured both before and after they read the essay to check whether individual differences in mood contributed to the findings.

A Type of Predominant Self-Discrepancy × Regulatory Focus of Event × Overall Valence of Event analysis of variance (ANOVA) was performed on the number of target events recalled. This analysis revealed a significant Type of Predominant Self-Discrepancy × Regulatory Focus of Event interaction. As shown in Table 1, this interaction reflected the fact that, as predicted, predominant actual/ideal discrepancy individuals tended to remember target events representing the presence or absence of positive outcomes better than did predominant actual/ought discrepancy individuals, whereas predominant actual/

Table 1

Mean Recall of Events Reflecting Different Types of Psychological Situations as a Function of Regulatory Focus of Event, Overall Valence of Event, and Individual's Type of Predominant Self-Discrepancy

| | Regulatory focus | | | |
| | Positive outcome focus | | Negative outcome focus | |
Self-discrepancy	Positive valence (PP)	Negative valence (AP)	Positive valence (AN)	Negative valence (PN)
Actual: Ideal	2.7	3.5	2.2	2.3
Actual: Ought	2.3	2.8	2.4	2.6

NOTE: PP = presence of positive outcomes; AP = absence of positive outcomes; AN = absence of negative outcomes; PN = presence of negative outcomes.

ought discrepancy individuals tended to remember target events representing the absence or presence of negative outcomes better than did predominant actual/ideal discrepancy individuals. No other interactions were significant, and the obtained interaction between type of predominant self-discrepancy and outcome focus of event was independent of any differences in mood. Thus, predominant actual/ideal discrepancy individuals and predominant actual/ought discrepancy individuals were differentially sensitive to the target events as a function of the events' regulatory focus but not as a function of the events' overall valence or the individuals' mood.

Our subsequent studies considered further cognitive consequences of regulatory focus, particularly the consequences of the distinct strategies and tactics associated with each focus. Self-regulatory systems can have either a desired end state functioning as the standard (i.e., a positive reference value), or an undesired end state functioning as the standard (i.e., a negative reference value). Both positive and negative reference values have been described in the literature (see, e.g., Carver &

Scheier, 1990; Markus & Nurius, 1986). The literature also distinguishes between different directions of motivated movement—between approaching a positive self state and avoiding a negative self state. Carver and Scheier (1990) proposed that when a self-regulatory system has a desired end state as a reference value, the system is discrepancy reducing and involves attempts to move the currently perceived actual-self state as close as possible to the desired reference point (an *approach system*). And when a self-regulatory system has an undesired state as a reference value, the system is discrepancy amplifying and involves attempts to move the currently perceived actual-self state as far away as possible from the undesired reference point (an *avoidance system*).

In a discrepancy-reducing system, people are motivated to move their actual self as close as possible to the desired end state. There are two alternative means to reduce the discrepancy between the actual self and a desired end state as reference point—approach self states that match the desired end state or avoid self states that mismatch the desired end state. For example, a person who wants to get a good grade on a quiz (a desired end state) can either study hard at the library the day before the quiz (approaching a match to the desired end state) or turn down an invitation to go out drinking with friends the night before the quiz (avoiding a mismatch to the desired end state).

In a discrepancy-amplifying system, people are motivated to move their actual self as far away as possible from the undesired end state. There are, again, two alternative means to amplify the discrepancy between the actual self and an undesired end state as reference point— approach self states that mismatch the undesired end state or avoid self states that match the undesired end state. For example, a person who dislikes interpersonal conflict (an undesired end state) could either arrange a meeting with his or her apartment mates to work out a schedule for cleaning the apartment (approaching a mismatch to the undesired end state) or leave the apartment when his or her two apartment mates start to argue (avoiding a match to the undesired end state).

Thus, by considering the alternative means for accomplishing discrepancy reduction in relation to desired end states and discrepancy amplification in relation to undesired end states, four different forms

Exhibit 2
Summary of Regulatory Forms as a Function of Valence of End State as Reference Point and Direction of Means

	Valence of end state as reference point	
Direction of means	Desired end state (discrepancy reducing)	Undesired end state (discrepancy amplifying)
Approach	Approaching matches to desired end states	Approaching mismatches to undesired end states
Avoidance	Avoiding mismatches to desired end states	Avoiding matches to undesired end states

of self-regulation can be identified. Exhibit 2 summarizes how valence of end state as reference point combines with direction of means to produce the four different regulatory forms.

One might expect that a positive outcome focus would be associated with a predilection for self-regulatory forms involving approach, whereas a negative outcome focus would be associated with a predilection for self-regulatory forms involving avoidance. This would also be reasonable if, as suggested earlier, the positive outcome focus system is nurturance oriented (i.e., obtaining nourishment), and the negative outcome focus system is security oriented (i.e., escaping danger). It follows that regulation in relation to ideal self-guides would involve approach-related self-regulatory forms, whereas regulation in relation to ought self-guides would involve avoidance-related self-regulatory forms. Self-discrepancy theory has considered only discrepancy reduction to desired end states as reference point. Thus, ideal self-regulation would involve a predilection for approaching matches to desired end states, whereas ought self-regulation would involve a predilection for avoiding mismatches to desired end states (see Exhibit 2). Does this difference in self-regulatory predilections have consequences for how social events are remembered? A study by Higgins, Roney, Crowe, and Hymes (1994) addressed this question.

A between-subjects manipulation of self-guide activation was used. The manipulation was based on the technique used by Higgins, Bond, Klein, and Strauman (1986, Study 2). Individuals were asked either to report on how their hopes and goals had changed over time (activating ideal self-guides) or to report on how their sense of duty and obligation had changed over time (activating ought self-guides). To examine memory effects, a free recall technique similar to that used in the Higgins and Tykocinski (1992) study was employed. Study participants read about 16 episodes that occurred over 4 days in the life of another student. Each of the four regulatory forms was exemplified by four different episodes. We expected that activating either the ideal or ought regulatory system would increase individuals' predilection for particular regulatory forms, which in turn would make them more sensitive to, and thus more likely to recall, those episodes that exemplified those particular forms.

In each of the episodes the target was trying either to experience a desired end state or not to experience an undesired end state. To experience a desired end state, the target either used means that would decrease the discrepancy to a desired end state (approaching matches to desired end states) or means that would avoid increasing the discrepancy to a desired end state (avoiding mismatches to desired end states). To avoid experiencing an undesired end state, the target either used means that would increase the discrepancy to an undesired end state (approaching mismatches to undesired end states) or used means that would avoid decreasing the discrepancy to an undesired outcome (avoiding matches to undesired end states). Following is an example of an episode exemplifying each of the regulatory forms:

1. Approaching matches to desired end states (e.g., "Because I wanted to be at school for the beginning of my 8:30 psychology class, which is usually excellent, I woke up early this morning.")
2. Avoiding mismatches to desired end states (e.g., "I wanted to take

Table 2

Mean Number of Episodes Recalled as a Function of Type of Self-Guide Activated, Valence of Stated End State, and Direction of Stated Means

| | Valence of stated end state | | | |
| | Desired end state | | Undesired end state | |
Direction of stated means	Approach matches	Avoid mismatches	Approach mismatches	Avoid matches
Type of activation				
Ideal guide	1.75	1.37	1.50	1.39
Ought guide	1.19	1.96	1.38	1.75

a class in photography at the community center, so I didn't register for a class in Spanish that was scheduled at the same time.")

3. Approaching mismatches to undesired end states (e.g., "I dislike eating in crowded places, so at noon I picked up a sandwich from a local deli and ate outside.")

4. Avoiding matches to undesired end states (e.g., "I didn't want to feel tired during my very long morning of classes, so I skipped the most strenuous part of my morning workout.")

An overall Type of Self-Guide Activated × Direction of Stated Means (approach, avoidance) × Valence of Stated End State (desired end state, undesired end state) × Story Version × Event Order ANOVA was performed on the number of episodes participants recalled for each type of episode in the story. Table 2 reports participants' recall of each type of episode in the story as a function of the type of self-guide that was activated.

The overall analysis revealed a significant Type of Self-Guide Activated × Direction of Stated Means interaction, reflecting that there was an overall tendency for individuals to remember better episodes exemplifying an approach direction of means when ideal self-guides were activated than when ought self-guides were activated, but to remember better episodes exemplifying an avoidance direction of means when ought self-guides were activated than when ideal self-guides were activated. The specific prediction that ideal self-regulation would involve approach forms and ought self-regulation would involve avoidance forms predicted a Type of Self-Guide Activated × Direction of Stated Means interaction for desired end states alone. As evident in Table 2, the predicted interaction was obtained. Participants remembered episodes exemplifying approaching matches to desired end states significantly better when ideal self-guides were activated than when ought self-guides were activated, whereas they remembered episodes exemplifying avoiding mismatches to desired end states significantly better when ought self-guides were activated than when ideal self-guides were activated. (It should be noted that the Type of Self-Guide Activated × Direction of Stated Means interaction was considerably weaker and nonsignificant for undesired end states.)

The results of these two studies suggest that personality differences at the general level of regulatory focus—a nurturance, positive outcome focus versus a security, negative outcome focus—can influence memory for social events. Moreover, this impact of personality on person memory occurred even when the events concerned another person and involved content unrelated to the content used to measure the perceiver's personality. The obtained relations between personality and memory did not concern specific beliefs or values. Rather, they concerned the general psychological situations emphasized by each regulatory focus and reflected in the events.

By distinguishing between different types of regulatory focus that emphasize different psychological situations, one can explain how society's values can become part of the very fabric of an individual's personality and influence his or her responses to the world. But what about the other problem raised by Jones and Gerard (1967), the fact that socialization effects are so difficult to study that it is unreasonable to suppose that the same kinds of effects could be produced in brief laboratory studies? I now turn to this issue.

REGULATORY FOCUS AS A SITUATIONAL
VARIABLE INFLUENCING COGNITION

It was noted earlier that both nurturance and security are fundamental survival needs. The positive outcome focus system would be responsive to people's nurturance needs and the negative outcome focus system would be responsive to people's security needs. Both systems for regulating pain and pleasure would be adaptive, and thus all people would possess both systems. The discussion thus far has considered how different socialization experiences can make one system predominant in self-regulation. In knowledge activation terms (see Higgins, 1996b), socialization can make either the positive outcome focus or the negative outcome focus more chronically accessible (as procedural knowledge). Still, both types of focus are available to individuals, and therefore situational factors should be able to make one focus or the other more accessible temporarily.

The "meanings" that other people assign to the events in one's life constitute an especially important situational factor in everyday life. For example, the way in which parents, teachers, and other socialization agents *frame* events when introducing them will assign particular meanings to the event. A parent, for instance, might emphasize safety and avoiding risks when introducing a new activity to his or her child or the parent might emphasize the fun of learning new skills. An employer might threaten employees with punishment for making mistakes or an employer might emphasize unfulfilled aspirations from failing to meet a standard. Even a momentary situation can be framed in different ways by another person such that the situation is assigned different meanings. It has been recognized for a long time, people respond to the meanings assigned to events rather than to the events per se (Weber, 1967), and it is the definition of a situation that intervenes between situations and responses (e.g., Thomas & Thomas, 1928). Given this, people's responses should vary if another person assigns different meanings to their current situation by placing them in different psychological situations.

A couple of recent studies investigated this proposal by framing a performance task with either a positive outcome focus or a negative outcome focus (see Roney, Higgins, & Shah, 1995). Higgins, Strauman, and Klein (1986) earlier noted a parallel between self-discrepancy theory and achievement motivation. According to Atkinson (see Atkinson & Feather, 1966), when confronted with an important achievement task, success-oriented persons focus on the possibility of experiencing "pride in accomplishment," whereas failure-threatened persons in the same situation focus on how they might experience "shame due to failure." One might reconceptualize this distinction in terms of a focus on possible positive outcomes versus a focus on possible negative outcomes, respectively. On the basis of previous research on achievement motivation, Roney et al. (1995) predicted that framing a performance task with a positive outcome focus would produce better performance and greater persistence than framing the same task with a negative outcome focus.

In one of the studies, undergraduates worked on a set of anagrams that included both solvable and unsolvable anagrams. The students were given feedback on each trial about their performance. In one condition the feedback was framed with a positive outcome focus, such as by telling students, "Right, you got that one" (when they solved an anagram) and "You didn't get that one right" (when they did not solve an anagram). In the other condition the feedback was framed with a negative outcome focus, such as by telling students, "You didn't miss that one" (when they solved an anagram) and "No, you missed that one" (when they did not solve an anagram). The study found that the students in the positive outcome focus framing condition solved more of the solvable anagrams and persisted longer in trying to solve the unsolvable anagrams than the students in the negative outcome focus framing condition.

Another study by Roney et al. (1995) examined motivational persistence. Undergraduates were told that they would perform two tasks. The first task was always an anagrams task that included anagrams pretested to be solvable by everyone as well as a set of unsolvable anagrams. The students were told that the second task would be either a computer simulation of the popular *Wheel of Fortune* game or a task called "Unvaried Repetition" that was described so as to appear very boring. Although the performance contingency for playing the fun game rather than the boring game as the second task was the same for all participants, the framing of the contingency was experimentally varied. In the contingency condition framed with a positive outcome focus, the students were told that if they solved 22 (or more) out of the 25 anagrams they would get to play the *Wheel of Fortune* game, otherwise they would do the Unvaried Repetition task. In the contingency condition framed with a negative outcome focus, the students were told that if they got 4 (or more) out of the 25 anagrams wrong, they would do the Unvaried Repetition task, otherwise they would play the *Wheel of Fortune* game. Again, this study found that the students in the positive outcome focus framing condition persisted longer in trying to solve the unsolvable anagrams than the students in the negative outcome focus framing condition.

These two studies demonstrate how a situational manipulation of regulatory focus can influence performance on an achievement task, presumably because the framing influenced the meanings assigned to the task. A recent study by Crowe and Higgins (1997) examined more directly how situational framing can influence cognition.

As part of a large survey held weeks before the experiment, all participants filled out a questionnaire in which they expressed their liking for different kinds of activities. For each participant an idiographic procedure was used to select one activity that the individual clearly liked (the positive valence [PV] task) and another activity he or she clearly disliked (the negative valence [NV] task). For the experiment, the participants arrived for a "memory" study and were told that they would first perform a recognition memory task and then would be assigned a second memory task. The participants were placed in different psychological situations with different regulatory orientations by framing the relation between the first and second tasks in different ways. The control participants were told that the second task would either be a PV task that measured a similar aspect of memory or an NV task that measured a different aspect of memory (where similarity was defined in relation to the recognition memory task that appeared first). They were told that the second task would be randomly assigned so that there was no contingent relation between the two tasks.

The experimental conditions all involved a contingent relation between the first and second memory tasks. The participants were told that depending on their performance on the recognition task they would be asked to do a PV task that measured a similar aspect of memory of an NV task that measured a different aspect of memory. Then the participants in each condition were given additional instructions that placed them in different contingency conditions, as follows:

1. Presence of positive outcome: "If you *do well* on the word recognition task, *you will get to do the PV task* instead of the other task."
2. Absence of positive outcome: "If you *don't do well* on the word recognition task, *you won't get to do the PV task* but will do the other task instead."
3. Presence of negative outcome: "If you *do poorly* on the word recognition task, *you will have to do the NV task* instead of the other task."
4. Absence of negative outcome: "If you *don't do poorly* on the word recognition task, *you won't have to do the NV task* but will do the other task instead."

After the memory tasks were described all participants were shown a set of nonsense words one at a time. Following a brief interference task, the participants were given "old" and "new" nonsense words and were asked to press a Y key for yes if they had seen the word before and to press an N key for no if they had not seen the word before. The decisional criteria used by participants are assumed to depend on the subjective utility of the different "payoffs" of the task. Individuals with a negative regulatory focus should experience a greater gain from "correct rejections" (i.e., avoiding a false distractor, or the absence of a negative) than from a "hit" (recognizing a true target, or the presence of a positive), and they should experience a greater loss from a "false alarm" (failing to avoid a false distractor, or the presence of a negative) than from a "miss" (omitting recognition of a true target, or the absence of a positive). The relative gains and relative losses of individuals with a positive regulatory focus should be the opposite. This leads to the prediction that participants with a negative regulatory focus should have a "no" bias (i.e., a conservative bias), whereas those with a positive regulatory focus should have a "yes" bias (i.e., a risky bias).

Overall, the participants in the four experimental "contingent" framing conditions were more accurate (higher sensitivity scores) than the participants in the "noncontingent" control condition, suggesting that, as expected, activating the regulatory systems generally increased motivation. The critical results concerned the effects of contingency framing on recognition memory biases. As shown in Figure 1, participants with a negative regulatory focus, as expected, had a no or conservative bias, whereas participants with a positive regulatory focus had a yes or risky bias. Participants in the noncontingency control condition fell in-between those two groups.

It is notable that only the regulatory focus variable was significant. There was no effect of the prospective valence of the framed contingency (i.e., the positive valence of the absence of a negative and the presence of a positive versus the negative valence of the presence of a negative and the absence of a positive), nor was there any interaction of regulatory focus and valence. Finally, the effects of regulatory focus on bias were independent of the participants' pretask mood and change in mood (posttask mood minus pretask mood). The results of this study provide further evidence that momentary situational manipulations (occurring in a brief laboratory study) can produce cognitive effects of regulatory focus that resemble the kinds of effects produced by socialization.

CONCLUSION

How does social regulation determine self-regulation? Jones and Gerard (1967) recognized that a strong foundation for the field of social psychology requires an answer to this fundamental question. Knowing how socialization produces internalization is also necessary to understanding how society's codes and values become part of the very

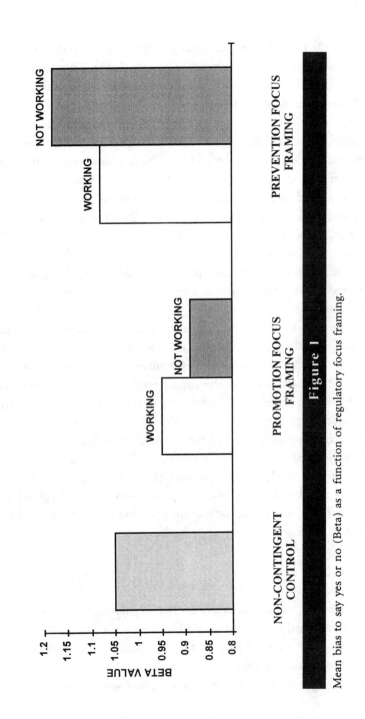

Figure 1

Mean bias to say yes or no (Beta) as a function of regulatory focus framing.

fabric of an individual's personality. Jones and Gerard's proposal took the classic position that beliefs and values "establish expectancies," and such expectancies produce a preparedness to respond to objects relevant to them. This chapter raised the following question: Given the specificity and distinctiveness of beliefs and values, as well as the expectancies they establish, how do general ways of responding to the world develop? How does one go from specific expectancies to general worldviews?

This chapter extended the classic position by highlighting the importance of different types of regulatory focus. According to the regulatory focus perspective, socialization has an impact beyond the acquisition of specific beliefs, expectancies, and goals. It was proposed that different modes of interaction between children and their significant others emphasize different types of regulatory focus, which in turn become general viewpoints on the world. By emphasizing either nurturance and a positive outcome focus or security and a negative outcome focus, caretakers' social regulation communicates to the child a world viewpoint. By learning to adapt their self-regulation to fit this viewpoint, children acquire a shared reality with their significant others about how the world works. In this way, the child can move from specific expectancies to general worldviews, and society's values can become part of the very fabric of an individual's personality during socialization.

I then presented evidence of how regulatory focus can function as a personality variable to influence responses to the world. Individuals with accessible ideal self-guides and a positive outcome focus were compared with individuals with accessible ought self-guides and a negative outcome focus. Several memory studies were described that found associations between which type of self-guide was accessible and which type of social event was remembered. Accessible ideal self-guides with their positive outcome focus were associated with better memory for events involving the presence or absence of positive outcomes and events involving approaching matches to desired end states. Accessible ought self-guides with their negative outcome focus were associated with better memory for events involving the absence or presence of negative outcomes and events involving avoiding mismatches to desired end states.

These studies demonstrated that personality differences at the general level of regulatory focus—a nurturance, positive outcome focus versus a security, negative outcome focus—can influence memory for social events. Moreover, this impact of personality on person memory occurred even when the events concerned another person and involved content unrelated to the perceiver's personality. The obtained relations between personality and memory were not for specific beliefs or values, but for the general psychological situations emphasized by each regulatory focus and reflected in the events.

This chapter also addressed a problem raised by Jones and Gerard (1967), who suggested that because socialization effects are so difficult to study, it is unreasonable to suppose that the same kinds of effects would be produced in brief laboratory studies. From the regulatory focus perspective, however, it should be possible to produce parallel effects on responses to the world through situational manipulations of regulatory focus. Because both nurturance with its positive outcome focus and security with its negative outcome focus are fundamental survival needs, all people must possess both systems. Therefore, just as socialization can make either the positive outcome focus or the negative outcome focus more chronically accessible, situational manipulations should be able to make one focus or the other more accessible temporarily.

A few studies were presented that used framing manipulations to accomplish this. These studies found that both achievement performance and recognition memory can be influenced by framing manipulations of regulatory focus. Level of performance and persistence was higher when the situation induced a positive outcome focus rather than a negative outcome focus. On a signal detection measure of recognition memory, framing with a positive outcome focus produced an approach risky bias for hits, whereas framing with a negative outcome focus produced an avoidance conservative bias for correct rejections.

In this chapter, I have described a psychological principle for which cognitive effects can arise from both socialization and brief laboratory manipulations—regulatory focus. In other studies I have described another psychological principle with cognitive effects that can have both chronic and momentary sources—knowledge accessibility (see Higgins, 1996b; Higgins & King, 1981). In both of these cases, the processes underlying the effects are assumed to be the same regardless of whether the source of the effect is chronic (like personality) or momentary (like the typical social psychology laboratory study). Moreover, the effects of such processes are relatively independent of specific content, which gives these principles broad applicability. Increasingly, social personality psychologists are exploring such principles at various levels of analysis (see Higgins & Kruglanski, 1996). The objective is to continue to build the foundations of social psychology. If we social personality psychologists do so with the same love for our field that is reflected in Jones and Gerard's (1967) classic book, or field will have an exciting future.

REFERENCES

Atkinson, J. W., & Feather, N. T. (Eds.) (1966). *A theory of achievement motivation.* New York: Wiley.

Bowlby, J. (1969). *Attachment* (Attachment and loss, Vol. 1). New York: Basic Books.

Bowlby, J. (1973). *Separation: Anxiety and anger* (Attachment and loss, Vol. 2). New York: Basic Books.

Bruner, J. S. (1957). On perceptual readiness. *Psychological Review, 64,* 123–152.

Carver, C. S., & Scheier, M. F. (1990). Principles of self-regulation: Action and emotion. In E. T. Higgins & R. M. Sorrentino (Eds.), *Handbook of motivation and cognition: Foundations of social behavior, Volume 2* (pp. 3–52). New York: Guilford Press.

Crowe, E., & Higgins, E. T. (1997). Regulatory focus and strategic inclinations: Promotion and prevention in decision-making. *Organizational Behavior and Human Decision Processes, 69,* 117–132.

Fazio, R. H. (1986). How do attitudes guide behavior? In R. M. Sorrentino & E. T. Higgins (Eds.), *Handbook of motivation and cognition: Foundations of social behavior* (pp. 204–243). New York: Guilford.

Gilligan, S. G., & Bower, G. H. (1984). Cognitive consequences of emotional arousal. In C. E. Izard, J. Kagan, & R. B. Zajonc (Eds.), *Emotions, cognition, and behavior* (pp. 547–588). Cambridge, England: Cambridge University Press.

Higgins, E. T. (1987). Self-discrepancy: A theory relating self and affect. *Psychological Review, 94,* 319–340.

Higgins, E. T. (1989). Self-discrepancy theory: What patterns of self-beliefs cause people to suffer? In L. Berkowitz (Ed.), *Advances in experimental social psychology, Volume 22* (pp. 93–136). San Diego, CA: Academic Press.

Higgins, E. T. (1991). Development of self-regulatory and self-evaluative processes: Costs, benefits, and tradeoffs. In M. R. Gunnar & L. A. Sroufe (Eds.), *Self processes and development: The Minnesota symposia on child psychology, Volume 23* (pp. 125–165). Hillsdale, NJ: Erlbaum.

Higgins, E. T. (1996a). Emotional experiences: The pains and pleasures of distinct regulatory systems. In R. D. Kavanaugh, B. Zimmerberg, & S. Fein (Eds.), *Emotion: Interdisciplinary perspectives* (pp. 203–241). Hillsdale, NJ: Erlbaum.

Higgins, E. T. (1996b). Knowledge activation: Accessibility, applicability, and salience. In E. T. Higgins & A. W. Kruglanski (Eds.), *Social psychology: Handbook of basic principles* (pp. 133–168). New York: Guilford.

Higgins, E. T., Bond, R. N., Klein, R., & Strauman, T. (1986). Self-discrepancies and emotional vulnerability: How magnitude, accessibility, and type of discrepancy influence affect. *Journal of Personality and Social Psychology, 51,* 5–15.

Higgins, E. T., & King, G. (1981). Accessibility of social constructs: Information processing consequences of individual and contextual variability. In N. Cantor & J. Kihlstrom (Eds.), *Personality, cognition, and social interaction* (pp. 69–121). Hillsdale, NJ: Erlbaum.

Higgins, E. T., & Kruglanski, A. W. (Eds.). (1996). *Social psychology: Handbook of basic principles.* New York: Guilford.

Higgins, E. T., Roney, C. J. R., Crowe, E., & Hymes, C. (1994). Ideal versus ought predilections for approach and avoidance: Distinct self-regulatory systems. *Journal of Personality and Social Psychology, 66,* 276–286.

Higgins, E. T., Strauman, T., & Klein, R. (1986). Standards and the process of self-evaluation: Multiple affects from multiple stages. In R. M. Sorrentino

& E. T. Higgins (Eds.), *Handbook of motivation and cognition: Foundations of social behavior* (pp. 23–63). New York: Guilford.

Higgins, E. T., & Tykocinski, O. (1992). Self-discrepancies and biographical memory: Personality and cognition at the level of psychological situation. *Personality and Social Psychology Bulletin, 18,* 527–535.

Isen, A. M. (1984). Toward understanding the role of affect in cognition. In R. S. Wyer & T. K. Srull (Eds.), *Handbook of social cognition* (Vol. 3, 179–236). Hillsdale, NJ: Erlbaum.

Jones, E. E., & Gerard, H. B. (1967). *Foundations of social psychology.* New York: Wiley & Sons.

Kelly, G. A. (1955). *The psychology of personal constructs.* New York: W. W. Norton.

Markus, H., & Nurius, P. (1986). Possible selves. *American Psychologist, 41,* 954–969.

Mowrer, O. H. (1960). *Learning theory and behavior.* New York: Wiley.

Olson, J. M., Roese, N. J., & Zanna, M. P. (1996). Expectancies. In E. T. Higgins & A. W. Kruglanski (Eds.), *Social psychology: Handbook of basic principles* (pp. 211–238). New York: Guilford.

Roney, C. J. R., Higgins, E. T., & Shah, J. (1995). Goals and framing: How outcome focus influences motivation and emotion. *Personality and Social Psychology Bulletin, 21,* 1151–1160.

Roseman, I. J. (1984). Cognitive determinants of emotion: A structural theory. *Review of Personality and Social Psychology, 5,* 11–36.

Stein, N. L., & Jewett, J. L. (1982). A conceptual analysis of the meaning of negative emotions: Implications for a theory of development. In C. E. Izard (Ed.), *Measuring emotions in infants and children* (pp. 401–443). Cambridge, England: Cambridge University Press.

Thomas, W. I., & Thomas, D. S. (1928). *The child in America.* New York: Knopf.

Weber, M. (1967). Subjective meaning in the social situation. In G. B. Levitas (Ed.), *Culture and consciousness: Perspectives in the social sciences* (pp. 156–169). New York: Braziller.

From Worldviews to Beliefs, Values, and Attitudes

Russell H. Fazio

Like Rohan and Zanna (this volume), I want to applaud Tory Higgins's (see chapter 5) quest to expand on the treatment of socialization that Jones and Gerard (1967) presented in their classic text *Foundations of Social Psychology*. Jones and Gerard's book is unquestionably a hallmark in the history of social psychology. It provides a fascinating and integrative treatment of the field—one that has influenced generations of students and researchers. Even today, nearly 30 years after its publication, the book remains a source of rich insights because Jones and Gerard were able to anticipate many of the directions in which the field would move.

For Jones and Gerard (1967), the interest in childhood socialization centered on the development of beliefs, values, and attitudes as a function of the child's effect dependence and information dependence on others, particularly parents. Higgins's theoretical efforts link socialization, not to specific beliefs, values, and attitudes, or in his terms *expectancies*, but to general worldviews. The essence of the argument is that

Preparation of this comment was supported by Research Scientist Development Award MH00452 and Grant MH38832 from the National Institute of Mental Health.

different socialization experiences lead to the predominance of distinct regulatory systems: one that is nurturance oriented in the sense that it stems from parental practices that emphasize the award or withdrawal of signs of affection and one that is security oriented in that it stems from the administration of sanctions for the child. The nurturance orientation is theorized to produce a self-regulatory system that emphasizes ideal standards (hopes and aspirations) and concern with the presence or absence of positive outcomes. In contrast, a security orientation emphasizes ought standards (duties and obligations) and concern with the presence or absence of negative outcomes.

The research that Higgins and his students have conducted has established the existence of a relation between these worldviews, on the one hand, and the memorability of specific classes of events, on the other hand. These classes of events are distinguished in terms of their involving the presence or absence of a positive outcome, or the presence or absence of a negative outcome. A predominant concern with ideal standards promotes a positive outcome focus, and a concern with ought standards a negative outcome focus. Thus, general worldviews, presumably dependent on socialization history, appear to ready the individual to perceive and remember particular kinds of events (e.g., Higgins & Tykocinski, 1992).

The major question that I would like to pose is how one might connect these theoretical and empirical efforts back to the emphasis that Jones and Gerard (1967) placed on beliefs, values, and attitudes. Here's what they have to say about the importance of beliefs, values, and attitudes:

> Especially in theorizing about man it is tempting to want to characterize his many-sided complexity or to construct an exhaustive inventory of his propensities. We propose to resist such temptations. Instead we shall seek to construct a useful *minimal person*—the socialized product of the conditions of effect and information dependence—having only those attributes needed to understand the major phenomena of social psychology . . . The minimal person for our purposes is a composite of beliefs, values, and attitudes. (p. 157)

What are the implications of Higgins's formulation for this level of analysis? Rohan and Zanna (this volume) have suggested that Higgins's distinctions with respect to self-regulatory systems may relate to individuals' priorities with respect to value systems. A security orientation may lead to a general emphasis on values representing conservatism; a nurturance orientation may promote a general emphasis on values reflecting an openness to change. I would like to suggest that Higgins's conceptual distinctions also may have implications for beliefs and attitudes and, in particular, for their representation in memory.

BELIEFS

Let's first consider beliefs. According to Jones and Gerard (1967), a "belief expresses the relations between two cognitive categories" and "concerns the associated characteristics of the object" (p. 158). This definition certainly remains acceptable today and, given the approach I have pursued to the study of attitudes as object–evaluation associations, I am especially comfortable with the characterization of a belief as an association between the object and an attribute of the object. The strength of this association may vary and will determine the likelihood that a given attribute will be activated from memory on observation of the object.

Higgins's formulation regarding positive versus negative outcome focus may have implications for the strength of such object–attribute associations. Individuals with a positive outcome focus (i.e., those who emphasize ideal self-guides and possess a nurturance orientation) may be especially likely to develop strong associations in memory for any attributes that concern the presence or absence of positive outcomes. In contrast, those with a negative outcome focus (i.e., those who emphasize ought self-guides and a security orientation) may be relatively more likely to develop strong associations for attributes that concern the presence or absence of negative outcomes.

To give a rather mundane example, consider the object "ice cream" and beliefs that it is tasty—a positive outcome—and yet at the same time, fattening—presumably a negative outcome. Would the positive outcome individual be more likely to develop a stronger association between ice cream and the attribute of tasty than between ice cream and the attribute of fattening? Likewise, would the negative outcome individual be relatively more likely to develop a stronger association with the attribute of fattening? If so, then what the two types of individuals perceive when presented with ice cream could be very different. Whether ice cream is categorized as and perceived as a tasty or a fattening substance could vary as a function of outcome focus. It is in this way that the general worldviews of which Higgins speaks could result in representations of objects in memory that emphasize different attributes of the objects. In other words, the worldviews themselves, or at least the same forces that shaped those worldviews, could have an influence on beliefs.

ATTITUDES

A similar argument can be made with respect to attitudes and their representation in memory. As mentioned earlier, I have proposed that attitudes can be viewed as object–evaluation associations in memory— a view that is quite compatible with Jones and Gerard's (1967) characterization of attitudes as essentially evaluative beliefs. According to the model that underlies my research program (see Fazio, 1995, for a review), the strength of the object–evaluation association in memory can vary and determines the likelihood that the evaluation or attitude will be activated from memory when the individual encounters the attitude object. Are individuals with differing worldviews likely to develop stronger object–evaluation associations and hence more accessible attitudes for different classes of attitude objects? I think they may— largely because it seems reasonable to classify attitude objects in the same way that Higgins has classified types of psychological events, as a function of outcome focus (see Exhibit 1).

By their very inherent function, some objects seem to involve largely the presence of a positive outcome (e.g., any desirable foods, wines, or otherwise generally appetitive object). Other objects clearly involve the presence of negative outcomes (e.g., snakes, insects, and the like). But,

Exhibit 1	
Examples of Objects Likely to Vary as a Function of Presence or Absence of Positive Versus Negative Outcomes	
Positive outcome	Negative outcome
Presence	
Any appetitive object	Any dangerous, harmful object
Absence	
Fasting	Condom
Diet	Flu shot
Legal drinking age	Sunblock
Losing lottery ticket	Balanced Budget Amendment

there also are objects whose inherent function is to prevent a negative outcome. For example, the purpose of condoms is to prevent sexually transmitted disease or pregnancy; a flu shot is intended to diminish the likelihood of catching the flu; sunblock is intended to prevent sunburn. Presumably, the Balanced Budget Amendment, at least according to Newt Gingrich, will prevent budget deficits. Thus, these are objects that, by their very nature, center on the prevention of a negative outcome. It also is possible to consider objects whose purpose involves the prevention or absence of positive outcomes. Fasting or dieting seem to be of this nature. Certainly, to a high school senior or a college freshman, a law imposing a legal drinking age might be viewed as an impediment to a positive outcome.

As a result of their negative outcome focus, individuals for whom a security orientation predominates may be more likely to develop accessible attitudes toward objects that inherently involve the presence or absence of *negative* outcomes. In effect, such objects may be, relatively speaking, more evaluatively laden for such individuals than are objects that inherently involve the presence or absence of positive outcomes. It may be those with a *positive* outcome focus who are more likely to develop relatively accessible attitudes toward this latter class of objects.

This line of reasoning leads to the suggestion that individuals' outcome focus may underlie the extent to which they become attitudinally expert in various domains. The negative outcome focus individuals may be more attitudinally expert—know their likes and dislikes better—for classes of objects that involve the presence or absence of negatives. Positive outcome focus individuals may be more attitudinally expert in those domains involving objects that involve the presence or absence of positives.

Obviously, these comments are largely speculative thoughts at this point. Nevertheless, if they have any validity, then some very interesting and reciprocal relations may exist among values, beliefs, and attitudes, on the one hand, and worldviews on the other. The worldviews may influence the representation of values, beliefs, and attitudes—representations that then may have consequences for the individuals' perception of, attention to, and behavior toward objects in the social world.

For example, it has been found that objects toward which an individual possesses highly accessible attitudes automatically and inescapably attract attention when they enter the visual field (Roskos-Ewoldsen & Fazio, 1992). Thus, of the multitude of objects in their daily environments, people will tend to notice those toward which they hold accessible attitudes. Accessible attitudes exert a similar influence on the categorization of objects. Many objects that people encounter can be thought of in multiple manners (i.e., they are multiply categorizable). For instance, yogurt can be viewed as a health food or as a dairy product, sunbathing as an activity that can lead to cancer or as something one does at the beach. The potential category toward which the individual has the more accessible attitude has been found to dominate the categorization process (Smith, Fazio, & Cejka, 1996). So, someone with a highly accessible attitude toward the beach is more likely to view sunbathing as related to the beach, whereas someone with a highly accessible attitude toward skin cancer is more likely to view sunbathing as related to cancer.

These findings point to potential mediating mechanisms by which differential worldviews may come to shape individuals' day-to-day experiences. If worldviews affect the accessibility of attitudes and beliefs in the manner that I have suggested, then security- and nurturance-oriented individuals may attend to, categorize, and perceive objects in the social world very differently. In effect, they may live in different social worlds. These resulting differential experiences, in turn, should serve to bolster the predominant worldview that characterizes these individuals. For example, an emphasis on negativity (i.e., a predilection to notice negative objects and to categorize as negative objects that could be construed in multiple ways) may enhance an individual's concerns for security. Likewise, a propensity to notice positively valued objects and to categorize objects positively may contribute to the individual's view of the world as revolving around concerns with nurturance.

In sum, Higgins's conceptualization may help us to understand not only how the socialized child moves from expectancies about interactions with his or her parents to worldviews, but also how those same socializing forces and worldviews may affect beliefs, values, and attitudes.

REFERENCES

Fazio, R. H. (1995). Attitudes as object–evaluation associations: Determinants, consequences, and correlates of attitude accessibility. In R. E. Petty & J. A. Krosnick (Eds.), *Attitude strength: Antecedents and consequences* (pp. 247–282). Hillsdale, NJ: Erlbaum.

Higgins, E. T., & Tykocinski, O. (1992). Self-discrepancies and biographical memory: Personality and cognition at the level of psychological situation. *Personality and Social Psychology Bulletin, 18,* 527–535.

Jones, E. E., & Gerard, H. B. (1967). *Foundations of social psychology.* New York: Wiley.

Roskos-Ewoldsen, D. R., & Fazio, R. H. (1992). On the orienting value of attitudes: Attitude accessibility as a determinant of an object's attraction of visual attention. *Journal of Personality and Social Psychology, 63,* 198–211.

Smith, E. R., Fazio, R. H., & Cejka, M. A. (1996). Accessible attitudes influence categorization of multiply categorizable objects. *Journal of Personality and Social Psychology, 71,* 888–898.

The "Products of Socialization": A Discussion of Self-Regulatory Strategies and Value Systems

Meg J. Rohan and Mark P. Zanna

Jones and Gerard (1967) discussed at length the "dispositional" or attitudinal outcomes of people's upbringing that result in differences in worldviews—the "products of socialization." In his contribution to this volume, Tory Higgins (see chapter 5) has built on the foundations provided by Ned Jones and Hal Gerard. In this chapter we discuss Higgins's contribution. We briefly summarize the ideas put forward by Higgins, discuss our own work as it relates to those ideas, consider some of the developmental issues involved, and, finally, ask questions that can be explored in future research.

We agree with Higgins that an emphasis on socialization needs to recapture the attention of social psychologists. Higgins has suggested that by paying attention to socialization we can begin to provide answers to one of the fundamental questions in social science: How does social regulation affect self-regulation?

Higgins noted that values and attitudes often are investigated as

Preparation of this comment was supported in part by a Social Sciences and Humanities Research Council of Canada (SSHRC) Doctoral Fellowship to Meg J. Rohan and an SSHRC grant to Mark P. Zanna. In addition to Tory Higgins, Russ Fazio, and John Darley, we thank Ziva Kunda for commenting on a draft of the manuscript.

relatively distinct mental elements. Because of this focus, there has been little exploration of the way people's attitudes—or the expectancies that arise from their specific value priorities—combine to become the basis of their worldviews. Higgins has put forward an impressive solution that bridges the gap between specific expectancies and general worldviews. It provides an approach for investigating the motivating foundations of people's worldviews.

SELF-REGULATORY STRATEGIES AS MOTIVATING FOUNDATIONS

According to Higgins (chapter 5), parents play a significant role in the development of their children's self-regulatory strategies. Parents, with their differing ways of communicating the hopes, expectations, or aspirations they have for their children, influence the development of their children's self-regulatory strategies. When parental hopes, expectations, or aspirations become rule-like and are enforced through sanctions and punishments, children learn to regulate their behavior using "ought" self-guides, and learn to focus on avoiding negative consequences. On the other hand, when fulfillment of parental hopes, expectations, or aspirations is nurtured through use of rewards for desirable behavior, children learn to regulate their behavior using "ideal" self-guides, and learn to focus on achieving positive consequences. So, as a result of parents' socialization techniques, children learn to regulate their own behavior with reference to an outcome orientation that has either a positive or negative focus. Positively focused individuals develop nurturance-oriented (or positive outcome) self-regulatory strategies, and negatively focused individuals develop security-oriented (or negative outcome) self-regulatory strategies. Although individuals are likely to develop the capacity for using both strategies, only one strategy will become their habitual mode of responding to the world.

Higgins therefore suggests that individuals' habitual responses to the world—and as a consequence, their worldviews—have their origins in the types of socialization experiences they had as children. In our own research, we also have operated on the assumption that parents have a strong, lasting influence on their children's habitual responses to the world, and we also have been interested in finding a way to comprehensively describe and examine the motivating foundations of individuals' worldviews. Like Higgins, we found that the examination of isolated attitudes or values does not allow a clear understanding of the connection between specific expectancies and general worldviews. Instead of examining isolated attitudes and values, we examined value systems. Why value systems? We discuss the answer to this question next.

VALUE SYSTEMS AS MOTIVATING FOUNDATIONS

Two features of value systems are important to us. First, following Shalom Schwartz (e.g., Schwartz, 1996), we assume that people possess integrated value systems in which priorities on one value type have consequences for priorities on all other value types. Second, we assume that values have important cognitive, affective, and behavioral consequences. Values function as "the criteria people use to select and justify actions and to evaluate people (including the self) and events" (Shwartz, 1992, p. 1). In other words, we propose that the value system is itself a basis for self-regulation and, as such, can be used to provide a comprehensive way of describing the motivating foundations of people's worldviews.

IS THERE A RELATION BETWEEN VALUE SYSTEMS AND SELF-REGULATORY STRATEGIES?

An obvious question to ask is whether there is a relation between self-regulatory strategies and value systems. What are the general similarities? First, both self-regulatory strategies and value priorities in an integrated value system are likely to be relatively stable. Second, Higgins has presented convincing evidence that demonstrates the pervasive effects of habitual self-regulatory strategies, and there exists similarly convincing evidence that value systems also have general and pervasive effects on the way people respond (e.g., Sagiv & Schwartz, 1995).

Another similarity follows from the fact that people have access to both types of self-regulatory strategies, and to all value types in the value system. This means, then, that situational pressures may stimulate the use of one or other of the self-regulatory strategies and may stimulate differing configurations of value priorities. This is a useful feature of both self-regulatory strategies and value systems because it may allow experimental examination of their motivating effects. Indeed, Higgins already has shown that situations can be arranged experimentally so that people use one or the other of the self-regulatory strategies.

There are other possible connections between self-regulatory strategies and value systems. Consider the organization of the value system (see Figure 1). According to Schwartz (see, e.g., 1992), the value system is structured by two underlying dimensions (which can be understood as underlying motivations), and the 10 value types that he has identified are located along the two dimensions.

Because an integrated system is proposed, adjacent value types should be related, and value types that have opposing underlying motivations will be in conflict. So, for example, to the extent that individuals place importance on the *Conformity* value type (which includes values relevant to self-restraint), they also can be expected to place importance on the *Tradition* value type (which includes values relevant to respect and acceptance of group customs and ideas) and the *Security* value type (which includes values relevant to safety, harmony, and stability), but are unlikely to place a high priority on *Self-Direction* (which includes values relevant to independent thought and creativity) or *Stimulation* (which includes values relevant to excitement, novelty, and challenge in life).

Intuition suggests that people who have self-regulatory strategies that are strongly security oriented (and who therefore are focused on avoiding negative consequences) may place high priorities on Conformity, Tradition, and Security. These value types all have the underlying motivation of conservatism, and all emphasize order and resistance to change. People who place high priorities on these value types are likely to self-regulate in terms of strong ought guides. As suggested earlier, people who self-regulate according to ought guides focus on avoiding negative outcomes and have self-regulatory strategies that are security-oriented.

The possible connections between self-regulatory styles that are nurturance, positive-outcome oriented also are implied by the structure of the value system. Again, intuition suggests a relation: nurturance-oriented individuals may very well place high priorities on value types that lie in direct conflict with Conformity, Tradition, and Security, namely Self-Direction and Stimulation. Underlying the Self-Direction value type (which includes priorities on, for example, creativity and

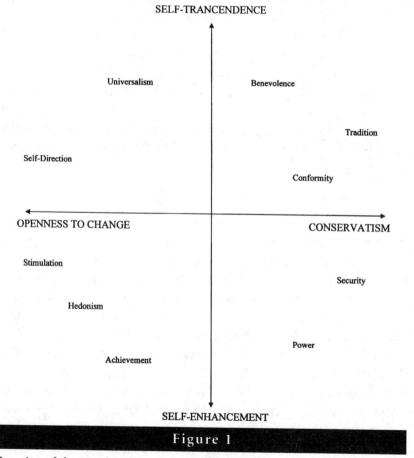

Figure 1

Location of the 10 value types along two dimensions.

independence) and the Stimulation value type (which includes priorities on, for example, having a varied life and having an exciting life) is an openness to change. People who place importance on these value types are likely to self-regulate in terms of strong ideal guides. As mentioned, people who self-regulate according to ideal guides focus on the potential for positive outcomes and have self-regulatory strategies that are nurturance oriented.

It is possible, then, that there are some interesting connections between value systems and self-regulatory strategies: Both value systems and self-regulatory strategies likely are relatively stable, both have pervasive effects on the ways people respond, and situational pressures may stimulate the use of one or other of the self-regulatory strategies and may stimulate differing integrated sets of value priorities. Furthermore, there may be predictable relations between habitually used self-regulatory strategies and value priorities within an integrated value system. A question to ask, then, in light of these possible connections, is whether changes in one system will be accompanied by changes in the other system. This will be an interesting question for future research.

VALUE SYSTEMS, WORLDVIEWS, AND SELF-REGULATORY STRATEGIES

Recall that one of the reasons Higgins has been investigating self-regulatory strategies and one of the reasons we have been focusing on people's value systems in our own research is to understand the relation between people's specific expectancies that arise from particular attitudes or values and their general worldviews. We have pursued this question. Specifically, we have examined the way value systems relate to particular types of worldviews (e.g., Rohan & Zanna, 1996). The three value types that we have just suggested might be related to a negative-outcome, self-regulatory orientation—that is, conformity, tradition, and security—are associated with one worldview, the right-wing authoritarian worldview (see Figure 2). People who subscribe to right-wing authoritarian worldviews (according to Altemeyer, 1988, 1994) adhere strongly to social conventions, submit unquestioningly to

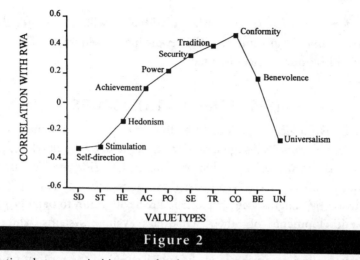

Figure 2

Correlations between priorities on each value type and right-wing authoritarianism (RWA). SD = self-direction; ST = stimulation; HE = hedonism; AC = achievement; PO = power; SE = security; TR = tradition; CO = conformity; BE = benevolence; UN = universalism.

authorities they perceive as legitimate, and are aggressive toward people they believe violate the authorities they respect.[1] In right-wing authoritarian worldviews, then, there is a focus on rules and regulations, and high priority is placed on values that are motivated by conservatism. It is possible, therefore, that people who have right-wing authoritarian worldviews will use self-regulatory strategies that focus on avoiding sanctions. Their strategies will be security-oriented.

A worldview that is not right-wing authoritarian can be described as egalitarian. Unlike people who have right-wing authoritarian worldviews, people who have egalitarian worldviews are open to change and are not conservative—they value diversity. Indeed, there is a negative correlation between the Self-Direction and Stimulation value types and right-wing authoritarianism (see again Figure 2). It is possible, then,

---

[1] Consider one item of Altemeyer's (1988) scale: "Once our government leaders and the authorities condemn the dangerous elements in our society, it will be the duty of every patriotic citizen to help stomp out the rot that is poisoning our country from within."

that people who have egalitarian worldviews will use self-regulatory strategies that focus on potentially rewarding consequences. Their strategies will be nurturance oriented.

DEVELOPMENTAL ISSUES

How do worldviews develop? Does the development of value priorities precede and cause self-regulatory strategies or does the development of self-regulatory strategies precede and cause value priorities? The emphasis on socialization that was proposed by Jones and Gerard (1967), and discussed by Higgins (see chapter 5), directs attention to parents' role in the development of their children's value systems and self-regulatory strategies to provide answers to this question. More generally, we can explore parents' role in the socialization of the motivating foundations of their children's worldviews. But socialization processes cover a vast territory—on what tractable questions can we focus our attention?

It is reasonable to assume that parents' aim is to socialize their children to view the world in a particular way. That way likely will be the parents' way. One first step toward understanding parental influence in the development of their children's worldviews may be to explore the nature of the relations between parental hopes, expectations, or aspirations and parents' worldviews. Do parents with differing worldviews have differing hopes, expectations, or aspirations for their children?

We have started to look at this question and have found that one worldview—again, the right-wing authoritarian worldview—is strongly related to parents' expectations for their children (Rohan & Zanna, 1995b). Specifically, expectations of right-wing authoritarian parents are more likely to serve predominantly instrumental, means–end goals rather than more expressive, relationship-oriented goals. Right-wing authoritarian parents are more likely, for example, to want their children to "have good manners" or to "be neat and clean," whereas egalitarian parents are more likely to want their children to "be considerate of others."[2]

---

[2]When we looked at the value type that is most strongly related to highly right-wing authoritarian worldviews—conformity—we found that parental priorities on this value type partially explained the relation between right-wing authoritarian worldviews and parents' child-related goals.

How do parents make their expectations known to their children? If parents have predominantly instrumental, means–end goals that are motivated by conservative values and focus on rules and regulations, they may be particularly sensitive to behavior in their child that might be viewed as "out of line" with their standards. They may be more likely to "lay down the rules" and tolerate no argument. In short, they likely will demand that their child behave in particular ways. As Higgins (chapter 5) pointed out, the result of parents' rule-bound demands may be that children learn to regulate their behavior by focusing on avoiding negative consequences. On the other hand, parents who have mainly expressive, relationship-oriented goals may make their expectations known in other ways. Rather than simply demanding that their children behave in particular ways, they may take the time to explain the reasons for their wishes. They also likely will make an effort to understand the reasons for their children's behaviors, and they are likely to be responsive to their children. Investigation of the ways (and whether) parents react to particular behaviors (e.g., when their children are not displaying good manners, or are not neat and clean, or are not being considerate of others) will be a useful direction for research.

Another important step in understanding parental influence is to examine the success parents have in transmitting their worldviews to their children. The question of tractability arises again: How can we measure the success of parents' socialization efforts? We decided that it was important to look at adults and their parents. If parents have been successful in their socialization efforts, then their children, as adults, will have similar worldviews. Furthermore, because value systems can be measured to provide a comprehensive description of the motivating foundations of people's worldviews (see Rohan & Zanna, 1995a), the comparison of parents' and their adult children's value systems provides a suitable—and tractable—way of measuring parents' success in their socialization efforts.

We compared the value systems of parents and their university-aged children, within families (Rohan & Zanna, 1996). For each family, we had a measure of mother's, father's, and their adult child's value systems. Specifically, we calculated an index of similarity among them on the basis of correlations among their value priorities on each of the 10 value types.[3] We found that when we looked at parents generally, they seemed not to be outstandingly successful in their value transmission. However, when we looked more closely, we found that successful value transmission was moderated by parental worldviews. Specifically, parents who had right-wing authoritarian worldviews were less successful than parents who had egalitarian worldviews.[4]

WHAT ABOUT REBELLIOUS CHILDREN?

Why are some parents more successful than others in transmitting their worldviews to their children? What socialization techniques are more likely to lead to successful transmission than others? Higgins has suggested, and we endorse his suggestion, that the key to understanding the development of the motivating foundations of people's worldviews lies in the interactions parents have with their children. We have implied that parents differ in the extent to which they demand their children live up to particular standards and in the extent to which they are responsive to their children. What then, do adults—who either do or do not endorse their parents' value systems—remember about the "demandingness" and responsiveness of their parents?

We asked university-aged adults (see Rohan & Zanna, 1996) to recall the way their parents interacted with them. The questionnaire we designed and administered was based on two underlying dimensions—parental demandingness and parental responsiveness. These dimensions also can be understood as representing control and warmth. To the extent that their parents had right-wing authoritarian worldviews, individuals reported that their parents had been demanding. In line with

[3]For each family, mothers' and fathers' value profiles were aggregated by averaging because of a high degree of similarity. For each family, then, we calculated a correlation coefficient (which, for use as data points, were transformed with a Fisher's r-to-z transformation) that described the degree of similarity between parents' and their adult children's value systems.

[4]Similarity of value systems between egalitarian parents and their adult children was significantly higher than in randomly matched parents and adult children (calculated to account for cultural similarity), whereas for right-wing authoritarian parents and their adult children it was no higher than this random baseline.

predictions made earlier, to the extent that right-wing authoritarian parents were perceived as being demanding, they were more likely to have had goals for the socialization of their children that were predominantly instrumental (e.g., that children have good manners or that they be neat and clean). In contrast, to the extent that parents had egalitarian worldviews, individuals reported that their parents had been responsive. Also in line with predictions made earlier, to the extent that egalitarian parents were perceived as being responsive, they were more likely to have had goals for their children that were predominantly expressive and relationship oriented (e.g., that children be interested in how and why things happen or that they be considerate of others).

To the extent that individuals remembered their parents as being responsive to them, they were more likely to endorse their parents' values. Responsive parents therefore were more successful in transmitting the values that provide the motivating foundations of their children's worldviews than were unresponsive parents. In addition, individuals' perceptions of their parents' responsiveness in large part explained why egalitarian parents were more successful than right-wing authoritarian parents in the transmission of their value systems. This finding supports a suggestion made by Jones and Gerard (1967) that "the greater the nurturance, the stronger the identification with the nurturant parent" (p. 119). Not surprisingly, perceptions of parental responsiveness also were linked to people's evaluations of their parents: Parents who were remembered as having been responsive were also more likely to be evaluated as having been trustworthy, fair, and not hypocritical. Perhaps when children cannot think well of their parents, they look for other adults of whom they can think well, and are then socialized according to values other than those upheld by their parents.

Do children who rebel against their parents, and who grow up to hold worldviews that differ from the worldviews of their parents, reorganize their value systems and develop new self-regulatory strategies? Although we have found that some adult children appear to have successfully discarded their parents' value systems, observation—and experience—alerts us to the possibility that complete overthrow of parents' value systems may not be possible. Just think of the times when we have done something that is completely in line with our own values but is out of line with our parents' values. How loudly did we hear our parents' disapproval?

Garrison Keillor (1986), in his novel *Lake Wobegon Days*, offers some insight. He tells of the former Lake Wobegon resident who rejects completely his parents' values, but who finds that he remains inextricably tied to his parents' ways of thinking. The character in the story concludes:

> I wasted years in diametrical opposition, thinking you were completely mistaken, and wound up living a life *based more on yours* than if I'd stayed home. (p. 329)

The character did not, however, share his parents' attitudes and values. It seems though, that his parents' values and attitudes were ever accessible—he seemed still to see the world through his parents' eyes. For example,

> For fear of what it might do to me, you never paid a compliment, and when other people did, you beat it away from me with a stick. "He certainly is looking nice and grown up." *He'd look a lot nicer if he did something about his skin.* "That's wonderful that he got that job." *Yeah, well, we'll see how long it lasts.* You trained me so well, now I perform this service for myself. I deflect every kind word directed at me. (p. 323)

Think of it this way. Rebellion implies knowledge of the opposing opinion. Therefore, is it possible that this knowledge remains conveniently available, even highly accessible, in case further rebellion is required? As a result of this chronic accessibility, will rebellious children pay closer attention to features of their worlds that are more relevant to their parents' value priorities than to their own? Furthermore, will this chronic accessibility mean that these individuals will need to exercise conscious cognitive control over their responses—because they will need to defend themselves against the motivating influence of their parents' value systems? If so, might this also mean that this control can be disrupted with increases in cognitive load?[5]

These questions imply that although it may be possible for children to grow up and embrace value systems that differ from their parents' value systems, it may not be so easy, in fact, for people to "turn their backs on" what they learned during their socialization. An interesting explanation for this inability may be implied by the relation between value systems and habitual self-regulatory focus. Recall that we proposed that there may be predictable relations between type of self-regulatory focus and value priorities in an integrated value system. Is it possible that for rebellious children who are unable to "shake off" their parents' influence—like the character in Garrison Keillor's novel—there is a mismatch between their newly embraced value system and the self-regulatory focus they developed during their socialization?

Questions about the enduring nature of the products of socialization bring us suspiciously close to the discussion by Jones and Gerard (1967) about the resistance to extinction of "dispositions" learned in childhood. The fact that our discussion concludes in territory that Ned Jones has already navigated provides another demonstration of Ned's influence.

The work of Higgins is in the Ned Jones tradition. True to this tradition, Higgins has provided some important insights. The questions he has raised, as we have tried to point out in our discussion, are likely to direct research in the area for quite some time to come.

REFERENCES

Altemeyer, B. (1988). *Enemies of freedom: Understanding right-wing authoritarianism.* San Francisco: Jossey-Bass.

Altemeyer, B. (1994). Reducing prejudice in right-wing authoritarians. In M.

---

[5]John Darley suggested a time when cognitive overload may allow "our parents' ghastly value systems" to be displayed in their full finery. Looking after children can—to say the least—consume incredible amounts of cognitive resource, and when the children do something that (with a clear mind) is just fine with us, but would not be so with our parents, we may hear ourselves yelling in what is a terrifying echo of our parents.

P. Zanna & J. M. Olson (Eds.), *The Ontario Symposium: The psychology of prejudice* (Vol. 7, pp. 131–148). Hillsdale, NJ: Erlbaum.

Jones, E. E., & Gerard, H. B. (1967). *Foundations of social psychology.* New York: Wiley.

Keillor, G. (1986). *Lake Wobegon days.* New York: Penguin.

Rohan, M. J., & Zanna, M. P. (1995a, June). *Husbands and wives sometimes but not always have similar value profiles.* Poster presented at the Seventh Annual Convention of the American Psychological Society, New York.

Rohan, M. J., & Zanna, M. P. (1995b, August). *Value priorities, worldviews, and the content and expression of goals.* Poster presented at the 103rd Annual Convention of the American Psychological Association, New York.

Rohan, M. J., & Zanna, M. P. (1996). Value transmission in families. In C. Seligman, J. M. Olson, & M. P. Zanna (Eds.), *The Ontario Symposium: The psychology of values* (Vol. 8, pp. 253–276). Mahwah, NJ: Erlbaum.

Sagiv, L., & Schwartz, S. H. (1995). Value priorities and readiness for outgroup social contact. *Journal of Personality and Social Psychology, 69,* 437–448.

Schwartz, S. H. (1992). Universals in the content and structure of values: Theoretical advances and empirical tests in 20 countries. In M. P. Zanna (Ed.), *Advances in Experimental Social Psychology* (Vol. 24, pp. 1–65). San Diego, CA: Academic Press.

Schwartz, S. (1996). Value priorities and behavior: Applying a theory of integrated value systems. In C. Seligman, J. M. Olson, & M. P. Zanna (Eds.), *The Ontario Symposium: The psychology of values* (Vol. 8, pp. 1–24). Mahwah, NJ: Erlbaum.

Toward the Relational Self

Kenneth J. Gergen

I f there is one critical issue the work of Edward E. Jones leaves as an intellectual challenge to the present scholarly community it is that of comprehending the self. In the corpus of his work treating self-presentation in general (Jones, 1965; Jones, Rhodewalt, Burglas, & Skelton, 1981), and ingratiation in particular (Jones, 1964), Jones paints a picture of an inscrutable master of subterfuge, one who might deceive oneself in the very process of deceiving others. When we are permitted a view behind the mask of public posture, it is only a momentary glance into possible motives and heuristics of calculation. Even in the single chapter of *Ingratiation* (Jones, 1964), treating cognitive and motivational determinants, Jones admits in conclusion that "we have continually emphasized the manipulable or detectable environmental conditions which are most likely to affect *p*'s cognitive and motivational state" (p. 115). The inner being disappears further into obscurity in Jones's offerings on attribution. In the classic study of the information effects of role-playing variations (Jones, Davis, & Gergen, 1961), we never learn of the *actual* opinions of the would-be astronaut and submariner. In the later work on correspondent inference (Jones & Davis, 1965) we come to appreciate how the perceiver might develop confidence in his or her attributions, but we are moved to doubt whether these attributions can ever be correspondent with the inner state of the other. Such doubt is fortified in arguments for *correspondent bias,* the tendency to attribute the cause of behavior to internal impulse as opposed to situational conditions. Yet, how are we to determine precisely when and where this tendency is mistaken? And, if our attributions to the self are generally mistaken, then what is to permit any confidence in our statements regarding inner life? At a more general level, if our conceptions of "inner life" generally result from misattributions, then what are we to make of the science of psychology? How are we to credit the vast array of cognitive attributions currently issuing from the recesses of myriad laboratories?

As such questions make clear, deliberation on the self is of the broadest consequence for psychology—both in terms of challenging content and the potentials of traditional research. Such discussion is pointed at nothing less than the fundamental conceptions of the person, at the metaphysical grounds on which we erect our theories, methods, and professional practices. Once we have fashioned a "picture of the self" we have essentially charted the parameters within which all further questions can be asked. We have established the implicative network within which answers can be framed. And in this way we have also established the kinds of meanings that will be communicated to the society, that contribute to the cultural future. Jones's puzzlements over the self can scarcely go unheeded.

In what follows I first consider the polarities of debate in which Jones's work is lodged, a debate that pits those committed to a belief in underlying processes of the self against those who find this position indefensible. Whereas those in the former domain champion specifically psychological answers to questions of human action, the latter are moved to more social (or external) forms of explanation. Because the weight of these arguments will favor the social account—albeit on grounds other than those articulated by Jones—we shall then consider two emerging attempts to reconceptualize the self in social terms. A sociocognitive view, attempting to integrate the polarities of debate, will first be considered. However, because of inherent problems, this position will finally be abandoned in favor of a relational account of the self. The latter account will serve as a positive answer to Jones's enigma.

THE FULL SELF: FROM MENTALISM TO COGNITIVISM

We may identify one cluster of assumptions about human functioning, firmly lodged in the philosophical tradition giving rise to psychology, which has guided psychological theory and research throughout the present century. This uniquely Western ethnopsychology first presumes the palpable existence of an array of mental processes, mechanisms, or structures—in effect, an ontology of the interior. Of course, the constituents of this interior have changed in important ways over the centuries. Whereas it was once fashionable to speak in terms of the soul, melancholy, or infirmities such as *mal de siecle*, we now opine effortlessly on information processing, computational systems, and schizophrenia. Yet, where the 19th-century mentalists and the 20th-century cognitivists agree—and where they are joined by psychoanalysts, trait theorists, emotions researchers, and attitude change investigators alike—is in the assumption that there are processes or mechanisms to be examined, and that to understand the functioning of these processes and mechanisms is to unlock the secrets of human action and the self.

To this belief the full self theorist will typically append three additional presumptions. At the outset, the ontology is typically imbued with universal properties. To understand the perceptual or memory processes of Smith is also to understand Brown, and to understand Smith and Brown here in the United States is to understand Misra in India and Hatanaka in Japan. Further, it is ventured, these universal processes or structures are open for systematic study. Whether through recent adventures in 19th-century introspection, 20th-century experimental triangulation, or contemporary computer modeling, it is assumed that research can furnish a more or less accurate or adequate picture of mental functioning. Finally, and by no means a necessary corollary of the aforementioned, it is often presumed that the constituents of the mental world are ideally integral and autonomous. That is, in the fully functioning person the various processes (memory, perception, emotion, etc.) will operate in concert (as opposed to conflict) and that this operation is inherent or natural (as opposed to culturally dependent). Or, as it is variously put, the "natural man" is self-contained or autonomous, capable of effective and adaptive action without benefit of cultural intervention. It is this conjury of assumptions that has served over the century to motivate and justify the great bulk of psychological research, if not the very claims of psychology to specifically scientific respectability.

THE EMPTYING OF SELF

For the most part, conceptions of the full self have occupied center stage in the drama of the discipline. Yet, the voices of a contrapuntal and contentious chorus—also resonating with early philosophic writing—have been sounded with regularity and intensity over the century. Again, the content has varied, but the black key stacatto has been unrelenting. There was first the influence of logical positivist philosophy and its insistence on word–object correspondence as the foundation for an empirical science. How are psychologists to forge such linkages, welding discriminate syllables with subjective states—the very states that positivism was designed to eliminate from the realm of a meaningful epistemology? It is this influence, of course, that formed the basis for radical behaviorism, and the view espoused by B. F. Skinner that mental predicates deserve no place in a mature science of human behavior. Similar misgivings emerged in the domain of ordinary language philosophy. Here, largely under the influence of Wittgenstein's (1953) *Philosophical Investigations*, philosophers began to explore the multiple and conflicting ways in which mental state terms are used within the culture and to worry about the function of such terms within a systematic science. Thus, for example, Gilbert Ryle's (1949) *The Concept of Mind* demonstrated the infinite regress of explanation into which the theorist enters when positing a mental state (a "ghost in the machine") as an explanation for a person's actions. To explain a person's effective actions in terms of "effective" thought preceding such actions simply shifts the site of explanation; it leaves open the question of why effective thought occurs. Such skepticism again burst on the scene with Stephen Stitch's (1983) critique of the use of folk terms (i.e., *thought* and *memory*) as the basis for a mature cognitive science. More radically, the eliminative materialism of Churchland (1981) calls for the abandonment of all mental state terms in favor of descriptions and explanations compatible with a materialist ontology.

In effect, the skeptical chorus has argued not for a full self, but an empty one, devoid of any specifically psychological processes, mechanisms, and the like. From this standpoint, there would be no specific psychological science. Inferences to a "psychological domain" would be little less than an exercise in mysticism. Rather, the understanding of human action would become a subcategory of ethological biology. Systematic observation of behavior—under controlled and natural circumstances—would inform us of the nature of human functioning. If there is no "mind within," then psychology is impossible and human action is simply a material or biological datum.

SHIFTING THE TERRAIN: THE SOCIAL SELF

As we find, the traditional pillars of debate leave us strapped between the Scylla of a fallacious full self and the Charybdis of a nihilistic non-self. One means of escaping this unsatisfying dilemma is through reconceptualization, through reconfiguring the binary. In particular, we may collapse these traditional rivals into a single unit and explore the potentials inherent in a new polarity. Interestingly, each of the traditional standpoints is distinctively *asocial*. That is, both full and empty self theorists tend to view the human organism as a self-contained entity, a bounded unit the capacities, characteristics, and functioning of which may be examined independent of its surrounds. As a significant contrast to such accounts, we may conceptualize the individual as inextricably social, not one whose major modes of action derive from processes inherently separated from culture and history, but one whose functioning is socially constituted. Here the removal of the individual from culture and history would essentially eradicate all those actions we identify as distinctively human. To put it otherwise, both the full and empty self conceptions tend to be lodged in an ontology of separation, natural man in the artificial circumstance of culture. In the present case, we shift to a view of human nature as culture, and human action as its artifact.

The attempt to articulate a social conception of the self is scarcely new. We possess a valuable legacy in Wundt's *Volkerpsychologie* (1900–1920), the works of George Herbert Mead, Charles Horton Cooley, Harry Stack Sullivan, and Lev Vygotsky, among others. Contemporary undertakings clearly bear the traces of preceding dialogues. Such historical reverberations are not insignificant in implication. For, as I attempt to demonstrate, because of their reliance on the past, the newly emerging accounts of the social self also carry with them a number of the tensions inherent in the antagonism between full and empty self theorists. Many of their assumptions and doubts resurface in the current undertakings, and though contemporary efforts "make history," they also grapple with its conundrums.

This latter comment is by way of introducing a distinction between two forms of conceptualizing the social self: *sociocognitive* and *relational.* In what follows I wish to sketch out the contours of these approaches and to demonstrate what I believe to be the superior potentials of the latter orientation.

SOCIOCOGNITIVE CONCEPTIONS OF SELF

In my view the major adventures into the social self of the past decade have been derivations—and simultaneously deviations—from the full self tradition. More specifically, in their presumption of internal processes, such as schemata, representations, meanings, or intentions, they derive much of their drama from cognitive psychology. Such processes or structures are presumed to exist and to parallel (even if analogically) some form of physiological processing. Further, as in the case of their cognitive predecessors, it is presumed that these structures or processes can be mapped by various methodological procedures; through experiments, questionnaires, interviews, and the like, the investigator may gain increasingly accurate understanding of their operation.

Yet, although sustaining these aspects of the full self tradition, sociocognitive formulations also deviate from them in significant ways. For illustrative purposes, it is useful to contrast Albert Bandura's (1977) efforts toward socializing the mental world and Lev Vygotsky's (1978) account. Bandura's theory of the social self places a strong emphasis on processes of operant conditioning and a cognitive theory of modeling. By virtue of these joint processes the individual comes to develop first the capacity to reward and punish self in the same manner as others have treated him or her. In effect, one internalizes what one observes in other's actions toward the self, and these internalizations become self-guiding in their effects. Second, the individual comes to engage in systematic interdependencies wherein sustaining the other (by virtue of one's actions) is to sustain self (by virtue of the other's patterns of response). Self and other are united by a system of feedback loops. In this account Bandura retains the entire range of full-self-conceptions save for the assumption of self-containment.

Bandura (1977) himself never explored the possibility that the admission of others into the mental compendium may have disruptive implications. Rather, it is assumed that the internal reinforcement mechanisms enable the individual to live more congenially in society. Further, the social feedback loops are not so much interferences in the natural order as they are forms of enlightened self-interest. ("If I wish my back scratched, I will have to watch how you get yours scratched.") In effect, Bandura moved only cautiously toward the brink of the social.

By contrast one may consider Vygotsky's (1978) work. Whereas full self theorists (including Bandura) operate on the presumption of naturalized mental process, Vygotsky replaced nature with culture. There is little of psychological significance given by nature, in terms of dictating the complex and significant actions of the individual. Rather, the mechanisms and processes of profound importance are given through immersion in the culture. The critical mental processes are, in effect, cultural processes carried out in the interior. With this conceptual step taken, not only is the commitment to universalized mental processes largely abandoned, but so is a view of the individual as self-contained and unified. Autonomy is abandoned, for on this account there is vir-

KENNETH J. GERGEN

tually no self without the preexistence of the other. There is no inherent self-direction, fundamental motive of self-interest, or natively endowed principle of high-order information processing. Further, there is no guarantee that the cultural incorporation will not lead to internal disharmony.

It is this move toward the preeminence of the social, and the accompanying diminishment of self-containment and natural harmony, that I see currently emerging in a family of social theories of self. Jerome Bruner (1990), in important respects a founding father of the cognitive movement, has now abandoned most of the full-self scaffolding. In his volume, *Acts of Meaning,* he laid out the rationale for a culturally based theory of cognition that extends to all that the individual might identify as self. Although less articulate concerning its broader assumptive base, much of the work on social representations, inspired by Serge Moscovici (1984), is congenial with the more socialized conception of self. According to this view there is little to distinguish between publicly shared conceptions and private mentality. Much of Richard Shweder's (Schweder & Miller, 1985) early work on cultural differences in self-conception adds strong support to the social view, emphasizing as it did the vastly different system of symbols by which Indian culture understands the person in contrast to the understandings in the West. (Shweder, in recent accounts, has given over to a universalized theory of cognition, holding that differing cultural conceptions are but idiosyncratic derivations from universal process derivations.) Similar in many respects is Marcus and Nurius's (1986) work on the cultural embedding of self-conception. In particular, her emphasis on multiplicity, as represented in the concept of "possible selves," begins to fill out a conceptual space in which self and culture are inherently intertwined. It is largely on the basis of conceptual moves such as these that Harre and Gillete (1994) have recently heralded the emergence of a "second cognitive revolution."

In many respects the sociocognitive view is much to be welcomed. For many it is a refreshing change from the culturally and historically challenged undertakings of the full-self theorists of the past. In many respects it invites the psychologist out of the sheltered laboratory and into the streets—to focus less on people's performance on artificially contrived tasks and more on their lives in specific cultural contexts. The approach enables the psychologist to escape the snares of an imperialistic biologizing and opens fruitful and enriching dialogues with anthropologists, sociologists, and historians. Further, in terms of its ideological implications, one senses here a significant softening of the grasp of possessive individualism (see Sampson, 1977, Bellah et al., 1985, for examples). From the sociocognitive standpoint the individual is neither isolated nor autonomously self-directing, but culturally constituted. And finally, in its political implications the sociocognitive alternative favors a liberal multicultural philosophy. It argues for the local validity of myriad cultural perspectives—each different, but functional within its own local and historical modes of life. Reins are placed on tendencies toward cultural imperialism.

Yet, although much to be welcomed, sociocognitive formulations also harbor significant conceptual problems. There are significant limitations inherent in the rush toward a second cognitive revolution. At the outset, the sociocognitive view falls prey to several criticisms generated by proponents of the empty self. On what grounds, for example, is the sociocognitivist to justify his or her particular claims to knowledge of the interior? Why are scientific beliefs in internal schemas, meaning systems, representations, and the like not so many folk concepts—merely formalized and projected into the individual by the unwitting scientist? And do not our experiments, questionnaires, and the like simply serve to affirm the consequent, objectifying, and otherwise unsupportable *a priori?* To these questions, the sociocognitivists—just as their full self predecessors—have no compelling answers.

Yet, there are still further lines of critique confronting the sociocognitivist that together form a daunting threat to full intelligibility and satisfaction. Consider but three of these lines of contention:

1. For over three centuries philosophers have struggled with the problem of mind–world dualism and particularly with the enigma of how events in the external or material world are accurately registered and transformed into mental representations or "thought molecules." From Locke to Kant to 20th-century philosophers of science, the prob-

lem has never yielded to solution. Following Wittgenstein's (1953) explorations into the problematic assumptions we make in posing the question of mind—world relations, many philosophers are now moved to abandon dualist presumptions altogether. In the most influential work of this kind, Richard Rorty (1979) argued that the entire mind—world problem is an outgrowth of an unnecessary and deeply flawed metaphysics; the question of how the world is represented in the mind is optional. Sociocognitivists inherit this problem in a vicious form. Simply put, the problem is that if (a) the theorist presumes that the world is understood through the deployment of cognitive processes and (b) the character of cognition is fashioned by or incorporated from the social world (and primarily through language), then (c) how could the individual ever comprehend the social processes through which he or she is said to understand? This was, in prototypical form, the basis of Giddens's (1984) critique of George Herbert Mead's symbolic interactionism. As Mead proposed, the I (or self) is not present at birth, but emerges through social experience—as "the response of the organism to the attitudes of others" (Mead, 1934, p. 175). Yet, if the I is a response, then who or what is comprehending and organizing the "attitudes of others?" Nor has the problem been solved by theorists such as Vygotsky, who simply imbue the organism with any array of "lower" or rudimentary psychological processes that are said to form the basis on which "higher order" processes—reflecting cultural process—are founded.

2. In spite of its democratic implications, the sociocognitive orientation remains a child of the Western intellectual and ideological tradition. Although it recognizes the local validity of multiple ways of comprehending the self, it continues to presume that all such modes of comprehension are fundamentally cognitive. The term *cognitive*, of course, carries with it—and indeed derives its meaning from—a history of discourse. This history includes such interrelated concepts as soul, consciousness, ratiocination, and knowledge—all peculiar to the Western tradition. Why, it may be asked, do we not presume a *sociokarmic* process, in let us say a Hindu way, or the sociogenises of *no mind* as a Buddhist might? In effect, the sociocognitive position never

fully escapes its Western roots and thus operates subtly as a form of Western imperialism.

3. Finally, the sociocognitive orientation cannot tolerate the invitation to self-reflexivity. As Norbert Groeben (1990) charged, because theories themselves are human action, then any scientific theory of human action should be able to render an account of its own emergence. If we apply such a challenge to the sociocognitive orientation, we confront difficult problems indeed. First, we should face the possibility that the position is itself the outcome of a particular social (cultural, historical) process. It represents a set of "cultural texts" that have become prevalent within a particular subculture of social scientists. The scientists, in turn, have framed their research in terms of this particular discourse and have interpreted their results in its terms, essentially making true or vindicating their own system of subcultural beliefs. How could we escape such a charge? Second, if an orientation such as the sociocognitive is the outcome of social processes, then how can we account for understanding those who do not share our theories? If understanding is always "through the lens" of a given cultural group, how could one ever comprehend the actions of those who do not share the lens? Would their actions always be understood through our own lens and thus never on their own terms? In effect, on the sociocognitive account, one would never be able to transcend the boundaries of his or her cultural mindset, and nothing in the way of genuine cross-cultural *understanding would ever occur.*

TOWARD A RELATIONAL CONCEPTION OF SELF

As we find, in spite of their advantages over earlier formulations, sociocognitive accounts do not finally yield a solution to Jones's (1964) enigma of the self. At the same time, the shift toward social formulations of the person include a second line of reasoning, one that begins to render intelligible a relational self. In terms of the abovementioned reasoning it is useful to view relational formulations as congenial outgrowths of empty-self critiques. This is so in two respects. First, consistent with the skepticism of empty-self theorists, there is an aversion to the primacy of the mental. That is, we may usefully close off the option of commencing analysis with a specifically psychological interest—in an attempt either to understand the inner workings or to use psychological predicates to explain human action. In doing so we escape the various problems of dualism, solipsism, individualism, and the recapitulation of the Western ontology that occupied us earlier. But more positively, there is a certain way in which a form of the empty-self argument points to an alternative departure.

Specifically, let us foreground language, public and concrete. Following Wittgenstein (1953) we may agree that words gain their meaning primarily from the language games in which they are embedded— games that require the coordinated action of two or more persons. We have words such as *intention, belief,* and *thought* in the Western vocabulary, but rather than viewing such terms in their referential capacity (as "signifiers" of a psychological "signified"), we may rather see them in terms of their function within language games—or more specifically, as they are constituted within and serve to sustain patterns of coordinated action. In this way, we find that psychological terms have an important cultural function: They serve to explain, excuse, indicate directions of action, and so on. Without terms such as *intention* and *foreknowledge,* the legal system would require major change; without the language of "individual choice," the concept of democracy would be incapacitated; without such terms as *reason, memory,* and *attention,* educational systems would lose their rationale. In contrast with empty-self theorists, then, we are not advised to rid our vocabularies of mental terminology. Rather, we realize that without this vocabulary much of social life would be eradicated.

From this standpoint we are invited to begin analysis with *processes of relationship* as opposed to the individual as the focal point. All that was heretofore conceptualized as psychological now becomes a byproduct of relationships. This is not to say that the psychological is thus the social now internalized. This would be to recapitulate the sociocognitive view. Rather, it is to say there is nothing outside of the relationship of signal importance in understanding most of the problems confronting the human sciences. To clarify, and to extend the implications, let me briefly draw from two lines of theoretical work in which I have been engaged:

Consider first the emotions. In the full-self account, emotions are viewed as biological universals, private possessions, but subject to the scrutiny of science. From the sociocognitive perspective, emotions continue to be private and individualized, but the mode of conceptualizing them may be derived from the cultural repertoire. (Schachter and Singer's 1962 work would be exemplary here.) However, from the relational standpoint, emotions are viewed as cultural constructions—as forms of patterned activity that emerge in certain cultures at certain times, and may accordingly pass from the social register (let us say, as the emotions *acidae* and *melancholy* have largely been lost from our own Western repertoire). Most important, such performances are embedded within conventional patterns of interchange. Thus, one cannot perform what we call "anger" at any time or place, and still remain intelligible within the culture. One may intelligibly do anger when someone steps on one's foot, but not on one's shadow. And once anger has entered the interchange, the target is not free to engage in any just activity. By virtue of the "rules of the game," he or she may apologize or rationalize, for example, but not talk about the weather or congratulate the angry one. And should apologies take place, again the angry player is restricted by dint of history and culture to certain kinds of actions. In effect, we may extricate from the hurly–burly of daily life a series of culturally sanctioned *emotional scenarios*—or modes of relational dances—of which the performance of anger is but a single integer (Gergen, 1994). Two or more persons are required to mutually constitute or "bring off" the scenario. In this sense, my emotions are not truly mine; I am but a performer in a dance that has long preceded me and out of which the "emotional" action is but a single component. Without your actions, my emotion is unintelligible; I would neither have a name for what I do nor a reason for doing it. Our error in the past has been to mistake the dancer for the dance.

Consider next the problem of understanding and specifically the issue of understanding others. As we found with the sociocognitive position, the problem of understanding other minds was insoluble.

Once the individual is said to be operating on the basis of internal category systems (schemas, thoughts, etc.), there is no means by which he or she can comprehend the mind of someone who does not already share this system. From the relational standpoint, however, we need not posit a mind behind the action; it is unnecessary to fathom another's mind before what we call understanding occurs. Rather, we first recognize that the concept of understanding is preeminently linguistic and as such carries out certain forms of relational work. We say "I understand," or "do not understand" at certain junctures in relationships and not others. We may intelligibly inform our students that they have understood an assignment, but not that they understand how to digest their food; a low mark on a quiz indicates that they do not understand the assignment, but their aching tummy does not indicate their failure in understanding how to digest. And when we signal to the student in this way, there are further forms of action, both on the student's part and on our own, that appropriately follow. Without the insertion of the comment, "you fail to understand," or its equivalent into the relationship, subsequent patterns of mutually coordinated action would not take place.

More generally, it may be said that the ascription of understanding is used to index certain forms of coordination (or its lack) within relationships. If the coordinations are smooth and unproblematic, by conventional standards, we may ascribe "understanding" to one or more of the participants. Failures will trigger the opposite. Thus, for example, if you step on my toe, I shriek in anger, and you apologize, I might say that you understood the situation, my pain, and so forth. In saying so, I am not thus referring to your mental state, but to the set of coordinated actions. And if you respond to my angry shriek by asking me for the time, I might blame you for your calloused incapacity to understand. This means that understanding from one subculture to another, or across subcultures, is not prohibited by virtue of cognitive inaccessibility. Rather, as I engage in multiple relations, differing patterns of coordination will emerge—each appropriate to its particular range of contexts. To understand, on this account, is not a private act of cognition, but the result of a public and relational coordination. Essentially, the sense of understanding is achieved through a process of mutual supplementation (Gergen, 1994).

At this juncture, it is impossible to see the full set of potentials (and the limits) or a relational approach. Because of the lack of a rich tradition, conceptual articulation proceeds slowly. The works of Potter and Wetherell (1987) on attitudes, Billig (1987) on thinking as public argumentation made private, Middleton and Edwards (1990) on communal memory, and Myerson (1994) on rationality as dialogue are all significant in pressing the standpoint into intelligibility. However, whether the orientation can so fully escape the problems of the past, and whether it can yield significant theoretical and cultural developments, will remain a challenge for the community of scholars. It is a pity that this colloquy will proceed without Edward E. Jones's probative discernment. While remaining a staunch theoretical and methodological individualist, I am certain that if the relational account gave rise to the kinds of subtle and ironic experimental outcomes that so earmarked his own contributions, Jones would set a welcoming place at his table.

REFERENCES

Bandura, A. (1977). Self-efficacy: Toward a unifying theory of behavioral change. *Psychological Review, 84,* 191–215.

Bellah, R. N., Madsen, R., Sullivan, W. M., Swidler, A., & Tipton, S. M. (1985). *Habits of the heart: Individualism and commitment in American life.* Berkeley: University of California Press.

Billig, M. (1987). *Arguing and thinking.* London: Cambridge University Press.

Bruner, J. (1990). *Acts of meaning.* Cambridge, MA: Harvard University Press.

Churchland, P. M. (1981). Eliminative materialism and propositional attitudes. *Journal of Philosophy, 78,* 11–19.

Gergen, K. J. (1994). *Realities and relationships.* Cambridge, MA: Harvard University Press.

Giddens, A. (1984). *The constitution of society.* Cambridge: Polity Press.

Groeben, N. (1990). Subjective theories and the explanation of human action. In G. Semin & K. J. Gergen (Eds.), *Everyday understanding* (pp. 19–44). London: Sage.

Harre, R., & Gillete, G. (1994). *The discourse mind.* Thousand Oaks, CA: Sage.

Jones, E. E. (1964). *Ingratiation, a social psychological analysis.* New York: Appleton-Century-Crofts.

Jones, E. E. (1965). Conformity as a tactic of ingratiation. *Science, 149,* 144–150.

Jones, E. E., Davis, K. E., & Gergen, K. J. (1961). Role playing variations and their informational value for person perception. *Journal of Abnormal and Social Psychology, 53,* 302–310.

Jones, E. E., & Davis, K. E. (1965). From acts to dispositions. The attribution process in person perception. In L. Berkowitz (Ed.), *Advances in experimental social psychology* (Vol. 2, pp. 220–266). San Diego, CA: Academic Press.

Jones, E. E., Rhodewalt, F., Burglas, S. E., & Skelton, J. A. (1981). Effects of strategic self-presentation on subsequent self-esteem. *Journal of Personality and Social Psychology, 41,* 407–421.

Markus, H., & Nurius, P. (1986). Possible selves. *American Psychologist, 41,* 94–96.

Mead, G. H. (1934). *Mind, self and society.* Chicago: University of Chicago Press.

Middleton, D., & Edwards, D. (1990). *Collective remembering.* London: Sage.

Moscovici, S. (1984). The phenomenon of social representations. In R. Farr & S. Moscovici (Eds.), *Social representations* (pp. 13–64). London: Cambridge University Press.

Myerson, G. (1994). *Rhetoric, reason and society.* London: Sage.

Potter, J., & Wetherell, M. (1987). *Discourse and social psychology: Beyond attitudes and behaviour.* London: Sage.

Rorty, R. (1979). *Philosophy and the mirror of nature.* Princeton, NJ: Princeton University Press.

Ryle, G. (1949). *The concept of mind.* London: Hutchinson.

Sampson, E. E. (1977). Psychology and the American ideal. *Journal of Personality and Social Psychology, 35,* 767–782.

Schachter, S., & Singer, J. L. (1962). Cognitive, social and physiological determinants of emotional states. *Psychological Review, 65,* 121–128.

Shweder, R., & Miller, J. (1985). The social construction of the person: How is it possible? In K. J. Gergen and K. E. David (Eds.), *The social construction of the person* (pp. 41–69). New York: Springer-Verlag.

Stitch, S. (1983). *From folk psychology to cognitive science.* Cambridge, MA: MIT Press.

Vygotsky, L. S. (1978). *Mind in society.* Cambridge, MA: Harvard University Press.

Wittgenstein, L. (1953). *Philosophical investigations.* (G. Anscombe, Trans.) New York: Macmillan.

Wundt, W. (1900–1920). *Volkerpsychologie.* Leipzig, Germany: Engelmann.

PART THREE

Social Interaction

6

Self-Handicapping

Robert M. Arkin and Kathryn C. Oleson

A defining feature of contemporary Western society is the extraordinary emphasis placed on achievement and success. Striving for success seems to pervade every aspect of human interaction from the classroom, to the playing field, to the corporate boardroom. This emphasis on achievement and success suggests that people might make every effort to ensure possession of the necessary resources to maximize performance. Individuals would be expected to reach for any and every advantage to facilitate performance, including eliminating obstacles or disabilities that might interfere with success. Nevertheless, Jones and Berglas (1978) predicted that individuals are sometimes willing to create impediments to performance, making failure more likely, and they termed the phenomenon *self-handicapping*.

It is nearly two decades since Ned Jones and Steve Berglas were collecting their first data on the topic of self-handicapping and writing a conceptual paper that framed the theoretical issues. The conceptual article appeared in *Personality and Social Psychology Bulletin* and the empirical article was published in the *Journal of Personality and Social Psychology*, both in 1978. One can read these works profitably the way many have read and continue to savor Heider (1958)—over and over, again and again, in search of ideas, hypotheses, nuance.

The roots of the concept of self-handicapping rest in attribution theory, and therefore with Fritz Heider. Although predominantly cognitive in its thrust, attribution theory incorporates motivational factors as well. To quote Jones (1990), "Heider hardly violated our common sense when he suggested that people are inclined to attribute their performances in a self-serving manner: the good things I caused; the bad things were forced upon me" (p. ix). Of course, violating common sense was not Heider's (1958) purpose.

The notion of self-handicapping added a proactive twist to this common-sense wisdom. People not only make excuses for their blunders after the fact (Snyder, Higgins, & Stucky, 1983) but also plan social occasions so that self-protective excuses are already in place and need not be merely retrospective. Using attributional rules and logic, circumstances are arranged so that flawed or even failing performances may not be interpreted in a way that threatens self-esteem or social esteem.

In self-handicapping, individuals strategically seek out or create a handicap (an external, inhibitory factor that interferes with performance) to obscure the link between performance and evaluation (at least in the case of failure). A persuasive handicap may diminish the likelihood of success but permit the handicapper to attribute a forthcoming failure to some source other than lack of competence. By self-handicapping, individuals can exert control over the types of attributions made for performance outcomes. Specifically, by acquiring or claiming a handicap, and blocking the expression of ability, an individual can diminish lack of ability as the most plausible attribution for flawed performance or failure. In attributional terminology, self-handicapping is a strategy designed to "discount" ability (Kelley, 1971) as an explanation for poor performance.

The ranking of various stigmas is defined by our culture in this attributional selection process. To illustrate, Jones (1990) put it bluntly: "It is better to fail because one is lazy than because one is stupid" (p. x). The persuasive handicaps are typically stigmatizing (e.g., procrastination, lack of effort, hangovers, and the like). Their use satisfies the short-range interest of preserving self-esteem when judgments about self-worth rest more on assessments of competence than on these other aspects of one's character. But, at the same time, these self-handicaps also defeat the long-range purpose of achieving successful outcomes.

INITIAL DEMONSTRATION

The initial demonstration of self-handicapping involved drug use as a self-handicap. Berglas and Jones (1978) gave their research participants who had previously succeeded at a task, but who did not expect to be able to repeat the success on a similar task, the opportunity to choose to protect themselves by ingesting a debilitating drug. By taking the drug, the individuals were able to manipulate the situation such that their first successful performance might be seen as based on their "true" abilities. Therefore, if failure occurred, it would be seen as attributable to the effects of the debilitating drug.

The most novel and comic feature of the study is surely the experimental basis for fostering individuals' low expectations concerning the second trial of the task (i.e., their uncertainty about repeating their early success). Half the participants were given a test composed largely of items for which there were no correct answers. Yet, the experimenter declared their performance to be quite good, just as was the case for participants who took a test made up of items for which there were discernible answers. They had succeeded at a very high level. However, the success almost surely felt unearned, even illegitimate. These individuals were expected to doubt their capacity to repeat the success, and their motivation to self-handicap their future performance was supposed to be high.

In support of the hypothesis, two studies showed that the noncontingent success participants (those who took the test with no actual correct answers) were more likely to select the drug Pandocrin, the debilitating drug (rather than Actavil, the performance-enhancing drug), than were the contingent success participants (who had taken the test composed of items for which there clearly were correct answers). However, this was true only for the male and not for the female participants in the study.

315

HISTORY AND CONTEXT

The concept of self-handicapping has a longer past than its mere two decades as a keyword in the psychological literature. As mentioned earlier, it is now 20 years since Ned Jones and Steve Berglas began their data collection on the topic and began writing a companion conceptual paper. Ned later acknowledged historical roots in the Adlerian and the Heiderian anchors for the concept of self-handicapping, but it required the flair of their studies and the counterintuitive but thoroughly compelling mix of attribution processes, social relations, and developmental issues to capture the imagination. Their characterization was also intriguing because it was at the intersection of social, personality, and clinical psychology. It is at the same time cognitive and motivational, interpersonal and intrapsychic. The phenomenon of self-handicapping also speaks directly to fundamental questions about human motivation: It addresses the relative importance of the signifying versus exchange value of positive and negative interpersonal evaluation and the centrality of people's investments in the question of self-worth as a motivational force in human action. These basic concerns, and dichotomies, are echoed throughout this volume, in Ned Jones's work and in his legacy, and they were thematic at the "Nedstock" festschrift held at Princeton University to honor Ned.

This chapter can only touch on the many ways that these fundamental matters emerge in the literature on self-handicapping. We attempt to highlight these, particularly where there is now evidence on the point. We also touch on some new directions in which we and others are now taking the literature. More than 50 journal articles, several literature reviews, and one book on self-handicapping have appeared since the phenomenon was first reviewed comprehensively (Arkin & Baumgardner, 1985). It is difficult in limited space to do justice to this body of research. Our brush is broad.

MOTIVATIONAL BASIS FOR SELF-HANDICAPPING

It seemed right to begin as purists, with the initial demonstration of self-handicapping provided by Berglas and Jones (1978). However, this initial pair of studies examines the restrictive case. A main theme in the self-handicapping literature, since the early 1980s, has concerned theoretical and empirical departures from this original, noncontingent success paradigm.

Berglas and Jones (1978) used an experimental protocol that provided a positive image (through noncontingent success) to protect. Rick Snyder and his colleagues (e.g., T. W. Smith, Snyder, & Handelsman, 1982) were willing to assume that individuals ordinarily have a positive image to protect, at least to some extent, even if the experimental protocol doesn't explicitly provide it. Consequently, they dispensed with the induction of uncertainty conveyed through the noncontingent success experience. (Since 1982, many other researchers have done the same.) Further, the original self-handicapping notion had applied only to an individual's attempt to avoid disconfirmation of a positive self-image; Snyder and his colleagues extended the range of the concept to include cases in which an individual avoids confirming a negative self-image.

In noting these distinctions, we run the risk of pointing out differences that matter little, if at all. Researchers find support for their predictions, uncovering patterns of findings that look like self-handicapping, without all the complicated, arcane uncertainty-induction procedures used by Berglas and Jones (1978). However, we think it wise to reserve the possibility that there is something special in the theory spelled out by Jones and Berglas (1978), and in the procedures that emerged from their theorizing.

The Conceptual Definition of Doubt

Specifically, everyone agrees that the motivational basis for self-handicapping is the presence of feelings of doubt. Doubt about achieving a positive outcome, or avoiding a negative outcome, runs through all the demonstrations of self-handicapping in the literature. However, future research may show that the nature of the feelings of doubt, and its consequences (affective, behavioral, and cognitive), are different depending on whether one is focusing on avoiding a negative outcome or achieving a positive outcome and whether the doubt is about oneself or merely about some transient outcome on some task.

Feelings of *self-doubt* drive self-handicapping in the Berglas and Jones (1978) initial, restrictive case. Participants in the original study were thought to harbor high estimates of their own self-worth, but they were also thought to be subject to a rather wide confidence interval around that positive self-evaluation (i.e., they worried that they were not so gifted as that). The test they took in the experiment was said to be an effective measure of distinctions in intellect at the very highest levels. Thus, participants were construed as entertaining two competing self-assessments: (a) They were special, among the nation's elite on an intellectual dimension, or (b) they weren't quite as good as that, perhaps not as smart as their peers at their distinguished university.

The nature of doubt, as the concept appears in other research, may lack that powerful reference to the core, stable self. Instead, the typical individual may have a high, but somewhat more modest and less emotionally charged self-evaluation, and the typical individual may have a narrower confidence interval, or latitude of acceptance, around that self-evaluation. Extremely positive outcomes and extremely negative outcomes are equally implausible to the typical individual, and both are likely to be seen as unreliable and attributable to chance. In the run-of-the-mill situation, with the typical undergraduate participant, a failure is surely to be avoided, and failure can shake one's confidence, particularly when it recurs. However, one failure can be explained away, and it would not be likely to shatter one's confidence and provoke worry or despair.

However, the Jones and Berglas (1978) conceptualization involves an asymmetrical confidence interval, in which most information points to very high performance levels, and intellect, and the danger is focused entirely on the occasional piece of information that shakes confidence in that self-evaluation and suggests that the individual isn't quite so extraordinary. It is as if one failure is sufficient to draw the individual's intelligence into question (Darley, 1995). The one negative instance, the poor performance, is used as "signifying" evidence—of questionable intellect—even against a history of otherwise exceptionally positive out-comes (Darley, 1995; Jones & Berglas, 1978).

Jones and Berglas (1978) viewed the sort of self-doubt they posed as a motivational skein, around which is woven a good deal of one's everyday behavior. For instance, they offered the example of the alco-holic, whose overinvestment in concerns about self-worth can manifest in the chronic use of alcohol as a life-pervading excuse for poor per-formance. By contrast, doubt of the garden-variety, as it typically ap-pears in other research paradigms and in everyday life, may be more about whether good outcomes are likely to be achieved, and poor out-comes avoided, in some transitory situation.

This transitory form of doubt may lack the "heat" generated by the implication that an outcome is central to one's core sense of self-worth, at least to some extent. Naturally, recurring failure could increase feel-ings of doubt, and garden-variety doubt could be converted into chronic self-doubt through unexpected, recurring experiences with fail-ure. However, it is important to remember that the self-doubt posed by Jones and Berglas (1978) stems, theoretically, from recurring expe-riences with noncontingent success, not failure; they theorized that the purest form of self-doubt would occur when noncontingent success is the norm in one's experience, and failure, when it occurs, is attribu-tionally ambiguous (i.e., cannot be attributed clearly to the situation or to the self).

In sum, we think it wise to reserve the possibility that there are different forms of self-handicapping. Some are based on garden-variety feelings of doubt. Others stem from powerful feelings of self-doubt. The ramifications of these two types of self-handicapping, and what they reflect about processes of self-evaluation, may prove enormously important.

Public Versus Private Basis of Self-Handicapping

Several studies examine the motivational basis of self-handicapping by drawing a theoretical distinction between its self-presentational, or interpersonal, and its intrapsychic, or personal, foundations. If stemming from self-presentation goals, the primary audience for self-handicapping acts would be significant others, rather than oneself, and self-handicapping would be found predominantly in public rather than private settings. If self-handicapping occurs more in private than in public contexts, or emerges equally in public and in private, the likely audience for self-handicapping is the self. (Interpersonal evaluation could suppress it, if self-handicapping is itself stigmatizing. We present more on this point later.)

One study found self-handicapping when both the self-handicapping act and the performance outcome were public, but not when one or the other was kept entirely private (Kolditz & Arkin, 1982). This finding suggests a self-presentational basis for self-handicapping. Later work also found that individuals high in public self-consciousness (Fenigstein, Scheier, & Buss, 1975) self-handicapped more than their low public self-consciousness counterparts (Shepperd & Arkin, 1989). In that public self-consciousness taps sensitivity to self-presentational concerns, this finding also points to an interpersonal, self-presentational basis for self-handicapping.

Although a public context enhances the likelihood and intensity of self-handicapping, it is premature to conclude that self-handicapping is exclusively a version of public impression management. This seems particularly true given the distinction discussed earlier between a gripping form of self-doubt, suggested by Jones and Berglas (1978), and a garden-variety form of doubt about performance outcomes. The laboratory investigations showing the impact of publicity of handicapping and performance outcomes on self-handicapping may have concerned the latter, garden-variety form of doubt, and could have failed to provoke any deep concern about the core, stable self.

The Roles of Self-Protection and Self-Enhancement

Another crucial distinction in assessing the precise motivational basis for self-handicapping concerns its self-protective (e.g., Arkin, 1981) versus self-enhancement objectives. Self-handicapping is capable of setting the stage for two attributional outcomes with the one strategy. Placing barriers in the way of one's own success provides a protective excuse for flawed or failing performance, if that occurs, but also enhances perceived personal responsibility for success should a positive outcome occur in spite of the handicap. In attributional terms, ability is "discounted" as a perceived cause of failure, whereas ability is "augmented" as a perceived cause of success (Kelley, 1971). A discounted ability attribution protects the self in the face of failure; an augmented ability attribution enhances the self if success occurs.

Most discussions of self-handicapping do not distinguish these two sources of motivation. The typical definition of self-handicapping includes both its self-protective and self-enhancement benefits. However, there now is some compelling work addressing this interesting distinction.

In four studies, Tice (1991) differentiated between self-enhancement and self-protection. She drew on a review of the self-esteem literature which concluded that high-self-esteem individuals are motivated to enhance their public and self-image, but that moderate- and low-self-esteem individuals are more concerned about protecting their public image and self-regard (Baumeister, Tice, & Hutton, 1989). She also made use of the distinction between acquisitive behavioral styles and protective behavioral styles in interpersonal relations (Arkin, 1981). In Tice's clever methodology, individuals were either offered a handicap that afforded enhancement of success but no protection against failure (which should appeal mainly to people with high self-esteem) or that offered protection against failure but no enhancement of success (appealing primarily to those with low self-esteem).

She found that low-self-esteem individuals only self-handicapped to protect against the esteem-threatening implications of failure, but that high-self-esteem participants also self-handicapped to augment the competence implications of their successes. Tice (1991) concluded that people with high self-regard self-handicap when an opportunity exists to appear outstanding, whereas low-self-regard individuals self-handicap exclusively to protect themselves from probable failure. Similar findings have been reported in an attribution context (Rhodewalt, Morf, Hazlett, & Fairfield, 1991). High-self-esteem and low-self-esteem individuals both discounted ability attributions in response to failure feedback. After success feedback, however, only individuals high in self-esteem augmented ability attributions.

Above, we drew a distinction between self and other as the target for the self-handicapping strategy and between self-protection and self-enhancement as the basis for it. It is tempting to map Tice's (1991) low-self-regard individuals on this two-dimensional scheme. They engaged in self-protection, and one might surmise that their target is the self (or self and other), even though target was not explicitly manipulated or measured in this set of studies.

Although plausible, this mapping of the findings might seem to equate low self-regard with the gripping sort of self-doubt posed by Jones and Berglas (1978), even though Jones and Berglas (1978) viewed self-doubt as deriving from high—but uncertain—estimates of self-worth. Clearly, there is no easy reconciliation of Tice's (1991) findings and Jones and Berglas's (1978) theorizing.

In this context, it is important to note that individual differences in certainty about self-regard and self-regard itself should not be equated (Kernis, 1995). Tice (1991) made no attempt to disentangle these variables, so her findings pertain only to individual differences in self-regard. Making matters more complex still, Harris and Snyder (1986) found that individual differences in certainty of self-esteem predicted self-handicapping, regardless of individuals' level of self-esteem. Overall, then, the relationships between self-esteem and self-handicapping, and between self-esteem certainty and self-handicapping, are not yet resolved.

For now, it seems wise to conclude from this research only that the distinction between self-protection and self-enhancement, and discounting and augmentation, is important. Further, the pattern of findings across various studies seems to underscore the point that there may be several types of self-handicapping, each with a motivational basis that differs in important ways from other forms of self-handicapping. This discussion is not meant to be critical of recent research, particularly of Tice's (1991) clever and useful contribution. We mean only to point out the value of noting the shift in emphasis in the self-handicapping literature from the original theoretical conception of self-handicapping (as driven by compelling feelings of self-doubt) toward research questions that are centered more on everyday versions of the behavior, with a different motivational basis.

Individual Differences

Rhodewalt (1990) posed the general question, Do certain individuals have a tendency to engage in self-handicapping behavior more than others? His answer is a clear yes.

The Self-Handicapping Scale (Jones & Rhodewalt, 1982; Strube, 1986) is a face-valid instrument that assesses the extent to which people report, or admit, engaging in excuse-making behavior of a self-handicapping sort. It asks respondents to indicate whether they agree with self-descriptive statements (e.g., "I am easily distracted by noises or my own creative thoughts when I try to read"; "I would do much better if I didn't let my emotions get in my way") and probes such behaviors as lack of effort, illness, procrastination, and emotional upset, in association with performance settings. The scale has adequate reliability and validity evidence collected to support it. Scores on the Self-Handicapping Scale are inversely related to academic performance and directly related to the withdrawal of effort, and the scale shows several other straightforward forms of predictive validity (Rhodewalt, 1990). For instance, high self-handicappers practice less than their non-self-handicapping counterparts prior to an important performance (Rhodewalt, Saltzman, & Wittmer, 1984).

For the most part, though, demonstrations of self-handicapping using the Self-Handicapping Scale have been limited to the domains of intellectual achievement and sports activities, and involve almost exclusively "claimed" rather than "acquired" (real, behavioral) self-handicaps (Arkin & Baumgardner, 1985). By *claimed*, we mean handicaps that would be meaningful in their implications (i.e., illness, fatigue, mood, lack of preparation) but that are merely asserted to be present and relevant. Claimed handicaps have no physical referent and are, in that regard, indisputable; however, they are likely to be far less impressive, attention-getting, and persuasive than actual, behavioral handicaps. The term *acquired* (Arkin & Baumgardner, 1985) is used to describe actual, observable handicaps (e.g., alcohol consumption, drug use, procrastination, lack of effort) that are also indisputable, but persuasive as well, in that they can be seen and tend to get attention when they occur in the face of some challenging and important task. The available evidence suggests that Rhodewalt's (1990) high self-handicappers translate their claims into actions and self-handicap behaviorally, but actual evidence on acquired self-handicaps in this research context is scant.

Next, Rhodewalt (1990) turned to an examination of the preconditions that might simultaneously cause people to be uncertain of their abilities and then to select self-handicapping over other alternatives in the range of potential coping strategies. He pointed to individual differences in attributional, or explanatory, style.

Rhodewalt's (1990) first clue was a strong correlation between scores on the Self-Handicapping Scale and the external, unstable attributional dimensions of the Attributional Styles Questionnaire (ASQ). The ASQ (Peterson, Semmel, Metalsky, Abramson, von Beyer, & Seligman, 1982) includes the three most common and theoretically important dimensions in causal attribution (internal–external, stable–unstable, global–specific) in one scale. It asks respondents to assign hypothetical positive and negative outcomes to causes and then to rate those causes on the three dimensions. High self-handicappers tended to rate daily life events, whether positive or negative, as more likely to be caused by external than internal factors and by unstable than stable factors. Such a pattern points high self-handicappers away from an ability attribution; ability is the prototypical internal and stable cause of achievement outcomes. Instead, self-handicappers appear to rate the causes of events as outside their control and as unpredictable.

Even more interesting, Rhodewalt (1994) found that beliefs about the mutability of ability itself, and one's style of approaching achievement goals, were both associated with individual differences in self-handicapping. Rhodewalt drew on Dweck and Leggett's (1988) model of implicit theories people hold and their role in judgments and reactions in performance settings. The model proposes that people's implicit theories about attributes shape the way they understand and react to behavior and its results. Specifically, when people believe that attributes (e.g., intelligence, moral character) are fixed, traitlike entities, they tend to construe actions and outcomes in fixed terms (e.g., "I failed the test because I am dumb"; "He lied because he is dishonest"). This is called an entity theory. In contrast, when people believe that qualities are more dynamic (malleable, changeable), they tend to think about and explain events more in terms of specific, changeable aspects of the person and the situation (e.g., "I failed the test because of my effort, or strategy"; "He lied because he was desperate"). This is called an incremental theory because, in the case of ability, the individual is construed as able to grow, to learn, to increase competence. In short, ability is not seen as fixed.

The Dweck–Leggett model is supported by extensive observation of children's "mastery-oriented" versus "helpless" reactions to personal setbacks, such as failure, and it has recently been extended to the adult population (Dweck, Chiu, & Hong, 1995). People who hold an entity theory tend to display the helpless pattern. They tend to avoid challenges and frequently give up in the face of failure. People who hold an incremental theory, by contrast, are mastery oriented. They tend to seek challenges and persist and even enhance effort in response to failure. Individuals displaying these two patterns do not differ in their actual ability; instead, these two patterns are associated with different achievement goals, goals that stem from the implicit theories they hold about the very nature of ability (e.g., Nicholls, 1984).

Specifically, the helpless pattern is associated with the pursuit of *performance goals* in achievement contexts. This term is shorthand for a concern with demonstrating ability and obtaining positive feedback that affirms one's competence. By contrast, the mastery-oriented approach is associated with *learning goals;* the mastery-oriented individual is predominantly interested in increasing competence, growing, and learning.

Helpless people focus on performance goals because they view competence as fixed; they believe that intellectual capability is largely immutable and can therefore be demonstrated, but not improved. Naturally, it is gratifying to demonstrate one's ability, but it is very threatening to attempt to demonstrate a fixed ability if there is much prospect of failure. By contrast, mastery-oriented individuals follow another theory, seeing competence as incremental, entirely open to cultivation and improvement. Consequently, those who hold an incremental theory seek challenges, treat them as learning opportunities, and show no dread when there is a prospect of failure.

In a questionnaire study, Rhodewalt (1994) found that individuals who scored high in self-handicapping believe that ability traits are innately determined; in contrast, low self-handicappers hold the more incremental view of ability. Self-handicappers pursue performance goals; low self-handicappers are more likely to pursue learning objectives. Further, the endorsement of performance goals among high self-handicappers was strongly related to a measure of work avoidance (the desire to "do almost no work and get away with it"). This suggests a preference to avoid rather than approach performance situations, and it is consistent with a self-protective motive rather than self-enhancement.

In sum, the evidence suggests important cognitive and motivational underpinnings to individual differences in self-handicapping. This difference in implicit theories held by high and low self-handicappers, and their performance goals, is consistent with a point made earlier in the context of characterizing types of doubt. Self-handicappers are inclined to doubt their intelligence on the basis of one poor outcome, even when it occurs against a background of exceptionally positive outcomes. They take the one poor performance as signifying questionable intellect (Darley, 1995). Consequently, there is no surprise in the seductive nature of self-handicapping as a self-protective measure for avoiding an unambiguous failure, at least for entity theorists. One unambiguous failure carries tremendous weight and can do significant damage to one's estimate of self-worth. Self-handicapping is most likely to seem counterintuitive to people who live their lives as incremental theorists and who therefore believe that one failure is not very meaningful.

Rhodewalt (1994) also found that people's implicit theories of ability were strikingly similar across the several domains sampled in the study (athletics, intelligence, social skills). This finding is perhaps surprising, but gratifying in a sense. It is consistent with Weiner's (1985) contention that ability domains are phenotypically different but share an underlying structure that is causally similar. That is, the ways in which individuals think about athletics, intelligence, and social skills all reflect an implicit theory about the very nature of ability, and one's theory about the nature of ability has an impact on goals and objectives in daily life, across domains (see also Dweck et al., 1995; Shepperd, Arkin, Strathman, & Baker, 1994).

The research using the Self-Handicapping Scale, developed by Jones and Rhodewalt (1982) and later shortened by Strube (1986), is intriguing in a number of respects. Among these is a paradoxical aspect to this individual difference approach to studying self-handicapping. The researcher identifies the self-handicapper through the respondent's willingness to admit the use of self-handicaps. The paradox is that the major theoretical perspectives on self-handicapping might seem to anticipate that a self-handicapper would fail to see, let alone admit, that she or he is the architect of the handicapping circumstances. The admission that the handicap is one's own doing, that such an excuse is prefabricated for strategic purposes, would seem to sap self-handicapping of its value—perhaps in the same way that a compliment is undermined, and can even backfire, if its purpose is seen as mere ingratiation.

However, we do not subscribe to this requirement that the effective self-handicapper fail to recognize, or admit, that he or she is a handicapper. First, the individual who cites handicaps, and indicates that he or she routinely calls on them for purposes of attributional self-protection, is not clearly admitting that the handicap is self-generated and created for strategic purposes. Second, even if the strategic nature of self-handicapping is acknowledged, it is still true that the handicap interferes with performance and makes a clear attribution for flawed or failing performance ambiguous; the self-handicapper who admits it may be stigmatized, but the handicapper is still protected from a clear attribution of incompetence and feelings of questionable self-worth based on judgments of competence. For instance, the self-handicapping alcoholic is willing to incur very high social costs, in the form of stigma and poor outcomes, to protect self-attributions about competence. This weighing of social costs and costs to the self may seem like a precarious house of cards, but that doesn't imply that people do not think and act in such terms.

Rhodewalt (1990) speculated that the Self-Handicapping Scale does not identify the more discreet, selective, or self-deceptive type of self-handicapper, identifying instead the acknowledged self-handicapping strategist. It seems possible that there are two types of self-handicapper: one identified by the scale, who acknowledges the presence and use of handicaps, and one based more in self-deception—that this face-valid scale cannot identify. This reconciliation, despite its elegance, has not yet been tested.

Sex Differences

From the outset, research on self-handicapping has uncovered fairly reliable sex differences. Male participants self-handicapped in the initial Berglas and Jones (1978) studies, whereas female participants did not. Women do self-handicap when only claims of self-handicaps, rather than behavioral handicaps, are involved (e.g., Baumgardner, Lake, & Arkin, 1985). Indeed, the link between behavioral handicaps for men and claimed self-handicaps for women is consistent throughout the literature.

In the most compelling work, Hirt and his colleagues (Hirt, Deppe, & Gordon, 1991) found that high-self-handicapping men and women showed evidence of self-reported self-handicapping. However, only high-self-handicapping men handicapped behaviorally. When both types of handicaps were available, both men and women preferred the self-reported (claimed) handicaps to the behavioral version.

The reason only male self-handicappers show evidence of behavioral self-handicapping is not yet clear. Snyder, Ford, and Hunt (1985) argued that men may be more acutely sensitive to the negative public implications of failure and may therefore be more willing to incur the costs associated with behavioral handicaps. Men might also be more likely than women to endorse entity theories of ability and feel more self-protective concerning their self-attributions when faced with the prospect of failure. However, Dweck and her colleagues (e.g., see Dweck et al., 1995) found that boys tend to attribute academic failure to lack of effort, whereas girls tend to cite lack of ability, a pattern suggesting that entity theories may actually be more robust for girls and women than for boys and men. Finally, women may use behavioral self-handicaps but may be less likely to do so in the intellectual domain than in other domains (e.g., social). To date, most research on self-handicapping presents individuals with tests of intellectual ability. If women perceive themselves, or are judged by others, as disadvantaged relative to men in the intellectual domain, then women would have no positive appraisal to protect through self-handicapping. Instead, a claim of a handicap, perhaps coupled with extra effort, would be a far more efficacious strategy for a woman when she is faced with the prospect of flawed or failing performance in the intellectual domain.

DOES SELF-HANDICAPPING WORK?

The question has recently been raised about the impact of self-handicapping. Does it work? Ten years ago there was "as yet no evidence bearing on the impact, or effectiveness, of self-handicapping" (Arkin & Baumgardner, 1985). Five years later, Snyder (1990) found a small group of studies bearing on the question. Today, the self-handicapping literature on this question is beginning to grow rapidly. Although mixed in some respects, the research suggests overall that it does work, perhaps surprisingly well.

One could use a number of different indexes of effectiveness in assessing the impact of self-handicapping. To begin, does the self-handicap "work" for the individual who is self-handicapping? What is the impact of self-handicapping on the self-esteem, behavior, health, and so forth, for the self-handicapper?

Effectiveness for the Self-Handicapper

Theoretically, self-handicapping is designed to protect a precarious sense of one's self-worth. When individuals self-handicap, they wish to believe that they are competent, yet they harbor self-doubt about their ability or uncertainty about their likely performance. The purpose in self-handicapping is to seek out or create a handicap to obscure the link between performance and evaluation and therefore to sustain the uncertainty. The critical questions, then, are whether self-handicapping, in practice, actually serves to protect one's estimate of self-worth, whether it effectively breaks the link between performance and evaluation, and whether it carries with it any additional costs or benefits.

In general, evidence is scant regarding the effectiveness, or impact, of self-handicapping for the handicapper. A few studies show some minor positive effects on self-esteem (Isleib, Vuchinich, & Tucker, 1988), anxiety-reduction (Harris & Snyder, 1986), self-perceptions of ability (Mayerson & Rhodewalt, 1988), and feelings of control (Rhodewalt & Davison, 1986). Rhodewalt et al. (1991) found that male research participants who handicapped and received failure feedback showed significantly higher self-esteem and more positive mood than did participants who received failure feedback without the presence of the handicap. Success feedback produced equally positive feelings of self-regard and mood regardless of the presence or absence of a self-handicap; that is, there was no augmentation of mood or self-regard uncovered in this study. More recently, Rhodewalt and Hill (1995) found similar results for male participants in a classroom setting: Male self-handicappers experienced higher self-esteem and made more external attributions for academic failure than low self-handicappers. Yet, the pattern of results for female participants was quite different: Women did not tend to claim self-handicaps and their self-esteem and attributions were unrelated to their self-handicapping behavior. Together, these studies suggest, at least for men, a mildly favorably protective function for self-handicapping.

At the same time, self-handicappers tend to report being in worse physical condition than nonhandicappers (Rhodewalt et al., 1984), and there is mounting evidence—not surprisingly—that self-handicappers tend to be underachievers (Poehlmann & Oleson, 1995; Rhodewalt, 1990). For instance, above and beyond the substantial ability of the American College Test (ACT) to predict college grade point average, scores on the Self-Handicapping Scale predict performance deficits in college grades (Poehlmann & Oleson, 1995). The overall range and impact of these shortfalls in real, consequential daily life outcomes—such as one's daily affective life, self-evaluation, and health outcomes—is unknown at this time.

Perhaps the most intriguing index of the effectiveness of self-handicapping would be a measure of sustained uncertainty and, relatedly, feelings of personal control (e.g., Arkin & Baumgardner, 1985; Rhodewalt, 1990). Arkin and Baumgardner (1985) speculated that self-handicapping driven by deep-seated feelings of self-doubt may be in the service of maintaining one's sense of personal control, or at least prospective personal control. In essence, the self-handicapper, caught in a frightening challenge to feelings of competence and self-worth, prefers the belief that he or she might be effective—were it not for the handicap—to a clear and diagnostic test of competence. This might be viewed as a sort of "enabling tactic" on the part of the handicapper, a strategy that permits the individual to maintain an illusion of control—really, an illusion of future control. The illusion is self-sustaining, and it rewards the individual through short-term benefits in the management of fear and anxiety. Jones and Berglas (1978) hinted at this sort of analysis in their characterization of the alcoholic as engaging in mañana fantasies. Naturally, the short-term management of affective life suggests a house of cards that, in the long-term, might lead to crisis.

A good test of the overall effectiveness of self-handicapping would require a clear distinction between self-handicapping driven by transitory, situation-specific forms of doubt and self-handicapping driven by more gripping feelings of self-doubt. Further, measures that can capture both the short-term and the long-term affective, cognitive, behavioral, and health outcomes would seem to be necessary. The occasional, casual type of self-handicapping must be distinguished from the chronic, life-pervading type.

A clear conclusion about the effectiveness of self-handicapping for the self-handicapper requires more research on the benefits to the handicapper's self-esteem and perceptions of ability. The studies in this domain find rather weak evidence. For instance, the Isleib et al. (1988) study used only male participants, found only a marginally significant main effect for self-esteem, and found that the self-esteem ratings did not relate well to the attribution ratings taken. Similarly, Mayerson and Rhodewalt (1988) found evidence suggesting that self-handicappers may believe that their poor performance is due to lack of ability; however, they included only male participants. Also, these findings were dependent on the use of internal analyses to classify self-handicappers and non-self-handicappers. Clearly, more evidence is needed to draw any confident conclusions.

Effectiveness of Self-Handicapping Interpersonally

To the extent that self-handicapping is public, in any sense, another index of its effectiveness is in terms of interpersonal evaluation. Despite the debate about the relative importance of the public (social esteem) versus private (self-esteem) determinants of self-handicapping, the impact of self-handicapping on interpersonal relations is important in its own right. It would be surprising if one's relationships with others were entirely unaffected by a self-protective strategy such as self-handicapping, particularly if it is chronic.

The interpersonal effectiveness of self-handicapping could be measured in a number of ways. One obvious analysis involves the interpersonal costs and benefits of handicapping. These include attributions of responsibility for undesirable behaviors, perceptions of an actor's ability, liking for the actor, attribution of stigmata (e.g., "alcoholic") to the actor, and so forth. If the costs outweigh the benefits in this domain of overall social esteem, then self-handicapping will be a dubious self-presentation strategy. If benefits exceed the costs, self-handicapping is effective, interpersonally.

However, even if the cost–benefit analysis within the domain of social esteem comes up short, self-handicapping may still be effective by a more encompassing index. The overall cost–benefit ratio in the domain of social esteem would have to be weighed against the overall benefits (short-term and long-term) and costs to self-esteem.

Still another way to explore the interpersonal effectiveness of self-handicapping is to examine whether observers infer that the self-handicapper is performing a strategic behavior. Do perceivers infer that the person is strategically creating or claiming various obstacles to protect or augment his or her esteem? If self-handicapping is identified as strategic, the handicapper may be seen as motivated by self-doubts about his or her ability. If self-handicapping is not seen as strategic, handicaps are more likely to be taken at face value. The handicapper may be stigmatized (e.g., seen as lazy, weak) or may be seen as challenged (e.g., by hardships, barriers, disabilities) rather than as manipulative, sleazy, or strategic.

The available evidence suggests a mix of costs and benefits to self-handicapping. First, concerning attribution of responsibility, there appear to be clear interpersonal benefits to self-handicapping. For instance, a small number of studies show that self-handicaps can help produce lower ratings of personal responsibility for an undesirable action. Depression (Schouten & Handelsman, 1987), alcohol consumption (Critchlow, 1985; Richardson & Campbell, 1980), and obesity (Schill, Beyler, Wehr, Swigert, & Tatter, 1991) are all effective self-handicaps in this sense.

Self-handicappers are also recipients of higher ability attributions than their non-self-handicapping counterparts (Luginbuhl & Palmer, 1991; Oleson, Riley, & Arkin, 1995). Indeed, quite ordinary behaviors (e.g., not studying for an exam) serve well as handicaps in that attribution of flawed or failing performances to ability are reduced (e.g., Luginbuhl & Palmer, 1991). In short, observers seem quite likely to use the discounting principle in making ability attributions (Oleson, Yost, Poehlmann, & Arkin, 1995).

Yet, it is not so straightforward as that. In the studies described above, participants were provided with specific performance outcome information (e.g., they learned that the person received either an *A* or an *F*). Rhodewalt, Sanbonmatsu, Tschanz, Feick, and Waller (1995) recently found that, if the performance outcome is ambiguous, self-handicapping may negatively color the interpretation of the performance. In their study, male participants rated performances— objectively the same—as more negative when they were done by someone who claimed a handicap than by someone who claimed no handicap. Further, these lower ratings of the outcome were translated into lower ratings of ability, too (at least for some of the handicaps used in this study). In sum, this research shows that, under certain conditions, self-handicappers may receive lower ability ratings than their non-self-handicapping counterparts.

Other research further suggests that, in some cases, self-handicappers may receive low ability ratings. Baumgardner and Levy (1988) found that high-self-esteem observers tended to make lower attributions of ability to a self-handicapping than to a non-self-handicapping actor. Low-self-esteem individuals did not distinguish between the ability levels of the self-handicapper and the non-self-handicapper. However, Baumgardner and Levy (1988) may have found different results than other researchers because of differences in the various ways of measuring ability. Their measure included a range of adjectives, including *intelligence, capable, smart,* and *unwise.* Some of these ratings might tap attributional dimensions quite apart from intelligence or ability, per se (e.g., this person uses poor judgment).

In addition to poor judgment, many other undesirable attributions could accompany self-handicaps, and therefore constitute interpersonal costs. Luginbuhl and Palmer (1991) found that self-handicapping can inspire negative attributions about the personal characteristics that foster the handicap (e.g., laziness). Other work suggests that self-handicappers who initiate their own handicaps are generally rated more negatively (Smith & Strube, 1991) and are liked less (Boris & Hirt, 1994; Oleson, Riley, & Arkin, 1995) than their counterparts who do not initiate the handicap and those who do not handicap at all. In sum, the overall impression-management outcome for self-handicapping seems to be mixed.

Do observers realize that an individual who self-handicaps is using a strategic, self-protective behavior? Do observers infer that the self-handicapping individual is doubtful about his or her ability and has selected a strategy designed to preserve either self- or social esteem? Recent work (Oleson, Riley, & Arkin, 1995) suggests that observers do not see the strategic nature of self-handicapping behavior. Indeed, despite heroic efforts on the part of the researchers to prime such a conclusion in participants' thinking, observers of self-handicapping so far seem virtually unable to discern its strategic nature. In some instances, self-handicapping is even seen by observers as stemming from bravado, rather than self-doubt, and observers link it with attributions of high— rather than low—expectations to the handicapper (Oleson, Riley, & Arkin, 1995). A student who goes to the movies rather than studies for a forthcoming exam was generally seen as confident, even cocky (Oleson, Riley, & Arkin, 1995).

There appear to be individual differences in the impressions of self-handicappers and their non-self-handicapping counterparts. For instance, Boris and Hirt (1994) uncovered sex differences. Only men tended to give the attributional benefit to the handicapper. D. S. Smith and Strube (1991) found that observers who were not themselves self-handicappers tended to be persuaded by self-handicapping; however, individuals high in self-handicapping tended to spot the self-handicapper and failed to grant the interpersonal benefits that their non-self-handicapping counterparts were willing to concede. Perhaps it takes one to know one.

Is self-handicapping an effective tool for self-presentation? The summary answer would seem to be yes and no, depending on how one defines effectiveness.

First, consider measures that reflect handicappers' objectives for the act: If effectiveness is measured by whether casual observers (e.g., strangers) discern that the self-handicapper is using a self-protective strategy, then it gets high marks. If effectiveness is defined by a weakening of perceived responsibility for negative behavior, and by garnering higher ability ratings (i.e., protecting interpersonal evaluation of competence), then self-handicapping gets mostly high marks.

At the same time, there are interpersonal costs: Self-handicappers are seen as more lazy, less likable, and weak when their handicaps reflect these flaws in character. Many if not most self-handicaps may be classified as acquisitions of impediments of an internal, personal, but ability-irrelevant nature. Taking a debilitating drug, consuming alcohol, and reducing effort all obscure the inference that poor performance is due to incompetence. But each reflects an internal "disposition" that itself is not particularly flattering.

Another class of handicap might include setting the stage so that a poor performance could be attributable to an external impediment. For instance, such a ploy could be used by the weekend athlete who socially compares solely with those obviously out of her league, such as marathon runners. Under such circumstances, losing a race could not be viewed as diagnostic of poor ability; the individual has merely selected an inordinately difficult goal. Poor equipment, inadequate time, and other "external" handicaps serve the same purposes: protecting attributions about competence and avoiding other negative attributions about one's character.

The key question concerns the boundaries (e.g., see Rhodewalt et al., 1995) of individuals' generally positive assessment of self-handicappers. Under what conditions, beyond those already specified, will observers fail to use the discounting principle in making interpersonal judgments about ability? When will the costs of self-handicapping outweigh the benefits? Under what conditions will observers realize that the person's behavior is strategic?

There is only preliminary evidence on these points. In our own current work, we are examining the chronicity of handicapping. If self-handicapping is used only minimally, then it appears to be fairly effective in the conventional sense. But if an individual continues to self-handicap (particularly when an individual continues to self-handicap and fails), then the benefits of self-handicapping may decline over time and the interpersonal costs may begin to outweigh the benefits (Oleson, Riley, & Arkin, 1995).

One sacrifices a great deal with habitual handicapping. In part, it implies that the handicapper is likely to continue to fail, and interpersonal investments (e.g., hiring the individual, selecting her for a team) in the handicapper increasingly seem unwise. Nevertheless, chronic forms of self-handicapping that are stigmatizing in this way (e.g., as in the case of the alcoholic) can be sustained by powerful feelings of self-doubt. The willingness to incur these high social costs to minimize costs to the self, in the form of damage to one's estimate of core self-worth is precisely what made Jones and Berglas's (1978) analysis of alcohol abuse so compelling.

Additional research is addressing whether priming observers with information about psychopathology could suggest an illicit motivational basis for self-handicapping and consequently undermine its value. Initial work suggests that observers do not realize that the individual's self-doubts may be fueling their behavior, even when the observers are aware of psychological disturbance rooted in self-doubts. Perhaps some combination of primes will prove necessary to cause observers to realize that an instance of self-handicapping is strategic in nature. Perhaps a longer term, more intimate relationship (friend, relative) and the knowledge, history, and sense of involvement that accompanies intimacy is required to produce recognition of self-handicapping.

NEW DIRECTIONS

The themes outlined herein are likely to provide years of future research questions for the researchers currently investigating facets of self-handicapping. Clearly, some of these issues have only begun to be resolved, and they deserve continued attention because they speak to fundamental questions about attribution processes, social relations, personality processes, and clinical applications. Nevertheless, two new directions have captured our imagination lately, and we say just a bit about each of these next.

"Other-Enhancement"

The point of self-handicapping is to provide a persuasive nonability explanation for a flawed or failing performance. In comparative or competitive contexts, where performance is judged largely by reference to one's standing relative to others, another closely related strategy is available. Rather than handicapping one's own performance, the same attributional goal (i.e., making the causes of flawed or failing performance ambiguous) can be achieved by providing advantages to one's competitors. Shepperd and Arkin (1991) termed this *other-enhancement.*

One advantage of other-enhancement is that the individual does nothing to interfere with his or her own performance. Instead, the opponent is provided with resources that promote better performance. Therefore, other-enhancement permits the individual to pursue optimal performance but at the same time protects the self from the threat inherent in a poor evaluation of performance relative to the comparison other. Further, other-enhancement offers the opportunity to foster an image of being altruistic, or unselfish (see Dolinski, 1988).

James Shepperd's (1988) doctoral dissertation concerned a purely cognitive version of other-enhancement. Like claimed handicaps, which are imagined to be present, one can also merely imagine advantages that others enjoy. Competitors can be seen as expending heroic effort, as better prepared, as more experienced, as taking short-cuts, and so forth. Such a belief sets the stage for attributional ambiguity about one's ability, should one fail relative to a competitor. Conjuring up such a belief may manage the threat to self-esteem associated with competition, reduce anxiety, and make it easier to engage in competition. After the fact, such a belief has also set the stage to explain away one's own shortcomings—as they are inevitably made clear in the course of everyday behavior.

Higgins, Snyder, and Berglas (1990) and Baumeister (Baumeister & Scher, 1988) have also placed self-handicapping in a broader, clinical context (self-defeating behavior), and they also explore the linkages of self-handicapping to related coping strategies. From both a theoretical and a practical standpoint, we view this mapping of cognitive gymnastics and interpersonal strategies for preserving illusions about the self to be extremely valuable.

Overachievement

Another strategy to protect one's self-worth is overachievement. As Jones and Berglas (1978) noted, ironically, that "the self-handicapper ... may in many ways be similar to the overachiever. Each is fearful that failure will implicate competence. Each has an abnormal investment in the question of self-worth. One succeeds in avoiding failure through persistent effort, the other embraces failure as an alternative to self-implicating feedback" (p. 205). Phenotypically, the self-handicapper and the overachiever could not look more different. For instance, the self-handicapper is likely to withdraw effort; the overachiever is likely to expend heroic effort. The overachiever avoids failure, seemingly at

all costs; the self-handicapper flirts with disaster, enhancing the probability of failure by the very act of self-handicapping. Yet, genotypically,
the two types of behavior may be inspired by the same motivational
force: self-doubt.

Because overachievers tend to do well and enjoy outcomes conven-
tionally regarded in American society as "success," little attention has
been paid to this group. More often, overachievers are merely included
in research, and in commentary, as an extreme comparison group for
the analysis of underachievers, a group that presents management problems for educators, parents, and other authorities. Yet, by at least some
definitions of optimal outcomes and well-being, overachievers would
seem to come up wanting. Once overachievement exceeds a certain
level, it probably does so only at the expense of some other facet of an
individual's life.

The existing research on overachievement typically defines it in
starkly objective terms, by comparing an individual's performance, such
as college grade point average, with his or her predicted performance
using a standardized test, such as the ACT. This objective definition of
overachievement misses the richness of the psychological experience,
however. By focusing on the objective outcome of performance, the
perspective of the overachieving individual is lost entirely. How does
the overachiever feel about success? What drives the overachiever to
expend such a great deal of effort? These and related questions have
prompted a program of research in which we explore the phenomenon
of overachievement from this more experiential, phenomenological perspective.

Following Jones and Berglas's (1978) lead, we propose that part of
the reason overachievers expend extra effort to perform well is because
they are uncertain that they have the ability to perform well without it.
They are doubtful of their ability, so they attempt to compensate for it
by putting in extra effort. But it also seems clear that overachievers have
an extremely high need for success (Strube, White, Shimabukaro, &
Bailey, 1988), coupled with this doubt about their ability to achieve it
(Yost, Poehlmann, & Arkin, 1994).

We have developed a scale to tap these two dimensions and have begun to explore the impact of being high on this two-dimensional scale on affect, cognition, and behavior related to over- and underachievement (Oleson, Yost, Poehlmann, & Arkin, 1995). It is important to note that we do not construe overachievers as the rough equivalent of high achievers. Although high achievers may work hard for their success, they do not necessarily share the phenomenology of the individuals we describe. The persons we describe as overachievers are those who have a high desire to be successful, who depend on symbols of their success to signal their self-worth, and who harbor self-doubts about their ability. Using conventional terminology, high achievers can be seen as intrinsically motivated, as deriving joy, pride, and pleasure from their work and its results. High achievers may well experience something akin to "flow" (Csikszentmihalyi, 1990) as they achieve and become absorbed in the experience of work itself and the joy it provides. Overachievement, by contrast, reflects extrinsic motivation (Amabile, Hill, Hennessey, & Tighe, 1994; Lynch, 1996). Achievement has a purpose, for the overachiever, the centerpiece of which is demonstrating success and shoring up feelings of self-worth.

In an initial series of studies we have demonstrated the predicted two-factor structure (self-doubt and need for success) of the individual difference measure we devised. We have also demonstrated the reliability and validity of the scale (Poehlmann & Oleson, 1995). Our results suggest that overachievers and nonoverachievers display distinct, meaningful cognitive and affective patterns that fit well with the current, phenomenological conceptualization of overachievers. This work suggests that although overachievers tend to believe that they must expend extra effort, they do not necessarily enjoy working hard (which would contrast this experience with the concept of flow). (This finding is reminiscent of Rhodewalt's, 1994, concerning explanatory styles of self-handicappers, in which there was a strong relationship between performance goals and work avoidance.) In addition, overachievers tend to experience strong negative emotions when they fail, and we find that they are not able to enjoy their successes (Poehlmann, Oleson, Yost, & Arkin, 1995).

Finally, several studies suggest that overachievers are distinguishable not only by their thoughts and feelings but also by their behaviors. Recent work examining both overachievers and chronic self-handicappers found that, whereas high self-handicappers reported that they studied less, overachievers reported studying more than their non-overachieving counterparts. In addition, the overachievers' level of studying seems to be predictive of more objective overachievement—scoring higher on their college grade point average than what would be predicted by their ACT score (Poehlmann & Oleson, 1995). Other work suggests that there may be an oscillation, on occasion, between the self-handicapping style of coping with the question of self-worth (e.g., withdrawal) and the overachieving style (heroic effort; Yost & Arkin, 1995; Yost, Lichtstein, Poehlmann, & Arkin, 1995) among overachievers.

In sum, as Jones and Berglas (1978) anticipated, we found that there are compelling linkages between overachievement and underachievement. Both styles of coping with uncertainty seem to reflect a powerful investment in questioning one's self-worth. Both styles rest on the fear that failure will implicate competence. Both rely on the attributional algebra of the discounting and augmentation principles. They differ mostly with respect to the behavioral styles that result from this mix of motives, affect, and cognition.

CONCLUSION

A decade ago, one of us had the distinct pleasure of pausing to reflect on and to review the theory and research concerning self-handicapping (Arkin & Baumgardner, 1985). Now, with two decades of research complete, the opportunity once again presents itself; the pleasure has been all ours.

Ned Jones often expressed surprise at the extremely positive reception for the idea and the findings concerning self-handicapping. When asked why he was surprised, he acted matter-of-fact and just said that he didn't think it would end up a big deal. But we think it did end up big. The topic of self-handicapping presents a rich tapestry of stories to tell in class; ideas at the intersection of social, personality, and clinical psychology; problems to resolve about the interpersonal versus intrapsychic bases for human motivation; a fine illustration of a rich mixture of basic cognitive and motivational issues; and a thoroughly compelling recipe for bringing together attribution processes, social relations, and developmental issues with flair. It includes a counterintuitive twist, a few paradoxes that both provide intrigue and beg for further research— and self-handicapping sheds important light on the meanings we give life.

Although much of Ned's work led to the contemporary focus on exchange relations, particularly the exchange value of positive and negative interpersonal evaluation described in many of the other chapters in this volume, self-handicapping theory and research points right at the self. In self-handicapping, Ned Jones told a wonderful story about the signifying value of positive and negative interpersonal evaluation and about the centrality of the quest for certainty in one's self-worth in understanding complex behavior. We feel sure that we, or others, will return to the pleasant task of pausing to reflect on this corner of the legacy of Ned Jones again, some 5 years after the millennium.

REFERENCES

Amabile, T. M., Hill, K. G., Hennessey, B. A., & Tighe, E. M. (1994). The Work Preference Inventory: Assessing intrinsic and extrinsic motivational orientations. *Journal of Personality and Social Psychology, 66,* 950–967.

Arkin, R. M. (1981). Self-presentation styles. In J. T. Tedeschi (Ed.), *Impression management and social psychological research* (pp. 311–333). San Diego, CA: Academic Press.

Arkin, R. M., & Baumgardner, A. H. (1985). Self-handicapping. In J. H. Harvey & G. W. Weary (Eds.), *Attribution: Basic issues and applications* (pp. 169–202). San Diego, CA: Academic Press.

Baumeister, R. F., & Scher, S. J. (1988). Self-defeating behavior patterns among normal individuals: Review and analysis of common self-destructive tendencies. *Psychological Bulletin, 104,* 3–22.

Baumeister, R. F., Tice, D. M., & Hutton, D. G. (1989). Self-presentational motivations and personality differences in self-esteem. *Journal of Personality, 57,* 547–579.

Baumgardner, A. H., Lake, E. A., & Arkin, R. M. (1985). Claiming mood as a self-handicap: The influence of spoiled and unspoiled public identities. *Personality and Social Psychology Bulletin, 11,* 349–357.

Baumgardner, A. H., & Levy, P. E. (1988). Role of self-esteem in perception of ability and effort: Illogic or insight? *Personality and Social Psychology Bulletin, 14,* 429–438.

Berglas, S., & Jones, E. E. (1978). Drug choice as a self-handicapping strategy in response to noncontingent success. *Journal of Personality and Social Psychology, 36,* 405–417.

Boris, H. I., & Hirt, E. R. (1994). *Audience reaction to self-handicapping.* Paper presented at the 66th Annual Meeting of the Midwestern Psychological Association, Chicago.

Critchlow, B. (1985). The blame in the bottle: Attributions about drunken behavior. *Personality and Social Psychology Bulletin, 11,* 258–274.

Csikszentmihalyi, M. (1990). *Flow: The psychology of optimal experience.* New York: Harper-Collins.

Darley, J. M. (1995). Mutable theories that organize the world. *Psychological Inquiry, 6,* 290–294.

Dolinski, D. (1988). Altruistic behavior as a self-handicapping strategy. *Polish Psychological Bulletin, 19,* 249–256.

Dweck, C. S., Chiu, C., & Hong, Y. (1995). Implicit theories and their role in judgments and reactions: A world from two perspectives. *Psychological Inquiry, 6,* 267–285.

Dweck, C. S., & Leggett, E. L. (1988). A social–cognitive approach to motivation and personality. *Psychological Review, 95,* 256–273.

Fenigstein, A., Scheier, M. F., & Buss, A. H. (1975). Public and private self-consciousness: Assessment and theory. *Journal of Consulting and Clinical Psychology, 43,* 522–527.

Harris, R. N., & Snyder, C. R. (1986). The role of uncertain self-esteem in self-handicapping. *Journal of Personality and Social Psychology, 51,* 451–458.

Heider, F. (1958). *The psychology of interpersonal relations.* New York: Wiley & Sons.

Higgins, R. L., Snyder, C. R., & Berglas, S. (1990). (Eds.). *Self-handicapping: The paradox that isn't.* New York: Plenum Press.

Hirt, E. R., Deppe, R. K., & Gordon, L. J. (1991). Self-reported versus behavioral self-handicapping: Empirical evidence for a theoretical distinction. *Journal of Personality and Social Psychology, 61,* 981–991.

Isleib, R. A., Vuchinich, R. E., & Tucker, J. A. (1988). Performance attributions and changes in self-esteem following self-handicapping with alcohol consumption. *Journal of Social and Clinical Psychology, 6,* 88–103.

Jones, E. E. (1990). Foreword. In R. L. Higgins, C. R. Snyder, & S. Berglas (Eds.), *Self-handicapping: The paradox that isn't* (pp. ix–xi). New York: Plenum Press.

Jones, E. E., & Berglas, S. (1978). Control of attributions about the self through self-handicapping strategies: The appeal of alcohol and the role of underachievement. *Personality and Social Psychology Bulletin, 4,* 200–206.

Jones, E. E., & Rhodewalt, F. (1982). *The Self-Handicapping Scale.* Available from F. Rhodewalt, Department of Psychology, University of Utah.

Kelley, H. H. (1971). *Attribution in social interaction.* Morristown, NJ: General Learning Press.

Kernis, M. (1995, July). *Toward understanding the factors that promote unstable self-esteem.* Paper presented as part of the "Fragile Self-Regard: Causes and Consequences" symposium (K. C. Oleson, Chair), American Psychological Society annual meeting, New York.

Kolditz, T., & Arkin, R. M. (1982). An impression management interpretation of the self-handicapping phenomenon. *Journal of Personality and Social Psychology, 43,* 492–502.

Luginbuhl, J. E. R., & Palmer, R. (1991). Impression management aspects of self-handicapping: Positive and negative effects. *Personality and Social Psychology Bulletin, 17,* 655–662.

Lynch, M. E. (1996). *Intrinsic and extrinsic motivation in overachievers.* Unpublished master's thesis, The Ohio State University, Columbus.

Mayerson, N. H., & Rhodewalt, F. (1988). The role of self-protective attributions in the experience of pain. *Journal of Social and Clinical Psychology, 6,* 203–218.

Nicholls, J. G. (1984). Achievement motivation: Conceptions of ability, subjective experience, task choice, and performance. *Psychological Review, 91,* 328–346.

Oleson, K. C., Riley, S., & Arkin, R. M. (1995, May). *Interpersonal impact of self-handicapping: Observers' impressions of a self-handicapper.* Paper presented at the 67th Annual Meeting of the Midwestern Psychological Association, Chicago.

Oleson, K. C., Yost, J. H., Poehlmann, K. M., & Arkin, R. M. (1995, May). *Overachievement and underachievement: The relationship of a new scale measuring self-doubt and need for successful outcomes to related concepts in the literature.* Paper presented at the 67th Annual Meeting of the Midwestern Psychological Association, Chicago.

Peterson, C., Semmel, A., Metalsky, G., Abramson, L., von Beyer, C., & Seligman, M. E. P. (1982). The Attributional Style Questionnaire. *Cognitive Therapy and Research, 6,* 287–289.

Poehlmann, K. M., & Oleson, K. C. (1995, June). *Psychological consequences of being an overachiever.* Paper presented at the 7th Annual Meeting of the American Psychological Society, New York.

Poehlmann, K. M., Oleson, K. C., Yost, J. H., & Arkin, R. M. (1995, May). *The phenomenology of overachievement.* Paper presented at the 67th Annual Meeting of the Midwestern Psychological Association, Chicago.

Rhodewalt, F. (1990). Self-handicappers: Individual differences in the preference for anticipatory, self-protective acts. In R. L. Higgins, C. R. Snyder, & S. Berglas (Eds.), *Self-handicapping: The paradox that isn't* (pp. 69–106). New York: Plenum Press.

Rhodewalt, F. (1994). Conceptions of ability, achievement goals, and individual differences in self-handicapping behavior: On the application of implicit theories. *Journal of Personality, 62,* 67–85.

Rhodewalt, F., & Davison, J. (1986). Self-handicapping and subsequent performance: Role of outcome valence and attributional ambiguity. *Basic and Applied Social Psychology, 7,* 307–323.

Rhodewalt, F., & Hill, S. C. (1995). Self-handicapping in the classroom: The effects of claimed self-handicaps on response to academic failure. *Journal of Research in Personality, 25,* 402–417.

Rhodewalt, F., Morf, C., Hazlett, S., & Fairfield, M. (1991). The role of discounting and augmentation in the preservation of self-esteem. *Journal of Personality and Social Psychology, 61,* 122–131.

Rhodewalt, F., Saltzman, A. T., & Wittmer, J. (1984). Self-handicapping among competitive athletes: The role of practice in self-esteem protection. *Basic and Applied Social Psychology, 5,* 197–209.

Rhodewalt, F., Sanbonmatsu, D. M., Tschanz, B., Feick, D. L., & Waller, A. (1995). Self-handicapping and interpersonal tradeoffs: The effects of claimed self-handicaps on observers' performance evaluations and feedback. *Personality and Social Psychology Bulletin, 21,* 1042–1050.

Richardson, D., & Campbell, J. L. (1980). Alcohol and wife abuse: The effect of alcohol on attribution. *Personality and Social Psychology Bulletin, 6,* 51–56.

Schill, T., Beyler, J., Wehr, J., Swigert, L., & Tatter, T. (1991). Self-handicapping and obesity: Is there a sympathetic audience out there? *Perceptual and Motor Skills, 72,* 1260–1262.

Schouten, P. G. W., & Handelsman, M. M. (1987). Social basis of self-handicapping: The case of depression. *Personality and Social Psychology Bulletin, 13,* 103–110.

Shepperd, J. A. (1988). *Cognitive other-enhancement.* Unpublished doctoral dissertation, University of Missouri, Columbia.

Shepperd, J. A., & Arkin, R. M. (1989). Self-handicapping: The mediating roles of public self-consciousness and task importance. *Personality and Social Psychology Bulletin, 15,* 252–265.

Shepperd, J. A., & Arkin, R. M. (1991). Behavioral other-enhancement: Strategically obscuring the link between performance and evaluation. *Journal of Personality and Social Psychology, 60,* 79–88.

Shepperd, J. A., Arkin, R. M., Strathman, A., & Baker, S. M. (1994). Dysphoria as a moderator of the relationship between perceived effort and perceived ability. *Journal of Personality and Social Psychology, 66,* 559–569.

Smith, D. S., & Strube, M. J. (1991). Self-protective tendencies as moderators of self-handicapping impressions. *Basic and Applied Social Psychology, 12,* 63–80.

Smith, T. W., Snyder, C. R., & Handelsman, M. M. (1982). On the self-serving function of an academic wooden leg: Test anxiety as a self-handicapping strategy. *Journal of Personality and Social Psychology, 42,* 314–321.

Snyder, C. R. (1990). Self-handicapping processes and sequelae: On the taking of a psychological dive. In R. Higgins, C. R. Snyder, & S. Berglas (Eds.), *Self-handicapping: The paradox that isn't* (pp. 107–150). New York: Plenum Press.

Snyder, C. R., Ford, C. E., & Hunt, H. A. (1985, August). *Excuse-making: A look at sex differences.* Paper presented at the 93rd Annual Convention of the American Psychological Association, Los Angeles.

Snyder, C. R., Higgins, R. L., & Stucky, R. J. (1983). *Excuses: Masquerades in search of grace.* New York: Wiley/Interscience.

Strube, M. J. (1986). An analysis of the self-handicapping scale. *Basic and Applied Social Psychology, 7,* 211–234.

Strube, M. J., White, A., Shimabukaro, J., & Bailey, J. (1988, August). *Development of a questionnaire for assessing self-appraisal motivation.* Paper presented at the 96th Annual Convention of the American Psychological Association, Altanta.

Tice, D. (1991). Esteem protection or enhancement?: Self-handicapping motives and attributions differ by trait self-esteem. *Journal of Personality and Social Psychology, 60,* 711–725.

Weiner, B. (1985). An attributional theory of achievement motivation and emotion. *Psychological Review, 92,* 548–573.

Yost, J. H., & Arkin, R. M. (1995, June). *Self-handicapping, overachievement, and the precarious competence image.* Paper presented at the 7th Annual Meeting of the American Psychological Society, New York.

Yost, J. H., Lichtstein, J., Poehlmann, K. M., & Arkin, R. M. (1995, May). *Overachievement and self-handicapping.* Paper presented at the 67th Annual Meeting of the Midwestern Psychological Association, Chicago.

Yost, J. H., Poehlmann, K. M., & Arkin, R. M. (1994, May). *An attributional model of overachievement.* Paper presented at the 66th Annual Meeting of the Midwestern Psychological Association, Chicago.

Would You Believe It's the Pandocrin? Comment on Self-Handicapping

Kelly G. Shaver

In many scientific endeavors it is simple to separate the content of the discipline from the processes by which that content is discovered, created, or revised. Not so in social psychology. Ours is a distinctly *social* enterprise. Experimenters construct elaborate social settings designed to produce between-condition differences in behavior. Research participants know they are on stage and try be helpful while maintaining their guard. Interpretation of the data collected can depend as much on the social intuition of the investigator as on the outcome of statistical analyses. Successful communication of the findings requires an ability to weave a tale that reviewers and readers will find convincing. Our field's stars can do all of this with ease; our legends can take the next step, learning as much about behavior from the research process itself as from the particular data collected. Ned Jones was a legend; his intellectual influence on social psychology has been both broad and deep, as indicated by two retrospective reviews of work that was dear to his heart (Oleson & Arkin, 1994; Shaver & Kirk, 1996). Concepts that Ned furthered, such as ingratiation, strategic self-presentation, and correspondence bias, apply to the research process every bit as much as they apply to ordinary social behavior.

One thread that runs through these diverse conceptual contributions is the idea of interpersonal competition. Those of us who played golf or tennis with Ned, or walked into his office with what we thought—mistakenly—was a pretty good idea, recognize that many of Ned's conceptual contributions are "noncommon" effects that reflected his underlying personal dispositions. In the evolutionary idiom that is becoming so popular, Ned was the old bull testing generation after generation of young challengers. There is just one problem for the old bull. Before embarking on competition, one must be prepared to *lose*. Ned was always willing to take this risk. But even here, Ned was phenomenally adept at translating his patter before a doubles match into an important theoretical idea: self-handicapping. In this commentary, I first review Jones and Berglas's (1978) original theoretical account of self-handicapping, touching on the unresolved debate about the importance of situational and personal factors in motivating self-handicapping behavior. I then turn to the distal (child development) and proximal cues that commence the self-handicapping motive, as well as the consequences extended over time of repeated enactment of self-handicapping. Finally, I discuss the theoretical relationship of self-handicapping to both expectancy theory (Vroom, 1964) and self-evaluation maintenance theory (Tesser, 1988).

SELF-HANDICAPPING: THE PERSON AND THE SITUATION

As originally proposed (Jones & Berglas, 1978), self-handicapping was a strategic form of self-presentation designed to maintain a positive self-conception: "People actively try to arrange the circumstances of their behavior so as to protect their conceptions of themselves as competent, intelligent persons" (p. 200). This interpersonal strategy encompassed both the discounting of failure and the augmentation of success: "An important reason why some people turn to alcohol is to avoid the implications of negative feedback for failure and to enhance the impact of positive feedback for success" (p. 201). As Arkin and Oleson note (see chapter 6), the essential ingredient in self-handicapping is the obscuring of the link between performance and evaluation, or in Jones and Berglas's words (1978), "we sometimes do things to *avoid* diagnostic information about our own characteristics and capacities" (p. 200). Finally, like so much of Ned's work, his conception of self-handicapping was informed not only by theory and research but also by his keen observations of himself and others. Social comparison theory (Festinger, 1954) and attribution theory (e.g., Kelley, 1972) are part of the picture, as is the experimental participant's choice of the presumably performance-debilitating drug Pandocrin (Berglas & Jones, 1978). But there is also one of my favorite lines, "Self-handicappers are legion in the sports world, from the tennis player who externalizes a bad shot by adjusting his racket strings, to the avid golfer who systematically avoids taking lessons or even practicing on the driving range" (Berglas & Jones, 1978, p. 201).

Arkin and Oleson's chapter shows how well many of Ned's ideas about self-handicapping have withstood experimental testing, but also identifies intrapsychic aspects of the phenomenon that have remained elusive. For example, there is wide support for the notion that weakening the performance–evaluation link is important in avoiding having to acknowledge self-doubt. Whether this avoidance—or for that matter, the self-doubt—is transitory or enduring remains an open question. There have been plenty of experimental demonstrations that self-handicapping choices can be made with conscious awareness, but Fred Rhodewalt's (1990) demonstration of individual differences in self-handicapping makes one wonder whether, outside the laboratory, the strategy is always that available to introspection. The existence of consciously chosen self-handicapping suggests the power of situations, the presence of individual differences suggests the power of personal styles. It would be interesting to compare the relative proportions of variance in self-handicapping behavior accounted for by situational, as opposed to personal, factors. Resolution of the intrapsychic issues awaits further research; Arkin and Oleson's chapter outlines some of the new directions being taken.

DISTAL AND PROXIMAL CAUSES AND CONSEQUENCES OF SELF-HANDICAPPING

In addition to intrapsychic issues, the fundamentally *interpersonal* quality of self-handicapping offers fruitful avenues for exploration. One excuse protects the self; a continuing string of excuses changes the perceptions held by an observer. If these perceptions are then internalized as a form of "looking-glass self" (Cooley, 1902) there could be serious consequences for self-esteem. Translated into more recent idiom, the looking-glass self involves our understanding of the perceiver's attributions about our motives, not just that individual's view of our outward appearance. As long as we dole out our excuses one at a time to different observers, we might be able to maintain a self-fiction of competence and responsibility. But consistent self-handicapping to the same target audience is likely to bring one's reflected shortcomings into sharper focus.

To be sure, in their original description of the phenomenon, Jones and Berglas (1978) emphasize that

> the public value of the strategy is not its original impetus. This lies in the exaggerated importance of one's own private conception of self-competence and the need to protect that conception from unequivocal negative feedback even in the absence of others. (p. 202)

Despite their concentration on the strategy's implications for the self, Jones and Berglas still identified interpersonal events in development that might contribute to an adult tendency toward self-handicapping. As Arkin and Oleson (this volume) note, this search for developmental origins of self-handicapping has continued. For example, Rhodewalt (1994) has suggested that adult variations in self-handicapping might be a consequence of childhood differences between mastery-oriented versus helpless reactions to challenge in childhood (Dweck & Leggett, 1988). In Dweck's opinion people come to hold one of two general "implicit theories" of ability and morality (Dweck, Chiu, & Hong, 1995). People who are *entity theorists* see human personal characteristics as relatively immutable, whereas people who are *incremental theorists* believe that change is always possible—even of personality characteristics and fundamental abilities. Faced with failure, entity theorists tend to become helpless (because nothing they might do would alter the outcome). Confronted by a similar predicament, incremental theorists concentrate on strategies designed to overcome what are perceived to be only temporary setbacks. The presumed relationship between worldview and self-handicapping can be taken as further evidence of just how difficult the parent's job really is. Will a parent's supportive assertion (e.g., "You're very smart; I'm *sure* you can do it") produce the sort of internal attributions for performance success that contribute to independence and a desire for mastery? Or will it produce an entity theorist who will self-handicap to avoid the possibility of failure that would be considered diagnostic of stupidity?

As important as developmental antecedents might be, the impression-management quality of self-handicapping leads us to wonder whether at least some of its causes might be more immediately proximal. Specifically, is there anything about *who else* is present that might enhance or diminish self-handicapping? Using one of Ned's favorite real-life pastimes, consider, as an example, a reasonably skilled weekend tennis player who also happens to be president of a major corporation. This individual might well engage in a bit of strategic self-handicapping right before a weekly match with equally qualified and competitive friends. Do we believe that comparable self-handicapping will emerge if the individual is playing in a pro-am fund-raising match against a tour professional? I doubt it. One doesn't need self-handicapping in the face of a real handicap. The company president's play could be comparable in both instances (indeed, it might even be better when playing against the professional), but the *attributions* made by the self and by any audience will change with the interpersonal context. In this situation, John Darley and Al Goethals would note that the company president was attributionally safe—even being able to hold one's own on the same court as a tour professional is a performance that is quite good enough, whatever the final score. But suppose that the tennis professional is replaced with the president of a Japanese corporation with which the CEO wishes to do business. Now the attributional stakes may be high, but we would still be surprised to learn that the CEO had failed to recognize that the social demands of this cross-cultural exchange precluded the garden-variety "American" version of self-handicapping.

The situation described in this example occurs rarely enough that we should not expend scarce theoretical resources to account for it. On the other hand, there are much more common interpersonal relationships in which the others present might make a substantial difference in the likelihood of self-handicapping. Continuing with the business metaphor, an intelligent subordinate realizes that one should not embarrass one's boss in public. Or for that matter, one should help one's boss keep from embarrassing himself or herself. Thus, there may be instances in which "civility" or "tact" requires self-handicapping by a subordinate to avoid diminishing the *other* instead of the more typical self-handicapping to avoid diminishing the self.

RELATING SELF-HANDICAPPING TO OTHER THEORETICAL DOMAINS

Self-Evaluation Maintenance

An additional opportunity for progress might be created by more directly comparing self-handicapping to related processes from other domains. A similar possibility to the earlier example of strategic self-handicapping by a subordinate can be seen in close romantic relationships, as suggested by Tesser's (1988) theory of self-evaluation maintenance (SEM; Tesser, 1988). In this theory Tesser identifies two dynamic processes, reflection and comparison, thought to affect judgments of self-worth in a context containing a psychologically close other person. When a performance dimension is of low relevance to the self, the reflection process occurs. One can "bask in the reflected glory" (Cialdini et al., 1976) of the other's successes, thus enhancing self-esteem. In a Heiderian (Heider, 1958) sense, this is advantage by association (through existence of a unit relation). Alternatively, when a performance dimension is highly relevant to the self, the comparison process engages. Now self-esteem can be maintained only if one's own performance is superior to that of the comparison other. Because the overall motivation ascribed to the self is maintenance of a positive sense of self-worth, relevance of the performance dimension and perceived psychological closeness of the other person can also be dependent variables, changing as needed on the basis of reflection or comparison.

In his review of the SEM model, Tesser (1988) mentioned self-handicapping only in passing, but I believe the two approaches have much more to say to one another than has been true in the past. Both SEM and self-handicapping are processes in the service of continued (or enhanced) self-esteem. Both concentrate on the outcomes of task performance. Both require all the agility at which the human cognitive gymnast excels. Finally, both processes are fundamentally interpersonal, and here some of the possibilities become apparent. How is the immediate choice of a self-handicapping strategy affected by the relationship that does or does not exist between performer and audience? To what extent does self-handicapping depend on knowledge of the other's standing on the dimension of comparison? For that matter, will two romantic partners with similar interests and capabilities last as a couple without both being adept at self-handicapping? In short, some of the processes inherent in the SEM model may suggest interpersonal conditions under which self-handicapping will occur; similarly, self-handicapping may be an important strategic choice for people who desire to maintain both themselves and their relationship. More extensive cross-fertilization between these two topic areas may be of significant conceptual and empirical value to each.

Expectancy Theory

Arkin and Oleson's chapter makes it clear that the objective of self-handicapping is to obscure the *link* between performance and attribution. A more complete understanding of self-handicapping awaits delineation of all of the conditions under which ambiguity in linkage is preferable to clarity. Indeed, one can imagine high-stakes performance-related activities (like free-climbing a sheer and dangerous rock face) in which self-doubt would be more personally valuable than self-handicapping could ever be. Merely inquiring about ability–performance clarity, however, suggests that *expectancy theory* (Porter & Lawler, 1968; Vroom, 1964) might have something valuable to say concerning self-handicapping.

Traditionally, expectancy theory has discussed the influence of four variables on motivated behavior: *effort–performance expectancy, performance–outcome expectancy, valence,* and *instrumentality.* The first of these is defined as belief concerning the likelihood that expending a particular level of effort will lead to successful completion of a particular task. The second is defined as the belief that successful task completion will lead to a specified end state. In the simplest terms, valence is the evaluation placed on the end state, and instrumentality refers to the difference between an end state desired for itself and one desired because of what other consequences it might have.

In a theoretical model designed to account for the motivation to begin a new business venture, Elizabeth Gatewood and I have suggested how attributions for the causes of success and failure might be inserted into the traditional expectancy framework (Gatewood & Shaver, 1991). The part of our model that is specifically relevant here concerns the effort–performance link. For example, if performance failures are attributed to unstable external factors, effort–performance expectancies do not change. (This, of course, is the situation created by self-handicapping.) But such an attribution also leaves performance–outcome expectancies and perceived instrumentality at the same (high) level that made undertaking the action desirable in the first place. For this reason, the actor would likely try again. What if there were self-handicapping prior to the second performance? The third? Would the actor come to believe his or her excuses? If that happened, would the instrumentality of the activity also change? These questions suggest that we do not know nearly enough about self-handicapping in the long-term. Whether or not the instrumentality change prediction is eventually confirmed, research on self-handicapping stands to gain from closer collaboration with research and theory on expectancy.

JONESIAN PROCESSES EXTENDED THROUGH SOCIAL TIME

From the infamous "unequivocal behavioral orientation," "correspondence bias," and "outgroup homogeneity effect" to the *shift* from category-based to target-based expectancies, Ned's work concentrated on processes extended through social time. In some cases the time extension is largely by implication; in others it is relatively explicit. For example, although the correspondence bias occurs when there is only one judgment being made, a debate coach's instructions about whether a speech should be pro-Castro or anti-Castro obviously had to come before the time at which the speech was given. This is the inclusion of time by implication. Alternatively, the repeated social interaction needed to change a category-based expectancy into a full understanding of what a target person may be like as a person must occur explicitly through an extended period of time. The process of self-handicapping may fall somewhere in-between these two extremes. Will there be self-handicapping on a task that is performed only once, in front of an audience the actor never expects to see again, and in a behavioral domain with which the actor has had virtually no prior experience? Probably not. But will self-handicapping effectively confuse either the self or the audience the 20th time the same excuses are used in a task setting? Again, probably not. Determining the time course of self-handicapping, and many of the other Jonesian behavioral principles, cannot be accomplished in the slice-of-time cross-sectional experiments Ned loved so much. This is why, despite how much Ned accomplished, there still remains much to do as, to paraphrase Dan Gilbert, we speed down the highway with Ned into the future.

REFERENCES

Berglas, S., & Jones, E. E. (1978). Drug choice as a self-handicapping strategy in response to noncontingent success. *Journal of Personality and Social Psychology, 36*, 405–417.

Cialdini, R. B., Borden, R. J., Thorne, A., Walker, M. R., Freeman, S., & Sloan,

L. R. (1976). Basking in reflected glory: Three (football) field studies. *Journal of Personality and Social Psychology, 34,* 366–375.

Cooley, C. H. (1902). *Human nature and the social order.* New York: Scribners'.

Dweck, C. S., Chiu, C., & Hong, Y. (1995). Implicit theories and their role in judgments and reactions: A world from two perspectives. *Psychological Inquiry, 6,* 267–285.

Dweck, C. S., & Leggett, E. L. (1988). A social–cognitive approach to motivation and personality. *Psychological Review, 95,* 256–273.

Festinger, L. (1954). A theory of social comparison processes. *Human Relations, 7,* 117–140.

Gatewood, E. J., & Shaver, K. G. (1991, August). *Expectancies for success and attributions for failure: Toward a theory of entrepreneurial persistence.* Paper presented at the meeting of the Academy of Management, Miami, FL.

Heider, F. (1958). *The psychology of interpersonal relations.* New York: Wiley.

Jones, E. E., & Berglas, S. (1978). Control of attributions about the self through self-handicapping strategies: The appeal of alcohol and the role of underachievement. *Personality and Social Psychology Bulletin, 4,* 200–206.

Kelley, H. H. (1972). Attribution in social interaction. In E. E. Jones, D. E. Kanouse, H. H. Kelley, R. E. Nisbett, S. Valins, & B. Weiner (Eds.), *Attribution: Perceiving the causes of behavior* (pp. 1–26). Morristown, NJ: General Learning Press.

Oleson, K. C., & Arkin, R. M. (1994). Slaying the empirical dragon. *Contemporary Psychology, 39,* 455–458.

Porter, L. W., & Lawler, E. E. (1968). *Managerial attitudes and performance.* Homewood, IL: Irwin.

Rhodewalt, F. (1990). Self-handicappers: Individual differences in the preference for anticipatory, self-protective acts. In R. L. Higgins, C. R. Snyder, & S. Berglas (Eds.), *Self-handicapping: The paradox that isn't* (pp. 69–106). New York: Plenum Press.

Rhodewalt, F. (1994). Conceptions of ability, achievement goals, and individual differences in self-handicapping behavior: On the application of implicit theories. *Journal of Personality, 62,* 67–85.

Shaver, K. G., & Kirk, D. L. (1996). The quest for meaning in social behavior:

Retrospective review of *Attribution: Perceiving the causes of behavior. Contemporary Psychology, 41,* 423–426.

Tesser, A. (1988). Toward a self-evaluation maintenance model of social behavior. In L. Berkowitz (Ed.), *Advances in experimental social psychology* (Vol. 21, pp. 181–227). New York: Academic Press.

Vroom, V. H. (1964). *Work and motivation.* New York: Wiley.

Reflections on
Self-Handicapping

David J. Schneider

One of the things about Ned Jones's research that was especially appealing was that he crossed so many boundaries. He worked on many topics, but many of the individual topics he studied also cast a wide shadow. The work initiated by Jones and Berglas (1978) on self-handicapping illustrates this breadth perfectly. At the heart of the phenomenon is, of course, the notion that people are motivated to behave in certain ways that may affect the ways others and they themselves come to think about them. This is a straightforward and simple idea, one that might become vacuous in its most general form. However, research on self-handicapping focused our attention on a particular manifestation of that general idea that has broad appeal. Even in their first short article on the topic Jones and Berglas (1978) drew on a range of formal and informal observations from not only garden-variety social behavior but also clinical areas. They obviously used attribution theory, but they also discussed, albeit briefly, addictions, alcoholism, child rearing, depression, and self-esteem theory. Self-handicapping is an intuitively engaging idea, but for me it is also interesting because it so clearly illustrates many of the themes of Ned's social psychology career. In this chapter, I touch on six of these themes: the motivated perceiver, social interaction, negotiation, common-sense and illumination of the everyday world, applied person perception, and paradoxes.

THE MOTIVATED PERCEIVER

For Jones the social actor was always a motivated one. The social world could not be understood without some sense of what animated the actors within it. He (thankfully) never escaped the intellectual climate of his Harvard days during the 1950s when Allport, Bruner, and others were deeply involved in trying to document the various ways motives affect cognition. Jones understood that in everyday life, motives, goals, and values were not merely messy accidental properties of the ways we cognize others; they are of the essence. While the bulk of his work focused on our cognitions of social events, a topic he (Jones, 1990) fortunately reviewed from his own unique perspective, he was always concerned with the motivational influences on social cognition. Indeed his early work with John Thibaut (Jones & Thibaut, 1958) on goals in person perception remains, to my mind, one of the more provocative studies in the field. Furthermore, at a time when the dominant tradition in social psychology insists on studying social stimuli as if they were not really social, Ned had a healthy respect for the fact that the most interesting manifestations of our cognitions take place in a social context, and he stressed that socially situated cognition could not be understood without considering motivation. He was not one to avoid the obvious.

In that context I need not elaborate the point that the self-handicapper is a profoundly motivated cognizer. Those who self-handicap are not content to take self-definitions as they come but are trying to affect the perceptions that others have of them, and perhaps ultimately that they have of themselves.

SOCIAL INTERACTION

As I have indicated we cannot separate Jones's emphasis on motivation from his deep concerns with the ins and outs of social interaction. His early work on ingratiation (Jones, 1964) illustrates this most clearly, but the social world of real people talking and listening, communicating and learning, hassling and being hustled, hurting and being hurt, was never far in the background of his thinking. Even at their most cognitive, his social perceivers were always trying to figure out real people with real dispositions that led to real proclivities to affect the perceivers. His attribution ideas (Jones & Davis, 1965; Jones & McGillis, 1976; Jones & Nisbett, 1971) stayed close to the important, socially saturated, questions initiated by Heider, and he stayed closer than most of the other glosses on Heider. Most attribution models have emphasized general attributions, and there are, indeed, times when we might be interested in issues of whether people performed some behavior for generic internal or external reasons, actor or entity attributions. However, Jones realized that in the real world what most of us care most about is whether the people we interact with are kind, hostile, lazy, or smart. It is, I think, much tougher, but also far more important, to know how we attribute traits and other specific dispositions to others than to solve internal–external causality questions. Ned focused on the real question of dispositions even though I think the final answers eluded him (and the rest of us). My claim is that it was precisely his connectedness to the world of everyday social interactions that kept him so focused on the real issues here and elsewhere.

Again, we see in the work on self-handicapping this theme in full relief. The self-handicapper is not engaged in solitary mental activity; he or she is using the social world in a particular way. The self-handicapper who may be passive in many ways is active in negotiating the image that others have of him or her. Self-handicappers, like the rest of us, must have a theory of how others will attribute motives and traits based on their behavior.

NEGOTIATION

Ned was generally interested in social interaction, but he had a particular focus on the art of negotiation. Obviously the ingratiation work fits this paradigm most closely, but I would argue that much of the other work did as well. For Jones social interaction was, in part, about gaining social advantage (although he certainly recognized other, more amiable, functions of social interaction). There are many ways of negotiating social advantage, but for Ned the essential currency of negotiation was information about identity, especially one's own identity as seen by others. A good deal of his work dealt in one way or another with how we produce clear and usable self-images through the give and take of everyday social interaction. Although Ned was obviously influenced by the seminal work of Erving Goffman (1959), it seems he never had Goffman's existential angst about the fragility of self. Ned did not agree with Goffman that people were in troubled seas of self in a small interaction boat without a cognitive compass, but he did imagine that we were moving at a fast clip down a small stream with only a few attributional tools to guide and steer us. The individual who entered a Jones experiment did not necessarily suffer deep anxieties about identity, but the typical individual was certainly motivated to seek whatever clarity was available about self, even if he or she did err in a positive direction.

Again, self-handicapping illustrates this theme perfectly. Those of us who are unsure of our own competencies will be motivated to protect our sense of self. The self-handicapper is negotiating a self-concept. In one sense, the self-handicapping idea was a return to his early work on ingratiation, but it was a return with a thick veneer of his subsequent concerns with attributional issues.

COMMON SENSE AND ILLUMINATION OF THE EVERYDAY WORLD

Ned liked the real world or at least respected its charms. He never was one to stress the notion that animated so much of the early days of experimental social psychology, namely that truth lies in the counterintuitive prediction. Many of Ned's theoretical notions could be easily explained to any layperson, and his findings often made a great deal of intuitive sense to the rest of us as well. In saying that, however, I do not mean to suggest that his work was intellectually lightweight or that he merely confirmed common sense. He did better than that—he illuminated our sense of the world. When I first read the manuscript of *Ingratiation* as a graduate student, I thought that it was both profoundly prosaic and quite exciting. Prosaic because there was no grand theory, no revealed secret passageways through the maze of social behavior, no hint of the unexpected insights genius often produces.

In fact in the arrogance of youth, I even imagined that I might have done as well. But I did not and could not have. Indeed I suspect that no on else could have got it right in precisely the way Ned did. What he was able to do better than almost anyone of his generation was harness research technologies to do the bidding of his ideas. *Ingratiation* was a perfectly reasonable set of propositions, set in a conceptual framework that reflected both the loosest (Goffman, 1959) and the tightest (Thibaut & Kelley, 1959) of our theoretical paradigms at the time. There was nothing terribly original about the ideas he set forth, and yet somehow one never had any doubt that Jones had captured one essential feature of how people negotiate their social worlds and that he had made us see the everyday social world in new ways. For example, in a precursor to later work on attribution, Jones, Gergen, and Davis (1962) and Gergen (1965) showed that people believe in the genuineness of the approval they gain even when they are deliberately and manipulatively seeking it. This is a nonsurprising result in some ways, but it is one that encourages considerable reflection about the pragmatics and epistemology of the evaluational foundations of everyday social life. The ingratiation model was tight enough to generate good predictions and clear experiments, and it was loose enough to capture enough essence of the real world that one could imagine the experiments actually shedding light on the real world. He didn't have the gripping insights of a Heider or Goffman or the experimental flair of a Festinger, but he had the unbeatable combination of good ideas and testable propositions that seemed to reinforce one another. And in so doing he helped create lines of research that have told us a great deal about our social world.

Self-handicapping is also one of those ideas that seems obvious once one hears it, and if one is not careful it can be too easily dismissed as something we have always known. The idea is simple enough; again, one could easily explain it even to a nonastute layperson. We've all seen self-handicapping done; some of us have even tried it more or less deliberately a time or two. It seems so obvious that it can be regarded as trivial. One might even be excused the "Why didn't I think of that?" reflection. But "one" didn't, and Ned's research in this area again documents his flair for taking simple ideas and making them experimentally tractable. Furthermore, as almost two decade's worth of follow-up research has made clear, self-handicapping is far from a trivial phenomenon. It has stimulated research that has forced us to recognize the complexity of the phenomenon, but it has done so while remaining relatively true to its real-world counterparts.

APPLIED PERSON PERCEPTION

Another feature of Ned's life work that has received little public recognition is the potential for combining his interests in social interaction and person perception in a particular kind of way. As most of us know Jones's first major research project was the study of impression management, or more broadly ingratiation. From there it may have seemed a large step sideways (or backward or forward depending on one's theoretical proclivities) to attribution work that was his next big project. But in one sense it is not such a large step because in effect he was examining the cognitive underpinnings of ingratiation.

Afterall, before one can create a good impression, one must have a clear sense of how one's behavior will be viewed by others. As I have argued before, ingratiation is really applied person perception (Schneider, 1981). One fascinating area that has thus far eluded the nets of formal social psychology is an analysis of the skills that make for various kinds of social interactions. Why is it that some people are interesting conversational companions (as Ned certainly was), and others clearly boring? Why do some people give good public talks, whereas others seem awkward and dull? Why can some people talk their way out of almost any scrape, while others become permanent losers in life's games? And how is it that some people seem able to negotiate a self-concept that is satisfactory, whereas others leave interactions feeling belittled, put-upon, and underappreciated? There are certainly large empirical literatures on leadership, depression, social skills analysis, and the like, and they are not irrelevant to the point I want to make. It is easy to see social skills in terms of ability, and I have no doubt that in the social as well as the more purely cognitive world raw G counts for something. I am even prepared to believe that there are more specific forms of intelligence that affect how easily we negotiate our social worlds. Obviously, some people have some traits such as introversion or shyness that make social interactions difficult, and others who seem to enjoy social interaction more find the same interactions seemingly effortless.

However, the Jones paradigm focuses our attention on two other aspects of social adroitness. First, when one asks why some people are more socially adept than others, surely information about social interactions, contexts, self, and other people is highly useful. If I wish to ask a colleague to take me to the airport, I must know which colleagues are most approachable about such matters, which would be least inconvenienced by my request, and perhaps which owe me favors of one kind or another. In more complex maneuvers I may have quite sophisticated information about what types of requests work with which people under which circumstances.

Second, asking a favor, trying to carry on a conversation, and simply going about one's day-to-day social activities involve forming and affirming social identities. When I ask my dean or department chair for a favor, I surely give some thought not only to how my request will be received but also with how I will be perceived as I ask for the favor. What attributions will the target make following this or that type of request? Of course, I care generally how such people perceive me, but presumably the knowledge also has strategic value in helping me fashion my request. One essential dilemma is how to make others think highly of me without diminishing others in the process (Jones, 1964). Some of us manage to pull this off, but there are social klutzs among us who simultaneously hurt self and others by portraying themselves as insensitive braggarts.

Early ingratiation research explicitly dealt with how the actor's knowledge about the roles and values of self and target influenced self-presentations (Jones, Gergen, & Jones, 1963; Jones, Gergen, Gumpert, & Thibaut, 1965). Here I am merely extending that idea by arguing that attribution knowledge is central for social smoothness. And the kind of knowledge that is required is not whether behavior is internally or externally caused but rather specific knowledge about likely outcomes of attribution processes—precisely the trait, motive, and ability attributions that correspondent inference theory emphasizes. What kinds of traits will my target infer if I behave in this or that way? Will her inferences be correspondent or not? How is she likely to interpret my behavior given my assumptions about what she already thinks of me?

Obviously, self-handicapping, which is, afterall, a form of impression management, requires these very same skills. The successful self-handicapper will have a clear sense that he will be held more responsible for lapses of motivation than for lack of ability. In everyday life, he may also have a clear sense of the best ways of conveying his "handicap" precisely so that it does not seem like a manufactured excuse. If he is really successful, he may even get people to feel sorry for him.

PARADOXES

Finally, I want to emphasize Ned's enjoyment of a good paradox. There are several examples in his work. For instance, in considering successful ingratiation he wondered how it was that people could come to believe the positive feedback that they had so cleverly engendered (Jones et al., 1962; Jones, Rhodewalt, Berglas, & Skelton, 1981). In his more famous work on correspondent bias (Jones, 1979), he was concerned for how people can so successfully avoid situational information in doing attribution work, especially when they so obviously engendered it (Gilbert & Jones, 1986).

And there is a further paradox in the work on self-handicapping. Basically the self-handicapper is willing to allow others to infer that she is lazy or alcoholic or a procrastinator rather than stupid. Put in the conventional language we would seem to prefer that others assign us unstable rather than stable internal qualities. At one level that makes considerable sense. Precisely because abilities are seen as relatively stable, one does not wish to be permanently assigned a negative quality that one will not easily be able to shake. And as Arkin and Oleson (this volume) pointed out, the ascription of high ability more or less commits one to a lifetime of high achievement, which may seem an overwhelming burden. Indeed, some of the most tragic cases of self-handicapping occur for those people who fail to live up to early promise or family destiny and who take to drink or drugs, partially as a kind of self-handicapping strategy.

And yet there is a kind of paradox involved. Why would one rather be seen as lazy than stupid? The paradox arises precisely because motives are generally assumed to be easier to change than abilities; therefore, in some sense we have more control and hence more responsibility for motives than for abilities. We have a soft spot in our hearts for the marginally gifted athlete who plays above his ability and feel angry at the gifted student who achieves well below his ability. It is always frustrating to have eager students whose abilities are not up to their ambitions, but it is even more frustrating to have students whose failures of will and effort leave them well below their potential. The gifted writer who drowns his doubts about his abilities in alcohol may go down in history as a person of great unfulfilled promise, but he will also be seen as a person who lacked elementary skills to control his own life chances. I am not so sure that I would not rather be seen as someone who tried and failed.

CONCLUSION

Ned Jones's intellectual life was full and rich, broadly focused and deep in its implications. I have tried to discuss several themes that I see as guiding his general research effort, and it seems to me that his initial model of self-handicapping illustrates these themes.

REFERENCES

Gergen, K. J. (1965). The effects of interaction goals and personalistic feedback on presentation of self. *Journal of Personality and Social Psychology, 1,* 413–425.

Gilbert, D. T., & Jones, E. E. (1986). Perceiver-induced constraint: Interpretations of self-generated reality. *Journal of Personality and Social Psychology,* 50, 269–280.

Goffman, E. (1959). *Self-presentation in everyday life.* New York: Doubleday/ Anchor.

Jones, E. E. (1964). *Ingratiation.* New York: Appleton-Century-Crofts.

Jones, E. E. (1979). The rocky road from acts to dispositions. *American Psychologist,* 34, 107–117.

Jones, E. E. (1990). *Interpersonal perception.* New York: Freedman.

Jones, E. E., & Berglas, S. (1978). Control of attributions about the self through self-handicapping strategies: The role of alcohol and underachievement. *Personality and Social Psychology Bulletin,* 4, 200–206.

Jones, E. E., & Davis, K. E. (1965). From acts to dispositions: The attribution process in person perception. In L. Berkowitz (Ed.), *Advances in experimental social psychology* (Vol. 2, pp. 219–266). San Diego, CA: Academic Press.

Jones, E. E., Gergen, K. J., & Davis, K. E. (1962). Some determinants of reactions to being approved or disapproved as a person. *Psychological Monographs,* 76 (Whole No. 521).

Jones, E. E., Gergen, K. J., Gumpert, P., & Thibaut, J. (1965). Some conditions affecting the use of ingratiation to influence performance evaluation. *Journal of Personality and Social Psychology,* 1, 613–626.

Jones, E. E., Gergen, K. J., & Jones, R. G. (1963). Tactics of ingratiation among leaders and subordinates in a status hierarchy. *Psychological Monographs,* 77 (Whole No. 566).

Jones, E. E., & McGillis, D. (1976). Correspondent inferences and the attribution cube: A comparative reappraisal. In J. H. Harvey, W. J. Ickes, & R. F. Kidd (Eds.), *New directions in attribution research* (Vol. 1, pp. 389–420). Hillsdale, NJ: Erlbaum.

Jones, E. E., & Nisbett, R. E. (1971). The actor and the observer: Divergent perceptions of the causes of behavior. In E. E. Jones, D. E. Kanouse, H. H. Kelley, R. E. Nisbett, S. Valins, & B. Weiner (Eds.), *Attribution: Perceiving the causes of behavior* (pp. 79–94). Morristown, NJ: General Learning Press.

Jones, E. E., Rhodewalt, F., Berglas, S. E., & Skelton, J. A. (1981). Effects of strategic self-presentation on subsequent self-esteem. *Journal of Personality and Social Psychology, 41,* 407–421.

Jones, E. E., & Thibaut, J. W. (1958). Interaction goals as bases of inference in interpersonal perception. In R. Taguiri & L. Petrullo (Eds.), *Person perception and interpersonal behavior* (pp. 151–178). Stanford, CA: Stanford University Press.

Schneider, D. J. (1981). Tactical self-presentations: Toward a broader conception. In J. T. Tedeschi (Ed.), *Impression management theory and social psychological research* (pp. 23–40). San Diego, CA: Academic Press.

Thibaut, J. W., & Kelley, H. H. (1959). *The social psychology of groups.* New York: Wiley.

7

Self-Presentation and the Phenomenal Self: The "Carryover Effect" Revisited

Frederick Rhodewalt

S elf-presentation is the act of strategically managing how one is perceived by others. It can be in the service of a number of different goals, including attempts to gain power and influence others, the communication of a desired identity, or the management of one's emotions. These presentations can be authentic portrayals of our "true selves," ruses in which we strive to convince others that we are what we are not, or exclusionary or evasive presentations (Leary, 1995) in which we try to conceal or avoid revealing aspects of the self. There are also many tacks that one may take in the pursuit of these self-presentational goals. Jones and Pittman (1982), in their chapter on strategic self-presentation, listed ingratiation, self-promotion, exemplification, intimidation, and supplication as ploys for shaping others' views of oneself.

Despite the variety of self-presentational goals, motives, and strategies, almost all self-presentational behaviors share one common element: They are constrained interpersonal acts (Jones, 1990). That is, our endeavors to lead others to believe something about ourselves, whether freely chosen or dictated by the audience, limit the range of thoughts, feelings, and actions appropriate to that activity. Although much of the research on self-presentation has been concerned with the effects of such behavior on the audience, the research reviewed in this chapter focuses on the implications of such constrained interpersonal behavior on the presenter's self-concept. Specifically, I argue that people's self-presentations play a unique and significant role in defining who they are. I review recent research that expands the literature on the interplay between public presentations and private self-conceptions and offer hypotheses to guide future research. The overarching message is that self-presentational behavior provides a valuable window through which the processes of self-concept maintenance and change can be examined.

THE "CARRYOVER EFFECT"

When Ned Jones and I began our research on the carryover effect, Ned was pondering the findings of two experiments he had recently completed with Steve Berglas and Andy Skelton. Although the two studies involved different presentation contexts (Jones, Rhodewalt, Berglas, & Skelton, 1981, Studies 1 and 2), both experiments asked participants to be self-enhancing during an interaction with an interviewer. Participants were provided with consensus information that indicated that others had been either self-enhancing or self-effacing during the interview. Following the interviews, research participants completed measures of self-esteem anonymously, in private, for a purpose that was allegedly unrelated to the study. When the consensus information was presented prior to the individual's own self-presentation two things happened. First, the consensus information influenced the participants' self-presentations: Participants who viewed others being self-enhancing were self-enhancing during the interview, and participants who saw others being self-effacing were self-effacing during the interview. More important, all participants displayed what we termed the *carryover effect*. That is, despite the clearly "manded" nature of their self-presentations, individuals' private self-evaluations changed to correspond with their public displays; aggrandizing self-presenters viewed themselves more positively than did modest self-presenters.

These were not the first nor last results to show the subtle influences of social context on individuals' subsequent self-conceptions (i.e., Fazio, Effrein, & Falender, 1981; Gergen, 1965; Kunda & Sanitioso, 1989; McGuire & Padawer-Singer, 1976; Morse & Gergen, 1970; Natale & Hantas, 1982; Rhodewalt & Comer, 1981; Snyder & Swann, 1978). Many factors can lead to momentary shifts in how people think or feel about themselves. What was striking to us was that such obviously constrained behavior could result in shifts in self-evaluations.

THE PHENOMENAL SELF, BIASED SCANNING, AND DISSONANCE

If self-presentations affect one's self-views, by what paths does this influence travel? This question bears on a more fundamental concern: How is the self to be conceived such that it can be simultaneously a stable element of the individual and yet reactive to contextual influences such as strategic self-presentation? Contemporary writings on the self focus on features of the self that would apparently foster self-concept stability. In the tradition of Markus (1977), social cognition research has portrayed the self as a highly complex, integrated mental representation of who one is (Kihlstrom & Cantor, 1985; Klein & Loftus, 1993; Linville & Carlston, 1994) that is stable and consistent across time (Cheek & Hogan, 1983).

This structural self-stability is augmented by motivational and interpersonal factors. Enlisting a set of cognitive biases, Greenwald (1980) argued the "totalitarian ego" filters social feedback to maintain desired self-views. Moreover, Swann (1983) argued compellingly that people strategically engineer their social interactions to create a "social reality" that sustains or verifies their beliefs about themselves.

Yet, despite all of the forces that should coalesce to promote self-stability, subtle contextual cues such as the relative uniqueness of one's features (McGuire & Padawer-Singer, 1976) or transitory moods (Natale & Hantas, 1982) alter one's momentary self-views. To accommodate the idea that the self is both stable and mutable or in flux, we adopted the Jones and Gerard (1967) notion of the *phenomenal self*. In our view, the phenomenal self is much like Markus's (Markus & Wurf, 1987) notion of the "working self-concept" in that we assume that people have available an integrated interpretation of who they are that may be used to guide present behavior and future acts. When in awareness, the phenomenal self represents a summary statement of self-relevant information currently accessible out of a vast array of potentially available self-knowledge. Contextual and motivational cues are like a spotlight on the self that through its beam can illuminate certain aspects of the self and make them more accessible than other areas of self-knowledge. Thus, these cues can foster moment-to-moment shifts in the self. At the same time our self-knowledge is bounded; that is, we may not be consistent about precisely who we are, but we know who we are not. Finally, we also recognize that the phenomenal self evolves over time, coming to incorporate one's actions and outcomes. This framework, then, accommodates moment-to-moment variations within an underlying stable self, a self albeit with the capacity for long-term modification of content.

Given this working definition of the self, we (Jones et al., 1981) proposed two separate pathways to the carryover effect. One possibility was a "biased scanning" variant of self-perception theory. In this view self-presentational behaviors make congruent self-knowledge more accessible, and, consequently, this knowledge is given more weight in subsequent self-reflections. This hypothesized process is consistent with the Markus and Wurf (1987) notion that the self is a vast, complex, and even potentially contradictory network of knowledge. The size of the network far exceeds normal attentional capacity so that only a limited subset of self-knowledge is activated and "working" at any given moment. Moment-to-moment shifts reflect changes in the self-knowledge that is included in active memory at the time.

The second possibility recognized that although the underlying knowledge base of the self is vast, well articulated, and stable, it is also bounded. That is, for any person there are any number of potential self-conceptions that are not represented as part of the self network. Self-presentations depicting such "nonself" attributes cannot influence one's self-conceptions through increased accessibility of congruent knowledge because presumably such information is not in the self

376

network. Rather, these presentations should arouse cognitive dissonance precisely because they are incongruent with existing self-knowledge. Factors such as choice, responsibility, foreseeability, commitment, and consequences should mediate the carryover effect when self-presentations are discrepant with existing self-views. In brief, the carryover effect can be explained as the outcome of dissonance reduction processes.

Ned and I decided to pit the biased scanning and cognitive dissonance explanations against one another by having individuals present themselves to another individual while we manipulated variables that should independently influence one process or the other. Accordingly, participants were led to believe that they were confederates helping us to evaluate the interviewing skills of naive graduate students who were enrolled in a clinical and personnel interviewing practicum. Participants were instructed to present themselves in a self-enhancing or self-deprecating manner during the interview. Within this pretext we were able to manipulate biased scanning by having half of the participants play the self-enhancing or self-deprecating role by thinking of themselves on a particularly good day or bad day and responding to the interviewers' questions from that perspective. Each self-referencing participant had a yoked partner who was matched on initial level of self-esteem and provided with the answers given by the self-referencing partner. The yoked participant's task was to provide the scripted answers as if they were his or her own extemporaneous responses to the interviewer's queries. Thus, for half the individuals the behaviors were connected to how they viewed themselves, and for half the presentation was equally enhancing or deprecating but not directly related to self-referent knowledge.

To manipulate dissonance we borrowed the choice manipulation from the induced-compliance attitude change paradigm (Linder, Cooper, & Jones, 1967). All participants were told that we recognized it might be objectionable for them to mislead another person. We told half that the choice was really up to them and told half that regrettably they could not be given a choice. After the interview participants completed a packet of questionnaires ostensibly to be seen and used by a researcher at another university. Embedded in the packet was a final measure of self-esteem.

The postinterview self-esteem results were quite surprising; both manipulations had an effect depending on whether the individual had portrayed a positive or negative image. For self-enhancing presentations, whether the presentation was improvised determined the carryover effect. Self-referencing participants displayed elevated self-esteem following their self-enhancing interactions; yoked participants did not. The choice manipulation made no difference for these individuals. In contrast, among self-deprecating participants the choice variable and not self-referencing accounted for declines in self-esteem. High-choice participants regardless or whether they improvised or role played the presentation displayed a decline in self-esteem. Low-choice participants appeared to be unaffected by their self-presentations.

We were impressed by the similarity of the pattern of our findings to data presented by Fazio, Zanna, and Cooper (1977) in their attempt to reconcile the dissonance-self-perception controversy. Specifically, we argued that people have a range of attributes, past behaviors, and experiences that underlie their present self-conceptions that when available in memory fall within their latitude of acceptance. People in our study (see Figure 1) who improvised their positive self-presentations displayed the carryover effect because this biased search of the self made positive aspects more accessible. It is as if self-referencing participants ask themselves leading questions (Swann, Giuliano, & Wegner, 1982) and then weight the answers more heavily in self-reflection. Such shifts in the phenomenal self should be transitory and last only until contextual cues shift self-attention elsewhere. We further argued that dissonance processes accounted for those self-presentations that were discrepant with our existing self-knowledge—presentations that presented a self in the latitude of rejection. Presumably, our self-deprecating participants' negative presentations were inconsistent with how they typically viewed themselves, and thus they displayed the carryover effect when they were made to feel responsible for their behavior. We would expect that in contrast to biased-scanning-produced transitory shifts in

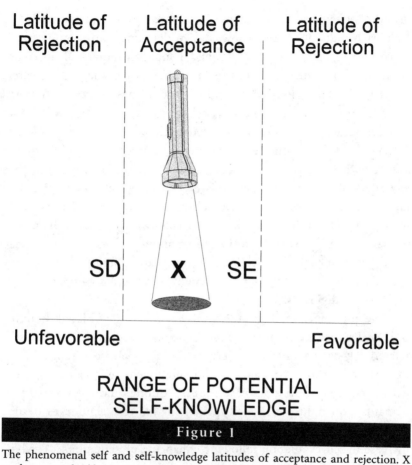

Latitude of Rejection | Latitude of Acceptance | Latitude of Rejection

SD   X   SE

Unfavorable   Favorable

RANGE OF POTENTIAL
SELF-KNOWLEDGE

Figure 1

The phenomenal self and self-knowledge latitudes of acceptance and rejection. X = phenomenal self; SE = self-enhancement; SD = self deprecation.

the self-concept, dissonance-produced changes should be longer lasting (cf. Higgins, Rhodewalt, & Zanna, 1979).

Given the admittedly post hoc flavor to this interpretation Sjofn Agustsdottir and I (Rhodewalt & Agustsdottir, 1986) conducted a replication study in which we attempted to show that positive self-presentations, if inconsistent with one's self-image, could produce dissonance-mediated carryover. Conversely, we wanted to demonstrate that negative self-presentations within one's latitude of acceptance could produce biased-scanning-mediated carryover. Rather than attempt to scale each individual's self-knowledge to determine latitudes of acceptance and rejection, Agustsdottir and I took an individual difference approach to the question. On the basis of clinical theory and research, we assumed that depressed individuals should possess relatively broad latitudes of acceptance for negative self-knowledge and narrow latitudes of acceptance for positive self-knowledge (Kuiper, MacDonald, & Derry, 1983). We predicted that self-enhancing presentations would be inconsistent with depressed individual's available self-knowledge, and thus any effect of self-enhancement on self-concept would be mediated by dissonance processes. Conversely, self-deprecating presentations would increase the accessibility of negative self-knowledge so that changes in the self would be the result of biased scanning processes. We examined these predictions by replicating the Jones and Rhodewalt procedure with a sample of mildly depressed individuals and a sample of nondepressed individuals.

The top panels of Figure 2 display the effects of biased scanning collapsed across the choice variable. As we predicted, nondepressed, self-referencing participants who were presenting a positive image during the interview showed an increase in subsequent self-evaluations (top left panel, replicating Jones et al., 1981). Among mildly depressed participants (top right panel), self-referencing led to a significant decline in self-evaluations following deprecating presentations and a modest increase in self-evaluation following enhancing presentations.[1] The bottom panels of Figure 2 show the effects of the dissonance manipulation (high or low choice) collapsed across the biased scanning variable. Again replicating Jones et al., nondepressed interviewees displayed a decline in self-esteem only when they believed that they had freely chosen to present a negative impression (lower left panel). In contrast and consistent with our model, mildly depressed participants (lower right

---

[1]Research suggests that as level of depression deepens, the availability of positive knowledge diminishes and the availability of negative knowledge increases (Kuiper et al., 1983). The mildly depressed participants in the Rhodewalt and Agustsdottir (1986) study undoubtedly had both positive and negative information available. Thus, the finding of carryover among both positive and negative presentation, self-referencing participants is not surprising.

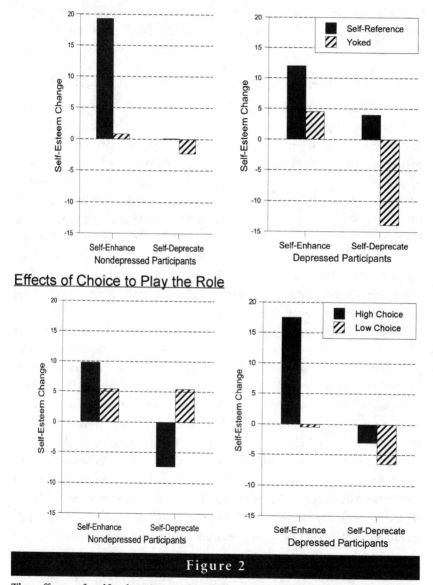

Figure 2

The effects of self-enhancing and self-deprecating presentations on the self-evaluations of nondepressed and depressed participants (originally adapted from Jones, 1990). From "Effects of Self-Presentation on the Phenomenal Self," by F. Rhodewalt and S. Agustsdottir, 1986, *Journal of Personality and Social Psychology, 50*, p. 49. Copyright 1986 by the American Psychological Association.

panel) showed a postinterview increase in self-esteem only when they believed that they had freely chosen to portray a positive image—presumably an image inconsistent with their negative self-views.

THE CARRYOVER EFFECT REVISITED

Since the publication of our findings in 1986, a number of investigators have attempted to replicate, qualify, or extend various aspects of our model. I am aware of seven published studies containing 13 experiments that have directly examined the effects of strategic self-presentations on private self-conceptions (Jones, Brenner, & Knight, 1990; Kelly, McKillop, & Neimeyer, 1991; Kowalski & Leary, 1990; McKillop, Berzonsky, & Schlenker, 1992; Schlenker, Dlugolecki, & Doherty, 1992; Schlenker, & Trudeau, 1990). All of these studies instructed participants to present themselves to an interviewer and then measured private self-conceptions. These investigations merit review because they provide a better understanding of the importantly social nature of the carryover effect.

Before turning our attention to individual studies, a general caution is in order. As the reader has undoubtedly surmised, complicated experimental designs are required to test the model. An investigation that sought to examine both biased-scanning and cognitive-dissonance-mediated effects of self-presentation on self-concept would need to include four elements. The study must (a) measure the individual's self-beliefs, (b) match individuals on those beliefs, (c) contrast those who self-reference with those who do not, and (d) vary perceived choice to enact the presentation. The results would also be more compelling if postpresentation self-beliefs were measured in a separate context. None of the studies contained all of these conditions. To be fair, in many instances particular investigations were not intended as overall tests of the model but rather were concerned with one specific issue or set of conditions. This microapproach to the study of the carryover effect has its limitations. For example, many of the studies were interested primarily in the biased-scanning component of the model and as almost an afterthought provided *all* participants with choice instructions. Thus, two factors could have promoted carryover, and this can lead to the spurious overattribution of the influence to biased scanning or, conversely, to the erroneous conclusion that biased scanning is not a viable explanation for the carryover effect.

These limitations not withstanding, what do these experiments tell us? First, we know that the carryover effect is very robust. The effect obtained in all studies, usually as a main effect for the self-presentation qualified by interactions with other variables. The carryover effect also seems to hold for strategic presentations outside the laboratory interview paradigm. Hannah, Hanson, Domino, and Hannah (1994) assessed the self-concepts of actors prior to then through the course of character development during rehearsals and performances of a play and finally one month after the play closed. Hannah et al. compared the actors' self-conceptions to personality profiles of the characters they portrayed provided by the director. Not surprisingly, the actors' self-concepts became more similar to the characters they portrayed as the play progressed. More important, the findings suggest that the actors' portrayal carried over to their self-conceptions measured 1 month after the close of the play. Although the authors did not report the actors' individual techniques for preparing for their roles, it is likely that "method acting" involves a substantial amount of biased scanning. Hannah et al.'s (1994) findings, although preliminary in many respects, suggest a potentially fruitful venue in which to examine the carryover effect. Returning to the main point, self-presentational behavior routinely and reliably influences private self-conceptions both within and outside the laboratory setting.

The second important conclusion from these studies is that the effect holds for specific self-beliefs as well as global self-evaluations. For example, self-presentations have been shown to carry over to self-conceptions of independence (Schlenker & Trudeau, 1990), emotional stability (Tice, 1992, Study 1), introversion–extraversion (Tice, 1992, Study 2 and 3), sociability (McKillop, Berzonsky, & Schlenker, 1992; Schlenker, et al., 1992), and depression (Kelly et al., 1991). Related to this point is the finding that the carryover effect is observed for trait-relevant behavior as well as self-conceptions (Schlenker et al., 1992; Tice, 1992; see also Fazio et al., 1981).

THE CARRYOVER EFFECT: COGNITIVE VERSUS INTERPERSONAL EXPLANATIONS

A great deal of the interest in the carryover effect has focused on our biased scanning propositions. There is some evidence that biased scanning does indeed produce carryover through the route of differential accessibility of self-knowledge. In line with the biased-scanning hypothesis, Ned and I (Jones et al., 1981, Study 3; Rhodewalt & Agustsdottir, 1986) predicted that the extremity of the self-presentation should be related to the magnitude of the carryover effect for self-referencing participants in the latitude of acceptance conditions. Presumably, the more the self-presentation diverged from baseline self-views the greater the amount of specific self-knowledge accessible in memory. Consistent with this prediction, extremity of the self-presentation correlated with self-concept change for self-referencing participants presenting an image within the latitude of acceptance. Among yoked participants and among those who presented an image within the latitude of rejection the relation was around zero.

Schlenker et al. (1992, Study 1) provided a more direct test of the biased-scanning hypothesis by asking half of their participants to self-reference and present a sociable self to an interviewer. The other half of the sample did not undergo the interview. All participants then performed a recall task in which they were asked to list behaviors from their past that were either very sociable, unsociable, or simply related to sociability (undirected recall). Finally, they all completed a measure of self-perceived sociability. In support of the biased-scanning hypothesis, "recall very sociable" and "undirected recall" participants listed significantly more examples of sociable behavior if they had been interviewed than if they had not been interviewed. Thus, the act of self-presenting rendered relevant self-knowledge more accessible in memory. Interviewed participants also displayed the typical carryover onto self-perceived sociability. However, the recall of examples of unsociable behavior appeared to negate the effect of the positive self-presentation in that these participants did not exhibit carryover to self-perceived sociability.

The Schlenker et al. (1992) findings also demonstrate that although self-presentations affect accessibility of self-knowledge, accessibility alone does not inevitably lead to change in the phenomenal self. This statement is supported by the fact that there were no differences in self-perceived sociability among participants who were not interviewed, regardless of the content of the recall task. That is, participants who recalled examples of particularly sociable behavior did not view themselves as more sociable than did participants who recalled examples of unsociable behavior.

These findings do not appear to jibe with the wealth of research demonstrating the effects of information accessibility on judgment (Higgins & King, 1981); however, they do foreshadow another conclusion about the effect of self-presentational behavior on the phenomenal self. There is something especially compelling about the interpersonal nature of self-presentational behavior. To illustrate this point, Schlenker et al. (1992, Study 3) had participants either present themselves as independent in a face-to-face interview or provide a written description of themselves as independent. Participants wrote the descriptions under one of three conditions: (a) They believed they would later provide the description in a face-to-face interview, (b) they initially expected to be interviewed but learned the interview was canceled after they wrote the description, or (c) they believed their description was anonymous. If participants were interviewed or expected to be interviewed they displayed the carryover effect on self-perceptions of independence. In contrast, if they believed the interview was canceled or that the description was anonymous, no carryover occurred. On the basis of these findings, Schlenker et al. argued that public commitment, "the binding of self to a particular public identity" (p. 31), is a critical element in producing the carryover effect.[2] In their view, public commitment, perhaps more

---

[2] These studies also illustrate the interpretive difficulties introduced by not carefully including all of the variables in the model. Choice to enact the role was confounded with interview condition. Those who actually were interviewed did so under high-choice instructions, whereas choice was not mentioned to those who were not interviewed. Thus, carryover in the interview conditions was probably enhanced through the contribution of dissonance effects from the subset of participants for whom the behavior was inconsistent with the self.

so than biased scanning, impels self-concept change in the direction of the presented image.

The importance of the interpersonal component of self-presentation was further illustrated by Dianne Tice (1992), who demonstrated that the presence of an audience, real or imagined, is a critical ingredient in the carryover effect. Tice (1992) had research participants go through the cognitive effort of a presentation in public or private. To accomplish this, she asked participants to tape record a self-presentation of introversion or extraversion in public or private. The carryover effect occurred in public and was attenuated or eliminated in private. I discuss more about the importance of interpersonal factors and the carryover effect in the closing section.

STRUCTURE AND CONTENT OF SELF-KNOWLEDGE AND THE CARRYOVER EFFECT

A second point that is eminently clear from the recent studies of the carryover effect is that self-presentations have greater impact on the self-concepts of some individuals than they do on the self-concepts of others. First, the extent to which a person's self-concept is based on social sources of knowledge is an important moderator of the extent to which self-presentations affect the self-concept. For example, individuals who are high in social identity—the tendency to root the self in social sources of experience, roles, and relationships (Cheek, 1989)—display greater carryover after self-presenting (McKillop et al., 1992) than those low in social identity. The same is true for self-monitors (Rhodewalt, 1986; Tice, 1992). Collectively, these findings again seem to point to the unique interpersonal significance of self-presentational acts for self-definition.

Other research suggests that people who seem most susceptible to the carryover effect are those who have a broad latitude of acceptance vis-à-vis a specific self-belief. The latitude may be broad because of high behavioral variability (Schlenker & Trudeau, 1990) or because of confusion about the attribute (Campbell & Lavallee, 1993), or it may be broad because of the complexity of the self-representations (Linville, 1985). There are a number of possibilities that warrant further consideration.

The importance of the structure of self-knowledge with regard to the carryover effect was nicely illustrated by Schlenker and Trudeau (1990). In their study, participants were induced to present themselves as more or less independent. A nice feature of the experiment was that Schlenker and Trudeau attempted to measure participants' latitudes of acceptance and rejection on the dimension of independence and have participants portray a self that was within or outside of the latitude of acceptance. They also asked participants how consistently they behaved on this dimension. Schlenker and Trudeau argued that the highly consistent individuals should be more resistent to change when the self presented was in the latitude of rejection. The results indicated that low-consistency individuals displayed carryover for presentations in both the latitude of acceptance and the latitude of rejection. High-consistency individuals changed their self-perceived independence only when their presentations were within the latitude of acceptance. It is interesting to note that high-consistency individuals felt less responsible for their highly discrepant acts and showed an arousal misattribution effect. This latter finding supports the notion that self-discrepant behavior is dissonance arousing even if it does not result in self-concept change.

Differences in self-reported behavioral consistency in the Schlenker and Trudeau (1990) study probably reflect differences in the clarity of the underlying self-representation.[3] One consequence of low-consistency behavior is that the boundary between "me" and "not me" is likely to be fuzzy and poorly defined. For low-self-consistency par-

---

[3] Schlenker and Trudeau (1990) reported that the width of the latitude of acceptance was unrelated to self-reported behavioral consistency. This finding is puzzling because one would predict that individuals with low behavioral variability would also report narrow latitudes of self-descriptive behavior. This finding may suggest that the latitudes analogy is not a useful way to characterize self-consistent versus self-discrepant behavior. The lack of relationship may also simply reflect insensitive measurement in the Schlenker and Trudeau study or something unique about the trait of independence. This latter possibility is intriguing because it may suggest that some traits translate more concretely into referents than do others. Thus, the latitudes framework may apply to more concrete attributes but not to more abstract ones.

ticipants, the carryover effect simply reflects biased scanning or, possibly, a simple self-perception effect. In contrast, high-consistency individuals because of their relatively homogenous prior experience know when a presented self is inconsistent with self-knowledge. Although these individuals resist the carryover effect, they experience dissonance over the portrayal of the public image.

Self-content considerations may bear on the carryover effect in a number of important and independent ways. For example, there are many identities or self-images that may often stand in contrast to the phenomenal self. A potentially rich vein for future research would be to examine the effects on the phenomenal self of presentations that communicate a "possible self" (Markus & Nurius, 1986), an "undesired self" (Ogilvie, 1987), or an "ideal or ought self" (Higgins, 1987). It is possible for instance, that presentations that reflect a small actual–ideal self-discrepancy trigger biased-scanning processes, whereas large actual–ideal self-discrepancies motivate dissonance reduction. An even more intriguing question concerns whether the negative affect resulting from the experience of a specific self-discrepancy would amplify dissonance arousal and, consequently, induce greater self-concept change. In brief, many self researchers suggest that the self is more accurately depicted as a collection of self-images. Undoubtedly, some of these selves reside in the latitude of acceptance, and some, perhaps undesired selves or ought selves, hide in the latitude of rejection and thus possess the potential to influence the phenomenal self.

Alternatively, the structure of self-knowledge may bear on the magnitude of the carryover effect. Several researchers have focused on the importance of the structure rather than the content of self-knowledge (Linville, 1985; Showers, 1992). For instance, Linville (1985) proposed that the complexity of one's self-representation is an important mediator of reactions to self-relevant feedback. People who are high in self-complexity have well-articulated, finely differentiated, multifaceted self-concepts. In contrast, low-complexity individuals think of themselves in simple, undifferentiated ways. With regard to the carryover effect, one might expect biased scanning to have a greater influence among low- than high-complexity individuals. For the former a larger library of self-relevant knowledge would be available for the biased scanner to browse. The latter individual's self-presentation would place him or her in a specialized "satellite" library with circumscribed self-knowledge.

I have sketched out only a few of many possible ways in which differences in self-knowledge might mediate self-concept change through the carryover effect. The critical point is that the structure, clarity, and content of the self must be considered in order to understand fully the reciprocal influences of public behavior on private self-conceptions. Moreover, not only do individuals differ in the makeup of their self-conceptions but there are also times, such as periods of transition or the beginning of new relationships, when all of us are a little uncertain about who we are and, thus, should be particularly susceptible to carryover effects.

SELF-PRESENTATION AND THE SOCIAL SELF

The research reviewed herein converges on the conclusion that constrained interpersonal behavior is often a powerful influence on how we experience ourselves. Self-presentation appears to be a behavioral bridge between our public images and private self-conceptions. I believe the carryover effect is clear evidence that the self exists largely on what Lewin called the "plain of social reality." At the same time, however, I do not think there is anything exclusively unique about self-presentational behavior that cannot be found in other activities. For example, many circumstances can prompt us to ruminate selectively about narrow aspects of ourselves. Many other conditions can lead us to commit to behavior so that it is self-relevant. What appears to be unique about self-presentational behavior is that so many forces combine to imbue it with intense self-relevance.

What are the properties of self-presentational behavior that cause it to have such impact on the phenomenal self? I believe the answer is that self-presentational acts are simultaneously self-focusing, powerfully vivid, and they commit us to specific identities. Self-focus, vividness, and commitment are all factors that have been shown to increase the relevance of behavior to judgments about the self.

With regard to self-focus, self-presentations by definition involve a real or imagined audience. The mere presence of others is self-focusing, which in turn increases the accessibility of self-referent knowledge—in particular knowledge of the "public self" (Froming & Walker, 1980)—and induces comparisons between self-standards and behavior. Self-focus also increases one's sense of involvement in, and causal responsibility for, outcomes (Arkin & Duval, 1975; Duval & Wicklund, 1973; see also Hull & Levy, 1979). Thus, audience-induced self-focus should amplify the carryover effect for presentations in both the latitudes of acceptance and rejection. Within the latitude of acceptance, self-focus increases the accessibility of relevant self-knowledge, which should later be given greater probative weight in self-reflection. Within the latitude of rejection, self-focus increases the extent to which the person feels responsible for the self-presentation, which, in turn, should increase dissonance motivation.

People's social interactions are also a source of highly vivid information, and vivid information is given more weight in judgment (Nisbett & Ross, 1980). Findings from Schlenker et al. (1992, Study 2) illustrate this point. Recall that individuals either presented themselves as sociable or were not interviewed and then were asked to recall examples of behaviors that were either very sociable, unsociable, or simply relevant to sociability. For the present discussion the finding of interest is from the condition in which individuals were asked to recall unsociable experiences after presenting a sociable self. These individuals still displayed self-presentation-congruent carryover. That is, they privately viewed themselves as more sociable than did individuals who were not interviewed, regardless of the intervening biased-scanning task.

Given that a wealth of data indicates that such "biased-scanning" activity can influence one's self-views, the question becomes why one type of biased-scanning task, the thought-listing exercise, did not negate the effects of another biased-scanning task, the self-presentation exercise. I believe the answer may be that information made accessible as a result of a social interaction is simply more vivid—and thus was given more attention and weight—than is information accessed through the more pallid thought-listing exercise.

In this light, Schlenker et al.'s (1992) findings may be viewed as a conceptual replication of Ross, Lepper, and Hubbard's (1975) perseverance effect in the debriefing paradigm. In Ross et al.'s (1975) investigation, participants received false feedback after each trial that they had performed well or poorly on an intelligence test. They were then "debriefed" and told that the feedback was bogus, random, predetermined, and in no way indicated their intelligence. Nonetheless, when participants were asked to indicate their true level of intelligence, successfeedback participants rated their intelligence more favorably than did failure-feedback participants.

Nisbett and Ross (1980) discussed a number of factors that contribute to the perseverance effect, but two are directly pertinent to the present discussion. First, they argued that the on-line experience of succeeding or failing the test is more vivid and powerful than is the rather dry debriefing communication. It is particularly important to note that although vivid information is given greater weight in any judgment, as Nisbett and Ross (1980) pointed out, vividness effects are most pronounced in judgments about the self. Nisbett and Ross also suggested that individuals engage in a confirmation-biased search of memory as they receive self-relevant feedback. The relevance of this observation to the carryover effect is the implication that people who are presenting a specific image—for example, a sociable, friendly self— are also searching self-knowledge for evidence that supports the public image. It is a motivated variant of biased scanning.

Public commitment is undoubtedly an active force in the carryover of self-presentations to the phenomenal self. But why is public commitment important? Stryker and Serpe (1982) suggested that commitment to a public identity is influential precisely because commitment increases the identity's salience, and salience, in turn, fosters role related thoughts and behaviors. Dianne Tice (1992) made a similar argument, suggesting that the public component of self-presentation promotes "magnified scanning." From Tice's perspective, the self-presentation increases the accessibility of pieces of self-knowledge, and the fact that others are aware of the information magnifies its importance in subsequent judgments about the self. In sum, Jones and Rhodewalt's (1986) model specifies two pathways by which constrained public behavior influences private self-conceptions: One is cognitive and one is motivational. Public commitment is pivotal to both pathways because commitment to specific identities amplifies biased scanning within the latitude of acceptance and stakes out ownership of the identity image within the latitude of rejection.

The research spawned by our analysis calls attention to the intimate dynamic between private cognitive processes and public interpersonal phenomena. It is possible that the relationship between self-cognition and social interaction is more intrinsic than is currently believed. An assumption guiding Jones and my (e.g., see 1990; Rhodewalt & Agustsdottir, 1986) research, and one embraced by many social cognitive researchers, is that the self is undergirded by a wealth of autobiographical knowledge. There is currently significant debate about the connection between autobiographical knowledge and the self-concept (Klein & Loftus, 1993). However, a number of researchers have argued that a large portion of self-knowledge is represented as "self-with-others" (Ogilvie & Ashmore, 1991) or as "social self" (Lord, 1993). For example, Charlie Lord (Lord, Desforges, Chacon, Pere, & Clubb, 1992) and colleagues demonstrated that our social reputations—what we believe others think of us—can prime and facilitate the processing of self-knowledge. Perhaps, then, the reason that self-presentations so powerfully push and pull our experience of self is because public identities and private beliefs are more isomorphic than many have assumed.

CONCLUSION

Over a decade of research attests to the fact that constrained interpersonal behavior "carries over" to shape one's current self-concept. This work emphasizes the important reciprocally determined relation between people's social interactions and their self-views. I have attempted to outline a number of questions of central importance to the social psychology of the self that I believe can be addressed by continued research on the carryover effect.

More broadly, I would like to contend that the model of the phenomenal self in social interaction that Ned and I sketched out and that I have expanded on in this chapter has heuristic value for exploring self-concept stability and change in emerging and ongoing relationships. This framework may prove useful in attempts to address the processes that drive self-concept change in identity negotiation, self-fulfilling prophecies, and self-verification (see also McNulty & Swann, 1991; Tice, 1994).

I would like to make one more observation in closing. This volume is a celebration of Ned Jones's unparalleled contributions to social psychology. Although Ned will most likely be remembered for his far-reaching theoretical contributions to the field, there is another aspect of his legacy that should be acknowledged. Ned taught his students and colleagues the joy and the value of conducting phenomenon-driven research. The carryover effect, correspondence bias, and self-handicapping are illustrations of the interesting quirks of social behavior that held Ned's fascination throughout his career. His lesson was that such puzzling behaviors can be a wellspring of social psychological knowledge when examined through the eyes of a careful social psychologist and insightful human being. I am confident that this part of Ned's legacy will live on through his students and his students' students.

REFERENCES

Arkin, R., & Duval, S. (1975). Focus of attention and causal attributions of actors and observers. *Journal of Experimental Social Psychology, 11,* 427–438.

Campbell, J. D., & Lavallee, L. F. (1993). Who am I? The role of self-concept confusion in understanding the behavior of people with low self-esteem. In R. Baumeister (Ed.), *Self-esteem: The puzzle of low self-regard* (pp. 3–20). New York: Plenum Press.

Cheek, J. (1989). Identity orientations and self-interpretations. In D. M. Buss & N. Cantor (Eds.), *Personality research for the 1990's.* New York: Springer-Verlag.

Cheek, J., & Hogan, R. (1983). Self-concepts, self-presentations, and moral judgments. In J. Suls & A. G. Greenwald (Eds.), *Psychological perspectives on the self* (Vol. 2, pp. 249–273). Hillsdale, NJ: Erlbaum.

Duval, S., & Wicklund, R. A. (1973). Effects of objective self-awareness on attribution of causality. *Journal of Experimental Social Psychology, 9,* 17–31.

Fazio, R. H., Effrein, E. A., & Falender, V. J. (1981). Self-perceptions following social interaction. *Journal of Personality and Social Psychology, 41,* 232–242.

Fazio, R. H., Zanna, M. P., & Cooper, J. (1977). Dissonance and self-perception: An integrated view of each theory's proper domain of application. *Journal of Experimental Social Psychology, 13,* 464–479.

Froming, W. J., & Walker, G. R. (1980). *Self-awareness and public versus private standards for behavior.* Unpublished manuscript.

Gergen, K. J. (1965). Interaction goals and personalistic feedback as factors affecting the presentation of the self. *Journal of Personality and Social Psychology, 1,* 413–424.

Greenwald, A. G. (1980). The totalitarian ego: Fabrication and revision of personal history. *American Psychologist, 35,* 603–618.

Hannah, M. T., Hanson, R., Domino, G., & Hannah, W. (1994). Acting and personality change: The measurement of change in self-perceived personality characteristics during the actor's character development process. *Journal of Research in Personality, 28,* 277–286.

Higgins, E. T. (1987). Self-discrepancy: A theory relating self to affect. *Psychological Review, 94,* 319–340.

Higgins, E. T., & King, G. (1981). Accessibility of social constructs: Information-processing consequences of contextual variability. In N. Cantor & J. F. Kihlstrom (Eds.), *Personality, cognition, and social interaction* (pp. 69–121). Hillsdale, NJ: Erlbaum.

Higgins, E. T., Rhodewalt, F., & Zanna, M. P. (1979). Dissonance motivation: Its nature, persistence, and reinstatement. *Journal of Experimental Social Psychology, 15,* 16–34.

Hull, J. G., & Levy, A. (1979). The organizational functions of the self: An alternative to the Duval and Wicklund model of self-awareness. *Journal of Personality and Social Psychology, 37,* 756–768.

Jones, E. E. (1990). Constrained behavior and self-concept change. In J. M.

Olson & M. P. Zanna (Eds.), *Self-inference processes: The Ontario Symposium* (Vol. 6, pp. 69–86). Hillsadale, NJ: Erlbaum.

Jones, E. E., Brenner, K. J., & Knight, J. G. (1990). When failure elevates self-esteem. *Personality and Social Psychology Bulletin, 16,* 200–209.

Jones, E. E., & Gerard, H. B. (1967). *Foundations of social psychology.* New York: Wiley.

Jones, E. E., & Pittman, T. S. (1982). Toward a general theory of strategic self-presentation. In J. Suls (Ed.), *Psychological perspectives on the self* (Vol. 1, pp. 231–262). Hillsdale, NJ: Erlbaum.

Jones, E. E., Rhodewalt, F., Berglas, S., & Skelton, J. A. (1981). Effects of strategic self-presentation on subsequent self-esteem. *Journal of Personality and Social Psychology, 41,* 407–421.

Kelly, A. E., McKillop, K. J., & Neimeyer, G. J. (1991). Effects of counselor as an audience on internalization of depressed and nondepressed self-presentations. *Journal of Counseling Psychology, 38,* 123–132.

Kihlstrom, J. F., & Cantor, N. (1985). Mental representations of the self. In L. Berkowitz (Ed.), *Advances in experimental social psychology* (Vol. 17, pp. 1–47). San Diego, CA: Academic Press.

Klein, S. B., & Loftus, J. (1993). The mental representation of trait and autobiographical knowledge about the self. In T. K. Srull & R. S. Wyer, Jr. (Eds.), *The mental representation of trait and autobiographical knowledge about the self. Advances in social cognition* (Vol. 4, pp. 1–49). Hillsdale, NJ: Erlbaum.

Kowalski, R. M., & Leary, M. R. (1990). Strategic self-presentation and the avoidance of aversive events: Antecedents and consequences of self-enhancement and self-deprecation. *Journal of Experimental Social Psychology, 26,* 322–336.

Kuiper, N. A., MacDonald, M. R., & Derry, P. A. (1983). Parameters of a depressive self-schema. In J. Suls & A. G. Greenwald (Eds.), *Psychological perspectives on the self* (Vol. 2, pp. 191–217). Hillsdale, NJ: Erlbaum.

Kunda, Z., & Sanitioso, R. (1989). Motivated changes in the self-concept. *Journal of Experimental Social Psychology, 25,* 272–285.

Leary, M. R. (1995). *Self-presentation: Impression management and interpersonal behavior.* Madison WI: Brown and Benchmark.

Linder, D. E., Cooper, J., & Jones, E. E. (1967). Decision freedom as a determinant of the role of incentive magnitude in attitude change. *Journal of Personality and Social Psychology, 6,* 245–254.

Linville, P. W. (1985). Self-complexity and affective extremity: Don't put all your eggs in one cognitive basket. *Social Cognition, 3,* 94–120.

Linville, P. W., & Carlston, D. E. (1994). Social cognition of the self. In P. G. Devine, D. L. Hamilton, & T. M. Ostrom (Eds.), *Social cognition: It's impact on social psychology.* San Diego, CA: Academic Press.

Lord, C. G., (1993). The "social self" component of trait knowledge about the self. In T. K. Srull & R. S. Wyer, Jr. (Eds.), *The mental representation of trait and autobiographical knowledge about the self. Advances in social cognition* (Vol. 4, pp. 91–100). Hillsdale, NJ: Erlbaum.

Lord, C. G., Desforges, D. M., Chacon, S., Pere, G., & Clubb, B. (1992). Reflection on reputation in the process of self-evaluation. *Social Cognition, 10,* 2–29.

Markus, H. (1977). Self-schemata and the processing of information about the self. *Journal of Personality and Social Psychology, 35,* 63–78.

Markus, H., & Nurius, P. (1986). Possible selves. *American Psychologist, 41,* 954–969.

Markus, H., & Wurf, E. (1987). The dynamic self-concept: A social psychological perspective. *Annual Review of Psychology, 38,* 299–337.

McGuire, W. J., & Padawer-Singer, A. (1976). Trait salience in the spontaneous self-concept. *Journal of Personality & Social Psychology, 33,* 743–754.

McKillop, K. J., Berzonsky, M. D., & Schlenker, B. R. (1992). The impact of self-presentations on self-beliefs: Effects of social identity and self-presentational context. *Journal of Personality, 60,* 789–808.

McNulty, S. E., & Swann, W. B. (1991). Psychotherapy, self-concept change, and self-verification. In R. C. Curtis (Ed.), *The relational self: Theoretical convergence in psychoanalysis and social psychology* (pp. 213–237). New York: Guilford Press.

Morse, S. J., & Gergen, K. J. (1970). Social comparison, self-consistency, and the presentation of self. *Journal of Personality and Social Psychology, 16,* 148–159.

Natale, M., & Hantas, M. (1982). Effects of temporary mood states on selective memory about the self. *Journal of Personality and Social Psychology, 42,* 927–934.

Nisbett, R. M., & Ross, L. (1980). *Human inference: Strategies and shortcomings of social judgment* (pp. 288–292). New York: Prentice Hall.

Ogilvie, D. M. (1987).The undesired self: A neglected variable in personality research. *Journal of Personality and Social Psychology, 52,* 379–385.

Ogilvie, D. M., & Ashmore, R. D. (1991). Self-with-other representation as a unit of analysis in self-concept research. In R. C. Curtis (Ed.), *The relational self: Theoretical convergences in psychoanalysis and social psychology* (pp. 282–314). New York: Guilford Press.

Rhodewalt, F. (1986). Self-presentation and phenomenal self: On the stability and malleability of the self-concept. In R. Baumeister (Ed.), *Public self and private self* (pp. 117–142). New York: Springer-Verlag.

Rhodewalt, F., & Agustsdottir, S. (1986). Effects of self-presentation on the phenomenal self. *Journal of Personality and Social Psychology, 50,* 47–55.

Rhodewalt, F., & Comer, R. (1981). The role of self-attribution differences in the utilization of social comparison information. *Journal of Research in Personality, 15,* 210–220.

Ross, L., Lepper, M. R., & Hubbard, M. (1975). Perseverance in self-perception and social perception: Biased attributional processes in the debriefing paradigm. *Journal of Personality and Social Psychology, 32,* 880–892.

Schlenker, B. R., Dlugolecki, D. W., & Doherty, K. (1992). The impact of self-presentations and behavior: The power of public commitment. *Personality and Social Psychology Bulletin, 20,* 20–33.

Schlenker, B. R., & Trudeau, J. V. (1990). Impact of self-presentations on private self-beliefs. *Journal of Personality and Social Psychology, 58,* 22–32.

Showers, C. (1992). Evaluatively thinking about characteristics of the self. *Personality and Social Psychology Bulletin, 18,* 719–729.

Snyder, M., & Swann, W. B. (1978). Behavioral confirmation in social interaction: From social perception to social reality. *Journal of Personality and Social Psychology, 36,* 1202–1212.

Stryker, S., & Serpe, R. T. (1982). Commitment, identity salience, and role behavior: Theory and research example. In W. Ickes & E. Knowles (Eds.), *Personality, roles, and social behavior* (pp. 199–218). New York: Springer-Verlag.

Swann, W. B. (1983). Self-verification: Bringing social reality into harmony with the self. In J. Suls & A. G. Greenwald (Eds.), *Psychological perspectives on the self* (Vol. 2, pp. 33–66). Hillsdale, NJ: Erlbaum.

Swann, W. B., Giuliano, T., & Wegner, D. M. (1982). Where leading questions can lead: The power of conjecture in social interaction. *Journal of Personality and Social Psychology, 42,* 1025–1035.

Tice, D. M. (1992). Self-concept changes and self-presentation: The looking glass self is also a magnifying glass. *Journal of Personality and Social Psychology, 63,* 435–451.

Tice, D. M. (1994). Pathways to internalization: When does overt behavior change the self-concept? In T. M. Brinthaupt & R. P. Lipka (Eds.), *Changing the self: Philosophies, techniques, and experiences* (pp. 229–250). Albany, NY: SUNY Press.

The Self Is Not a Bowling Ball

William B. Swann, Jr.

Reading Fred Rhodewalt's chapter (see chapter 7) was gratifying in several respects. Most obviously, the program of research that he and Ned pursued so imaginatively has offered penetrating insights into the delicate interplay between social behavior and self-knowledge. More generally, Rhodewalt has described some good science; the ideas are rich, the studies are elegant, and the data are compelling and important.

But Rhodewalt's chapter also was personally gratifying because it gave me fresh insight into a remark that Ned once made. We were at a small conference on the self, and the opening talks had proceeded uneventfully. Then, late in the morning, Ned suddenly sprang to life, incensed by something someone had said. With an air of someone who has just endured a malicious personal insult, he blurted out, "Well, for Christ's sake. The self is not a bowling ball, you know."

I had forgotten about Ned's bowling ball analogy until I read Rhodewalt's chapter. The critical passage centered on Rhodewalt's conclusion that carryover effects tend to disappear in the absence of an audience. His remark gave me a fresh perspective on Ned's comment.

What Ned meant, I think, was that self-views are not autonomous structures that reside inside us like our livers, spleens, hearts, or other physical objects. Rather, self-views are not things at all; they are abstractions that are derived from, and nourished by, our social interactions. If our self-views fail to receive nutriment in the form of support from the social environment, they die. We can sustain our self-views only with the "permission" of our lovers, our friends and acquaintances, and society at large. Unlike bowling balls, whose existences are largely unaffected by the people and objects they encounter, our self-views are acutely sensitive to the nuances of everyday experience. In fact, our interactions with others represent the essence of the processes whereby we sustain self-knowledge.

Recognizing the fundamentally social nature of self-knowledge allows us to avert certain paradoxes and problems that would otherwise arise. Consider, for example, what happens when one pairs Rhodewalt's work with the research on self-enhancement that has been championed so effectively by one of Ned's other students, Roy Baumeister. If people are constantly presenting themselves in an extremely positive manner, as Baumeister (1982) would have us believe, and if they internalize such self-presentations into their self-views, as Rhodewalt would argue, then people's self-views should get more positive over the life span. Yet as far as I know, no such thing occurs. Rather, people's self-views seem instead to remain remarkably stable over their lives (e.g., Block & Robins, 1993; Block, Gjerde, & Block, 1991; Blyth, Simmons, & Carlton-Ford, 1983; O'Malley & Bachman, 1983; for related discussions, see Kernis & Waschull, 1995; Sroufe & Jacobvitz, 1989). Here, then, lies a paradox: Why is there no evidence for the infinite and soliplistic upward adjustment of self-views implied by the Baumeister–Rhodewalt formulation? Why aren't we happier with ourselves today than we were yesterday?

Ned's concept of an interpersonal self provides an intriguing answer to this question. Specifically, our self-views may fail to grow steadily more positive because our relationship partners won't hear of it. In what follows, I consider some evidence for this proposition.

FROM INTERNALIZATION OF OTHERS' REACTIONS TO EXTERNALIZATION OF SELF-VIEWS

The symbolic interactionists told us long ago that we don't just "know" who we are; we infer our self-views from our experiences with others, especially the treatment we receive from those who are important to us and whose opinions we trust (Cooley, 1902; Mead, 1934; Rosenberg, 1973). Research inspired by attachment theory (Bowlby, 1969) supports the idea that people internalize the treatment of others into their self-views: Children whose caregivers are warm and sensitive to their needs develop positive self-views, whereas children whose caregivers are cold or insensitive to their needs will develop negative self-views (e.g., Arend, Gove, & Sroufe, 1979; Cassidy, 1988).

Once formed, self-views tend to persist over time, whether they are positive or negative. In part, people cling to their self-views for practical reasons—dramatic changes in these self-views would be disruptive to their relationships. Witness, for example, the troubles that ensue when adolescent children strike out in new directions and refuse to honor identities (e.g., the obedient or respectful child) that they have negotiated in the past. Although some identities can be more readily renegotiated than others, any such negotiation is disruptive to the relationship because it requires partners to shift their expectations and associated behaviors (e.g., Athay & Darley, 1981; Goffman, 1959).

Yet pragmatic concerns are not the only ones that cause people to cling to their self-views. Our self-views provide the "glue" that holds our perceptions of reality together, giving us a vital sense of psychological coherence. Murphy (1947) likened self-views to a map or chart:

> The self-picture has all the strength of other perceptual stereotypes *and in addition* serves as the chart by which the individual navigates. If it is lost, he can make only impulsive runs in fair weather: The ship drifts helplessly whenever storms arise. (p. 715)

Deprived of the "chart by which we navigate," we lack a reliable basis for action. Even our most basic propensities, such as our desire for positive evaluations, would have little adaptive value. Although we would be able to distinguish favorable evaluations from unfavorable ones at the superficial level, if we were unsure of who we were we would lack a reference point for determining if the evaluations we encountered could be taken at face value.

To avoid changing their self-views, people may gravitate toward and remain in relationships in which they receive confirmation for their self-views. One troubling implication of such self-verification processes is that if people happen to develop negative self-views, they will pick relationship partners who help keep their self-views negative. For example, people with negative self-views are more inclined to seek and receive unfavorable evaluations than are people with positive self-views. Similarly, people with negative self-views prefer interaction partners who appraise them unfavorably, whether the alternative is interacting with those who appraise them favorably or participating in a different experiment. Moreover, if people wind up in relationships with partners who see them differently than they see themselves, they become less committed to the relationship (for recent reviews of this work, see Swann, 1996, 1997).

A study of women from central Texas suggests that the consequences of self-verification strivings may be more than merely academic. Buckner and I (Buckner & Swann, 1995) found that women with negative self-views form close relationships with men who are high in a trait that Spence and her colleagues have called negative instrumentality (Spence, Helmreich, & Stapp, 1974). These men tend to be arrogant, condescending, egotistical, cynical, hostile, dictatorial, and look out only for themselves. Not only are these men likely to derogate their relationship partners, they are actually inclined to verbally and physically abuse them (as reported by the women). What better formula for maintaining negative self-views than getting in relationships in which one receives a steady supply of verbal and physical abuse?

KEEPING SELF-ENHANCERS IN THEIR PLACE

Even if we have positive self-views and choose verifying partners, if our self-views grow too positive, our behavior may erode the favorable impressions that others have of us initially. Colvin, Block, and Funder (1995), for example, identified men and women who rated themselves more favorably than trained evaluators on a wide range of attributes, such as energetic, adventurous, cheerful, dependable, and responsible. When engaged in informal conversation with another student, such self-enhancing men spoke quickly, interrupted their partner, bragged, and expressed hostility; nonenhancing men expressed sympathy and affection toward their partners. Similarly, self-enhancing women sought reassurance and acted in an irritable and awkward fashion; nonenhancing women were socially skilled, enjoyed their interaction partners, liked and were liked by their partners, and appeared relaxed and comfortable.

The tendency of self-enhancers to alienate others seemed to be fairly stable. When self-enhancing men were contacted again 5 years later, trained evaluators perceived them as more guileful, deceitful, and distrustful than their nonenhancing counterparts. Similarly, trained evaluators considered self-enhancing women thin-skinned, defensive, and conflicted relative to non-enhancing women. Even the friends of self-enhancers expressed their disgruntlement, describing them as condescending, hostile, inconsiderate, and unsympathetic (for related research, see John & Robins, 1994).

In short, self-enhancers seem to displease their relationship partners in a systematic way. This should prompt their partners either to withdraw from the relationship or to provide them with negative feedback. In either case, it is unlikely that their self-views will grow more positive, as the Baumeister–Rhodewalt formulation implies.

HOW OPPRESSION CONSTRAINS THE SELF

Even if our friends and intimates fail to keep our self-views in check, the larger society may place limits on the positivity of particular self-views by limiting the kinds of persons we can aspire to become. Members of groups who are oppressed, for example, may be systematically encouraged to develop self-views that are in keeping with the oppression. As a result, they may feel frustrated and diminished and may react in ways that perpetuate the stereotype.

Claude Steele and his colleagues have documented one such process through which, as Claude's brother Shelby put it, "self-doubt works to duplicate the oppression" (S. Steele, 1990, p. 54). C. Steele and Aronson (1995) speculated that because most Blacks are socialized to doubt their ability to excel in academic settings, they may become anxious when pursuing academic tasks. To test this idea, C. Steele and Aronson (1995) observed the performance of Whites and Blacks on aptitude tests. They discovered that Blacks performed more poorly than Whites when they were reminded of their racial identity prior to taking such tests but that Blacks and Whites performed equally well when they received no reminder of their racial identity (see also Kaplan, Peck, & Kaplan, 1994). Steele believes that reminding Blacks of their race while they are in performance contexts "activates their stereotype" (i.e., makes their supposed inferiority salient to them). This makes them anxious about failing, which in turn causes them to perform poorly.

Spencer and Steele (1994) demonstrated the existence of a parallel phenomenon among women. They discovered that, true to the cultural stereotype, in the baseline control condition male Stanford University students outperformed women on the math section of an aptitude test but performed no differently on the English section of the test. When the experimenter took steps to deactivate the gender stereotype by telling students that the exam was gender neutral, however, no gender differences emerged on either version of the test.

Both racial and gender stereotypes, then, seem to undermine performance by engendering self-doubt among the targets of those stereotypes. Although such a process would not necessarily lead to low global self-esteem, it could readily place an upper limit on people's self-views within certain areas.

SUMMARY AND IMPLICATIONS

Of course, there are surely many other processes that ensnare people's self-views and ensure that they do not grow steadily more positive over the life span. My point here, however, is simply to emphasize, as Ned would have, how the intrapsychic processes that he and Rhodewalt and others have studied so fruitfully are constrained by the interpersonal context in which those processes are embedded. The concept of an interpersonal self clashes sharply with those contemporary accounts that suggest that we can learn about ourselves by peering inward. Such accounts are based on a logical fallacy that involves mistaking an abstraction for a thing. Self-knowledge is not a physical object that lurks inside us somewhere. Rather, self-knowledge is a fiction we construct to make sense of who we are, what others think of us, and how we should behave. This fiction is no more "inside us" than the concept of time or knowledge of mathematics is inside us. Rather, the basis of self-knowledge is very much outside us, in our relations with others. George Herbert Mead (1934) put it this way,

> No hard and fast line can be drawn between our own selves and the selves of others, since our own selves exist and enter as such into our experience only insofar as the selves of others exist and enter as such into our experience also. (p. 164)

Mead's words undoubtedly have a certain power and grace. Yet, on the balance, I prefer Ned's more economic way of putting it: "The self is not a bowling ball."

REFERENCES

Arend, R., Gove, F., & Sroufe, L. A. (1979). Continuity of individual adaptation from infancy to kindergarten: A predictive study of ego-resiliency and curiosity in preschoolers. *Child Development, 50,* 950–959.

Athay, M., & Darley, J. M. (1981). Toward an interaction centered theory of personality. In N. Cantor & J. F. Kihlstrom (Eds.), *Personality, cognition, and social interaction* (pp. 281–308). Hillsdale, NJ: Erlbaum.

Baumeister, R. F. (1982). A self-presentational view of social phenomena. *Psychological Bulletin, 91,* 3–26.

Block, J., Gjerde, P. F., & Block, J. H. (1991). Personality antecedents of depressive tendencies in 18-year-olds: A prospective study. *Journal of Personality and Social Psychology, 60,* 726–738.

Block, J., & Robins, R. W. (1993). A longitudinal study of consistency and change in self-esteem from early adolescence to early adulthood. *Child Development, 64,* 909–923.

Blyth, D. A., Simmons, R. G., & Carlton-Ford, S. (1983). The adjustment of early adolescents to school transitions. *Journal of Early Adolescence, 3,* 105–120.

Bowlby, J. (1969). *Attachment and loss. Vol. 1: Attachment.* New York: Basic Books.

Buckner, C. E., & Swann, W. B., Jr. (1995, August). *Physical abuse in close relationships: The dynamic interplay of couple characteristics.* Paper presented at the 103rd Annual Convention of the American Psychological Association, Washington, DC.

Cassidy, J. (1988). Child–mother attachment and the self in six-year-olds. *Child Development, 59,* 121–134.

Colvin, C. R., Block, J., & Funder, D. C. (1995). Overly positive self evaluations and personality: Negative implications for mental health. *Journal of Personality and Social Psychology, 68,* 1152–1162.

Cooley, C. H. (1902). *Human nature and the social order.* New York: Scribners'.

Goffman, E. (1959). *The presentation of self in everyday life.* New York: Anchor Books.

John, O. P., & Robins, R. W. (1994). Accuracy and bias in self-perception: Individual differences in self-enhancement and the role of narcissism. *Journal of Personality and Social Psychology, 66,* 206–219.

Kaplan, D. S., Peck, B. M., & Kaplan, H. B. (1994). Structural relations model of self-rejection, disposition to deviance, and academic failure. *Journal of Educational Research, 87,* 166–173.

Kernis, M. H., & Waschull, S. B. (1995). The interactive roles of stability and level of self-esteem: Research and theory. In M. P. Zanna (Ed.), *Advances in experimental social psychology* (Vol. 27, pp. 94–141). San Diego, CA: Academic Press.

Mead, G. H. (1934). *Mind, self and society.* Chicago: University of Chicago Press.

Murphy, G. (1947). *Personality: A biosocial approach to origins and structure.* New York: Harper & Brothers.

O'Malley, P. M., & Bachman, J. G. (1983). Self-esteem: Change and stability between ages 13 and 23. *Developmental Psychology, 19,* 257–268.

Rosenberg, M. (1973). Which significant others? *American Behavioral Scientist,* *16,* 829–860.

Spence, J. T., Helmreich, R. L., & Stapp, J. (1974). The Personal Attributes Questionnaire: A measure of sex role stereotypes and masculinity and femininity. *JSAS: Catalog of Selected Documents in Psychology, 4,* 43–44.

Spencer, S. J., & Steele, C. M. (1994). *Under suspicion of inability: Stereotype vulnerability and women's math performance.* Manuscript submitted for publication.

Stroufe, L. A., & Jacobvitz, D. (1989). Diverging pathways, developmental transformations, multiple etiologies, and the problem of continuity in development. *Human Development, 32,* 196–203.

Steele, C. M., & Aronson, J. (1995). Contending with a stereotype: African-American intellectual test performance and stereotype vulnerability. *Journal of Personality and Social Psychology, 69,* 797–811.

Steele, S. (1990). *The content of our character.* New York: Harper Perennial.

Swann, W. B., Jr. (1996). *Self-traps: The elusive quest for higher self-esteem.* New York: Freeman.

Swann, W. B., Jr. (1997). The trouble with raising self-esteem. *Psychological Science, 3,* 177–180.

Effects of Self-Presentation Depend on the Audience

Dianne M. Tice

In this comment I examine the impact the audience has on self-presentation and discuss how different audiences can differentially impact the self, emphasizing the finding that audiences consisting of strangers affect the presenter differently than audiences consisting of people known to the presenter. I also discuss self-presentations in relationships, especially as they relate to the five self-presentational strategies identified by Jones and Pittman (1982), and I describe two mechanisms by which audiences can affect the impact of the self-presentation on the presenter's self-concept.

Fred Rhodewalt's (see chapter 7) summary of the research on the carryover effect emphasizes the importance of the social nature of the behavior that impacts on the self-concept. This interpersonal emphasis reflects a significant and recent change in the self-presentation and self-concept change literature (see Tice, 1992) and is nicely summarized in Rhodewalt's chapter. Briefly, theorizing about the mechanism behind the carryover effect has focused on intrapsychic processes, particularly biased scanning and dissonance (e.g., Jones, Rhodewalt, Berglas, & Skelton, 1981; Rhodewalt, 1986; Rhodewalt & Agustdottir, 1986). In principle, these patterns of cognitive processes occur inside the individual and do not involve other people. However, the published studies that demonstrate carryover effects invariably included the presence of other people to create public, interpersonal contexts. Thus, the empirical findings raise the issue of how much the basically intrapsychic theories should be revised to incorporate interpersonal processes.

All published work demonstrating the carryover effect indicates that public behavior (that is, behavior that the person believes others are aware of) impacts the self-concept (see, e.g., Fazio, Effrein, & Falender, 1981; Jones et al., 1981). Recent articles attempting to discriminate between social and intrapsychic explanations for the carryover effect have demonstrated the importance of the presence of others for self-image change (Schlenker, Dlugolecki, & Doherty, 1992; Tice, 1992). Although a cognitive, intrapsychic mechanism may still contribute to the effect, as Rhodewalt pointed out in his chapter in this volume, the importance of an audience for the carryover effect has been clearly established (e.g., Rhodewalt, this volume; see also Tice, 1994). In plain terms, people internalize their public behaviors, but a cognitive explanation may help describe the interpersonal process.

AUDIENCES AFFECT SELF-PRESENTATION

Now that general agreement exists that social aspects of the self are important for understanding how self-presentation affects the self-concept, it may be time to start examining more carefully how the term *social* is construed and, in particular, who makes up the audience of the self-presentation or behavior. In many of the studies reviewed in Rhodewalt's chapter, the audience is merely the experimenter who is aware of the participant's responses, or else some naive graduate student the experimenter and participant are trying to fool according to some cover story. I believe that it is time to look more closely at the audience to understand how self-presentations affect self-concepts.

Self-presentation occurs between strangers, but it also occurs between people who know each other well. Teenagers present themselves differently to their parents than they do to their friends (and indeed, parents present themselves differently to their teenagers than to their own colleagues and friends), people present themselves differently to colleagues than to spouses, and my own work has demonstrated that people present themselves differently to friends than they do to strangers (Tice, Butler, Muraven, & Stillwell, 1995).

Past research has focused almost entirely on self-presentation to strangers (Tedeschi, 1986; Tice et al., 1995; see Leary et al., 1994, for a major exception). This one-sided approach is understandable. For both methodological and conceptual reasons, it made sense for self-presentation researchers to start by focusing heavily on how people present themselves to strangers. The construction of first impressions is important in its own right for many contexts, such as new romantic encounters and employment interviews. In addition, there are fewer complications that enter into interactions among strangers. Researchers can study self-presentation to strangers in the laboratory without having to deal with confounds such as prior knowledge, affective bonds, shared past experiences, and so forth. Also, of course, if the first impression is not managed effectively, the person may not have much opportunity to correct the impression in further interactions, because the other person may not want any further interactions. Probably because of these practical and conceptual reasons, most of social psychology's knowledge about self-presentation is based on studies of interactions between strangers.

However, evidence is accumulating that suggests that people self-present more often to people they know than to strangers. The majority of social interactions occur between people who already know each other, rather than between strangers. For example, Wheeler and Nezlek (1977) found that the vast majority of meaningful interactions are with the same six people, and DePaulo, Kashy, and Kinkendol (1995) and Kashy and DePaulo (1996) found that people spend more time with those they know better and are closer to than they do with strangers. The sheer volume of social life that occurs within relationships makes it important to understand those interaction processes and their effects on the self-concept as well as the effects of stranger interactions. Moreover, although carryover effects from self-presentations to strangers may be an important first step in the process of constructing identity, a person may only feel that he or she has claimed an identity when relationship partners have accepted that definition of the person and will interact with the person on that basis (e.g., Baumeister, 1982, 1986; Goffman, 1959; Mead, 1934; Tice, 1992, Tice et al., 1995; Wicklund & Gollwitzer, 1982).

SELF-PRESENTATIONS IN RELATIONSHIPS

Many of the findings and principles that researchers have uncovered about self-presentations to strangers may hold true for interactions with friends, but it is not safe to assume that all aspects of self-presentation will apply equally well to people in relationships as to strangers. Pre-existing relationship may at least be a boundary condition for some of those effects.

Jones and Pittman (1982) identified five self-presentational strategies that people use to try to create an impression on an audience: self-promotion, ingratiation, intimidation, exemplification, and supplication. Jones and Pittman's description of these five strategies included the goals and motivations for engaging in these different self-presentational styles. Thus, the goal of self-promoters is to induce others to respect them for their intelligence and competence; the goal of ingratiators is to get others to like them; exemplifiers attempt to persuade others that they are moral, worthy, and have integrity; people engaging in supplication try to elicit sympathy and support from others by acting weak and helpless; and intimidators are motivated to induce others to fear them.

Although people may use any of these strategies with either strangers or relationship partners of any kind, different strategies might work better with different audiences. Of the five self-presentational strategies that Jones and Pittman identified, two of them, ingratiation and self-promotion, have received the most support from laboratory research. In fact, they may occur so often in the laboratory that some researchers have claimed that they can contaminate findings of experiments done to examine other phenomena, because people may engage in a variety of behaviors to try to make a likable or competent impression on the experimenter (e.g., Tedeschi, Schlenker, & Bonoma, 1971; Tetlock & Manstead, 1985; see also Baumeister, 1982; Leary, 1995). Eliciting liking and respect from strangers (and perhaps especially high-status strangers such as experimenters) may be a stronger motivation than eliciting fear or pity from strangers in laboratory settings, which may be why more laboratory evidence for self-promotion and ingratiation exists than for intimidation, exemplification, or supplication.

It is possible to set up situations in which people engage in supplication, exemplification, or intimidation with strangers in the laboratory, but these strategies may be more common in close relationships such as friendships, families, and other ongoing interactions. In fact, most of the examples of supplication, exemplification, and intimidation that Jones and Pittman (1982) described occur in ongoing relationships such as employee–employer, parent–child, and married couples. Exemplification, for example, may be a more successful self-presentational strategy in ongoing relationships than with strangers because it may take time to build a reputation for integrity.

In addition, engaging in the actions that elicit fear or pity from others may be costly to the self-presenter, so it may be more sensible to use intimidation and supplication with relationship partners rather than with strangers. In an ongoing relationship, the self-presenter may only have to engage in the costly self-presentation early on in the relationship (or perhaps occasionally throughout the relationship) to reap the benefits of the strategy over time (e.g., Jankowski, 1991). For example, the convict in the prison yard or the bully in the schoolyard may only have to engage in risky, threatening behavior in the initial stages of establishing a reputation for violence. Once the others in the yard are convinced that the bully is willing and able to be violent, the bully is able to take what he wants with little fear of reprisal. Likewise, a parent may need to punish a child for a temper tantrum by sending her to her room only once or twice; after that when the child starts to have a tantrum the parent may only have to give the child "the look" to induce compliant behavior. Worchel, Cooper, and Goethals's (1991) textbook cites the example of Jack Tatum of the Oakland Raiders to demonstrate the benefits of an intimidating self-presentational style. In his book *They Call Me Assassin,* Tatum described establishing an intimidating reputation among fellow ball players. Once his reputation was established, Tatum capitalized on the fear his opponents had of him. More systematic observations to this effect were furnished by Jankowski (1991). In street gangs, the members with the reputations for being the fiercest, wildest fighters were not the most common fighters and in fact hardly fought at all. New gang members usually did not want to fight but recognized that it was necessary to do so to build the reputation that would protect them; if they were seen to back down from one challenge or potential fight, then everyone would pick on them and they'd end up fighting more.

Supplication also requires the self-presenter to engage in risky actions to elicit the desired response from the audience. Portraying oneself as helpless and powerless may actually increase the power the audience has over the supplicator. Thus, in some cases the supplicator may prefer to use the strategy only in relationships where the supplicator believes the power is least likely to be abused, perhaps because the audience is constrained by the bounds of love or duty.

Using intimidation or supplication as a self-presentational strategy with strangers requires the self-presenter to continually engage in more costly, dangerous behavior. The mugger that uses intimidation to elicit fear and compliance in victims must take the risk that each new victim will respond to the threat by fighting back rather than by complying and handing over the money.

In sum, the reason ingratiation and self-promotion have received far more laboratory support in social psychology than the other strategies of self-presentation identified by Jones and Pittman (1982) may be because ingratiation and self-promotion are likely to occur between strangers, and most social psychology laboratory situations involve interactions between strangers (e.g., the individual and a confederate, the individual and the experimenter, two unrelated individuals). If intimidation, supplication, and exemplification are strategies that are more likely to be used with friends, family, or other relationship partners than with strangers, the field of social psychology may benefit from a closer examination of self-presentation within relationships. Recent work

(Leary et al., 1994; Tice et al., 1995) suggests that people self-present differently to different audiences. People use different strategies with different audiences, and the goals and motivations behind the self-presentations differ depending on the relationship between the self-presenter and the audience.

THE CARRYOVER EFFECT IN RELATIONSHIPS

If people self-present differently to relationship partners than to strangers, the impact of the self-presentation on the self-concept is also likely to differ. If people are more modest with people they know than with strangers, and if people spend more time with people they know than with strangers, then they are likely to internalize more modest than self-enhancing behavior. The fact that self-presentation to friends and acquaintances is so common may help to keep people's self-concepts in line with reality.

The finding that self-enhancing forms of self-presentation (self-promotion and ingratiation) might be more common in self-presentations to strangers than in self-presentations to friends (Tice et al., 1995) suggests that modest self-views might be beneficial to relationships. Self-enhancement and the resultant high self-esteem from the carryover of self-enhancement to the self-concept may be beneficial to individuals, because it makes them feel good (especially about themselves). However, self-enhancement may be problematic for relationships and groups if it leads individuals to overvalue themselves. Any group member that overvalues his or her own contribution to the group puts pressure on the rest of the group members and makes claims on an unfair proportion of group resources. For example, if one partner at a law firm overestimates his or her value and responsibility for the firm's reputation and expects to be compensated accordingly, less funds are available for the bonuses of other partners. If one marriage partner overestimates the value of his or her share of the household tasks and claims to be contributing 50% of the effort to household management when in fact the contribution is considerably less, then the spouse is left with the majority of the housework. If one member of a sports team overestimates his or her own contributions and claims most of the credit for a win, then fewer accolades are available for the remaining team members. As Baumeister, Smart, and Boden (1996) proposed, the benefits of self-esteem accrue mainly to the self, whereas the costs are born by other people. Social groups may therefore want to discourage egotism, because although individually beneficial it is socially disruptive and costly.

Because egocentric biases may predispose people to overestimate their own contributions and because this overestimation can be costly to other group members, the group may prosper best if a norm of modesty prevails. Thus, groups may pressure people to be modest in their self-presentations. My own work (Tice et al., 1995) suggests that the norm of modesty prevails when interacting with relationship partners or friends.

FUTURE RESEARCH ON THE AUDIENCE AND THE CARRYOVER EFFECT

Many of the principles that have been shown to affect the carryover effect may be applicable to audiences as well as self-presenters. For example, the internalization of behavior can occur either through dissonance processes or through self-perceptual processes (Jones et al., 1981; Rhodewalt, 1986; Rhodewalt & Agustdottir, 1986). If the self-presentational behavior is uncharacteristic of the presenter, or "outside the latitude of acceptance," the self-presented behavior can only be internalized through dissonance reduction. If the self-presentational behavior seems to the self-presenter to be an acceptable presentation of the self and "within the latitude of acceptance," the behavior is internalized through self-perceptual processes. Audiences may affect self-presentational carryover of behavior by altering cognitive processing. The latitudes of acceptance and rejection may change depending on the self-schemas made accessible by different audiences. For example, a delinquent self-presentation may be within the latitude of acceptance when a teenager is interacting with his peer group but in the latitude of rejection when that same teenager is interacting with his parents and different self-schemas are activated.

In addition, when people self-present to audiences they know, the audiences may also have a latitude of acceptance and a latitude of rejection for the self-presenter's behavior. There are some behaviors that the audience won't let the self-presenter get away with unchallenged if the audience is well-known to the presenter. For example, a tone deaf person may be able to claim at least some musical ability when interacting with strangers, but friends who are familiar with the person's degree of tone deafness may express skepticism regarding any musical claims made by the person. Thus, in this example a self-presentation of musical ability falls in the audience's latitude of rejection. People are constrained by others' knowledge of them in how they can self-present and how others accept the self-presentation. This constraint may impact on the carryover effect and thus on people's self-concepts.

The actual beliefs that the audience has about the self-presenter may be less important than what the self-presenter thinks are the audience's beliefs about him or her. Research has demonstrated that the correlations between self-concepts and the beliefs others have about a person are low, but the correlations between what a person thinks others think of him or her and what he or she thinks of himself or herself are much higher (e.g., Felson, 1989; Kenny & DePaulo, 1993). In other words, the internally generated audience (Cooley, 1902; Mead, 1934) may be more important than the actual audience in constraining self-presentations and self-concepts.

Thus, there seem to be at least two mechanisms by which audiences can affect the carryover effect. First, audiences can constrain self-presentational behavior so that the person actually behaves differently with different audiences. A person may feel constrained to present a polite self to the neighbors, a sexy and uninhibited self to a date, and an assertive and powerful self at work because the person believes that this is what neighbors, dates, and employees expect (regardless of whether these groups actually hold such expectations). The person may feel that self-presentations of modesty and timidity at work, for example, would be rejected by employees whose past experience with the person would lead them to expect a very different kind of behavior. Likewise, the person's beliefs about what the generalized audience of "neighbors" expects may lead to polite behavior, even if the person does not know the neighbors well enough to know what they really expect.

Second, even if self-presentational behavior is held constant, the carryover effect may differ depending on the audience of the self-presentation. For example, a person may self-present in an ingratiating fashion, but the impact on the self-concept may differ depending on whether the audience has any power over the self-presenter. If the self-presenter has something to gain by getting the audience to like him or her, then he or she may discount the behavior and the self-concept may be less affected than if the self-presenter sees the behavior unconstrained by the audience.

SUMMARY AND TRIBUTE TO NED

The social context of self-presentations may tremendously influence the carryover effect. People internalize their public behavior and self-presentations (e.g., Fazio, Effrein, & Falender, 1981; Gergen, 1965; Jones et al., 1981; Kulik, Sledge, & Mahler, 1986; Rhodewalt & Agustdottir, 1986; Schlenker & Trudeau, 1990), and people's self-presentations are affected by social relationships (Tice et al., 1995). Thus, understanding the social context of self-presentation may be crucial to understanding the impact of the behavior on the self-concept.

Part of Ned Jones's genius in social psychology was his ability to operationalize almost anything, develop new methodologies, and apply existing methodologies to new issues. Contributing to the conference and volume dedicated to the memory of Ned gave me a chance to reflect on how Ned would think about the future of many of the issues covered. I am grateful to have the chance to comment on Fred Rhodewalt's chapter because it gave me the opportunity to imagine what Ned would think about the future of research on self-presentation and self-concept change. Discussing research with Ned was always exciting and instructive, and discussing Ned's interest areas with other students and colleagues of Ned's in his honor seemed to be an especially fitting tribute to one of the field's greatest researchers.

REFERENCES

Baumeister, R. F. (1982). A self-presentational view of social phenomena. *Psychological Bulletin, 91,* 3–26.

Baumeister, R. F. (1986). *Identity: Cultural change and the struggle for self.* New York: Oxford University Press.

Baumeister, R. F., Smart, L., & Boden, J. M. (1996). Relation of threatened egotism to violence and aggression: The dark side of high self-esteem. *Psychological Review, 103,* 5–33.

Cooley, C. H. (1902). *Human nature and the social order.* New York: Scribners'.

DePaulo, B. M., Kashy, D. A., & Kinkendol, S. E. (1995). *Lying in everyday life.* Manuscript in preparation.

Fazio, R. H., Effrein, E. A., & Falender, V. J. (1981). Self-perceptions following social interactions. *Journal of Personality and Social Psychology, 41,* 232–242.

Felson, R. B. (1989). Parents and the reflected appraisal process. A longitudinal analysis. *Journal of Personality and Social Psychology, 56,* 965–971.

Gergen, K. J. (1965). Interaction goals and personalistic feedback as factors affecting the presentation of self. *Journal of Personality and Social Psychology, 1,* 413–424.

Goffman, E. (1959). *The presentation of self in everyday life.* New York: Anchor Books.

Jankowski, M. S. (1991). *Islands in the street: Gangs and American urban society.* Berkeley, CA: University of California Press.

Jones, E. E., & Pittman, T. S. (1982). Toward a general theory of strategic self-presentation. In J. Suls (Ed.), *Psychological perspectives on the self* (pp. 231–263). Hillsdale, NJ: Erlbaum.

Jones, E. E., Rhodewalt, F., Berglas, S., & Skelton, J. A. (1981). Effects of strategic self-presentation on subsequent self-esteem. *Journal of Personality and Social Psychology, 41,* 407–421.

Kashy, D. A., & DePaulo, B. M. (1996). Who lies? *Journal of Personality and Social Psychology, 70,* 1037–1051.

Kenny, D. A., & DePaulo, B. M. (1993). Do people know how others view them? An empirical and theoretical account. *Psychological Bulletin, 114,* 145–161.

Kulik, J. A., Sledge, P., & Mahler, H. I. M. (1986). Self-confirmatory attribution, egocentrism, and the perpetuation of self-beliefs. *Journal of Personality and Social Psychology, 50,* 587–594.

Leary, M. R. (1995). *Self-presentation: Impression management and interpersonal behavior.* Madison, WI: Brown & Benchmark.

Leary, M. R., Nezlek, J. B., Downs, D., Radford-Davenport, J., Martin, J., & McMullen, A. (1994). Self-presentation in everyday interactions: Effects of target familiarity and gender composition. *Journal of Personality and Social Psychology, 67,* 664–673.

Mead, G. H. (1934). *Mind, self, and society.* Chicago, IL: University of Chicago Press.

Rhodewalt, F. (1986). Self-presentation and the phenomenal self: On the stability and malleability of the self-concept. In R. F. Baumeister's (Ed.), *Public self and private self* (pp. 117–142). New York: Springer-Verlag.

Rhodewalt, F., & Agustdottir, S. (1986). Effects of self-presentation on the phenomenal self. *Journal of Personality and Social Psychology, 50,* 47–55.

Schlenker, B. R., Dlugolecki, D. W., & Doherty, K. (1992). The impact of self-presentations and behavior: The power of public commitment. *Personality and Social Psychology Bulletin, 20,* 20–33.

Schlenker, B. R., & Trudeau, J. V. (1990). Impacts of self-presentations on private self-beliefs: Effects of prior self-beliefs and misattribution. *Journal of Personality and Social Psychology, 58,* 22–32.

Tedeschi, J. T. (1986). Private and public experiences of the self. In R. Baumeister (Ed.), *Public self and private self* (pp. 1–20). New York: Springer-Verlag.

Tedeschi, J. T., Schlenker, B. R., & Bonoma, T. V. (1971). Cognitive dissonance: Private ratiocination or public spectacle? *American Psychologist, 26,* 685–695.

Tetlock, P. E., & Manstead, A. S. R. (1985). Impression management versus intrapsychic explanations in social psychology: A useful dichotomy? *Psychological Review, 92,* 59–77.

Tice, D. M. (1992). Self-presentation and self-concept change: The looking glass self as magnifying glass. *Journal of Personality and Social Psychology, 63,* 435–451.

Tice, D. M. (1994). Pathways to internalization: When does overt behavior change the self-concept? In T. M. Brinthaupt & R. P. Lipka (Eds.), *Changing the self.* Albany, NY: State University of New York Press.

Tice, D. M., Butler, J. L., Muraven, M. B., & Stillwell, A. M. (1995). When modesty prevails: Differential favorability of self-presentation to friends and strangers. *Journal of Personality and Social Psychology, 69,* 1120–1138.

Wheeler, L., & Nezlek, J. (1977). Sex differences in social participation. *Journal of Personality and Social Psychology, 35,* 742–754.

Wicklund, R. A., & Gollwitzer, P. M. (1982). *Symbolic self-completion.* Hillsdale, NJ: Erlbaum.

Worchel, S., Cooper, J., & Goethals, G. R. (1991). *Understanding social psychology.* Chicago, IL: The Dorsey Press.

8

The Heterogeneity of Homogeneity

Patricia W. Linville

Ned Jones was involved in some of the earliest work on out-group homogeneity—that is, people perceive members of their out-group to be more homogeneous than members of their in-group. For example, to a psychologist, sociologists appear "all alike," whereas psychologists appear quite diverse. In his work with students at Duke University and Princeton University, Ned showed the out-group homogeneity effect (OHE) in a variety of social groups (e.g., people perceive members of their own race, age, university, profession, and eating club to be more diverse than comparable out-groups).

As I began thinking about progress in this research field, it was like writing no other chapter. I imagined myself sitting in Ned's big office at Duke, drinking my tea as I did during our meetings, with Ned sitting relaxed in his chair. In my mind, I described the progress of the field,

This chapter emerged from a 1995 conference at Princeton University celebrating the life and work of Ned Jones. I thank Joel Cooper, John Darley, and Gregory Fischer for their helpful feedback on this chapter; Joel Cooper and John Darley for organizing the conference; and Marilynn Brewer and Diane Mackie for stimulating my thinking as discussants of my conference paper. Finally, I am grateful to Ned Jones for sharing and inspiring in me his enthusiasm and love for social psychology, his deep interest in the mind of the active perceiver, and his belief that good social psychology tells a good story.

then Ned reacted. The process of preparing this chapter was like having periodic conversations with Ned. In this chapter, I share some of this conversation.

NED'S CONTRIBUTION

Conceptualizing and Measuring Group Variability

Ned was one of the first to explore various conceptions of group variability, including dimensional complexity, the range across a single trait, and number of subgroups. For example, Linville and Jones (1980) used a trait-sorting procedure to measure dimensional complexity for a group. White participants were more complex in their thinking about Whites than Blacks (Linville & Jones, 1980), and college-age and retired participants were more complex about their own age group (Brewer & Lui, 1984; Linville, 1982; Linville & Salovey, 1982). Jones, Wood, and Quattrone (1981) had members of four eating clubs at Princeton estimate the range on a trait scale (e.g., introvert-extravert) within which members of a club fell. Members perceived a greater range for their own eating club. Quattrone and Jones (1980) had premedical and nursing students form subtypes of each medical group. Both groups perceived more subtypes within their own group.

Consequences of Perceived Variability

Ned was also involved in some of the first work exploring consequences of perceived variability, including evaluation and generalization processes. Linville and Jones (1980) found that the less complex one's thinking about a group, the more extreme one's evaluations of individual members—more extremely positive about a positive member and more extremely negative about a negative member. For example, White participants read and evaluated several law school applications, some weak and some strong, that contained incidental information on the race of the applicant. We found out-group extremity. When reading a strong application, White participants rated a Black applicant higher than a comparable White applicant; when reading a weak application, they rated a Black applicant lower than a comparable White applicant. Similar results were found using age as the group variable: Both young and old people rated vignettes about members of the other age group more extremely (Linville, 1982; Linville & Salovey, 1982). At the individual participant level, those less complex in their thinking about an age group were more extreme in their ratings of specific group members (Linville, 1982). Finally, when we manipulated complexity by drawing participants' attention to two versus six features of stimuli, such as features of law school essays, those attending to fewer features made more extreme evaluations (Linville, 1982; Linville & Jones, 1980).

George Quattrone and Ned (Quattrone & Jones, 1980) were the first to focus on the generalization consequences of variability. People are more likely to generalize from the behavior of a single group member to the group as a whole when the member is from the out-group (Quattrone & Jones, 1980). Princeton and Rutgers students viewed a tape of either a Princeton or a Rutgers student making a choice during a psychology experiment (e.g., to wait alone or with others). After viewing the choice of one student, student participants then estimated the proportion of students from that university who would make the same decision as that particular student. Participants made stronger generalizations about out-group members (e.g., Princeton students were more willing to infer things about Rutgers students in general from the behavior of the single Rutgers student).

WAVES OF INTEREST

Since this early work, there has been continued interest in group variability. As evidence of this continued interest, at least 11 reviews of group variability have appeared since 1986 (e.g., Linville & Fischer, 1993a; 1997; Linville, Salovey, & Fischer, 1986; Messick & Mackie, 1989; Mullen & Hu, 1989; Ostrom & Sedikides, 1992; Park, Judd, & Ryan, 1991; Quattrone, 1986; Sedikides & Ostrom, 1993; Simon, 1992a; Wilder, 1986). In 1992, a symposium on group variability was held at the Society for Experimental Social Psychologists (SESP). In 1993, a special edition of *Social Cognition* was devoted to the topic. Finally, group

PATRICIA W. LINVILLE

variability became a context for several lively debates on competing models and approaches (e.g., prototype vs. exemplar categorization, on-line vs. memory-based processing, cognitive vs. social/motivational influences; e.g., for a summary of these debates see *Annual Review of Psychology* chapters by Brewer & Kramer, 1985; Hilton & von Hippel, 1996; Messick & Mackie, 1989; Schneider, 1991; Sherman, Judd, & Park, 1989).

There have been at least four waves of interest in group variability. The initial interest was in simply demonstrating the OHE in a variety of social groups. The effect appears robust among a range of natural social groups, including profession, nationality, race, religion, age, college major, sorority-fraternity affiliation, and so forth (see Ostrom & Sedikides, 1992). Groups or contexts in which the effect is relatively weak or reversed have stimulated lively theoretical debates (e.g., gender, minimal groups created in the laboratory, contexts with high social identity needs). The second wave focused on broadening our operationalization and measurement of perceived variability. In cases where new measurement was tied to new models, this stimulated theoretical progress.

In a third wave, the OHE became a catalyst for thinking about broader issues regarding how group knowledge is represented, including knowledge of a group's diversity. This led to the application of categorization models to explain the OHE. Why this shift in our research agenda? Was it really our interest in group variability that was the catalyst for addressing broader issues of stereotyping and social categorization? I believe so. Previous interest in stereotyping focused on central tendency, and all categorization models deal well with the representation of central tendency. It was only when the focus turned to issues of variability that it became evident that different categorization models made different processing predictions. I believe this pushed us to take categorization models seriously and to focus on the different predictions of competing models.

Fourth, although work on basic issues of categorization continues, theorizing from a social and motivational perspective has also developed. A central focus is how people's social identity with a group influences their perceptions of the group's variability. What is the next likely wave? I believe we will see more research linking cognitive models of group variability with motivational and social identity theories.

WHY CARE ABOUT GROUP VARIABILITY?

There are several reasons why we should care about group variability. First, people are sensitive to variability information in their environment, and they make reasonable estimates of group variability (e.g., Judd, Ryan, & Park, 1991; Nisbett & Kunda, 1985). Second, people use it in their inferences, evaluations, and behavior toward group members (e.g., Linville, 1982; Linville & Jones, 1980; Linville & Fischer, 1993b; Nisbett, Krantz, Jepson, & Kunda, 1983; Park & Hastie, 1987; Quattrone & Jones, 1980). Third, the tendency to view out-groups as more homogeneous appears distinct from in-group favoritism, thus highlighting the separate contribution of various cognitive and social/motivational processes. Fourth, an understanding of group variability is important in understanding basic issues in social categorization processes (e.g., prototype vs. exemplar processing, social identity needs). Fifth, to the extent that perceiving the out-group as homogeneous contributes to greater conflict, stereotyping, and prejudice toward out-group members, then creating experiences that lead to more differentiated impressions of out-groups may contribute to better social and organizational decisions as well as to better intergroup relations.

Finally, an understanding of perceived group variability is central to understanding stereotyping. For example, Hamilton and Sherman (1994) opened their handbook chapter on stereotyping with five questions: What is a stereotype? How do people develop stereotypes? When and how are they used? Why do they persist? How can we change them? I believe perceptions of variability are involved in each of these central questions about stereotyping. To give a few examples:

1. *What is a stereotype?* The definition of a stereotype is expanding to include not only the central tendency or most typical features of a

PATRICIA W. LINVILLE

group as a whole but also perceptions of the diversity within the group. As Hamilton and Sherman (1994) suggested, people perceive differences among group members, the degree of similarity or diversity among members, and how much members vary around a stereotype or specific trait.

2. *How do people develop stereotypes?* Group stereotypes are formed using the central tendency as well as the variability of features, particularly basing the stereotype on features that have low (rather than high) within-group variability because of their diagnostic value (Ford & Stangor, 1992). Also, learning about a group initially from abstracted prototypes (Park & Hastie, 1987) or second-hand exemplars conveyed by friends or the media (Linville & Fischer, 1993a) facilitates developing strong stereotypes, whereas learning about a group from individual exemplars facilitates developing a differentiated view of a group.

3. *When and how are stereotypes used?* People rely more on the stereotype in judging an individual member when a group is homogeneous, particularly when the individual performs an act typical of a homogeneous group (Krueger & Rothbart, 1988; Lambert, 1995; Lambert & Wyer, 1990; Park & Hastie, 1987; Park et al., 1991; Ryan, Judd, & Park, 1996).

4. *Why do stereotypes persist and how can we change them?* When a group is homogeneous, people are more likely to generalize from the stereotypic behavior of a single member to the group as a whole, but they are less likely to generalize from counterstereotypic behavior (Park & Hastie, 1987). They are also less likely to categorize a person with atypical characteristics of a group as a member of that group (Park & Hastie, 1987). Thus, the stereotype of a homogeneous group is less susceptible to change.

In summary, an understanding of perceptions of group variability sharpens our understanding of theoretical as well as real-world issues. The next sections look at the progress made in the area of group variability on several fronts—cognitive and social theoretical models, measurement, and determinants and consequences of perceived variability.

428

PROGRESS: THEORIES OF PERCEIVED GROUP VARIABILITY

Great progress has resulted from linking perceptions of group variability to basic models of mental representations on the one hand and to models of social identity on the other hand. This has enriched understanding of both group variability and categorization and social identity theories.

Progress in Cognitive Models

Research on perceived group variability has given rise to lively debates pitting different models of social categorization against one another. One type of cognitive model holds that information about the variability within a group is abstracted and updated on-line as the group stereotype or prototype is abstracted. Thus, variability information is stored at the group level, with the group prototype. Another type of model holds that variability information is derived from the retrieval of group exemplars. I now briefly describe the theoretical aspects of each type of model as it pertains to variability knowledge.

Prototype or Property Abstraction Models

In prototype or abstraction models, categories are represented by abstracted properties of the category. In the original, simple *prototype model*, this only included a list of prototypic features representing the central tendency of the group on relevant features (Posner & Keele, 1968). For example, a student's professor prototype might be "Professors dress casually, wear glasses, and are intelligent, curious, concerned with small distinctions, always busy, and disconnected from real-world problems." This traditional model is limited because it fails to represent the variability that perceivers see within the category. For example, the student may believe that although some professors are unconcerned with practical considerations, others are highly involved in social, political, and economic issues. Thus, more recent abstraction models such as Fried and Holyoak's (1984) *category density model* assume that people abstract the variance along with the prototypic (mean) value of each feature (e.g., intelligence). This model assumes that each feature is completely summarized by two parameters—its mean and variance. A critical assumption is that the mean and variance of a feature are abstracted and updated on-line each time a new instance is encountered. Thus, variability information stored with the group level information can be retrieved without accessing exemplars.

Bernadette Park and Chick Judd adapted this model to account for the OHE (Judd & Park, 1988; Park & Judd, 1990). They proposed a *prototype-plus-exemplar* model in which out-group variability judgments are based on abstracted variability stored with the group prototype, whereas in-group judgments are based on this stored variability qualified by retrieved in-group exemplars. Park and Judd reported two findings in support of the notion that retrieval processes play a bigger role in in-group than out-group variability judgments—first, a positive correlation between self-judgments and in-group but not out-group judgments; second, a relationship between retrieved in-group members and in-group judgments but not between retrieved out-group members and out-group judgments (Park & Judd, 1990). However, the OHE still remained when controlling for the effect of self and retrieved group members, suggesting that other factors also contribute to the OHE.

Kraus, Ryan, Judd, Hastie, and Park (1993) proposed a new property abstraction model in which perceivers abstract a frequency distribution on-line representing where group members fall along different levels of an attribute (e.g., the number of members of high, medium, and low intelligence). The OHE occurs because in-group members are classified along more finely grained attribute levels than out-group members (e.g., five vs. two attribute levels).

Multiple Exemplar-Based Models

The impetus for turning to exemplar models in representing social groups was their natural ability to deal with people's knowledge of the variability within a group. In these models, category knowledge consists of a set of exemplars of specific instances or subtypes of the category. Thus, a natural way of dealing with variability is through a process of retrieving a set of relevant exemplars (Linville & Fischer, 1993a; Linville, Fischer, & Salovey, 1989; Linville, Fischer, & Yoon, 1996; Linville et al.,

1986). Exemplar models thus highlight the role of memory-based judgments in which specific instances play a key role.

Category judgments, including judgments of variability, are based on the retrieval of a set of exemplars. Linville et al. (1989) developed PDIST, a computer simulation model of how people generate perceived distributions of category features (e.g., the distribution of values of intelligence among professors). PDIST relies on a probe-echo mechanism like that proposed by Hintzman (1986). A memory probe (e.g., intelligent professors) is formed in working memory and activates in parallel a set of traces in long-term memory, each trace being activated in proportion to its similarity to the probe. This set of activated traces is the echo. For example, to make judgments about the intelligence of professors, one might form three memory probes—"professor, high intelligence," "professor, average intelligence," and "professor, low intelligence." Each probe activates a set of traces in memory. The strength of each echo reflects the number and strengths of the traces activated by the probe. PDIST uses the relative strengths of these echoes as a basis for constructing a perceived distribution of the characteristics of group members. If the memory probe "professor, high intelligence" evokes a strong echo, whereas the probes "professor, average intelligence" and "professor, low intelligence" evoke very weak echoes, then PDIST will judge that the typical professor is high in intelligence and that professors do not vary much in that regard.

In this and in other exemplar models, retrieval is a parallel and implicit process that need not be accessible to consciousness. Thus, it may involve a large number of exemplars without time or cognitive resource concerns, and it may not be revealed by traditional recall measures (Hintzman, 1986). As a consequence, such a process will not necessarily produce a correlation between judged variability and the exemplars that are explicitly recalled (see Smith & Zarate, 1992). Moreover, parallel activation of a large number of exemplars need not take longer than activation of a smaller number.

How does this type of model account for the OHE? Other things being equal, the greater the number of retrieved exemplars, the greater the perceived variability of the group. Greater familiarity with one's in-groups will lead to the storage and retrieval of more exemplars re-garding in-groups. Thus, in the context of a multiple exemplar model like PDIST, greater familiarity provides one mechanism leading to the OHE.

Evidence for this type of model with social groups comes from several sources (Linville et al., 1989). First, our computer simulation PDIST showed that the retrieval of a greater number of exemplars from a group resulted in greater perceived variability of group members. Second, perceived variability was greater for in-groups on the basis of age and nationality, but not when groups had approximately equal con-tact with in-group and out-group members (men and women). Third, perceived variability increased as contact with a group increased. Fourth, perceived variability increased over time as group members had more contact with one another (perceived variability of class members increased over the semester).

One critical issue for distinguishing between abstraction and ex-emplar models is whether judgments of variability are made on-line (at the time when stimuli are initially encountered) or are memory based (formed by retrieving exemplar information from memory). Park and Hastie (1987) examined this issue using a training paradigm in which some training exemplars were repeated. Participants were instructed to ignore repeated exemplars when making variability judgments. Park and Hastie found that repetition improved recall but did not affect judgments of variability, from which they concluded that variability judgments were made on-line. However, as Mackie, Sherman, and Worth (1993) noted, the Park and Hastie study involved few stimuli, which made it easy for participants to keep track of what they had seen twice, and thus to discount repeated exemplars when making variability judgments.

Diane Mackie and her colleagues addressed the on-line versus memory-based judgment issue using a reaction time paradigm (Mackie et al., 1993). In one experiment, individuals made judgments of a group's variability, a judgment of liking (assumed to be on-line), and a judgment of religiousness (assumed to be memory based). Variability judgments were made slower than on-line judgments and at the same speed as memory-based judgments. In a second experiment, amount of similarity information recalled was significantly related to both the latency and extremity of recall judgments. Mackie et al. concluded that these findings support the hypothesis that variability judgments are memory based.

Progress in Social and Motivational Models

Social identity concepts (e.g., Tajfel, 1978, 1982) have inspired several recent theoretical contributions to the homogeneity field. In Marilynn Brewer's (1991, 1993) optimal distinctiveness theory, perceived group variability is subject to motivational forces associated with needs for self-identity and for differentiation from others. Optimal distinctiveness involves identifying with social categories in such a way as to achieve a balance between two needs: feeling assimilated and feeling differentiated from others. Perceptions of in-group variability are due to motivational forces related to self-identity. In a large, highly inclusive in-group, the need to differentiate oneself (me vs. us comparison) results in perceiving the in-group as heterogeneous. In a small, distinctive or exclusive in-group, identifying with the in-group (us vs. them comparison) results in perceiving the in-group as homogeneous. This model predicts a relationship between strong social group identification and in-group homogeneity.

Bernd Simon, Rupert Brown, and their colleagues (e.g., Brown & Wootton-Millward, 1993; Simon, 1992b; Simon & Brown 1987; Simon & Pettigrew, 1990) have demonstrated circumstances under which in-group (rather than out-group) homogeneity occurs. In general, this occurs when social identity needs are strong. First, relative group size can shift the basic OHE. Smaller in-groups perceive themselves as more homogeneous than larger out-groups, presumably to bolster their social group identity (e.g., see Mullen & Hu, 1989; Simon, 1992b, for reviews). Second, attribute relevance can also shift the effect to in-group homogeneity. In-groups perceive themselves as more homogeneous than out-groups on attributes relevant to the identity of the in-group (Kelly, 1989; Simon, 1992a). For example, nurses showed an in-group homogeneity effect for nurse-related attributes but an out-group homogeneity effect for doctor-relevant attributes (Brown & Wootton-Millward, 1993). And members of a British political party showed an in-group homogeneity effect for attitudes central to the party's ideology (e.g., private health care), but an out-group homogeneity effect for personality traits (e.g., loyal; Kelly, 1989). Thus, out-group homogeneity is not as universal as once thought.

Other social and motivational mechanisms play a role in perceptions of group variability. First, variability perceptions depend on temporal factors such as degree of socialization of a group's identity or amount of time with a group (Brown & Wootton-Millward, 1993; Linville et al., 1989). A second important social factor is the relationship between an in-group and an out-group, particularly the advantaged versus disadvantaged status of a group and power differential (Brewer, 1993; Brown & Wootton-Millward, 1993; Linville et al., 1989; Lorenzi-Cioldi, Eagly, & Stewart, 1995; Sedikides, 1997). For example, both men and women tend to see women as more homogeneous, which may reflect men's greater status and power (Lorenzi-Cioldi et al., 1995). A related third factor involves differential values of social groups that result in different patterns of group perceptions. For example, Black college students viewed White students as more stereotypic and less favorable than Black students, as one would expect from the typical out-group stereotypicality and in-group favoritism effects. White college students, however, showed no such effects, and in some cases perceived White students to be more stereotypic and less favorable than Blacks (Judd, Park, Ryan, Brauer, & Kraus, 1995). Judd et al. (1995) interpreted their results in terms of differential socialization, suggesting that White youths increasingly value ethnic equality and a color-blind society that deemphasizes ethnic differences, whereas Black youths increasingly value ethnic pride and ethnic differences.

PROGRESS: MEASUREMENT OF PERCEPTION OF GROUP VARIABILITY

Progress in measurement has also been substantial. Group variability has been conceptualized in a variety of ways, and new measures continue to emerge. In this section, I briefly summarize the major measurement approaches, which can be grouped into three clusters—overall intragroup similarity, within-attribute variability, and cross-attribute variability or covariance (for reviews see Linville & Fischer, 1993a; Linville et al., 1989; Park et al., 1991; Quattrone, 1986).

Overall Intragroup Similarity

An early measure that is still used with success asks people to make overall judgments of the extent to which the members of a given group resemble one another, without reference to any particular feature (e.g., Mackie & Asuncion, 1990; Park & Judd, 1990; Park & Rothbart, 1982; Quattrone & Jones, 1980). For example, how similar or dissimilar are physicians to one another (using a scale from 1 to 9, where 1 indicates *extremely similar* and 9 indicates *extremely dissimilar*)?

Within-Attribute Variability

Single-Feature Variability

Perceived variability has been predominantly measured with respect to single attributes of the group (e.g., How variable is the interpersonal skill of physicians?). A common way to tap this is to have people construct a perceived frequency distribution of group members along various features such as intelligence and friendliness (e.g., Linville et al., 1989; Linville et al., 1986; Park & Judd, 1990). For example, imagine 100 randomly chosen physicians and distribute them over seven levels of interpersonal skill. From these distributions, Linville et al. (1986; Linville et al., 1989) calculated two measures of perceived variability—the standard deviation (SD) and the perceived differentiation (P_d) of attribute values of each feature.[1]

A conceptually similar measure is the perceived range of a feature

---

[1] (P_d) measures the probability that a perceiver will distinguish between two randomly chosen category exemplars with respect to the attribute in question. The more uniform (flatter) the distribution of perceived attribute values, the greater P_d will be.

for a group. Here people specify low and high values of a feature that capture a specified percentage (e.g., 90%) of group members (e.g., Jones et al., 1981; Park & Judd, 1990; Park et al., 1991).

Stereotype Endorsement

Stereotypicality reflects the extent to which the group is seen to possess stereotypic versus counter-stereotypic attributes (Judd et al., 1995; Park & Judd, 1990; Park et al., 1991; Park & Rothbart, 1982). For example, people are asked to estimate the percentage of women who are nurturant or violent (i.e., attributes pretested to be stereotypic or counter-stereotypic of women). Higher stereotypicality reflects ascribing a high proportion of stereotypic and a low proportion of counterstereotypic attributes to a group. Because these measures are based on the means of distributions, not their variances, we have argued that such measures are not measures of variability in the usual statistical sense (Linville & Fischer, 1993a; see Simon, 1995, for a similar point). Consistent with this, Park and Judd (1990) reported that measures of stereotypicality are uncorrelated with dispersion measures of variability such as perceived range or standard deviation of a group. Research generally shows an out-group stereotypicality effect in which people perceive their out-groups to be more stereotypic than their in-groups (e.g., Park & Judd, 1990; Park & Rothbart, 1982). An interesting exception may be race, where Black college students viewed Whites as more stereotypic than Blacks, as one would expect from the out-group stereotypicality effect, whereas White students showed no out-group stereotypicality bias (Judd et al., 1995).

Cross-Attribute Variability and Covariation

Number of Subtypes

People perceive a variety of subtypes within both in-groups and out-groups, but they perceive more subtypes within their in-group. For example, participants perceived more in-group subtypes when they directly listed group subtypes (Goethals, Allison, & Frost, 1979; Kraus et al., 1993; Park, Ryan, & Judd, 1992; Quattrone & Jones, 1980), sorted traits into piles representing subtypes (Linville, 1982; Linville & Jones, 1980;

Linville & Salovey, 1982), sorted pictures (Brewer & Lui, 1984), and generated subtypes in a feature covariation task (Linville et al., 1996). People have knowledge not only of the variety of subtypes within a group, but also of the relative frequencies of the various subtypes (Linville et al., 1996).

Complexity

A simple count of the number of subtypes in one's category representation makes no discrimination among types; for example, are two subtypes very similar or highly distinct? A measure of dimensional complexity attempts to capture the degree to which the subtypes that comprise a category are similar or distinct from one another (Brewer & Lui, 1984; Linville, 1982; Linville & Jones, 1980; Linville & Salovey, 1982). The task involves sorting features (or pictures) into piles describing various subtypes within a group. The H statistic is an information theory measure that reflects the dimensional complexity of thinking about a group. It is a function of both the number and distinctiveness of the features underlying the trait sort (e.g., one might think of physicians in terms of two dimensions—their technical expertise and their interpersonal skill). Complexity is positively related to the number of subtypes used in describing a category (Linville, 1982; Linville & Jones, 1980).

Covariation Among Attributes

Apart from research on category complexity and subtyping, the predominant focus of out-group homogeneity research has been on measures of the perceived variability of single features (e.g., the variance or range of specific traits such as intelligence). Believing, however, that people represent social group knowledge in terms of clusters of features describing individuals and subtypes, we have recently shifted our focus to the covariation one perceives among features representing subtypes within a group (e.g., the perceived correlation between the technical and social skill of physicians; Linville & Fischer, 1996, 1997; Linville et al., 1996). Research participants generated various subtypes of a group by using a list of 18 features, each feature having multiple possible levels (e.g., interpersonally communicative, average, noncommunicative). From the patterns of features describing various subtypes (e.g., one subtype might be communicative, relaxed, less technical, family practitioners; another subtype might be noncommunicative, uptight, technically skilled, specialists), we calculate both an individual's average absolute correlation ($Avg\ |R|$) between pairs of features reflecting covariation per se and the average correlation ($Avg\ R$) reflecting degree to which features covary in an evaluatively consistent fashion. Larger values of either measure reflect greater homogeneity in the sense that the category attributes are more redundant. On both measures, participants showed an out-group-covariation effect: They perceived greater covariation among features of out-group members (Linville & Fischer, 1993b; Linville et al., 1996). For age groups, both young and older people perceived greater covariation among features of out-group members. For occupation, undergraduates perceived greater covariation among features of business subtypes than did MBAs.

In summary, group variability has been conceptualized and measured in a variety of ways. In addition, more research is now including multiple measures of group variability in a single study (e.g., Linville & Fischer, 1996; Park & Judd, 1990). Different measures of variability do not always correlate highly (e.g., stereotypicality and single-feature variability; single-feature variability and covariance). This leads to two suggestions. First, one should not casually pick a variability measure or only include one type. Second, more attention should be given to theoretical links between specific measures and specific models. For example, exemplar and abstraction models have different process explanations regarding how people perform variability tasks, for instance, how people generate frequency distributions for an attribute, how they form a group stereotype, what they retrieve to make a rating of overall similarity among group members, and how they make stereotypicality judgments (Linville & Fischer, 1993a). In this light, future research needs to explore whether different variability measures are sensitive to different mechanisms of the OHE (e.g., group familiarity, attention to individuating features, and social identity needs; see Brewer, this volume; Sedikides & Ostrom, 1993).

PROGRESS: DETERMINANTS OF
PERCEIVED VARIABILITY

From the early work in this area, a major focus has been the mechanisms underlying perceived group variability. Progress is reflected in the variety of determinants that have been identified and the theoretical links between specific determinants and specific models. The roots of group variability lie partly in the information environment of perceivers, partly in fundamental cognitive processes regarding perceptions of social categories, and partly in motivational and social factors. Because few studies have examined multiple determinants in the same study, exploring such interactions would be fruitful for future research. A good example of multiple determinants is found in the work of Islam and Hewstone (1993), who looked at the interactions of quantity and quality of contact and intergroup anxiety as predictors of perceived group variability and favorability.

Categorization Processes Per Se

An initial question is whether any of the prototype or exemplar categorization models developed in cognitive psychology are sufficient to account for group variability differences; that is, if a perceiver was exposed to identical samples of information about members of an in-group and out-group, would the models predict perceptions of less out-group variability? I believe the answer is no. Group membership per se plays no role in the basic cognitive models, so there is no basis for perceiving a difference between the variability of the in-group and out-group if one's information regarding exemplars of the groups is identical (Linville & Fischer, 1993a). None of the categorization models alone directly produces the OHE. So other factors within the perceiver or the perceiver's environment (e.g., biased information, a bias in memory and judgment processes, motivational and social influences) interact with basic categorization processes to produce the effect. The literature suggests several mechanisms underlying group variability effects, including greater familiarity with the in-group, greater second-hand exemplars of the out-group, prototype-first learning about out-groups, greater attention to individuating features of in-group members, different representations of in-groups and out-groups, greater incentives to make distinctions among in-group members, and social/motivational factors such as social identity needs.

Greater Familiarity With the In-Group

Familiarity with a group is one natural mechanism for explaining group differences in perceived variability. According to statistical sampling theory, if one retrieves a small number of exemplars from memory, this sample will tend to underestimate the variance of the actual population. Other things being equal, as one retrieves a larger number of exemplars from memory, the variance of this retrieved set becomes larger and closer to the actual population variance. An analogous state of affairs arises in memory-based judgments about social groups. The set of category exemplars stored in memory is a sample of the population of potential exemplars of the social group. As one becomes more familiar with a social group, one will be exposed to more exemplars from it and therefore store and retrieve a larger set of exemplars from memory. So other things being equal, greater familiarity with a social group should lead to greater variability in the sample of exemplars retrieved from long-term memory. In fact, familiarity has a stronger effect on variability in an imperfect memory-based process than in a pure statistical sampling process (Linville et al., 1989). Thus, one natural explanation for why people tend to perceive greater variability in their in-groups is that they are more familiar with their in-groups.

Empirical studies provide support for several elements of this interpretation. First, people report greater frequency of contact with in-groups defined by age, nationality, race, and profession (e.g., Linville et al., 1989; Linville et al., 1996; Zebrowitz, Montepare, & Lee, 1993). Second, in cases where people are more familiar with their in-group, people perceive greater single-feature variability among members of their in-group than out-group (e.g., groups based on age and nationality in Linville et al., 1989). And people perceive greater trait differentiation among faces of their racial in-group than among out-groups and greater differentiation among faces of a familiar compared with a less familiar racial out-group (Zebrowitz et al., 1993). Third, the familiarity hypothesis implies that if there is little difference in familiarity with the in-group and out-group, then differences in perceived variability should be relatively weak. College students report approximately equal levels of familiarity with members of both genders. As predicted by the familiarity hypothesis, differences in perceived variability of gender groups are relatively weak and frequently nonsignificant (Linville et al., 1989; Linville et al., 1996; Park & Judd, 1990). Finally, the predicted link between frequency of exposure and perceived variability is supported at the individual level. In a study of Irish and American students, perceived out-group variability correlated .49 with the number of out-group people they had met and correlated .40 with the number of people they knew well (Linville & Fischer, 1993a). Similarly, in a study of Hindu and Muslim students in Bangladesh, the quantity of contact with the religious out-group was the best predictor of perceived out-group variability (Islam & Hewstone, 1993). There are exceptions to this pattern (e.g., Jones et al., 1981), but on the whole, evidence regarding natural social groups supports a link between greater familiarity and greater perceived variability.

Research also supports a link between familiarity and another measure of homogeneity—perceived covariation among the features of group members (Linville et al., 1996). Individuals perceived greater covariation among features of out-group members. In more direct tests of the link, those with greater familiarity or experience with a group perceived lower covariation among features of the group. For example, for both young and older participants, those with greater familiarity with an age group perceived lower covariation among features for the group. Also, for business people, those with a greater number of years of business experience perceived lower covariation among features of types of people in business. Controlling for familiarity or experience eliminated all significant group differences in perceived covariation, suggesting that familiarity is a mediator of perceived covariation.

Our PDIST computer simulation model of exemplar processing provides a working model of how greater familiarity might lead to greater variability in perceived distributions (Linville et al., 1989).

PDIST combines a simple exemplar memory model with plausible assumptions about storage and retrieval. Computer simulation experiments show that the greater the number of category exemplars to which PDIST is exposed, the greater the variability and differentiation of the perceived distributions of features (e.g., intelligence) it generates (Linville et al., 1989). Thus, PDIST implies that greater familiarity with in-groups is sufficient to lead to an out-group homogeneity effect.

There has been some confusion about this point, partly because of confusion about the analogy between statistical sampling and memory-based judgment. It is well-known that sample variance underestimates population variance by a factor of $(n - 1)/n$, where n is the sample size. In a social perception context, the set of category exemplars stored or activated in memory can be viewed as a sample from a larger population of exemplars potentially describing the social group. Those with greater familiarity with a group are likely to have a larger sample of stored exemplars. Linville et al. (1989) assumed that people generate perceived frequency distributions of feature values using the sample of category exemplars retrieved from memory. The variance of a perceived frequency distribution constructed in this fashion naturally underestimates the population variance. The smaller the sample of exemplars, the greater the degree of underestimation. Because greater familiarity leads to the retrieval of more exemplars in memory, familiar categories are perceived to be more variable than unfamiliar ones.

The tendency to underestimate the variance of unfamiliar groups arises not because the sample variance statistic is biased, as Park et al. (1991) suggested, but rather because people base their judgments about a group on a small sample of exemplars from the larger group. This can be viewed as another instance of the well-documented "law of small numbers" (Kahneman & Tversky, 1972). People fail to adjust their judgments to allow for the effects of sample size. Instead, they estimate probabilities and generate frequency distributions on the basis of the data that are accessible in memory. In the present context, this contributes along with other mechanisms to the out-group homogeneity effect. Because PDIST generates perceived distributions using only information from the set of exemplars retrieved from memory, it provides a plausible mechanism that explains both out-group homogeneity and the law of small numbers.

Greater Exposure to Second-Hand Exemplars of the Out-Group

Learning conditions may differ for in-groups and out-groups, thus leading to biases in perceived variability. Knowledge of social groups is acquired from (a) *first-hand exemplars*, or experiences arising from direct observation or interaction with group members, and (b) *second-hand exemplars*, or indirect experiences conveyed in statements by family, friends, and others, or images and stories depicted in news and entertainment media (e.g., movies, TV, literature, folk tales; Linville & Fischer, 1993a). Second-hand exemplars are often stereotypic in nature, failing to convey the real diversity of groups. For example, a person whose knowledge of physicians is based primarily on characters depicted on television series might conclude that most physicians live from medical crisis to medical crisis. Similarly, the view of minorities on television greatly underrepresents true diversity of these groups. Linville and Fischer (1993a) suggested that second-hand exemplars comprise a higher proportion of people's knowledge of out-groups. Because second-hand exemplars tend to be more stereotypic in nature, this should cause people to perceive less variability in the out-group. Park, Judd, and Wolsko (1997) suggest that learning about stereotypes through abstract knowledge rather than actual contact leads to more extreme stereotyping of the group, more subtyping of a disconfirming member, and thus less stereotype.

Prototype-First Learning Conditions

Another difference in learning conditions concerns whether people's first knowledge of a group is based on socially conveyed stereotypes or on direct experience with members of a group. Park and Hastie (1987) compared variability estimates under two conditions. In the first, individuals learned the category prototype, then they were shown a set of exemplars. In the second, individuals were exposed to a set of exemplars, then they were shown the prototype. Persons who saw the

443

prototype first perceived less variability in the group. Apparently, learning the prototype first makes it more salient and thus leads to lower estimates of variability. One interesting implication is that people are more likely to learn prototypic information first for out-groups but exemplar information first for in-groups. If so, this provides a possible mechanism leading to greater perceived homogeneity among out-group members. This mechanism is related to the second-hand exemplars mechanism (Linville & Fischer, 1993a) because a group prototype is an extreme form of a second-hand exemplar.

Greater Attention to Individuating Features of the In-Group

Attentional factors also contribute to perceived variability. People give greater attention to individuating features of in-group members, leading to the perception that in-group members are less similar to one another, which is one manifestation of the out-group homogeneity effect. For example, people encode and thus recall group membership (e.g., gender) equally for in-groups and out-groups, but they recall individuating features that distinguish among members (e.g., profession) better for in-groups (Park & Rothbart, 1982).

Tom Ostrom, Constantine Sedikides, and their colleagues provided further evidence that perceivers individuate in-group members more than out-group members (Ostrom, Carpenter, Sedikides, & Li, 1993; Sedikides, 1996). They found that in-group information is organized in terms of person categories, whereas out-group information is organized in terms of stereotypic attributes. Searching such cognitive structures produces individuated information for the in-group and attribute-based similarities for the out-group, resulting in greater perceived in-group variability. Differential familiarity appears to be one mediator of this effect (Sedikides, 1996). Gender-typed people individuate their gender in-group more than their out-group, as suggested by the model; however, androgynous people are equally likely to individuate both the in-group and out-group (Carpenter, 1993). Group status also appears to be an important factor. Members of a high-status group individuate more their in-group, but members of a low status group individuate more the out-group (Sedikides, 1997).

Differential Processing of In-Group and Out-Group Variability

Park and Judd (1990) proposed that people use different processes when judging the variability of in-groups and out-groups. They suggested that judgments of out-group variability are based mainly on on-line abstractions of the variability of the group, whereas judgments of in-group variability are based on a combination of group level abstraction and exemplars retrieved from memory. Two questions naturally arise. First, why are people more likely to retrieve exemplars of the in-group? Judd and Park (1988, Park & Judd, 1990) suggested that people naturally think of the self as an exemplar of the in-group and that this evokes retrieval of other in-group exemplars. As suggested by this hypothesis, Park and Judd (1990) found that perceived in-group variability was significantly correlated with the extent to which a perceiver's self-description deviated from the perceiver's prototype for the in-group. In a similar spirit, Linville et al. (1989) suggested that the large number of exemplars of the self (in varied contexts) is likely to lead to greater perceived variability of in-groups. In short, the presence of the self in the in-group is likely to evoke exemplar processing when considering the in-group.

A second question concerning Judd and Park's (1988) hypothesis is why should considering a mix of exemplars and abstracted variability lead to greater perceived variability than considering abstracted impressions of variability alone? Judd and Park's model implicitly assumes that exemplar-based variability judgments are larger than on-line abstractions of variability. It is not clear why, however. This is an interesting but untested assumption of their model.

Incentives to Make Distinctions

Because people usually have more contact with in-group members, they tend to have greater incentives to make distinctions among in-group members; for example, psychologists have more incentives to make distinctions among types of psychologists than do sociologists (Linville et

445

al., 1989; Linville et al., 1986). This could lead to the OHE if people tend to lump a large proportion of out-group members into a few categories. As suggested by this hypothesis, Kraus et al. (1993) showed that people spontaneously generate more feature levels regarding in-groups than out-groups, a finding they argue provides at least a partial explanation for the OHE.

Social Identity

Ostrom and Sedikides (1992) discussed a number of need-based explanations for perceived group variability, including a need for social identity (see Simon, 1992b, for a review), a need for uniqueness (Brewer, 1993; Quattrone & Jones, 1980; Snyder & Fromkin, 1980), and a need to justify in-group favoritism and out-group hostility (Wilder, 1986). Most of the empirical research from a social/motivational perspective has focused on the role of social identity processes (Brown & Wootton-Millward, 1993; Simon, 1992b; Tajfel, 1978).

As noted earlier, a reversal of the OHE—perceived in-group homogeneity—occurs in at least two situations. One involves relative group size—smaller in-groups perceive themselves to be more homogeneous than larger out-groups; the other involves attribute relevance—people show in-group homogeneity on attributes central to the group's identity. Social identity has been proposed as the mechanism underlying both of these effects.

In terms of the group-size effect, Simon and Brown (1987) suggested that in-group homogeneity may be a way a minority group boosts its solidarity and identity in response to a threat to group identity posed by its smaller size and (in many cases) lack of power. As this suggests, minority or smaller groups show greater group identification (Brown & Smith, 1989; Simon & Brown, 1987; Simon & Pettigrew, 1990). More direct evidence comes from the positive relationship between strength of group identification and in-group homogeneity (Kelly, 1988; Simon & Brown, 1987; Simon & Pettigrew, 1990). The motivational impact of social identity is illustrated in a study by Simon and Brown (1987). They varied the size of the groups to which participants were assigned, but also included a control condition in which participants acted as observers instead of members of a particular group. Even though this control group observed the same group size information as the group members, they failed to rate the smaller group as more homogeneous. Actual group members did show this group-size effect, suggesting that the group identity of belonging to one of these minimal groups had an impact on perceived group variability.

These findings stimulated a debate over the source of in-group homogeneity among minority group members. On the basis of social identity theory, members of a minority group faced with a large, dominant out-group should be motivated to view themselves as relatively homogeneous. Bartsch and Judd (1993; Judd & Bartsch, 1995) pointed out that demonstrations of the effect have confounded strong social identity with the minority status of the in-group and presented data suggesting that smaller in-group size is the key to the in-group homogeneity effect. Simon (1995) and Haslam and Oakes (1995) disputed Bartsch and Judd's conclusions by pointing to other findings that cannot be accounted for on the basis of minority status alone. Whatever the resolution to this controversy, it appears that when the in-group is a minority group and also is central to social identity, then in-group homogeneity often occurs.

In terms of the relevance-of-group-attributes effect, Brown and Wootton-Millward (1993) discussed how social identity forces lead to in-group homogeneity on key group attributes. As group membership becomes psychologically salient, members may perceive themselves to be "psychologically interchangeable" or "depersonalized," particularly on key attributes for defining that group (Turner, Hogg, Oakes, Reicher, & Wetherell, 1987). This may increase perceived in-group homogeneity. Lee (1995) manipulated the salience of ethnic identity for a group of Chinese students studying in the United States using group membership items on a questionnaire. Those experiencing the group salience manipulation perceived higher in-group homogeneity.

These findings for both factors increasing in-group homogeneity support Brewer's (1993) theory of optimal distinctiveness. As people balance the competing needs for social identity and social distinctiveness, in-group homogeneity should arise when identity with the in-group is strong and the in-group is distinctive (or attention is on features that are distinctive of the group).

PROGRESS: CONSEQUENCES OF PERCEIVED VARIABILITY

Although the field has made substantial progress in terms of cognitive and social theoretical models, measurement, and determinants of perceived variability, we have made only limited progress toward learning the consequences of variability. Greater attention to consequences, however, is likely to be fruitful given the results of several initial lines of research. For example, perceiving a group as more homogeneous (e.g., the out-group) influences aspects of stereotyping and group perception, including generalization, categorization, and evaluative judgments.

Generalization

Some of the earliest and most studied consequences involve generalization inferences. Generalizations from an individual to the group are important because encountering a counterstereotypical member may change one's group stereotype, or overgeneralizing the behavior of one member may lead to inaccurate perceptions of the characteristics of the group. Generalizations from the group to an individual have important implications for applying group stereotypes to individual members. Logical considerations as well as the laws of probability imply that the more homogeneous a group, the more one should generalize from an individual to the group as a whole and from the group to an individual member. In the individual-to-group case, characteristics of a single member are quite informative about the prototypical characteristics of the group when the group is homogeneous. In the group-to-individual case, one can more confidently apply the group stereotype to a single member when the group is homogeneous. Research supports these intuitions.

Individual-to-Group Generalization

Early research shows that people are more likely to generalize from the characteristics of a single member to the group as a whole when the member is from the out-group. For example, Princeton and Rutgers students viewing a student making a choice during a psychology experiment estimated that a higher proportion of students from that university would make the same decision as the one they observed when the student was an out-group member. That is, Princeton students made stronger generalizations about Rutgers students, and Rutgers students made stronger generalizations about Princeton students (Quattrone & Jones, 1980). Nisbett and his colleagues extended this finding (Nisbett et al., 1983). After inducing participants to contemplate the central tendency of the group (which should make the homogeneity of the group even more salient), participants increased their generalizing from one member to the group as a whole.

More recent findings suggest that generalization depends on the stereotypicality of the information as well as group membership. When a group is homogeneous, people are more likely to generalize stereotype-consistent information about an individual to the group as a whole and less likely to generalize from counterstereotypic information about an individual to the group (Park & Hastie, 1987). Participants read a series of behaviors performed by a group, reflecting either a high or low degree of variability among the members in terms of intelligence and sociability. When told of a member who was honest (which is consistent with the group stereotype), individuals estimated that a larger number of members were also honest when the group was homogeneous. When the member was hostile (inconsistent with the group stereotype), individuals estimated that fewer other members were hostile when the group was homogeneous. Thus, when a group is homogeneous, people are more likely to generalize a typical trait of one member to the rest of the group and less likely to generalize an atypical trait of one member to the rest of the group.

Group variability similarly influences revision in one's belief about group attributes (Rehder & Hastie, 1996). Participants saw a set of group exemplars from 1985 and were asked to make mean and 95% confidence range estimates. Then they were shown one, two, or three new exemplars from the group in 1995 and asked to make new mean and range estimates for 1995. The more variable the group in 1985, the less people revised their beliefs about the mean and range of the 1995 distribution. Again, greater group variability reduced the degree to which people revised their beliefs in light of new data about individual group members.

Group-to-Individual Generalization

A similar pattern occurs for generalizations from the group to an individual. When a group is homogeneous, people are more likely to apply group attributes (e.g., the group stereotype) to an individual member (Krueger & Rothbart, 1988; Ryan et al., 1996). For example, the more stereotypic people perceived Asian Americans or African Americans, the more they generalized a group stereotype to individual members who performed ambiguous actions (Ryan et al., 1996). Greater perceived group variability moderated this effect, reducing the tendency to generalize group stereotypes to individual members. Thus, greater stereotypicality and greater homogeneity leads to stronger group-to-individual generalization of stereotypes.

Typicality plays an important role in group-to-individual generalizations (Lambert, 1995; Lambert & Wyer, 1990). When a group is homogeneous, typicality plays a "gatekeeper" role. If a member of a homogeneous group performs an act typical of the group, perceivers ascribe other group attributes to the member, but if the member performs an atypical act, no such inferences are made. For example, people liked an individual who performed an act typical of a homogeneous, liked group, but disliked an individual who performed an act typical of a homogeneous, disliked group (Lambert, 1995). When the group was heterogeneous, however, typicality had no effect (atypical acts are expected if a group is heterogeneous). Instead, liking of the individual depended only on liking for the group and the behavior.

Categorization

Basic categorization research revealed that the greater the variability of a category, the more likely a somewhat atypical new exemplar is to be classified as an instance of the category (for reviews, see Medin, 1989; Smith & Medin, 1981). Similar effects arise in judgments of social category membership. When a group is homogeneous, people are less likely to classify a person with atypical group attributes as a member of the group (Park & Hastie, 1987), and they are quicker to judge an atypical member to be atypical (Lambert, 1995). This implies that atypical out-group members are unlikely to be classified as members of their group, reinforcing out-group homogeneity as well as the group stereotype.

Evaluative Judgments

Complexity–Evaluative Extremity

Early work has also focused on evaluative consequences of category variability. For example, the less complex people perceive a category, the more extreme they evaluate category members: the complexity–extremity effect. Greater complexity entails using more independent features to represent category members and thus making greater distinctions among members and subtypes within a category, which is closely akin to variability. The more distinct features one uses to represent category members, the more likely one is to perceive a category member as good in some respects but bad in others, which will tend to moderate overall judgment.

In support of this, those less complex in their thinking about the category of older adults were more extreme in their rating of specific members ($r = -.65$), more positive about a favorable older person, and more negative about an unfavorable older person (Linville, 1982). Because people tend to have less complex representations of out-groups, they make more extreme judgments about out-group than in-group members, judgments that are more extremely positive toward a favorable member and more extremely negative toward an unfavorable member (Linville, 1982; Linville & Jones, 1980; Linville & Salovey, 1982). For example, White individuals rated a strong Black law school applicant higher than a comparable White applicant, yet rated a weak Black applicant lower than a comparable White applicant (Linville & Jones, 1980). Similarly, both young and older people rated members of their age out-group more extremely. For example, young people rated a favorable older person more positively and an unfavorable older person more negatively than a comparable younger person (Linville, 1982), and older people rated young people more extremely than comparable older people (Linville & Salovey, 1982). Finally, when complexity was manipulated by drawing people's attention to two versus six features of stimuli, such as chocolate chip cookies (or law school essays), those attending to fewer features made more extreme evaluations—more positive about the cookies (essays) they liked most and more negative about the cookies (essays) they liked least (Linville 1982; Linville & Jones, 1980). Thus, the complexity–extremity effect emerges when lower complexity is manipulated by out-group membership, measured as an individual difference in category representation, or manipulated by directing attention to a smaller number of features. In each case, lower complexity leads to more extreme overall judgments about individual members.

Covariation–Evaluative Extremity

Current research shows another evaluative consequence—a covariation–extremity effect. The greater covariation people perceive among features for a group, the more extremely they evaluate individual members (Linville & Fischer, 1993b; Linville & Fischer, 1996). Why should perceived covariation be linked with judgmental extremity? If one perceives high covariation among features, especially in the sense of perceiving group members as having evaluatively consistent profiles of features, then a new target may be encoded as more consistent—either good in most respects, bad in most respects, or average in most respects. The result is more extreme overall judgments about targets. On the other hand, if one perceives low covariation among features, then a new target may be encoded as good in some respects but bad in others. The result is more moderate overall judgment.

In support of this finding, participants generated subtypes of college-aged and retired adults. From these patterns of features describing various subtypes, we calculated both an individual's average absolute correlation ($Avg|R|$) between pairs of features reflecting covariation per se and the average correlation ($Avg\ R$) reflecting degree to which features covary in an evaluatively consistent fashion. Larger values reflect greater homogeneity in the sense that category features are more redundant. Participants also constructed perceived frequency distributions over each single feature. From these we calculated the standard deviation (*SD*) of their perceived distributions, a traditional measure of single-feature variability. Finally, participants read a series of vignettes, each describing a generally positive person (e.g., a target overcame a fear of heights to join friends on a picnic) or generally negative person (e.g., a target was awkward and withdrawn at a dinner party), and then made an overall favorability rating of each target. Pretesting showed the vignettes to be equally descriptive of young or older people.

Supporting a covariation–extremity effect, those perceiving higher covariation among features of a group were more extreme in their evaluations (Linville & Fischer, 1996). They displayed a greater range between their evaluations of the positive and negative targets, judging a positive target more positively and a negative target more negatively. As expected, the covariation–extremity effect was stronger for *Avg R*, reflecting evaluative consistency. In terms of a mechanism, familiarity with a group was a key factor. Those less familiar with a group perceived greater covariation among features of its subtypes and also were more extreme in judging individual members. Path analyses supported the hypothesis that perceived covariation mediated the link between familiarity and judgmental extremity. In contrast, perceived variability (*SD*) of individual features was not a mediator of the familiarity–judgment link.

This new research suggests that perceived covariation may have at least as much impact as perceived single-feature variability on intergroup judgment and behavior. Greater familiarity with a group leads to lower perceived covariation and less extreme judgments of group members, with perceived covariation an important mediator of this link between familiarity and judgmental extremity.

NED'S REACTIONS TO HOW THE FIELD HAS PROGRESSED

I am mentally back in Ned's office at Duke, and he has listened to me describe changes in the field. Let me end by sharing what I think Ned would be telling me in his reactions. As these examples illustrate, there is vitality—including lively debates in the field, more than one would expect from the original, simple out-group homogeneity effect. Trying to understand the OHE has been a catalyst, first for taking categorization models seriously in understanding stereotyping and second for integrating cognitive and motivational factors.

But I hear the advice that Ned gave me early in my career when we were writing a draft of our first article. "Tell a story," he advised. In applying his advice to the field, I think we have missed parts of the variability story. I believe that his critique would be less about what we have done than about what we have so far left out of the story. From Ned's perspective, let me suggest several of the missing pieces of the story.

1. *Focus more on the consequences of perceived variability.* Ned's work on attribution, person perception, and self-presentation, as well as his early work on group variability, focused on the consequences of perceptions. Most models and empirical work in the group variability area have focused on determinants of perceived variability. Far less attention has been paid to a range of potential consequences of perceived variability, for example, effects on judgment, evaluation, inference, attribution, choice, affect, and behavior. Currently there is more speculation than empirical fact. The field will benefit from research that fills this gap. By exploring consequences of perceived variability, we may also establish closer links with other research areas in social psychology that grabbed Ned's attention—research on the self, social interaction, attributions, and attitudes.

2. *Integrate cognitive and motivational mechanisms.* In his work on attribution biases, person perception, self-handicapping, and ingratiation, Ned painted us a picture of an active perceiver. In the variability area, the perceiver is also an active player, and the in-group perceiver is actually part of what is being perceived—the in-group. Thus, the interaction of cognitive factors with social identity needs is important. For example, when group identity is important, people may attend more to the common features shared by most mem-

bers; when group identity is not important, people may attend to features that individuate members from one another (e.g., Smith & Zarate, 1992). This interaction of cognitive, social, and motivational mechanisms will be a central focus of future work.

3. *Where is the behavior?* The field has progressed theoretically to a point where we should be focusing more on links between perceptions of variability and intergroup behavior. For example, how does perceived variability influence outcomes such as prejudice, discrimination, intergroup conflict, nonverbal behavior, resource allocation, judgment and evaluation, competitive versus cooperative behavior, power strategies, persuasion strategies, or hiring and promotion decisions?

There is a second place where attention to behavior may be fruitful. For Ned, a major appeal of attribution theory was its focus on how people perceive and interpret behavioral information. By focusing mainly on perceived variability of the traits of group members, the in-group/out-group area may have overlooked the perceived variability of the behavior of individual group members (e.g., the variability in the average number of hours professors spend working per week). We may also have overlooked variability in the behavior performed by a single group member over time (e.g., variability in the number of beers an Irish student consumes per week over the course of a semester).

So the group variability story is not yet complete. Overall, though, I think Ned would be pleased, and a little surprised, at the heterogeneity of the theories, measures, and findings that grew out of a simple out-group homogeneity effect.

REFERENCES

Bartsch, R. A., & Judd, C. M. (1993). Majority–minority status and perceived ingroup variability revisited. *European Journal of Social Psychology, 23*, 471–483.

Brewer, M. B. (1991). The social self: On being the same and different at the same time. *Personality and Social Psychology Bulletin, 17*, 475–482.

Brewer, M. B. (1993). Social identity, distinctiveness, and in-group homogeneity. *Social Cognition, 11,* 150–164.

Brewer, M. B., & Kramer, R. M. (1985). The psychology of intergroup attitudes and behaviors. *Annual Review of Psychology, 36,* 219–243.

Brewer, M. B., & Lui, L. (1984). Categorization of the elderly by the elderly: Effects of perceiver's category membership. *Personality and Social Psychology Bulletin, 10,* 585–595.

Brown, R., & Smith, A. (1989). Perceptions of and by minority groups: The case of women in academia. *European Journal of Social Psychology, 19,* 61–75.

Brown, R., & Wootton-Millward, L. (1993). Perceptions of group homogeneity during group formation and change. *Social Cognition, 11,* 126–149.

Carpenter, S. (1993). Organization of in-group and out-group information: The influence of gender-role orientation. *Social Cognition, 11,* 70–91.

Ford, T. E., & Stangor, C. (1992). The role of diagnosticity in stereotype formation: Perceiving group means and variances. *Journal of Personality and Social Psychology, 63,* 356–367.

Fried, L. S., & Holyoak, K. J. (1984). Induction of category distributions: A framework for classification learning. *Journal of Experimental Psychology: Learning, Memory, and Cognition, 10,* 234–257.

Goethals, G. R., Allison, S. J., & Frost, M. (1979). Perceptions of the magnitude and diversity of social support. *Journal of Experimental and Social Psychology, 15,* 570–581.

Hamilton, D. L., & Sherman, J. W. (1984). Stereotypes. In R. S. Wyer, Jr. & T. K. Srull (Eds.), *Handbook of social cognition* (2nd ed., Vol. 2, pp. 1–68). Hillsdale, NJ: Erlbaum.

Haslam, S. A., & Oakes, P. J. (1995). How context–independent is the outgroup homogeneity effect? A response to Bartsch and Judd, *European Journal of Social Psychology, 24,* 469–475.

Hilton, J. L., & von Hippel, W. (1996). Stereotypes. *Annual Review of Psychology, 47,* 237–271.

Hintzman, D. L. (1986). "Scheme abstraction" in a multiple–trace memory model. *Psychological Review, 93,* 411–428.

Islam, M. R., & Hewstone, M. (1993). Dimensions of contact as predictors of intergroup anxiety, perceived out-group variability, and out-group attitude: An integrative model. *Personality and Social Psychology Bulletin, 19,* 700–710.

Jones, E. E., Wood, G. C., & Quattrone, G. A. (1981). Perceived variability of personal characteristics in in-groups and out-groups: The role of knowledge and evaluation. *Personality and Social Psychology Bulletin, 7,* 523–528.

Judd, C. M., & Bartsch, R. A. (1995). Cats, dogs, and the OH effect: A reply to Simon and to Haslam and Oakes. *European Journal of Social Psychology, 25,* 477–480.

Judd, C. M., & Park, B. (1988). Out-group homogeneity: Judgments of variability at the individual and group levels. *Journal of Personality and Social Psychology, 54,* 778–788.

Judd, C. M., Park, B., Ryan, C. S., Brauer, M., & Kraus, S. (1995). Stereotypes and ethnocentrism: Diverging interethnic perceptions of African American and White American youth. *Journal of Personality and Social Psychology, 69,* 460–481.

Judd, C. M., Ryan, C. S., & Park, B. (1991). Accuracy in the judgments of in-group and out-group variability. *Journal of Personality and Social Psychology, 61,* 366–379.

Kahneman, D., & Tversky, A. (1972). Subjective probability: A judgment of representativeness. *Cognitive Psychology, 3,* 430–454.

Kelly, C. (1988). Intergroup differentiation in a political context. *British Journal of Social Psychology, 27,* 319–332.

Kelly, C. (1989). Political identity and perceived intragroup homogeneity. *British Journal of Social Psychology, 28,* 239–250.

Kraus, S., Ryan, C. S., Judd, C. M., Hastie, R., & Park, B. (1993). Use of mental frequency distributions to represent variability among members of social categories. *Social Cognition, 11,* 22–43.

Krueger, J., & Rothbart, M. (1988). Use of categorical and individuating information in making inferences about personality. *Journal of Personality and Social Psychology, 55,* 187–195.

Lambert, A. J. (1995). Stereotypes and social judgment: The consequences of group variability. *Journal of Personality and Social Psychology, 68,* 388–403.

Lambert, A. J., & Wyer, R. S., Jr. (1990). Stereotypes and social judgment: The effects of typicality and group heterogeneity. *Journal of Personality and Social Psychology, 59,* 676–691.

Lee, Y. (1995). Perceived in-group homogeneity as a function of group membership salience and stereotype threat. *Personality and Social Psychology Bulletin, 21,* 612–621.

Linville, P. W. (1982). The complexity–extremity effect and age-based stereotyping. *Journal of Personality and Social Psychology, 42,* 193–211.

Linville, P. W., & Fischer, G. W. (1993a). Exemplar and abstraction models of perceived group variability and stereotypicality. *Social Cognition, 11,* 92–125.

Linville, P. W., & Fischer, G. W. (1993b). *Perceived variation, covariation, and extremity of judgment about group members.* Paper presented at the Duck Conference on Social Cognition, Duck, NC.

Linville, P. W., & Fischer, G. W. (1996). *Perceived variability, covariance, and judgments about group members.* Unpublished paper, Duke University, Durham, NC.

Linville, P. W., & Fischer, G. W. (1997). Group variability and covariation: Effects on intergroup judgment and behavior. In C. Sedikides, C. A. Insko, & J. Schopler (Eds.), *Intergroup cognition and behavior* (pp. 123–150). Mahwah, NJ: Erlbaum.

Linville, P. W., Fischer, G. W., & Salovey, P. (1989). Perceived distributions of the characteristics of ingroup and outgroup members: Empirical evidence and a computer simulation. *Journal of Personality and Social Psychology, 57,* 165–188.

Linville, P. W., Fischer, G. W., & Yoon, C. (1996). Perceived covariation among the features of ingroup and outgroup members: An outgroup covariation effect. *Journal of Personality and Social Psychology, 6,* 123–150.

Linville, P. W., & Jones, E. E. (1980). Polarized appraisals of out-group members. *Journal of Personality and Social Psychology, 38,* 689–703.

Linville, P. W., & Salovey, P. (1982). *The complexity–extremity effect: Age-based perceptions of the elderly.* Unpublished manuscript, Yale University, New Haven, CT.

Linville, P. W., Salovey, P., & Fischer, G. W. (1986). Stereotyping and perceived distributions of social characteristics: An application to ingroup-outgroup perception. In J. Dovidio & S. L. Gaertner (Eds.), *Prejudice, discrimination, and racism* (pp. 165–208). San Diego, CA: Academic Press.

Lorenzi-Cioldi, F., Eagly, A. H., & Stewart, T. L. (1995). Homogeneity of gender groups in memory. *Journal of Experimental Social Psychology, 31*, 193–217.

Mackie, D. M., & Asuncion, A. G. (1990). On-line and memory-based modification of attitudes. *Journal of Personality and Social Psychology, 59*, 5–16.

Mackie, D. M., Sherman, J. W., & Worth, L. T. (1993). On-line and memory-based processes in group variability judgments. *Social Cognition, 11*, 44–69.

Medin, D. L. (1989). Concepts and conceptual structure. *American Psychologist, 44*, 1469–1481.

Messick, D. M., & Mackie, D. M. (1989). Intergroup relations. *Annual Review of Psychology, 40*, 40–45.

Mullen, B., & Hu, L. (1989). Perceptions of ingroup and outgroup variability: A meta-analytic integration. *Basic and Applied Social Psychology, 10*, 233–252.

Nisbett, R. E., Krantz, D. H., Jepson, C., & Kunda, Z. (1983). The use of statistical heuristics in everyday intuitive reasoning. *Psychological Review, 90*, 339–363.

Nisbett, R. E., & Kunda, Z. (1985). Perceptions of social distributions. *Journal of Personality and Social Psychology, 48*, 297–311.

Ostrom, T. M., Carpenter, S. L., Sedikides, C., & Li, F. (1993). Differential processing of in-group and out-group information. *Journal of Personality and Social Psychology, 64*, 21–34.

Ostrom, T. M., & Sedikides, C. (1992). Out-group homogeneity effects in natural and minimal groups, *Psychological Bulletin, 112*, 536–552.

Park, B., & Hastie, R. (1987). Perception of variability in category development: Instance-versus abstraction-based stereotypes. *Journal of Personality and Social Psychology, 53*, 621–635.

Park, B., & Judd, C. M. (1990). Measures and models of perceived group variability. *Journal of Personality and Social Psychology, 59*, 173–191.

Park, B., Judd, C. M., & Ryan, C. S. (1991). Social categorization and the representation of variability information. In W. Stroebe & M. Hewstone

(Eds.), *European review of social psychology* (Vol. 2, 211–245). Chichester, England: Wiley.

Park, B., Judd, C. M., & Wolsko, C. (1997, October). *Stereotype change as a function of stereotype acquisition, group perceptions, and the judged typicality of new disconfirming group members.* Paper presented at the Society for Experimental Social Psychologists, Toronto, Canada.

Park, B., & Rothbart, M. (1982). Perception of out-group homogeneity and levels of social categorization: Memory for the subordinate attributes of in-group and out-group members. *Journal of Personality and Social Psychology, 42,* 1051–1068.

Park, B., Ryan, C. S., & Judd, C. M. (1992). Role of meaningful subgroups in explaining differences in perceived variability for in-groups and out-groups. *Journal of Personality and Social Psychology, 63,* 553–567.

Posner, M. I., & Keele, S. W. (1968). On the genesis of abstract ideas. *Journal of Experimental Psychology, 77,* 353–363.

Quattrone, G. A. (1986). On the perception of a group's variability. In S. Worchel & W. Austin (Eds.), *The psychology of intergroup relations* (Vol. 2, pp. 25–48). Chicago: Nelson-Hall.

Quattrone, G. A., & Jones, E. E. (1980). The perception of variability within ingroups and outgroups: Implications for the Law of Small Numbers. *Journal of Personality and Social Psychology, 38,* 141–152.

Rehder, B., & Hastie, R. (1996). *The moderating influence of variability on belief revision.* Unpublished manuscript, Department of Psychology, University of Colorado, Boulder.

Ryan, C. S., Judd, C. M., & Park, B. (1996). Effects of racial stereotypes on judgments of individuals: The moderating role of perceived group variability. *Journal of Experimental Social Psychology, 32,* 71–103.

Schneider, D. J. (1991). Social cognition. *Annual Review of Psychology, 42,* 527–561.

Sedikides, C. (1996). *Differential processing of ingroup and outgroup information: The role of familiarity.* Unpublished manuscript, University of North Carolina, Chapel Hill.

Sedikides, C. (1997). Differential processing of ingroup and outgroup information: The role of relative group status in permeable boundary groups. *European Journal of Social Psychology, 27,* 121–144.

Sedikides, C., & Ostrom, T. M. (1993). Perceptions of group variability: Moving from an uncertain crawl to a purposeful stride. *Social Cognition, 11,* 165–174.

Sherman S. J., Judd, C. M., & Park, B. (1989). Social cognition. *Annual Review of Psychology, 40,* 281–326.

Simon, B. (1992a). Intragroup differentiation in terms of in-group and out-group attributes. *European Journal of Social Psychology, 22,* 407–413.

Simon, B. (1992b). The perception of ingroup and outgroup homogeneity: Reintroducing the intergroup context. In W. Stroebe & M. Hewstone (Eds.), *European review of social psychology* (Vol. 3, pp. 1–30). Chichester, England: Wiley.

Simon, B. (1995). The perception of ingroup and outgroup homogeneity: On the confounding of group size, level of abstractness and frame of reference: A reply to Bartsch and Judd. *European Journal of Social Psychology, 25,* 463–468.

Simon, B., & Brown, R. (1987). Perceived homogeneity in minority–majority contexts. *Journal of Personality and Social Psychology, 53,* 703–711.

Simon, B., & Pettigrew, T. F. (1990). Social identity and perceived group homogeneity: Evidence for the in-group homogeneity effect. *European Journal of Social Psychology, 20,* 269–286.

Smith, E. E., & Medin, D. L. (1981). *Categories and concepts.* Cambridge, MA: Harvard University Press.

Smith, E. R., & Zarate, M. A. (1992). Exemplar–based model of social judgment. *Psychological Review, 99,* 33–21.

Snyder, C. R., & Fromkin, H. L. (1980). *Uniqueness: The human pursuit of difference.* New York: Plenum Press.

Tajfel, H. (1978). *Differentiation between social groups.* San Diego, CA: Academic Press.

Tajfel, H. (1982). Social psychology of intergroup relations. In M. R. Rosenzweig & L. W. Porter (Eds.), *Annual review of psychology* (Vol. 33, pp. 1–39). Palo Alto, CA: Annual Reviews.

Turner, J. C., Hogg, M. A., Oakes, P. J., Reicher, S. D., & Wetherell, M. S. (1987). *Rediscovering the social group: A self-categorization theory.* Oxford: Basil Blackwell.

Wilder, D. A. (1986). Social categorization: Implications for creation and reduction of intergroup conflict. In L. Berkowitz (Ed.), *Advances in experimental social psychology* (Vol. 19, 293–355). San Diego, CA: Academic Press.

Zebrowitz, L. A., Montepare, J. M., & Lee, H. K. (1993). They don't all look alike: Individual impressions of other racial groups. *Journal of Personality and Social Psychology, 65,* 85–101.

The Out-Group Homogeneity Effect and Beyond: On Linville's "The Heterogeneity of Homogeneity"

Marilynn B. Brewer

I n many ways, the out-group homogeneity effect is characteristic of the "Jones influence" on the course of research and theory in social psychology. The spreading activation begins with identifying an intriguing phenomenon; this engages a search for mechanisms that underlie the phenomenon and ultimately results in a reconceptualization that embeds the original phenomenon in some broader theory of social behavior.

Linville's (see chapter 8) excellent review of research on the out-group homogeneity effect provides a faithful history of the multi-directional influence of the seminal studies by Jones and Quattrone (Jones, Wood, & Quattrone, 1981; Quattrone & Jones, 1980) that led social psychologists down the path toward understanding the perception of group variability. In this brief commentary, I expand on several of the points made in Linville's chapter that illustrate how far we have progressed along the road to a general theory of how information about social groups and social categories is encoded and represented in memory. More specifically, I place the out-group homogeneity effect (OHE) in the context of two major themes that are currently prominent in social cognition theory and research—*motivated cognition* (cf. Fiske,

1992, 1993; Levine, Resnick, & Higgins, 1993) and *dual process* models of person memory (cf. Brewer, 1988; Fiske & Pavelchak, 1986; Ostrom, Carpenter, Sedikides, & Li, 1993; Wyer & Martin, 1986).

OHE AS MOTIVATED COGNITION

A number of the research findings associated with experimental studies of the OHE indicate that the perception of variability of social groups is not simply a product of information availability but a reflection of a perceiver's processing goals and his or her relationship to the target group. This is particularly evident in the work cited by Linville demonstrating the presence of *in-group homogeneity effects*—conditions under which in-groups are perceived as less heterogeneous than comparison out-groups (e.g., Kelly, 1989; Simon, 1992).

Elsewhere (Brewer, 1993) I have discussed some of the implications of this reversal effect for reconceptualizing the original phenomenon. Given that the OHE is defined in terms of the difference between perceived variability of in-groups and out-groups, it could just as well have been dubbed the "in-group heterogeneity effect." The labeling tends to shift the focus of attention from questions of why groups are perceived as homogeneous to why they are perceived as heterogeneous. It is possible that the two questions reflect different motivational systems. Motives to attend to information about intragroup variability may derive from needs for self-definition and differentiation from others. Perceived homogeneity, on the other hand, may be driven by motivations to see the group as a single, coherent, or united entity.

The motivation to establish a distinctive or differentiated representation of the self is more likely to affect perceptions of in-groups than of out-groups. Hence, when such motives are engaged, one would expect to observe the characteristic OHE, wherein out-groups are judged to be more homogeneous and in-groups as more heterogeneous. However, motives to perceive groups as coherent entities can apply equally to in-groups and to out-groups (Brewer & Harasty, 1996). Thus, when motives for perceived homogeneity are engaged, one can get any combination of relative variability effects: relative out-group homogeneity, relative in-group homogeneity, or equal homogeneity.

DUAL REPRESENTATIONS

When the OHE was initially documented, explanations implicitly assumed a single-mode representation of group variability information. Variability was presumed to derive either from the set of exemplars that constitute the category representation or from the information embodied in an abstract representation of the category as a whole. In effect, perceived variability was presumed to be a relatively fixed property of the way in which category information was encoded and represented in memory.

The cumulative results of research on the OHE (see Linville, chap. 8), however, are consistent with models of social cognition that hold that the same information can be processed and encoded in different ways simultaneously. For instance, recent research supports the idea that two kinds of representations of information about individual persons are available in memory—one representation that is behavior-based and another that is trait-based—and that these may be accessed independently (Klein & Loftus, 1990; Petzold & Edeler, 1995).

The dual-processing model of person representations (Brewer, 1988) makes a similar argument with respect to the way in which social category information may be stored and utilized. On the one hand, information about an individual's membership in certain social groups can be represented as a *feature* of that individual, a subcomponent of the information associated with the "person node" in memory. On the other hand, the same categorical classification can be stored as part of the information associated with the representation of the category itself, as a component of the "category node" in memory.

Take, as an example, the statement that "Robert is a nurse." This particular piece of information can be associated with other things that are known about Robert and organized in terms of its relationship to other trait and behavioral information that has been encoded about this specific person. This mode of representation is what Brewer (1988) referred to as *person-based* information processing. Alternatively (or in addition), the same piece of information can be associated with information that is known about nurses in general and processed in terms of its consistency or inconsistency with the category prototype (e.g.,

465

nurses are usually women, but some nurses are men, which constitutes a subtype of the general category). This mode of representation is what Brewer (1988) referred to as *category-based* information processing.

AVAILABILITY AND ACCESSIBILITY

If one accepts the argument that category information may have dual representations, then the determinants of perceived category variability will include what representations of that category are available in memory and which of the available representations are accessed at the time the judgment is being made. Accessing categories by searching through individual person representations for category exemplars is more likely to generate information on diversity and variability than accessing a stored prototypic representation of the group as a whole (Judd & Park, 1988), particularly if the category is represented as an undifferentiated entity rather than differentiated into subtypes (Park, Ryan, & Judd, 1992).

Both availability and accessibility are likely to be products of motivated cognition. According to Brewer's (1988) dual process model, person-based information processing is determined by processing goals and the nature of the interaction between the perceiver and the target at the time the information is received. As Linville suggests, first-hand information acquired during the course of personalized interactions is more likely to be stored as person-based representations than second-hand information about social categories or category representatives. Given what is known about social exchange patterns, opportunities for personalized interactions with in-group members are typically greater than for out-group members. Although personalized representations of some out-group members may be formed as well, the greater number of person-based in-group exemplars may make exemplar-based judgments of in-groups more likely than of out-groups.

Even when person-based and category-based representations are both equally available, various motives and processing goals may influence which representation is retrieved at the time a judgment of group variability is called for. Research on in-group homogeneity, for instance, suggests that needs for social identity and intergroup comparison may prime category representations of both in-group and relevant out-groups. Karasawa and Brewer (1996) have argued that the nature of the judgment task or measurement that is used to assess variability may also prompt different retrieval strategies. Measures that call for summary judgments, such as direct ratings of intragroup similarity or stereotype endorsement, may encourage reliance on abstract category representations, whereas measures that rely on estimations of frequency distributions may engage a search for specific category exemplars. These arguments help to account for why different measures of perceived variability are not always highly correlated and may help to explain the apparent "heterogeneity of homogeneity."

BACK TO NED: WHERE'S THE BEHAVIOR?

When Ned Jones agreed to comment on my original dual process model (Brewer, 1988), many of his points were characteristic of the concerns that Linville projects in the closing section of her chapter. To quote Ned (Jones, 1988) directly, "The present dual process model leaves out too much of the point of entry. So many of the really fascinating things that go on in the process of forming an impression happen as information is generated and *initially encoded* (p. 85, emphases added)."

As a closing tribute, I would like to address, at least partially, this challenge from Ned's perspective. The arguments I am making about dual representation suggest that encoding is a multipronged process. Simultaneous with how a behavioral event is encoded is the issue of where that behavior is encoded. In terms of the ultimate consequences of cognitive representations, it may make a great deal of difference whether a behavior is attributed to the actor and stored and integrated into an organized representation of that particular person or whether it is incorporated into a general representation of the social category to which the actor belongs. Ultimately, it is not just a matter of whether a particular behavior is interpreted as "aggressive" but whether the semantic representation of that act is encoded as "he is aggressive" or as "they are aggressive."

REFERENCES

Brewer, M. B. (1988). A dual process model of impression formation. In T. Srull & R. Wyer (Eds.), *Advances in social cognition* (Vol. 1, pp. 1–36). Hillsdale, NJ: Erlbaum.

Brewer, M. B. (1993). Social identity, distinctiveness, and in-group homogeneity. *Social Cognition, 11,* 150–164.

Brewer, M. B., & Harasty, A. S. (1996). Seeing groups as entities: The role of perceiver motivation. In R. M. Sorrentino & E. T. Higgins (Eds.), *Handbook of motivation and cognition: The interpersonal context* (Vol. 3, pp. 347–370). New York: Guilford Press.

Fiske, S. T. (1992). Thinking is for doing: Portraits of social cognition from daguerreotype to laserphoto. *Journal of Personality and Social Psychology, 63,* 877–889.

Fiske, S. T. (1993). Social cognition and social perception. *Annual Review of Psychology, 44,* 155–194.

Fiske, S. T., & Pavelchak, M. A. (1986). Category-based vs. piecemeal-based affective responses: Developments in schema-triggered affect. In R. M. Sorrentino & E. T. Higgins (Eds.), *Handbook of motivation and cognition* (pp. 167–203). New York: Guilford Press.

Jones, E. E. (1988). Impression formation: What do people think about? In T. Srull & R. Wyer (Eds.), *Advances in social cognition* (Vol. 1, pp. 83–89). Hillsdale, NJ: Erlbaum.

Jones, E. E., Wood, G. C., & Quattrone, G. A. (1981). Perceived variability of personal characteristics in in-groups and out-groups: The role of knowledge and evaluation. *Personality and Social Psychology Bulletin, 7,* 523–528.

Judd, C. M., & Park, B. (1988). Out-group homogeneity: Judgments of variability at the individual and group levels. *Journal of Personality and Social Psychology, 54,* 778–788.

Karasawa, M., & Brewer, M. B. (1996). Category size and judgments of variability: The effects of seeing the trees in the forest. *Japanese Psychological Research, 38,* 213–223.

Kelly, C. (1989). Political identity and perceived intragroup homogeneity. *British Journal of Social Psychology, 28,* 239–250.

Klein, S. B., & Loftus, J. (1990). Rethinking the role of organization in person memory: An independent trace store model. *Journal of Personality and Social Psychology, 59,* 400–410.

Levine, J. M., Resnick, L. B., & Higgins, E. T. (1993). Social foundations of cognition. *Annual Review of Psychology, 44,* 585–612.

Ostrom, T. M., Carpenter, S. L., Sedikides, C., & Li, F. (1993). Differential processing of in-group and out-group information. *Journal of Personality and Social Psychology, 64,* 21–34.

Park, B., Ryan, C. S., & Judd, C. M. (1992). Role of meaningful subgroups in explaining differences in perceived variability for in-groups and out-groups. *Journal of Personality and Social Psychology, 63,* 553–567.

Petzold, P., & Edeler, B. (1995). Organization of person memory and retrieval processes in recognition. *European Journal of Social Psychology, 25,* 249–267.

Quattrone, G. A., & Jones, E. E. (1980). The perception of variability within in-groups and out-groups: Implications for the law of small numbers. *Journal of Personality and Social Psychology, 38,* 141–152.

Simon, B. (1992). Intragroup differentiation in terms of in-group and out-group attributes. *European Journal of Social Psychology, 22,* 407–413.

Wyer, R. S., Jr., & Martin, L. L. (1986). Person memory: The role of traits, group stereotypes and specific behaviors in the cognitive representation of persons. *Journal of Personality and Social Psychology, 50,* 661–675.

Integrating Social and Cognitive Processes Underlying the Out-Group Homogeneity Effect: The Homogeneity of Homogeneity

Diane M. Mackie

A s the chapters in this volume attest, Ned Jones's research accom plishments illuminated an extraordinarily broad spectrum of social psychological topics. Even so, his work on what came to be called the out-group homogeneity effect (OHE; Jones, Wood, & Quattrone, 1981; Linville & Jones, 1980; Quattrone & Jones, 1980) stands out. After all, in a career devoted to understanding *inter-personal* perception, Ned touched only very few times on *intergroup* influences on impressions (Jones, Davis, & Gergen, 1961; Jones & Mc-Gillis, 1976). Although the Jonesian individual was always socially situated—and indeed could only be perceived through social action and interaction—social situations determined by group memberships were but rarely the focus of his attention. Whereas the OHE focused on the fact that perceivers saw more variability in their own group than in groups to which they did not belong, the rest of Ned's work was

The author acknowledges the support of National Science Foundation Grant SBR-9209995; the helpful comments made by Mina Ahn, Marilynn Brewer, David Hamilton, Sarah Hunter, Patricia Linville, Karen Neddermeyer, Sarah Queller, Dianne Ruble, and Crystal Wright; and the assistance of Crystal Wright in preparing the manuscript.

more attuned to attributions made about individuals by other individuals.

The apparent disparity between the intergroup nature of the OHE and the more typically interpersonal nature of Ned's other work was heightened by the way in which OHE research developed. As Patty Linville's review (this volume) makes clear, the initial demonstration of the OHE triggered extensive investigation of how group variability information is represented and much less concern with the processes by which group characteristics are inferred. This focus on group variability coincided with and was intensified by two other developments. First, criticism of then popular prototype-based theories of categorization was based partly on the fact that perceivers were demonstrably sensitive to variability information (Posner & Keele, 1968; Smith & Medin, 1981). Second, perceived homogeneity gained notoriety as one of the most pernicious consequences of stereotyping (Wilder, 1978). With these developments as a backdrop, OHE researchers turned more and more to investigation of the cognitive categorization processes that determine variability judgments. Their effort has been well rewarded. The wide variety of theoretical perspectives that have been bought to bear on this issue and the very careful attention that has been paid to measurement issues along the way has made this one of the most productive and actively researched areas in social psychology (see Linville, Salovey, & Fischer, 1986; Messick & Mackie, 1989; Park & Judd, 1990; Sedikides & Ostrom, 1993, for reviews). The heterogeneity that Linville (see chapter 8) refers to in the title of her chapter thus appears to be true in two different ways: The very existence of the research topic attests to the heterogeneity of Ned's contribution to social psychology, and, in addition, our understanding of perceived variability has itself been enriched by a heterogeneity of approaches to its study.

Despite the substantial progress made in understanding both the nature of perceived variability and the cognitive processes that underlie those perceptions, however, a full explanation of the OHE remains intriguingly illusive. As Linville points out, basic categorization mechanisms cannot alone explain why people usually see the groups to which they belong as more variable than do nonmembers of the groups. To explain out-group homogeneity, basic cognitive processes need to be informed by social processes—the kinds of processes that arise from interactions and relations among people. If abstract or specific inferences are made about one group or another, if people encode greater numbers of one group's exemplars than another, if initial judgments about one group are elaborated or not, the next question again must be, "Why?" With a clearer understanding of the contributing cognitive mechanisms in hand, the field needs to return its attention to the important task of determining how these social influences interact with them to produce perceptions of out-group homogeneity (see also Brewer's commentary, this volume).

As it does so, researchers will find that just such a social–cognitive analysis of the OHE was sketched out by Quattrone and Jones (1980) and is awaiting re-discovery. In suggesting explanations for their finding that perceivers were more likely to generalize an individual member's behavior to the out-group than to the in-group, Quattrone and Jones considered a range of possible ways in which *relations* between groups can constrain their *interactions* with and in turn their *inferences* about each other. In fact, Quattrone and Jones described and discussed the OHE as embodying the same fundamental principles that were so central to the rest of Ned's research concerns.

Their approach suggests the major thesis for this commentary: Despite superficial differences, the OHE and other social phenomena that interested Ned have much in common at the process level. Considered this way, in fact, a substantial degree of "homogeneity" can be seen in the causal contributors to the OHE and other social phenomena. To point out these commonalities, I first review four process principles that seem to permeate a Jonesian understanding of social behavior. In each case, relevant explanations offered by Quattrone and Jones (1980) and more recent theoretical and empirical treatments of the OHE that reflect that principle are discussed. To the extent that the principles focus on relational and interactive processes, this approach also indicates new directions in which the study of the OHE might profitably develop. Finally, I note, as Ned often did, some of the integrative benefits offered by a focus on the homogeneity of underlying processes, rather than the heterogeneity of social behavior.

JONESIAN PRINCIPLES IN EXPLAINING OUT-GROUP HOMOGENEITY

Correspondent Inferences in the Pursuit of Attributional Understanding

Consider, first, the pervasiveness of attributional processing in social life. To perceive others is to try to make sense of them, to confer meaning and stability on the social world (e.g., Jones, 1990, pp. 39–40). And if the goal of perception is to make sense of the world, then correspondent inferences—seeing behavior as reflecting the actor's personal dispositions, even in the face of equally viable and obviously compelling situational pressures—offer the most predictive power. The *primacy of attributional processing* and *the pervasiveness of correspondent inferences* are of course the most central themes in Jones's work.

Not surprisingly, then, Quattrone and Jones (1980) saw the most viable explanations for the OHE in the combined effects of fundamental attributional processes (a cognitive process) and differential opportunities for in-group and out-group interaction (a social process). They noted, for example, that intergroup interaction can differ from intragroup interaction both in terms of quantity (how much interaction occurs) and quality (what kind of interaction occurs), and either might produce the OHE.

Focusing on how much interaction took place, Quattrone and Jones (1980) suggested two ways in which differences in sheer quantity of in-group and out-group encounters might produce the effect. First, if encounters with the out-group are rare, the need for prediction dictates that the most stable information possible must be abstracted from each interaction. This quest for maximal stability in attributions thus promotes the drawing of trait inferences (rather than more fluid and mutable situational explanations) about the out-group, which in turn increases perceived homogeneity. In contrast, interaction with the in-group is not so numerically infrequent, encounters with in-group members do not have such attributional urgency, and thus homogenizing trait attributions need not be made so readily. Second, because out-group members are encountered only rarely, the very few behaviors observed in those rare encounters are attributed to equally few correspondent trait dispositions. In contrast, the many behaviors observed in frequent in-group interaction imply many characteristic trait dispositions. Note that these particular possibilities assume that the actual variability of in-group and out-group behavior might be equivalent (in contrast to explanations based on quality of interaction). The out-group seems less dispositionally complex, however, because fewer of their behaviors are observed. Thus, a dirth of opportunities to interact with the out-group produces an OHE.

In focusing on the effect of quality of interaction on the OHE, Quattrone and Jones (1980) relied most closely on the notion of correspondence bias. They pointed out that intergroup interactions occur in constraining situations: roles of superiority or subservience, positions of resource allocation or resource dependence, or contexts requiring intergroup competition. Because they are relatively impervious to constraining roles, however, observers mistakenly attribute the behavioral uniformity they observe to the out-group's dispositional invariance. Although correspondence bias obviously operates when in-group members other than the self are observed (after all, other individuals from in-groups are targets in most experimental investigations of attribution), the much wider range of situations and roles in which in-group members are encountered leads naturally to more complex and varied inferences about in-group characteristics.

Quattrone and Jones's (1980) concern with quantity and quality of interactions foreshadowed many contemporary explanations of the OHE. First, differential familiarity with in-groups and out-groups has been well investigated as a contributor to the effect (Linville, Fischer, & Salovey, 1989; Linville et al., 1986), although its influence has typically been thought about in terms of the *number* of group members or exemplars encountered and represented. As Quattrone and Jones made clear, however, encountering and representing fewer out-group members also means making fewer correspondent *inferences* about out-groups than about in-groups.

Second, Alice Eagly's (Eagly & Steffen, 1984; see also Hoffman & Hurst, 1990) analysis of stereotypes as developing from role-constrained correspondence bias bears out Quattrone and Jones's (1980) speculations. Perceivers attribute role-consistent characteristics to natural properties of the groups that perform those roles, while overlooking the social constraints that distribute different roles to different groups. Surprisingly, although these mechanisms are widely accepted as contributing to stereotyping, they have not been specifically considered as an explanation of the OHE.

Third, making correspondent inferences in situations of infrequent and invariant interaction leads naturally to the conclusion that very few "types" of out-group members, but many types of in-group members, exist, as Quattrone (1976) first pointed out. Theories about the number of in-group and out-group types are currently extremely popular explanations of the OHE effect (Kraus, Ryan, Judd, Hastie, & Park, 1993; Park, Ryan, & Judd, 1992). Quattrone and Jones's analysis reminds us, however, that the fundamental question is why these differences in types exist.

The Irony of Perceiver-Induced Constraint

Perhaps the most fascinating aspect of interpersonal attribution for Jones and his students was *the irony of perceiver-induced constraint:* Not only do perceivers overlook the constraints of the situation, but also they remain heedless of their own contribution to those constraints (Jones, 1990, p. 158; Gilbert & Jones, 1986). Quattrone and Jones (1980) suggested three ways in which this was particularly likely to occur in the case of intergroup interactions. First, the constraining situations in which out-groups act are often imposed by the perceiver's in-group (Eagly & Steffen, 1984; Claire & Fiske, in press). Nevertheless, the in-group's role in creating the behaviors that trigger dispositional inferences about the out-group is typically overlooked.

Second, the impact of expectancy effects means that out-group stereotypes constrain the interpretation of out-group behaviors, again making them seem less variable. Lack of stereotypic expectancies about one's own group, in contrast, has a liberating effect on inferences, leading to a rich and complex characterization of the in-group. In support of this idea, Quattrone and Jones (1980) reported that attention to dimensions relevant to category performance inhibits observation of variability on other dimensions (Jones & Thibaut, 1958; Zadny & Gerard, 1974). These ideas anticipated recent demonstrations that the OHE can be reflected in beliefs that more out-group members than in-group members have stereotypic traits (Park & Judd, 1990), that perceptions of variability differ depending on whether stereotypic defining traits or less central traits are considered (Park & Judd, 1990), that perceivers pay differential attention to category relevant and nonrelevant information about in-groups and out-groups (Park & Rothbart, 1982), and that perceivers typically have greater and earlier exposure to abstract "second-hand" exemplars and prototypes of the out-group than of the in-group (Linville & Fisher, 1993), which promotes perceptions of homogeneity (Park & Hastie, 1987).

Third, armed with their impoverished views of the out-group, perceivers interpret neutral behaviors as verifying their inferences or elicit behaviors that further consolidate this limited number of dispositions (Jussim, 1991; Word, Zanna, & Cooper, 1974), this confirming perceptions of out-group homogeneity. In the case of the OHE, attributional processes thus constitute a form of triple jeopardy. Not only does the in-group partially constrain intergroup interactions and thus overrely on stereotype-congruent correspondent inferences about the out-group, but also those inferences then constitute the basis for self-fulfilling prophecies.

At first glance, finding evidence of OHE in minimal groups seems to argue against an important role for perceiver-induced constraints and stereotypic expectancies in producing the effect. After all, the minimal group paradigm is designed to ensure lack of interaction (and thus inability to constrain) and lack of stereotypes (because the conditions for group assignment are minimal). However, social psychologists are far from understanding the meaning that such minimal groups have for individuals. First, even supposedly arbitrary classifications are apparently readily imbued with meaning using trait inferences (Diehl, 1988, 1990). Second, even minimal groups may induce expectations. In one experimental demonstration of this effect, for example, Worth (1988) found that individuals publicly reported expecting minimal in-groups and out-groups to be equally similar (as might be expected). However, these same individuals then processed information about the minimal in-group as if they expected heterogeneity while processing information about the minimal out-group as if they expected homogeneity. That is, they sought variability information about the in-group and homogeneity information about the out-group, mirroring the effects of expectancies found in other domains (Darley & Gross, 1983). Thus, it is no longer clear that the minimal group paradigm allows researchers to study the impact of categorization without expectancy constraints interfering.

The Crucial Impact of Interaction Goals

Quattrone and Jones (1980) reserved a special place for explanations that focus on differences in in-group and out-group members' motivations and incentives for going beyond abstract generalizations. In the Jonesian perspective, perceiving is for doing, and *"interaction goals . . . have a crucial impact on perceptions and inferences"* (Jones, 1990, p. 169). In fact, Quattrone and Jones suggested that the OHE might be adequately explained by considering the goals of interaction: Perceivers seek uniformity to provide them with an unequivocal hypothesis about how to behave toward the unknown out-group, and thus the OHE occurs. Thus, it is not just that lack of familiarity imbues every interaction with attributional urgency but that people need most to make uniform and stable inferences about groups about which they are ignorant.

Considering the consequences of interaction also suggests potential mediators of the OHE. Independent of group membership interactions can provide motivations to distinguish among individuals (Messick & Mackie, 1989). For example, those who have incentives to make distinctions—the desire for continued relationships, dependence for resources, finer grained interweaving of interaction—will usually make them. Typically, these incentives work to the differentiation benefit of the in-group, but they are also important in explaining conditions under which the effect does not hold. For example, intergroup conflict often exacerbates perceptions of out-group homogeneity (Sherif, 1967). Yet there may be occasions on which conflict provides incentives for differentiating—attempts to eliminate out-group leaders, for example, or to conquer by dividing. Relationships between majority and minority groups can also provide motivations that interact with the typical OHE. For example, minority groups might differentiate majority out-groups because they need to interact safely with them—treating individual members of a powerful out-group as equivalent may have even life-threatening effects. At the same time, minority groups might homogenize perceptions of the in-group to bolster identity (Simon, 1992; Simon & Brown, 1987). Demonstrations that power differentials between groups affect the magnitude of the OHE (Brewer, 1993; Linville et al., 1986) bear out the importance of motivational processes and underscore the need for more systematic application of dependency theories (e.g., Fiske, 1995) to investigation of the OHE.

The Centrality of the Self

Quattrone and Jones (1980) also foreshadowed current interest in the role of the self in producing the OHE. They proposed that in dealing with other in-group members, perceivers seek variety because of its benefits to the self. First, variety in the in-group frees the self from uniform expectations that might otherwise constrain one's own behavior. Second, variety in the in-group is necessary so as to avoid being indistinguishable from others. These explanations turn suggestions that OHE results from motivated perception of homogeneity in the out-group on their head, arguing instead that the OHE results from *motivated heterogeneity within the in-group*. Indeed the desire of individuals to differentiate themselves from other group members helps explain why people recall more distinguishing information about in-group than out-group members (Park & Rothbart, 1982) and why they might organize in-group information by individual members (Sedikides & Ostrom, 1993). Such ideas about distinctiveness have recently been extended to the group level, and Brewer (1993) has suggested that such processes are especially likely when in-groups are large and inclusive. When in-groups are small and distinctive, however, there is no need to differentiate oneself, and the OHE is reduced, or even reversed (Simon & Brown, 1987).

This on-going concern with the important role of the self in mediating impressions of others makes an apparent omission in Quattrone and Jones's (1980) list of possible explanations for the OHE very surprising. Nowhere do they suggest that the OHE might be caused by the kinds of fundamental attributional differences between actors (selves) and observers (others). It is well established, for example, that observers attribute to personal dispositions many actions that actors see as caused by the situation (see Jones, 1990, for a review). Yet if one assumes that in-group members are more likely to be *observers* of out-group action and *participants* in in-group actions, the actor–observer difference offers a perfect explanation for the OHE and a possibility that warrants considerable research attention.

There are two reasons why Quattrone and Jones (1980) may not have considered actor–observer differences an adequate explanation of the effect. First, the actor–observer difference was perhaps seen as too fundamental to interpersonal interaction to provide an explanation for intergroup interaction. After all, observers make different attributions when the actors they observe are in-group members, so the difference does not immediately present itself as an appropriate explanation of differences in attributions made about in-groups and out-groups. Nevertheless, its oversight both in 1980 and since is surprising, as some of the same factors have been posited as contributors to both the actor–observer difference and the OHE. Actors are usually assumed to have a greater quantity and variety of behavioral information about themselves, garnered from acting and interacting in a wider range of situations. This greater awareness of the impact of people, places, and events reduces actors' likelihood of making correspondent inferences, contributing to actor–observer differences in attribution (Baxter & Goldberg, 1987). At the same time, many researchers have recognized the special role that self-knowledge might play in making in-groups more variable. Specifically, people have far greater quantity and variety of behavioral information about themselves and thus the self is a highly accessible, highly variable member of the in-group, contributing to the perception that the in-group is varied. The important potential role of this special self-knowledge has been of particular interest in attempts to explain OHEs in minimal groups (Judd & Park, 1988; Mackie, Sherman, & Worth, 1993). Thus, the fact that different attributions are made about the self can also contribute to the OHE.

A second reason why self–other differences were not seen as relevant to in-group–out-group differences may have been the dirth of theorizing about the impact of group membership on the self-concept at that time. In the last decade, however, intergroup theories (such as social identity theory, Tajfel & Turner, 1986, and self-categorization theory, Turner, Hogg, Oakes, Reicher, & Wetherell, 1987) have described the process by which the group becomes part of the psychological self so that the self and in-group membership are often indistinguishable (Smith & Henry, 1996). This means that under certain conditions other members of the in-group become interchangeable with the self (about whom "actor" attributions are made), whereas out-group members are treated as the other (about whom dispositional "observer" attributions are made). From this perspective, then, even when intergroup encounters include identical in-group and out-group behavior, in-group actors are more likely to see their own actions as situationally caused and thus potentially more variable, while observing the out-group's behavior as dispositionally caused and thus more invariant.

As Linville (chapter 8) points out, social identity approaches have recently become popular as explanations of the OHE. However, much of this theorizing focuses on social identity motivations to differentiate the in-group from the out-group (Simon & Brown, 1987). Similarly, the impact of group membership in attribution theory has been largely to investigate in-group bias in attributions such that favorable behaviors are attributed internally for the in-group and externally for the out-group, whereas negative behaviors are attributed internally for the out-group and externally for the in-group (Maass, Salvi, Acuri, & Semin, 1989; Pettigrew, 1979). Generalizing actor–observer differences to the intergroup situation, however, suggests a more fundamental interaction of the processes that guide attributions and those triggered by group membership. To the extent that the in-group is psychologically synonymous with the self and the out-group with the other, the OHE will result from operations of the same principles that underlie actor–observer differences.

This also means that many of the same principles that undermine actor–observer differences in attributions should undermine out-group homogeneity effects. For example, taking the perspective of the other and increasing the perceived similarity between self and other can undermine actor–observer differences. In the same way, manipulations that decrease in-group and out-group differences and manipulations that increase in-group–out-group empathy should both eliminate the OHE. Indeed, Wright and Mackie (1996) provided a preliminary demonstration that instructing research participants to put themselves in the place of out-group members before making inferences about behaviors reduces the magnitude of the OHE.

CONCLUDING COMMENTS

In addition to demonstrating an effect that has intrigued researchers for more than 15 years, Jones and his colleagues also attempted to place that effect in a tightly woven mesh of interacting social and cognitive variables. As this brief review of the explanations Quattrone and Jones (1980) initially offered for the OHE makes clear, the same process principles underlie both this effect and many of the other foci of Ned's research. Thinking about the OHE as resulting from correspondent inferences that overlook the role of perceiver-induced constraint while reflecting interactional and self-preservational motivations makes clear the extent to which the OHE is a coherent part of Ned's body of research. In addition, however, this perspective points out ways in which the basic cognitive processes that contribute to the OHE are informed by social processes that arise from interactions and relations and thus suggests some of the new directions for OHE research that both Linville (chapter 8) and Brewer (this volume) call for.

Recognizing the coherence of Ned's explanatory approach to topics as diverse as the OHE, first impressions, ingratiation, and self-handicapping highlights another of his significant contributions to our field. Although singlehandedly responsible for broadening the field of social psychological inquiry, Ned sought constantly to integrate it as well. In one of the seminars he taught on interpersonal perception in the early 1980s, Ned spoke often of his belief that social psychology would progress only to the extent that the diversity of human behavior could be explained by capturing the underlying processes that describe individuals' cognitive and motivational activity in the social context.

More than a decade later, Quattrone and Jones still have much to offer those interested in doing just that in the context of explaining the OHE. Some of the mechanisms they propose as contributors to the OHE are currently well researched, but many have been all but ignored. The time is right to return to some of those ideas and refocus on the combination of relational, interactional, and cognitive processes they afford. Like Linville, I suspect that Ned's reaction would be, "Finally!"

REFERENCES

Baxter, T. L., & Goldberg, L. R. (1987). Perceived behavioral consistency underlying trait attributions to oneself and another: An extension of the actor–observer difference. *Personality and Social Psychology Bulletin, 13,* 437–447.

Brewer, M. B. (1993). The role of distinctiveness in social identity and group behaviour. In M. A. Hogg & D. Abrams (Eds.), *Group motivation: Social psychological perspectives* (pp. 1–16). London, England: Harvester Wheatsheaf.

Claire, T., & Fiske, S. T. (in press). A systemic view of behavioral confirmation: Counterpoint to the individualistic view. In C. Sedikides, J. Schopler, & C. A. Insko (Eds.), *Intergroup cognition and intergroup behavior.* Hillsdale, NJ: Erlbaum.

Darley, J. M., & Gross, P. H. (1983). A hypothesis-confirming bias in labeling effects. *Journal of Personality and Social Psychology, 44,* 20–33.

Diehl, M. (1988). Social identity and minimal groups: The effects of interpersonal and intergroup attitudinal similarity on intergroup discrimination. *British Journal of Social Psychology, 27,* 289–300.

Diehl, M. (1990). The minimal group paradigm: Theoretical explanations and empirical findings. In W. Stroebe & M. Hewstone (Eds.), *European review of social psychology* (Vol. 1, 263–292). Chichester: Wiley.

Eagly, A. H., & Steffen, V. J. (1984). Gender stereotypes stem from the distribution of women and men into social roles. *Journal of Personality and Social Psychology, 46,* 735–754.

Fiske, S. T. (1995). Controlling other people: The impact of power on stereotyping. In N. R. Goldberger & J. B. Veroff (Eds.), *The culture and psychology reader* (pp. 438–456). New York: New York University Press.

Gilbert, D. T., & Jones, E. E. (1986). Perceiver-induced constraint: Interpretation of self-generated reality. *Journal of Personality and Social Psychology, 50,* 269–280.

Hoffman, C., & Hurst, N. (1990). Gender stereotypes: Perceptions or rationalization? *Journal of Personality and Social Psychology, 58,* 197–208.

Jones, E. E. (1990). *Interpersonal perception.* New York: Freeman.

Jones, E. E., Davis, K. E., & Gergen, K. J. (1961). Role playing variations and their informational value for person perception. *Journal of Abnormal and Social Psychology, 63,* 302–310.

Jones, E. E., & McGillis, D. (1976). Correspondent inference and the attribution cube. In J. H. Harvey, W. J. Ickes, & R. E. Kidd (Eds.), *New directions in attribution research* (Vol. 1, pp. 389–420). Hillsdale, NJ: Erlbaum.

Jones, E. E., & Thibaut, J. W. (1958). Interaction goals as bases for inferences in interpersonal perception. In R. Taguiri & L. Petrullo (Eds.), Person perception and interpersonal behavior (pp. 151–178). Palo Alto, CA: Stanford University Press.

Jones, E. E., Wood, G. C., & Quattrone, G. A. (1981). Perceived variability of personal characteristics of in-groups and out-groups: The role of knowledge and evaluation. *Personality and Social Psychology Bulletin, 7,* 523–528.

Judd, C. M., & Park, B. (1988). Out-group homogeneity: Judgments of variability at the individual and group levels. *Journal of Personality and Social Psychology, 54,* 778–788.

Jussim, L. (1991). Social perception and social reality: A reflection–construction model. *Psychological Review, 98,* 54–73.

Kraus, S., Ryan, C. S., Judd, C. M., Hastie, R., & Park, B. (1993). Use of mental frequency distributions to represent variability among members of social categories. *Social Cognition, 211,* 22–43.

Linville, P. W., & Fischer, G. W. (1993). Exemplar and abstraction models of perceived group variability and stereotypicality. *Social Cognition, 11,* 92–125.

Linville, P. W., Fischer, G. W., & Salovey, P. (1989). Perceived distributions of the characteristics of in-group and out-group members: Empirical evidence and a computer simulation. *Journal of Personality and Social Psychology, 57,* 165–188.

Linville, P. W., & Jones, E. E. (1980). Polarized appraisals of out-group members. *Journal of Personality and Social Psychology, 38,* 689–703.

Linville, P. W., Salovey, P., & Fischer, G. W. (1986). Stereotyping and perceived distributions of social characteristics: An application to in-group–out-group perception. In J. Dovidio & S. L. Gaertner (Eds.), *Prejudice, discrimination, and racism* (pp. 165–208). San Diego, CA: Academic Press.

Maass, A., Salvi, D., Acuri, L., & Semin, G. (1989). Language use in intergroup contexts: The linguistic intergroup bias. *Journal of Personality and Social Psychology, 57,* 981–993.

Mackie, D. M., Sherman, J. W., & Worth, L. T. (1993). On-line and memory-based processes in group variability judgments. *Social Cognition, 2,* 44–69.

Messick, D. M., & Mackie, D. M. (1989). Intergroup relations. *Annual Review of Psychology, 40,* 45–81.

Mullen, B. (1987). Self-attention theory: The effects of group composition on the individual. In B. Mullen & G. R. Goethals (Eds.), *Theories of group behavior* (pp. 125–146). New York: Springer-Verlag.

Park, B., & Hastie, R. (1987). Perception of variability in category development: Instance- versus abstraction-based stereotypes. *Journal of Personality and Social Psychology, 53,* 621–635.

Park, B., & Judd, C. M. (1990). Measures and models of perceived group variability. *Journal of Personality and Social Psychology, 59,* 173–191.

Park, B., Judd, C. M., & Ryan, C. S. (1991). Social categorization and the representation of variability information. In M. Hewstone & W. Stroebe

(Eds.), *European review of social psychology* (Vol. 2, pp. 211–245). Chichester, England: Wiley & Sons.

Park, B., & Rothbart, M. (1982). Perception of out-group homogeneity and levels of social categorization: Memory for the subordinate attributes of in-group and out-group members. *Journal of Personality and Social Psychology, 42,* 1051–1068.

Park, B., Ryan, C. S., & Judd, C. M. (1992). Role of meaningful subgroups in explaining differences in perceived variability for in-groups and out-groups. *Journal of Personality and Social Psychology, 63,* 553–567.

Pettigrew, T. F. (1979). The ultimate attribution error: Extending Allport's cognitive analysis of prejudice. *Personality and Social Psychology Bulletin, 5,* 461–476.

Posner, M. I., & Keele, S. W. (1968). On the genesis of abstract ideas. *Journal of Experimental Psychology, 77,* 353–363.

Quattrone, G. A. (1976). *They look alike, they think alike, they dress alike: We don't: Ingroup/outgroup differences in the perception of variability.* Unpublished manuscript, Duke University.

Quattrone, G. A., & Jones, E. E. (1980). The perception of variability within in-groups and out-groups: Implications for the law of small numbers. *Journal of Personality and Social Psychology, 38,* 141–152.

Sedikides, C., & Ostrom, T. M. (1993). Perceptions of group variability: Moving from an uncertain crawl to a purposeful stride. *Social Cognition, 11,* 165–174.

Sherif, M. (1967). *Group conflict and cooperation.* London: Routledge & Kegan Paul.

Simon, B. (1992). The perception of ingroup and outgroup homogeneity: Reintroducing the intergroup context. In W. Strobe & M. Hewstone (Eds.), *European review of social psychology* (Vol. 3, pp. 1–30). Chichester, England: Wiley & Sons.

Simon, B., & Brown, R. (1987). Perceived homogeneity in minority–majority contexts. *Journal of Personality and Social Psychology, 53,* 703–711.

Smith, E. R., & Henry, S. (1996). An in-group becomes part of the self-response time evidence. *Personality and Social Psychology Bulletin, 22,* 635–642.

Smith, E. E., & Medin, D. L. (1981). *Categories and concepts.* Cambridge, MA: Harvard University Press.

Tajfel, H., & Turner, J. C. (1986). An integrative theory of intergroup relations. In S. Worchel & W. G. Austin (Eds.), *Psychology of intergroup relations* (pp. 7–24). Chicago: Nelson Hall.

Turner, J. C., Hogg, M. A., Oakes, P. J., Reicher, S. D., & Wetherell, M. S. (1987). *Rediscovering the social group: A self categorization theory.* Oxford: Blackwell.

Wilder, D. A. (1978). Perceiving persons as a group: Effects on attributions of causality and beliefs. *Social Psychology, 13,* 253–258.

Word, C. O., Zanna, M. P., & Cooper, J. C. (1974). The nonverbal mediation of self-fulfilling prophecies in interracial interaction. *Journal of Experimental Social Psychology, 10,* 109–120.

Worth, L. T. (1988). *The role of prior expectations and selective information processing in outgroup homogeneity.* Unpublished doctoral dissertation, University of California, Santa Barbara.

Wright, C. L., & Mackie, D. M. (1996, April). Empathy and perceived group variability. Paper presented at the meeting of the Western Psychological Association, San Jose, CA.

Zadny, J., & Gerard, H. B. (1974). Attributed intentions and informational selectivity. *Journal of Experimental Social Psychology, 10,* 34–52.

9

Caricature Theory

Robert P. Abelson

At the memorial held for Ned Jones in Princeton in 1995, I spoke of his recurring interest in the tension between opposing selves: the ingratiating self versus the true self, the perceived self versus the experiencing self, and so on. I think his fascination with awkward conjunctions was part of his general appreciation of the absurd.[1] The theme of this chapter is the systematic occurrence of psychosocial absurdity; I call it *caricature theory*. It concerns social processes that cumulate to transform normal situations into ridiculous ones.

My analysis is at the level of social institutions and social groups, with individuals essentially reduced to unlabelled, interchangeable statistical molecules under pressure from big social forces, or in the thrall of motives and emotions shared with other members of a social group.

---

[1]Something bizarre always seemed to happen when Ned and I were at the same conference. We both suffered lost luggage coming home from Prague in 1968, and the customs officials were very suspicious of our story. Two years earlier, it was a vodka-soaked, midnight, 5-mile walk in Moscow, when Leon Festinger almost got run over by an off-duty taxicab. Other adventures included the memorable takeover of an American Psychological Association business meeting by militant student admirers of Che Guevara, whom I heckled loudly, much to Ned's delight; the Greek torch singer in a DC restaurant who claimed, implausibly, that her name was Nelda Jones; the private exchanges of barbs with Ned through coded implications on lecture slides; and more.

Thus the type of evidence—both what little of it there is at present, and the much larger body waiting to be pursued—is hardly ever experimental, but instead must come from news accounts and archival records, and perhaps occasional survey data. My chapter is totally unlike anything Ned might ever have done, both in its level of analysis and in its empirical methodology. Nevertheless I think my theme is one he would have enjoyed. Despite Ned's reputation as something of a lovable curmudgeon from the Walter Matthau prototype factory, I always found in my conversations with him that he was open-minded, curious, and encouraging. If he were to have 10 lives to live, all as an academic social psychologist, I believe he could carve out 10 different specialties that between them would cover the entire enormous territory. One gets a sense of Ned's otherwise hidden scholarly breadth from the sensitive handbook chapter he wrote on the history of social psychology (Jones, 1985).

CARICATURE: THE RIDICULOUS AS A SOCIAL OUTGROWTH OF THE ORDINARY

Consider some of the phenomena in modern life that have become caricatures of themselves, ranging from the harmlessly absurd to the appallingly lunatic: Christmases that begin in September; the escalation of crude, negative political campaigns; the ultra-outrageousness of TV and radio talk shows; the preposterous inflation of athletes' salaries; centuries-old ethnic hatreds that reappear with amazing virulence; the legitimation of murder as a protest device; the decay of human decency in sensitive situations because of the fear of lawsuits;[2] computers that

---

[2]The astronomical insurance costs associated with the likelihood of litigation have unwanted institutional and occupational side effects, for example, the closing of small restaurants with steep back staircases, and the aversion of new MD's to suit-prone specialties, such as obstetrics. What I more have in mind here is the wide variety of episodes of people and institutions behaving with astonishing bad grace—one might even call it a *norm of necessary rudeness*—because people are actuarially terrified by a possible lawsuit. For example, a nurse refuses to help an immobilized patient remove a speck from his eye because she "doesn't do eyes." The father of a boy who has just knocked over an elderly woman with his bike stonewalls discussion of the matter with neighbors because "the evidence was circumstantial." A university committee has unexpectedly rejected a strong departmental recommendation for a senior appointment and refuses ever to give any explanation to anybody, on advice of university lawyers.

take over your brain when you are merely telephoning to find out when the next train leaves, and so on.

Examples like these could keep a gaggle of political scientists, economists, historians, and cultural anthropologists gainfully employed for a long time without bothering to call in psychologists at all. Nevertheless, the essence of processes of social distortion and caricature strikes me as heavily psychological, and I would like to bring a psychological voice to the analysis of social absurdity.

My central proposition is that over time, every social construction comes to caricature itself. By *caricature* I mean the ludicrous exaggeration of the distinctive features of a thing, whether it be a political idea, a technical development, an art form, a depiction of an enemy or an ex-spouse, and so on.

With caricature thus defined, I immediately confess that I am caricaturing my central proposition. I do not really suppose that every social construction becomes in time ludicrously exaggerated. Some things stay much the same as time passes, and some others become duller and duller, with their features leveled rather than sharpened (Allport & Postman, 1947). What I really want to do is to identify the prototypic conditions and social dynamics foreshadowing eventual absurdity. This chapter is a first try at that intention.

SOCIAL PROCESSES POTENTIALLY LEADING TO ABSURDITY

Behavior Arenas and the Initiating Event

The general scenario I have in mind involves behaviors over time in a given setting, or *arena*. Associated with each arena are a few fixed descriptive parameters, such as the nature of its actors, and a variety of dynamic variables, such as the number of actors involved at any given time, their rates of behavior, the extremity of their behaviors, and so on.[3] Within an arena, a possible caricaturing process starts when a subset of actors behave in such a way that particular variables become more extreme. (For example, if media promotion increases the attractiveness of a product or service, more people will want it, and the price will go up.)

After the initial stage, other factors can either restrain or intensify the growth of the exaggerated variables. The central psychological factors are the degree of actors' exposure to the change(s), and if exposed, the nature of the effect on their motivations. Actors might find the change sufficiently aversive to diminish their interest in repeating their behavior (e.g., the price becomes too high). On the other hand, the new situation may have emergent properties that further encourage the behavior (e.g., a lot of people have bought the attractive product, and failure to buy creates an impression of social deviance). This latter circumstance creates a positive feedback loop, so that in the absence of restraining forces, a cycle of escalating behaviors would in time produce absurdly extreme parameters in the arena—that is to say, a caricature (e.g., Super Bowl tickets selling at $1000 or more).

As another relatively simple example, picture the growing popularity of a new restaurant. The first patrons like it and tell their friends about it, who go and then tell their friends. The fact that it is popular becomes an attraction itself: It is the "in" place to go. At some point, the process slows when the number of patrons becomes bothersomely large. An equilibrium may be reached, or the place may fall out of favor, with the process reversing itself. As Yogi Berra once said about a ballplayers' hang-out, "Nobody goes there any more; it's too crowded." The most interesting possibility is that by the time equilibrium is finally approached, the consequences of the level of demand are already ludicrous. Without connections or bribery, you may have to make reservations 6 months in advance.

---

[3]The term *dynamical systems* has recently entered the social psychological literature (Vallacher & Nowak, 1993). It is an inclusive term, referring to systems of interdependent variables that manifest changes over time. Mathematically, such systems can have a wide range of general properties, of which the most exotic is *chaotic* behavior, that is, an intrinsic lack of predictability despite deterministic dynamics. Here I am not referring to chaos, but rather to the occurrence of very extreme values on particular variables.

I outline three types of motivated processes that have the potential to give rise to caricatures: concurrence, competition, and animus,[4] devoting most attention to the third type.

THREE SOCIAL MOTIVES GIVING RISE TO CARICATURING PROCESSES

Concurrence

The crowded restaurant example is but one of a big catalogue of situations in which a large number of actors increasingly behave in concurrence with each other. As people become more and more disposed to drive through red lights, or want tickets to the Super Bowl, or visit Yosemite National Park, the potential for ludicrous consequences lurks. Of course, excess of any kind tends to recruit restraining forces; the question is whether these restraints will dampen the concurrence process.

I use the bland term *concurrence* rather than *conformity* because there may or may not be social influence in the accretion of ever larger numbers of new actors performing (more of) the behavior. Incentives to act may appeal concurrently to many individuals who hardly influence one another at all, or there may be social monitoring and reward of conforming behavior, and punishment for nonconformity.

In either case, the escalation of the process might be restrained by the reality of clearly negative consequences. But continuance of the escalating behavior may be quite attractive, producing an ongoing contest between incentives and restraints. An assumption that the degree of eventual caricature depends linearly on the relative strengths of incentives and restraints would be neither interesting nor correct, however. It is known from many strands of the literature on attitudes and attitude change that important attitudes are resistant to change (Abelson, 1995; Zuwerink & Devine, in press); they are *sticky*. Behaviors

---

[4]A fourth type, involving the motivated social avoidance of particular problems or threats, might also be considered, although I do not do so here.

supported by group-anchored, thus important, attitudes therefore tend to persist despite challenge. That is, when attitudes in a group grow stronger and more popular, the corresponding behaviors become more stubbornly habitual and widespread, despite the negative consequences they might produce.

I seek the causes of stickiness of oversubscribed behavior, whereby a group of individuals newly performing it are resistant to arguments that they should refrain, or switch to innocuous alternatives. The factor of commitment comes to mind (Brehm & Cohen, 1962), particularly in the strong form of *public* commitment to one's in-group (Baron, Amazeen, & Beek, 1994; Kanter, 1972; Moreland & Levine, 1982). This suggests the proposition that conformity-induced commitment to particular behaviors will tend to prevent reversal, and make it more likely for the concurrence process to escalate to the caricature level.[5] Radical action groups, whether on the political left or on the right, offer good illustrations of this dynamic, with the additional feature of increased extremity of behavior over time. The deepening commitments of new members follow a kind of "group-in-the-door" process, such that a sequence of actions of increasingly radical nature successively become justifiable and self-defining. This mechanism, among others promoting extremitization and resistance to change, is discussed in more detail by Abelson (1995).

Competition

Suppose the actors in an arena are motivated by competitiveness with each other rather than by conformity. Actors might take turns topping each other in some type of performance. For example, a cohort of modern artists of a particular era might break out of a prevailing style, say, by using natural objects protruding from a surface. Novelty being

---

[5] Behaviors vary in their centrality to a group's long-term values and purposes. Faddish behaviors, such as the use of "in" verbal expressions, or of the latest dance wiggle, are at some level recognized by most conformers as only temporary badges of group belongingness. Today's dweeb was yesterday's nerd, and yesteryear's square. Such behaviors thus command conformity on a transient basis. When the charm of the fad peaks, eager change replaces resistance to change; the behavior is now *unsticky*.

valued (Martindale, 1989), many of the artists would seek to present a bolder realization of the new style to the public (or more pointedly, to each other). After shoes and fishnets became old hat, someone would try unnatural objects, and seemingly absurd assemblages of junk would soon dominate the galleries.

Similar examples occur in the entertainment arena: movie directors, pop artists, and TV and radio talk show hosts present ever more strident, violent, and erotic material, seemingly without restraint by moral standards or by good taste. If outrageousness increases audience size, as it often does, then economic motives in addition to psychological ones would drive and escalate the process.[6]

Under what conditions are spiraling competitive processes restrained before absurd caricatures occur? One set of such conditions is cultural. Restraints would presumably be stronger in societies that are heavily oriented toward tradition, or that value collective well being above individual performance.

A second type of restraint is more specific to the content of the escalation. Take gourmet cooking, for example. A set of outstanding chefs can one-up each other only so far before they meet the reality that their most exotic creations do not taste very good at all. A chef whose specialty is scallops with blueberries is in serious trouble.

Reality testing seems generally to be the key factor behind successful restraint of competitive escalation. Arenas lacking clear, direct ways to tell good from bad are more likely to produce caricatures, as with modern art, music, or deconstructionism. The taste of food is immediately definitive if negative, whereas the arts may bewilder most people because people are not sure they know what to look at or listen to. The restraining power of the taste test may explain why guardians of societal stability are at pains to define what behaviors are in "good taste." The attempt is to demarcate boundaries that, like firewalls, will intercept dangerous escalations. Commentators on the ills of the '90s are apt to

---

[6]Economic advantage does not always accrue to the most extreme presentation. As wedding receptions get more and more ludicrously lavish, or table settings for gourmet tailgate parties grow increasingly effete, brides' parents and tailgate party-goers (on a much smaller scale) pay bigger and bigger bills (which may indeed be the point: to display how rich or sophisticated one is).

decry the present lack of vivid, consensual boundaries on what is socially and morally permissible.

Animus

Let me turn now to the type of absurdity arising from intergroup or interpersonal conflicts that are driven by hatred, or *animus*.[7] Social psychologists have long been disinterested in the psychology of hate, even though as private citizens we shake our heads at terrorist plots and ethnic slaughters and seem at a loss for explanations.

Imagine two actors, A and B, each monitoring and reacting to the statements and behavior of the other, and motivated by strong negative attitudes. Focus on the bundles of features comprising the traits, attitudes, and typical behaviors and activities of the two respective actors. Some of the features are common to Actors A and B, and each actor also has distinctive features. Following Amos Tversky's (1977) model of similarity, overall feature similarity of the two actors is a positive function on the set of common features, and a negative function on the set of distinctive features.

A high degree of similarity between actors produces feelings of attraction between them. Conversely, attraction tends to motivate an increase in similarity, which can be achieved by enlarging the set of similar features (e.g., by participating in shared activities, or by attitude change toward greater agreement). It can also be achieved by shrinking the set of distinctive features (say, by suppressing attitudes that arouse disagreement, by curtailing activities in which the other has no interest, and so on).

What happens when instead of attraction, there is mutual animus between the actors? I use the term *animus* for a negative attitude intense enough to resist ordinary persuasive argument. *Hatred* is a very closely related term; in fact, legal definitions of *hate crimes* often refer to *animus* toward the victim's race, religion, ethnicity, or sexual orientation.

In a previous paper (Abelson, 1995), I discussed 13 social psycho-

---

[7]The author is indebted to Joel Cooper for suggesting that other potentially intense negative emotions such as disgust or fear could produce the same spiral of effects as animus.

logical processes that tend to increase the polarization of intergroup conflicts, that is, to produce more and more negative attitudes in each group toward the other, along with more and more unrestrained aggressive behaviors. The list includes thought polarization, group polarization during discussion, exchanges of insults, and so on. Despite this long list (or perhaps because of it), I wasn't sure of the motor that made all these processes start to run. Ned, along with most other social psychologists, would posit that expectations and attributions drive feelings and behaviors. With apologies to Ned, I follow the recommendation of Silvan Tomkins (1981)—my favorite professor when I was a graduate student at Princeton from 1950 to 1952—and try a theoretical orientation in which affect is primary, and cognition is in a supporting role. In this view, social conflict processes enter a serious, "hot" phase when there are insults, threats, contempt, or outrages of sufficient intensity to create animus.

Imagine, then, a situation of mutual animus between Actors A and B. Presumably A would want to become less similar to B, and vice versa, because points of similarity would imply to any observer that each actor was at least somewhat attracted to the other.[8]

From an actor's point of view, there are four strategies for decreasing perceived similarity to another actor, two of them behavioral, and two of them attributional. The behavioral methods are to decrease things you do or say in common with the other, and to increase distinctive behaviors. The attributional strategies are to construe the outgroup other as having less in common with in-group members than is actually the case, or to exaggerate the other's distinctive features.

Of these four devices, the one that is most likely to be costly to an actor is to abandon in-common behaviors. Initiating distinctive behaviors may also be relatively costly, though perhaps less so. Meanwhile, attributional distortion is relatively cost-free, particularly in attributions of distinctive features to the other. Though there may be some small

---

[8]In a personal vein, whenever I used to consume jelly beans in public, someone would inevitably make the irritating remark, "just like Ronald Reagan," whereupon I would indignantly respond that I liked them before I had even heard of Ronald Reagan, and perhaps even before he could distinguish them from Easter eggs.

reality constraint on what the actor can accuse the other of actually doing, there is unlimited scope for imagining the heinous personality traits and the evil intentions of the other, and no amount of reasonable argument has a chance against such animus-driven projection.

Consider also the situation from the point of view of the other actor. While A is applying strategies to increase dissimilarity with B, the latter also is likely to be trying to achieve greater psychological distance from A. Given the relative ease of manipulating distinctiveness, the major consequence of active between-actor animus would be mutually distinctive behaviors and mutual caricaturing, that is, further exaggeration of the already distinctive features of the other. Self-justification motives would lead each actor to evaluate positively the distinctive behaviors of self, and to evaluate negatively the distinctive behaviors and attributed features of the other.

If the caricaturing mechanism were part of a positive feedback loop, over time the mutual caricatures would become more and more ludicrous. Such a loop could occur if each actor's behavior included new insults, threats, outrages, or gratuitous accusations. This would further fuel the existing animus, mutually reactivate the motives to be different, and stimulate even greater increases in distinctiveness, that is, more extreme caricature.

There are at least two novel theoretical connections that emerge when two-actor conflicts are conceived in terms of escalation of the motive to be distinctive. For one thing, the process of stereotyping flows naturally out of the analysis. Here, *stereotypes* are gross exaggerations of preexisting features with a kernel of truth, real or apparent. In this view, stereotyping is more than a motivationally neutral misapplication of principles of categorization. It involves cognitive distortion, right enough, but is driven by animus toward the stereotyped other.

A second windfall from the analysis is a possible explanation of the mysterious battles often fought over mere symbols in political and social conflicts—for example, the ruckuses caused by displays or desecrations of partisan flags. The most unambiguously distinctive features of social actors are the symbols that uniquely identify them. Thus the public display and celebration of one's flag, logo, or slogans is a quick and effective way to assert one's distinctiveness. Conversely, the destruction of, or interference with the other's symbols—*symbol deprivation*—threatens to curtail the opportunity for the hated other to proclaim distinctiveness, and this typically produces outrage.

SUMMARY

It is no accident that there are so many absurdities of the human condition. My claim is that a great many of them are brought about by lawful dynamical processes (Vallacher & Nowak, 1993) of a largely social psychological nature. I have outlined three such processes, driven by concurrence, competitiveness, and animus, respectively.

Social comparisons and social influence enter all three processes. *Concurrence* involves horizontal comparison, such that everybody wants what everybody else wants, with the potential consequences of overuse and overcrowding and their byproducts. *Competitiveness* thrives on downward comparison of abilities, with everyone wanting to perform better than everyone else, often leading eventually to stylistically grotesque extremes of performance. *Animus* creates social distancing, accompanied by downward moral comparison, setting up conditions conducive to unbridled aggression. Animus is similar to concurrence in the role played by in-group influence: egging individuals forward under the threat of social ostracism, and ignoring the larger negative consequences of the escalating process. In a competitive process, direct conformity is not a factor as such, but there is social modeling of a behavioral style in which the competitors vie at downputting each other, or at least convincing themselves that they have done so, as standards of judgment of quality may be extremely loose.

Reality tests provide important potential restraints against inexorable trends toward absurd and destructive consequences. However, in-group conformity, solidified by behavioral commitment and especially by animus, encourages individuals to disregard restraints. In the competitive process, clear standards of performative success and well-defined moral boundaries—a "taste test"—could conceivably cap asymptotic outcomes short of absurdity.

WHAT WOULD NED HAVE SAID ABOUT THIS?

That is about as far as I've gotten with this line of thought. I have asked myself what Ned would have said about all this, and here is my simulation of his reaction:

"Abelson, where are your [expletive] data?![9] I sure as hell wish you had some data! I don't know what to think without experimental tests. Hell, even if you *had* some new data, I still wouldn't know what to think. People weren't asked to honor me with papers about the dynamics of *groups*! Who invited you?!" [*Sotto voce*] "Bob, I'm only insulting you because I know you can handle it. . . . But how about that animus process? I like it. You should say something about inter*personal* animus. . ."

Here, Ned might give me a crinkly smile, pausing to wipe his glasses and wait for my response.

I am ready. There is no reason why everything I have said about an animus-driven distinctiveness race could not apply equally to a relationship between two individuals as to two groups. Prototypic cases are teen-age rebellion against one's parent, bitter divorce, or the acrimonious break-up of a professional partnership. In the final stages of these melodramas, the actors frequently rant and rave about the unbelievable duplicity and viciousness of their ex's. The description of the other is often unrecognizable to neutral observers, although it may occasionally occur (as in the play, "The Sunshine Boys") that each person is really distinctively obnoxious, and becomes even more so in the caricaturing process.

"Well, how did you like it now, Ned?"
"I don't believe any of it, Bob, but it's great, just great!"
Gee, thanks, Ned . . . I think.

---

[9]Ned and I both had pet peeves about common misuses of language. The one that drives me most bananas is, "I could care less." (If you *could* care *less*, then you haven't hit bottom yet. The correct expression—which has been corrupted with incredible speed—is of course, "I *couldn't* care less.") Ned's hackles would rise when anybody singularized *data*. He would sooner have slept on a bed of nails than be overheard saying, "Where *is* your data?"

REFERENCES

Abelson, R. P. (1995). Attitude extremity. In R. E. Petty & J. A. Krosnick (Eds.), *Attitude strength: Antecedents and consequences.* Mahwah, NJ: Erlbaum.

Allport, G. W., & Postman, L. (1947). *The psychology of rumor.* New York: Henry Holt.

Baron, R. M., Amazeen, P. G., & Beek, P. J. (1994). Local and global dynamics of social relations. In R. R. Vallacher & A. Nowak (Eds.), *Dynamical systems in social psychology.* New York: Academic Press.

Brehm, J. W., & Cohen, A. R. (1962). *Explorations in cognitive dissonance.* New York: Wiley.

Jones, E. E. (1985). Major developments in social psychology during the past five decades. In G. Lindzey & E. Aronson (Eds.), *Handbook of social psychology* (3rd ed., pp. 47–108). New York: Random House.

Kanter, R. M. (1972). *Commitment and community: Communes and utopias in sociological perspective.* Cambridge, MA: Harvard University Press.

Martindale, C. (1989). Stylistic trends in British and French painting. *Visual Arts Research, 15*(2), 1–20.

Moreland, R. L., & Levine, J. M. (1982). Socialization in small groups: Temporal changes in individual-group relations. In L. Berkowitz (Ed.), *Advances in experimental social psychology* (Vol. 15, pp. 137–192). New York: Academic Press.

Tomkins, S. S. (1981). The quest for primary motives: The biography and autobiography of an idea. *Journal of Personality and Social Psychology, 41,* 306–329.

Tversky, A. (1977). Features of similarity. *Psychological Review, 84,* 327–352.

Vallacher, R. R., & Nowak, A. (Eds.). (1993). *Dynamical systems in social psychology.* New York: Academic Press.

Zuwerink, J. R., & Devine, P. (in press). Attitude importance and resistance to persuasion: It's not just the thought that counts. *Journal of Personality and Social Psychology.*

The Published Writings of Edward E. Jones

BOOKS

1964

Ingratiation. New York: Appleton-Century-Crofts.

1967

Foundations of social psychology. New York: Wiley. (Authored with H. B. Gerard)

1972

Attribution: Perceiving the causes of behavior. New York: General Learning Press. (Authored with D. Kanouse, H. H. Kelley, R. Nisbett, S. Valins, & B. Weiner)

1984

Social stigma: The Psychology of marked relationships. New York: W. H. Freeman. (Authored with A. Farina, A. Hastorf, H. Markus, D. Miller, & R. Scott)

1990

Interpersonal perception. New York: W. H. Freeman.

ARTICLES AND CHAPTERS

1954

Expectancy in apparent visual movement. *British Journal of Psychology,* 45, 157–165. (Authored with J. S. Bruner)

Authoritarianism as a determinant of first-impression formation. *Journal of Personality,* 23, 107–127.

1956

The learning and utilization of contravaluant material. *Journal of Abnormal and Social Psychology,* 53, 27–33. (Authored with J. Aneshansel)

1957

Changes in social perception as a function of the personal relevance of behavior. *Sociometry,* 20, 75–85. (Authored with R. deCharms)

1958

Interaction goals as bases of inference in interpersonal perception. In R. Tagiuri & L. Petrullo (Eds.), *Person perception and interpersonal behavior* (pp. 151–179). Stanford: Stanford University Press. (Authored with J. W. Thibaut)

The organizing function of interaction roles in person perception. *Journal of Abnormal and Social Psychology,* 57, 155–164. (Authored with R. deCharms)

Some effects of feedback from the experimenter on conformity behavior. *Journal of Abnormal and Social Psychology,* 57, 207–213. (Authored with H. H. Wells & R. Torrey)

The effects of plausibility on the learning of controversial statements. *Journal of Abnormal and Social Psychology,* 57, 315–320. (Authored with R. Kohler)

1959

Political orientation and the perceptual effects of an anticipated interaction. *Journal of Abnormal and Social Psychology,* 59, 340–349. (Authored with B. Daugherty)

Reactions to unfavorable personal evaluations as a function of the evaluator's perceived adjustment. *Journal of Abnormal and Social*

Psychology, 59, 363–370. (Authored with S. L. Hester, A. Farina, & K. E. Davis)

1960

Effect of group support on the evaluation of an antagonist. *Journal of Abnormal and Social Psychology, 61,* 73–81. (Authored with L. H. Strickland & W. P. Smith)

Changes in interpersonal perception as a means of reducing cognitive dissonance. *Journal of Abnormal and Social Psychology, 61,* 402–410. (Authored with K. E. Davis)

1961

Role playing variations and their informational value for person perception. *Journal of Abnormal and Social Psychology, 63,* 302–310. (Authored with K. E. Davis & K. J. Gergen)

1962

Some determinants of reactions to being approved or disapproved as a person. *Psychological Monographs, 76*(Whole No. 521). (Authored with K. J. Gergen & K. E. Davis)

1963

Some conditions affecting the evaluation of a conformist. *Journal of Personality, 31,* 270–288. (Authored with R. G. Jones & K. J. Gergen)

Tactics of ingratiation among leaders and subordinates in a status hierarchy. *Psychological Monographs*(Whole No. 566). (Authored with K. G. Gergen & R. G. Jones)

Mental illness, predictability and affective consequences as stimulus factors in person perception. *Journal of Abnormal and Social Psychology, 67,* 95–104. (Authored with K. J. Gergen)

1964

Optimum conformity as an ingratiation tactic. *Journal of Personality, 32,* 436–458. (Authored with R. G. Jones)

1965

Some conditions affecting the use of ingratiation to influence performance evaluation. *Journal of Personality and Social Psychology, 1,* 613–625. (Authored with K. J. Gergen, P. Gumpert, & J. W. Thibaut)

Conformity as a tactic of ingratiation. *Science, 149,* 144–150.

From acts to dispositions: The attribution process in person perception. In L. Berkowitz (Ed.), *Advances in experimental social psychology* (Vol. 2, pp. 219–266). San Diego, CA: Academic Press. (Authored with K. E. Davis)

1967

The attribution of attitudes. *Journal of Experimental Social Psychology, 3,* 1–24. (Authored with V. A. Harris)

Decision freedom as a determinant of the role of incentive magnitude in attitude change. *Journal of Personality and Social Psychology, 3,* 245–254. (Authored with D. E. Linder & J. Cooper)

1968

Evaluation of an ingratiator by target persons and bystanders. *Journal of Personality, 36,* 349–385.

Pattern of performance and ability attribution: An unexpected primacy effect. *Journal of Personality and Social Psychology, 10,* 317–340. (Authored with L. Rock, K. G. Shaver, G. R. Goethals, & L. M. Ward)

1969

Modesty versus self-enhancement as alternative forms of ingratiation. *Journal of Experimental Social Psychology, 5,* 172–188. (Authored with L. K. Stires)

Opinion divergence as a strategy to avoid being miscast. *Journal of Personality and Social Psychology, 13,* 23–30. (Authored with J. Cooper)

1971

Prior expectancy and behavioral extremity as determinants of attitude attribution. *Journal of Experimental Social Psychology, 7,* 59–80. (Authored with S. Worchel, G. Goethals, & J. Grumet)

The bogus pipeline: A new paradigm for measuring affect and attitude. *Psychological Bulletin, 76,* 349–364. (Authored with H. Sigall)

Order effects in impression formation: Attribution context and the nature of the entity. New York: General Learning Press. (Authored with G. Goethals)[1]

The actor and observer: Divergent perceptions of the causes of behavior. New York: General Learning Press. (Authored with R. Nisbett)[1]

1972

Attitude similarity, expectancy violation, and attraction. *Journal of Experimental Social Psychology, 8*, 222–235. (Authored with G. A. Wein)

The reciprocation of attraction from similar and dissimilar others: A study in person perception and evaluation. In C. C. McClintock (Ed.), *Experimental social psychology* (pp. 142–179). New York: Holt. (Authored with L. Bell & E. Aronson)

Attribution, dissonance and the illusion of uniqueness. *Journal of Experimental Social Psychology, 8*, 45–57. (Authored with J. Cooper & M. Tuller)

Primacy and assimilation in the attribution process: The stable entity proposition. *Journal of Personality, 40*, 250–274. (Authored with G. R. Goethals, G. E. Kennington, & L. Severance)

The timing of self-disclosure and its effects on personal attraction. *Journal of Personality and Social Psychology, 24*, 358–365. (Authored with E. Gordon)

1973

Where there is ignis, there may be fire. *Psychological Bulletin, 79*, 260–262. (Authored with H. Sigall)

Delay of consequences and the riskiness of decisions. *Journal of Personality, 41*, 613–637. (Authored with C. Anderson Johnson)

Ingratiation: An attributional approach. New York: General Learning Press. (Authored with C. Wortman)

1974

Expectancy and apparent duration as determinants of fatigue. *Journal*

---

[1]This module also appears in *Attribution: Perceiving the causes of behavior* (1972). New York: General Learning Press. (Authored with D. Kanouse, H. H. Kelley, R. Nisbett, S. Valins, & B. Weiner)

of Personality and Social Psychology, 29, 426–434. (Authored with
M. Snyder & R. Schulz)

Attitude attribution when behavior is constrained. *Journal of Experimental Social Psychology, 10,* 585–600. (Authored with M. Snyder)

1976

Are there special effects of personalistic self-disclosure? *Journal of Experimental Social Psychology, 12,* 180–193. (Authored with R. Archer)

Correspondent inferences and the attribution cube: A comparative reappraisal. In J. H. Harvey, W. Ickes, & R. Kidd (Eds.), *New directions in attributional research* (Vol. I). New York: Erlbaum. (Authored with D. McGillis)

A recency effect in attitude attribution. *Journal of Personality, 44,* 433–448. (Authored with S. Berglas)

How do people perceive the causes of behavior? *American Scientist, 64,* 300–305.

Defensive attribution and the Kelley Cube. *Journal of Personality and Social Psychology, 34,* 809–820. (Authored with L. Stevens)

The self-monitor looks at the ingratiator. *Journal of Personality, 44,* 654–674. (Authored with R. Baumeister)

1978

Control of attributions about the self through self-handicapping strategies: The appeal of alcohol and the role of under-achievement. *Personality and Social Psychology Bulletin, 4,* 200–206. (Authored with S. Berglas)

Drug choice as a self-handicapping strategy in response to noncontingent success. *Journal of Personality and Social Psychology, 36,* 405–417. (Authored with S. Berglas)

When self-presentation is constrained by the target's knowledge: Consistency and compensation. *Journal of Personality and Social Psychology, 36,* 608–618. (Authored with R. Baumeister)

Selective self-disclosure with and without correspondent performance. *Journal of Experimental Social Psychology, 14,* 511–526. (Authored with G. Quattrone)

A conversation with Edward E. Jones and Harold H. Kelley. In J. H. Harvey, W. Ickes, & R. Kidd (Eds.), *New directions in attribution research* (Vol. 2, pp. 371–388). Hillsdale, NJ: Erlbaum.

Update of "From acts to dispositions: The attribution process in person perception." In L. Berkowitz (Ed.), *Cognitive theories in social psychology.* San Diego, CA: Academic Press.

1979

The rocky road from acts to dispositions. *American Psychologist, 34,* 107–117.

Observer bias in the attitude attribution paradigm: Effect of time and information order. *Journal of Personality and Social Psychology, 37,* 1230–1238. (Authored with J. M. Riggs & G. Quattrone)

1980

The perception of variability within in-groups and out-groups: Implications for the law of small numbers. *Journal of Personality and Social Psychology, 38,* 141–152. (Authored with G. Quattrone)

The social psychological perspective. In G. Kimble, N. Garmezy, & E. Zigler, (Eds.), *General psychology* (pp. 306–329). New York: Wiley.

Polarized appraisals of out-group members. *Journal of Personality and Social Psychology, 38,* 689–702. (Authored with P. Linville)

1981

Perceived variability of personal characteristics in in-groups and out-groups: The role of knowledge and evaluation. *Personality and Social Psychology Bulletin, 7,* 523–528. (Authored with G. C. Wood & G. Quattrone)

A robust attribution error in the personality domain. *Journal of Experimental Social Psychology, 17,* 587–600. (Authored with A. G. Miller & S. Hinkle)

Effects of strategic self-presentation on subsequent self-esteem. *Journal of Personality and Social Psychology, 41,* 407–421. (Authored with F. Rhodewalt, S. Berglas, & J. A. Skelton)

1982

Toward a general theory of strategic self-presentation. In J. Suls (Ed.),

Psychological perspectives on the self (Vol. 1, pp. 231–262). Hillsdale, NJ: Erlbaum. (Authored with T. Pittman)

Choice and attitude attributions: The influence of constraint information on attributions across levels of generality. *Social Cognition, 1,* 1–20. (Authored with N. Cantor & T. Pittman)

1983–1984

Perceptions of moral expectancy violation: The role of expectancy source. *Social Cognition, 2,* 273–293. (Authored with J. Schwartz & D. Gilbert)

1984

Social cognition and behavior. In G. A. Kimble, N. Garmezy, & E. Zigler (Eds.), *General psychology* (6th ed., chap. 18). New York: Wiley. (Authored with C. G. Lord)

Social influence and group processes. In G. A. Kimble, N. Garmezy, & E. Zigler (Eds.), *General psychology* (6th ed., chap. 19). New York: Wiley. (Authored with C. G. Lord)

1985

History of social psychology. In G. A. Kimble & K. Schlesinger (Eds.), *Topics in the history of modern psychology.* Hillsdale, NJ: Erlbaum.

Major developments in social psychology since 1930. In G. Lindzey & E. Aronson (Eds.), *Handbook of social psychology* (3rd ed.). Reading, MA: Addison-Wesley.

Social psychology. In A. Kuper & J. Kuper (Eds.), *The social science encyclopedia* (pp. 780–782). London: Routledge & Kegan Paul.

Sterotypes. In A. Kuper & J. Kuper (Eds.), *The social science encyclopedia* (pp. 827–828). London: Routledge & Kegan Paul.

Stigma. In A. Kuper & J. Kuper (Eds.), *The social science encyclopedia* (pp. 829–830). London: Routledge & Kegan Paul.

1986

Self-promotion is not ingratiating. *Journal of Personality and Social Psychology, 50,* 106–115. (Authored with D. Godfrey & C. G. Lord)

When stigma confronts stigma: Some conditions enhancing a victim's tolerance of other victims. *Personality and Social Psychology Bulletin, 12,* 169–177. (Authored with C. Galanis)

Perceiver-induced constraint: Interpretations of self-generated reality. *Journal of Personality and Social Psychology, 50,* 269–280. (Authored with D. Gilbert)

Exemplification: The self-presentation of moral character. *Journal of Personality, 54,* 593–615. (Authored with D. Gilbert)

Interpreting interpersonal behavior: The effects of expectancies. *Science, 234,* 41–46.

1987

How "naive" is the naive attributor?: Discounting and augmentation in attitude attribution. *Social Cognition, 5,* 108–130. (Authored with L. E. Ginzel & W. Swann)

Influence and inference: What the active perceiver overlooks. *Journal of Personality and Social Psychology, 52,* 861–870. (Authored with D. T. Gilbert & B. W. Pelham)

Heider's "The psychology of interpersonal relations": A retrospective review [Review of The psychology of interpersonal relations]. *Contemporary Psychology, 32,* 213–216.

1988

Impression formation: What do people think about? In T. K. Srull & R. W. Wyer (Eds.), *Advances in social cognition* (Vol. 1, pp. 83–90). Hillsdale, NJ: Erlbaum.

1989

Expectancies, actions and attributions in the interaction sequence. In J. P. Forgas & J. M. Innes (Eds.), *Recent advances in social psychology: An international perspective* (pp. 63–80). Norton-Holland: Elsevier Science.

The framing of competence. *Personality and Social Psychology Bulletin, 15,* 477–492.

1990

Constrained behavior and self-concept change. In J. Olson & M. Zanna (Eds.), *Self-inference processes: The Ontario Symposium* (Vol. 6, pp. 69–86). Hillsdale, NJ: Erlbaum.

When failure elevates self-esteem. *Personality and Social Psychology Bulletin, 16,* 200–209. (Authored with K. J. Brenner & J. G. Knight)

1992

Inferring abilities after influencing performance. *Journal of Experimental Social Psychology, 28*, 277–299. (Authored with J. M. Aronson)

1993

Expectancy disconfirmation and dispositional inference: Latent strength of target-based and category-based expectancies. *Personality and Social Psychology Bulletin, 19*, 563–574. (Authored with C. Weisz)

Afterword: An avuncular view. *Personality and Social Psychology Bulletin, 19*, 657–661.

The social in cognition. In G. Harman (Ed.), *Conceptions of the human mind: Essays in honor of George A. Miller* (pp. 85–98). Hillsdale, NJ: Erlbaum.

Author Index

Numbers in italics refer to listings in reference sections.

Subject Index

About the Editors

John McConnon Darley, PhD, received his bachelor's degree from Swarthmore College in 1960. He did his graduate work in the Department of Social Relations at Harvard University and received his doctoral degree in 1964. Dr. Darley was then appointed assistant professor in the Department of Psychology at New York University (NYU), where he taught from 1964 to 1968. He later left NYU to become an associate professor of social psychology at Princeton University. Dr. Darley was made professor in 1972, and from 1980 to 1985 served as chairman of the Department of Psychology. In 1989, he was named Dorman T. Warren Professor of Psychology.

Dr. Darley is presently a fellow of the American Psychological Association (APA), the Society for the Psychological Study of Social Issues, and the American Psychological Society. In 1989–1990, he served as president of the Society for Personality and Social Psychology (Division 8 of APA). Dr. Darley is a member of the Society of Experimental Social Psychologists, the American Association for the Advancement of Science (AAAS), and the American Sociological Association.

With Bibb Latane, Dr. Darley received the AAAS Sociopsychological Essay Prize and the Appleton-Century-Crofts Manuscript Prize. During 1985–1986, Dr. Darley was a fellow at the Center for Advanced Study in the Behavioral Sciences. In 1990, he received a Guggenheim Fellowship, and in 1997 Dr. Darley was awarded the Distinguished Research Career Award by the Society of Experimental Social Psychologists.

Joel Cooper, PhD, received his bachelor's degree from the City College of New York in 1965 and his doctoral degree from Duke University in 1969. Dr. Cooper met Ned Jones in the fall of 1965, and a friendship that was to last for nearly 30 years was begun. Dr. Cooper went to

Princeton University as an assistant professor in 1969 and is currently professor of Psychology at Princeton University. Dr. Cooper has served in visiting professorship positions at University College London, Hebrew University, the East–West Center, Auckland University, and the University of Queensland.

Dr. Cooper is coauthor of an introductory social psychology text and has published numerous articles in the areas of attitude change, cognitive dissonance, gender equity in computer technology, and psychology and law.

Dr. Cooper is a fellow of the American Psychological Society, the American Psychological Association, and the Society for Personality and Social Psychology. He has served as chair of the Society of Experimental Social Psychologists and is a member of several other organizations, including the Society for Psychological Studies of Social Issues.